THE
German-American
EXPERIENCE

THE
German-American
EXPERIENCE

Don Heinrich Tolzmann

Humanity
Books

an imprint of Prometheus Books
59 John Glenn Drive, Amherst, New York 14228-2197

Published 2000 by Humanity Books, an imprint of Prometheus Books

04 03 02 01 00   5 4 3 2

Library of Congress Cataloging-in-Publication Data

Tolzmann, Don Heinrich, 1945–
     The German-American experience / Don Heinrich Tolzmann.
         p.   cm.
     Includes bibliographical references and index.
     ISBN 1–57392–731–7 (pbk. : alk. paper)
     1. German Americans—History. 2. German Americans—Miscellanea.
I. Title.
E184.G3T65   1999
973'.0431—dc21   99–045800
                                                                      CIP

Printed in the United States of America on acid-free paper

Contents

Preface

In 1909 Albert B. Faust, a German-American historian, observed that the prominence of German-Americans in American history suggests the need "of a record of the essential facts in their history, from the earliest period of their settlements in this country to the present time."[1] The "prominence" of German-Americans is underscored by the fact that they constitute the nation's largest ethnic group and that their history reaches back to the very beginnings of American history. Furthermore, the German heritage is readily apparent across the United States, especially in those states that became known as the "German Belt."

The German-American Experience aims to provide a basic outline of German-American history together with a discussion of the major influences German-Americans have exerted in American history since the seventeenth century. It is intended for use as a text on the topic as well as a general historical introduction.

The term "German-American" is used to refer to immigrants and their offspring from Germany, Austria, Switzerland, and other German-speaking areas of Europe. Hence, the term "German" is used here in a linguistic, cultural, and ethnic sense to cover the totality of German-speaking immigrants and their descendants.

My motivation for publishing this work was the need for an up-to-date history of the German-American experience—for a work that would serve as a basic introduction, as well as a text. Although Albert B. Faust's *The German Element in the United States* (1927) had served as a standard work for many years, it had been quite out of date for some time. Of the works completed since Faust's, Theodore Huebener's *The Germans in America* (1962) had aimed to summarize the encyclopedic work fo Faust, but by now was also clearly out of date.[2] In making plans for a new history, I originally had aimed to merely add a few chapters to Huebener's work, but upon closer examination of the work I found that there were many gaps, as well as areas in need of revision, further amplification, or clarification. I thus decided to prepare a new history, which would be based on Huebener as well as Faust. I leaned heavily on Huebener especially for the period from the American Revolution through the Civil War but included much new material for this time period dealing with immigration, settlement, and community life. Thereafter, I have tried to bring the history of the German-American experience as up-to-date as possible.

I also completed several appendices and have provided a bibliography with references to basic sources. Although this is basically a new work, it is one that rests on the shoulders of its predecessors, and I would like to particularly acknowledge my indebtedness to the work of Huebener, as well as Faust. In addition to incorporating the findings of more recent research in the field of German-American studies, I have also sought out the works of earlier historians, especially those of Heinrich A. Rattermann, and have made use of the German-American press by means of the bibliographical guides of Karl J. R. Arndt.

I would like to express gratitude to Juergen Eichhoff of the Max Kade Institute for German-American Research at Pennsylvania State University for permission to include the map indicating the locations of German immigrants in 1890 and the chart of the various immigrant groups in American history. Also, I would like to thank Ruth and Eberhard Reichmann of the Max Kade German-American Center at Indiana University—Indianapolis for permission to include the map showing where German-Americans live according to the 1990 U.S. Census.

I would also like to thank my students, who in courses and seminars at the University of Cincinnati have explored with me many of the topics discussed in this work, and several of whom have gone on to publish

IMMIGRATION BY COUNTRIES,[3] 1820–1985

Source: 1986 Statistical Yearbook of the Immigration and Naturalization Service

Country	Total 1820–1985	Top Decade	# That Decade
Germany	7,031,370	1881–90	1,452,970
Italy	5,330,064	1901–10	2,045,877
Great Britain	5,040,000	1881–90	807,357
Ireland	4,697,290	1851–60	914,119
Canada	4,204,027	1921–30	924,515
Soviet Union	3,420,772	1901–10	1,597,306
Mexico	2,568,449	1971–80	640,294
Norway, Sweden, Denmark	2,504,943	1881–90	656,494
France	767,899	1841–50	77,262
China, Taiwan	735,095	1971–80	124,326
Philippines	703,212	1971–80	354,987
Greece	683,155	1911–20	184,201
Austria	617,565	1911–20	453,649
Cuba	603,206	1971–80	264,863
Poland	555,037	1921–30	227,734
Hungary	536,232	1911–20	442,693
Portugal	482,231	1971–80	101,710
Korea	473,449	1971–80	267,638
Japan	436,119	1901–10	129,797
Turkey	400,329	1901–10	157,369

A production of German House Research, Madison, Wisconsin, © 1988 Juergen Eichhoff

Reprinted by permission of Juergen Eichhoff.

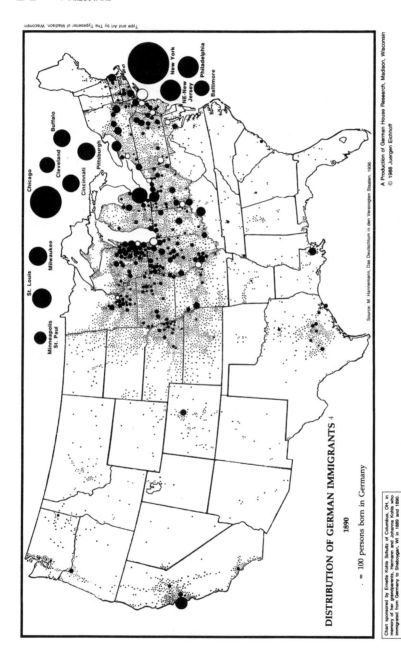

DISTRIBUTION OF GERMAN IMMIGRANTS [4]

1890

. = 100 persons born in Germany

Source: M. Hannemann, Das Deutschtum in den Vereinigten Staaten, 1936.

A Production of German House Research, Madison, Wisconsin
© 1988 Juergen Eichhoff

Chart sponsored by Ernette Kohls Schultz of Columbus, OH, in memory of her grandparents, Hermann and Johanna Kohls who immigrated from Germany to Sheboygan, WI in 1889 and 1890.

Reprinted by permission of Juergen Eichhoff.

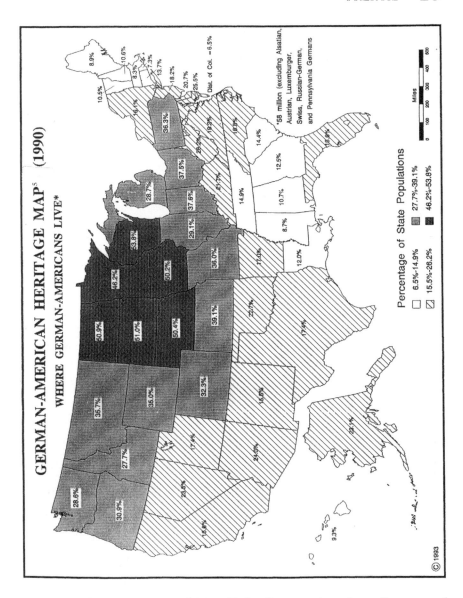

GERMAN-AMERICAN HERITAGE MAP[5] (1990)
WHERE GERMAN-AMERICANS LIVE*

Percentage of State Populations

6.5%–14.9%   27.7%–39.1%
15.5%–26.2%   46.2%–53.8%

*58 million (excluding Alsatian, Austrian, Luxemburger, Swiss, Russian-German, and Pennsylvania Germans

Dist. of Col. = 6.5%

© 1993

Reprinted by permission of Max Kade German-American Center and Indiana German Heritage Society, Inc.

monographs dealing with German-American history, which I have cited in the notes of this work.

Finally, a special word of gratitude to my family for its enduring support.

Don Heinrich Tolzmann

Notes

1. Albert B. Faust, *The German Element in the U.S.* (New York: Steuben Society of America, 1927), vol. 1, p. v.

2. Huebener's work appeared as: *The Germans in America* (Philadelphia: Chilton, 1962).

3. Juergen Eichhofff, *Immigration by Countries, 1820–1985* (Madison, Wisc.: German House Research, 1988).

4. Juergen Eichhoff, *Distribution of German Immigrants 1890* (Madison, Wisc.: German House Research, 1988).

5. Ruth Reichmann and Eberhard Reichmann, *German-American Heritage Map (1990): Where German-Americans Live* (Indianapolis: Indiana University-Purdue University, Max Kade German-American Center, 1993).

Introduction

President John F. Kennedy called America "a nation of immigrants." This is an appropriate designation, since 55 million people have immigrated to America since the founding of Jamestown, Virginia, in 1607.[1] This represents the greatest migration of people in world history. Everyone in the United States is either an immigrant or a descendant of one. In approximately four centuries, a nation of immigrants and their descendants has grown to a population of two hundred and fifty million.

Oscar Handlin once observed that he had set out to write a history of the immigrants in America and then discovered that the immigrants were American history.[2] This points to the importance of immigration and ethnicity in American life. In short, to understand America, it is necessary to understand the history of the immigrations and the various ethnic groups that make up American society. Poet Walt Whitman wrote:

> These states are the amplest poem,
> Here is not a nation but
> a teeming nation of nations.[3]

Of the 55 million immigrants who have come to America, 70 percent came from Europe, or 38.5 million. Of this European immigration, one-fifth, or 8 million, came from one of the German-speaking countries or regions of Europe, hence German immigrants constituted the largest single immigrant group in American history.

Clearly, on a statistical basis alone, it is important to study the history of German immigration and settlement in America. The impact of the German-American heritage has, however, more than sheer statistical significance. In all periods of American history, the presence of German-Americans and their contributions to this country can be registered.

The 1990 U.S. Census indicated that close to sixty million Americans reported that they were of German descent, thereby making German-Americans the largest single ethnic group in the United States. In twenty-three states of the Union they form at least 20 percent of the population and are the largest single group in those particular states. These states stretch from Pennsylvania in the East across the Midwest and the Great Plains all the way to Oregon and Washington in the West, forming what has become known as the German Belt.[4]

In his book *A Nation of Immigrants* (1964), President Kennedy highlighted some of the influences and contributions German-Americans have made in the last four centuries.[5] Among them were the following:

Almost every state has profited from German-Americans' intellectual and material contributions. In rural areas they pioneered scientific farming, crop rotation, and soil conservation. In urban areas they entered the ranks of educators, engineers, scientists, and artists. They established industrial enterprises in the fields of lumbering, food-processing, brewing, steelmaking, electrical engineering, piano-making, railroading, printing, publishing, and more.

Kennedy noted that American society owes the mellowing of the Puritan influence to the German-American concept of the "Continental Sunday." The celebration of Christmas and the New Year was mainly shaped by German-Americans as well. The presence of a symphony orchestra in most large cities is another German-American innovation, and community singing and glee clubs derive from the German singing societies.

In the area of education, German-Americans helped form the American educational system as we know it today. They introduced the *kindergarten* to prepare children for schooling. They promoted state-sponsored universities, based on the German model of the university. They introduced physical education into the public schools and also pioneered German instruction by means of the first bilingual programs in the country.

American English, as H. L. Mencken, the German-American sage of Baltimore, once wrote, varies greatly from European English, and this is due in no small part to German-Amerians, whose German language greatly influenced English as it is spoken in the United States today. German words are not only common, but an integral part of the daily vocabulary, giving us such words as *hamburger, frankfurter,* and *delicatessen.*

Such a large ethnic group would, of course, gain political influence. Indeed, in 1688 German-Americans in Germantown, Pennsylvania, issued the first protest against slavery in America. From that time to the present German-Americans have been actively involved in American politics at all levels. In times of war, even during the trying years of the world wars, German-Americans have been at the forefront.

Kennedy's introductory survey was important for two reasons. First, it signified a long-overdue recognition of the role played by German-Americans, America's largest ethnic group, in American history. Second, Kennedy's survey not only provides us with a brief overview of the German-American experience, but also serves as a convenient point of departure for an introduction to this history of the German-Americans.

Notes

1. See John F. Kennedy, *A Nation of Nations* (New York: Harper & Row, 1986). For a history of immigration to America, see Roger Daniels, *Coming to America: A History of Immigration and Ethnicity in American Life* (New York: Harper Collins, 1990).

2. Oscar Handlin, *The Uprooted: The Epic Story of the Migrations That Made the American People* (New York: Grosset & Dunlap, 1951), p. 3.

3. Kennedy, *Nation*, p. 3.

4. A basic and major problem with the Census with regard to statistics pertaining to German-Americans is that it lists only those from, or descended from

immigrants from Germany, and then lists separate statistics for ethnic Germans from other states and areas. As Roger Daniels notes, "This means that German speakers from Switzerland, Austria, the Austro-Hungarian Empire, and so on, are not included. . . . This counting by nationality rather than ethnicity continues to create problems in American immigration data." Daniels, *Coming to America*, p. 147. Also, see Don Heinrich Tolzmann, "The 1980 U.S. Census and the German Element," *Society for German-American Studies Newsletter* 5, no. 2 (1984): 2.

    5. Kennedy, *Nation*, pp. 51–55.

The Age of Discovery

German-American history begins in 1608 with the arrival of the first permanent German settlers at Jamestown, Virginia. However, any discussion of the beginnings of German-American history must include reference to any and all possible precursors and contacts between America and Germany. The earliest possible connection is found in the realm of Germanic legend, where Tyrker was the first German in America. Additionally, Germans played an important role in the discovery and exploration of America in the fifteenth and sixteenth centuries prior to the Jamestown settlement, which cannot be overlooked.

The Legendary First German

According to Germanic legend, Tyrker, a German explorer, reached North America around the year 1000, or close to five centuries before Columbus. At that time, the Norsemen, or Vikings, led by Leif Ericson, reached the New World, where they attempted to establish several colonies, one of which was Vinland (Wineland). The exact location of these settlements is unknown; however, it is now felt that Vinland was probably located in Newfoundland's northern shore at a site known as L'Anse aux Meadows.

21

Accompanying Erickson was the Norse leader's own foster father, Tyrker, a German. According to legend, he was the first German to reach America. Furthermore, he is credited with having discovered grapes on the new land and with having named this new land Vinland. Norse saga provides us with the following account of this legendary first German in America and his discovery:

> It was discovered one evening that one of their company was missing and this proved to be Tyrker, the German. Leif was sorely troubled by this for Tyrker had lived with Leif and his father for a long time, and had been very devoted to Leif, when he was a child. Leif severely reprimanded his companions, and prepared to go in search of him, taking twelve men with him. They had proceeded but a short distance from the house, when they were met by Tyrker, whom they received most cordially. Leif observed at once that his foster-father was in lively spirits . . . Leif addressed him, and asked: "Wherefore art thou so belated, foster-father mine, and astray from the others?" In the beginning Tyrker spoke for some time in German, rolling his eyes and grinning, and they could not understand him; but after a time he addressed them in the Northern tongue: "I did not go much further than you, and yet I have something of novelty to relate. I have found vines and grapes." "Is this indeed true, foster-father?" said Leif. "Of certainty it is true," quoth he, "for I was born where there is no lack of either grapes or vines."
>
> They slept the night through, and on the morrow Leif said to his shipmates: "We will now divide our labors, and each day will either gather grapes or cut vines and fell trees, so as to obtain a cargo of these for my ship." A cargo sufficient for the ship was cut, and when the spring came, they made their ship ready, and sailed away; and from its products Leif gave the land a name, and called it Wineland.[1]

The early Norse settlements established by Ericson were short-lived but pointed to the future interest Europe would have for America. Little is known about Tyrker other than the above details that can be extracted from Germanic legends and sagas. Although there appears to be solid ground for the fact that there were Norse settlements in America prior to Columbus, there is no evidence that Tyrker actually existed other than the references to him in Germanic legend, and it must therefore be assumed that he is a mythical character until such time that his actual existence can be documented. On the other hand, the notion that Tyrker may have actually existed should not be totally rejected, so perhaps the most that can be said is that there is a Germanic legend that he was the first German in America.

The Beginnings of the Age

Ever since 1295, when Marco Polo returned to Italy with immense wealth after having spent years at the court of Kublai Khan as well as in China, Japan, and various East Indian islands, there was a great interest, especially among navigators, in finding a water route to the El Dorado, or the city of gold, which had been described by Marco Polo. However, the greatest obstacle in the way of any maritime exploration was the lack of any method by which the navigator could tell his ship's location when it was out of sight of land. The problem was not solved until the German mathematician Johannes Müller (Regiomontanus) of Königsberg calculated and published his *Ephemerides*, or *Nautical Almanac*, in 1474. This was based on his astronomical observations and consisted of a collection of tables showing the present state of the heavens for every day of the year at noon. Another German innovation of great value and use for navigation was the astrolabe of Martin Behaim of Nürnberg. This was an instrument used for determining the altitude of the sun or stars when at sea.[2]

There have been reports of various pre-Columbian discoveries of America, including that of the arrival of a German explorer twenty years before Columbus. In 1473 Didrik Pining, a German in the service of Christian I of Denmark, led an expedition in search of a passage to the Far East, and he apparently reached Greenland, Labrador, and perhaps also Newfoundland. Pining, however, was not aware of the fact that he had landed in the New World and did not follow up on this expedition due to the inability of the Danes to finance such expeditions. However, in 1478 he was appointed the Danish governor of Iceland. Also, reports on his trip remained state secrets at the time and were not publicized, so his discovery remained unknown.

A quick glance at a world globe reveals how close Greenland is to

Iceland and that once in Greenland, the voyage to Newfoundland would not have been all that difficult. This northern route, therefore, was one that could be traversed as if by stepping-stones from Iceland to Greenland and varied from the Atlantic over-the-ocean route to Central American, which was reached by Columbus.

In 1481 the king of Portugal established a board of commission of scientists to examine the different nautical instruments, almanacs, calculations, and maps of the period, and to report on their utility. One of the five persons appointed to this body was Martin Behaim, a student of Johannes Müller. He also belonged to a subcommittee charged with discovering some sure method of navigating the seas according to the altitude of the sun and constructing mathematical and nautical instruments suitable for this purpose.

On this occasion, Behaim brought forth the calculations and tables of his former teacher. He also produced his improved astrolabe, which was of metal and could be attached in a vertical position to the main mast of a sailing vessel. This was the first application of the portable astrolabe for navigation, and together with the Jacob-staff, also introduced by Behaim, it taught sailors how to discover the position of a vessel at sea without the use of the magnetic needle and long, intricate calculations. It was the introduction of these instruments into Portugal, together with the tables of Behaim's teacher, which gave the navigators of that land so great an advantage. Columbus, who was at that time a resident of Lisbon, was well acquainted with the German Behaim and his research. It is an unquestionable fact that the success of the Portuguese in discovering the Atlantic islands, and of Behaim's voyage down the African coast, sustained Columbus in the hope of a western discovery, if indeed it had not instigated him to undertake the voyage. When finally the dream of Columbus was realized under the patronage of Ferdinand and Isabella of Spain, it was made possible only with the aid of three great factors, all of which were of German origin: the astrolabe of Martin Behaim, the mariner's compass from Nürnberg, and the nautical almanac of Johannes Müller.

When Columbus sailed to America in 1492, several Germans were with him, taken as interpreters, for in addition to the European languages they were well versed in Hebrew, Chaldaic, and Arabic. Of the many expeditions that left Spain and Portugal in the 1490s, the greater number were either projected or fitted out by the merchants of Germany, or the Hanseatic League, and there were many German adventurers on board with these voyages as well.

Germany as a nation did not play an active role in these explorations, as Germany did not establish a colonial empire. Indeed, Germany was not a seafaring nation during the Age of Discovery. The glory days of the old Hanseatic League, a commercial alliance of northwest German cities, were long since past, and Germany's location in the heart of Europe, with but a narrow strip of seacoast in the north, put it at a distinct disadvantage in comparison to the English, French, Dutch, Spanish, and Portuguese. Moreover, the Holy Roman Empire of the German nation was preoccupied in the 1500s with internal affairs revolving around the Reformation and the Counter-Reformation, which were followed in the 1600s by the disastrous Thirty Years' War (1618–48).

While not conspicuous as a leader in the great voyages of discovery, Germany occupied an important position in the area of scholarship, especially in cosmography and cartography. From this scholarship there emerged the crucial tools and instruments without which the voyages to the New World would have been impossible.[3] Also, there were many examples of Germans who were members of voyages organized by the Latin nations, and those German participants came as explorers, adventurers, sailors, soldiers, missionaries, miners, and craftsmen.

Although Germans laid the foundations for discovery in the areas of cosmography and cartography, they played a minor role in Columbus's discovery of 1492, as only a few accompanied Columbus on this voyage. However, Germans did play a major role in spreading information regarding this monumental event, and this was due to their predominance in the field of printing.[4] In 1455 Johannes Gutenberg had completed his first great work, and the effects of the invention of movable type were widespread throughout Europe, where in almost every case the printing press was introduced by German craftsmen. By 1600 over one hundred works had been published in Germany that dealt with, or mentioned, the New World.

Across Europe, printing presses were usually not without German printers. In 1493 Stefan Planck in Rome printed the letter of Columbus, *Der Kolumbusbrief*, which was called a little book or pamphlet since it consisted of a few pages. This was the first publication about the New World. It found its way to Anton Koberger in Nürnberg, who included it in his 1497 edition of the *Nürnberg Chronicle*, the first book to mention the discovery.[5]

The letter of Columbus was printed across Europe by German printers and was perhaps the first real best-seller. It told of "gold and pearls in the islands, treasures that would one day dwarf those of Solomon." In the next few years, German presses worked overtime to supply the great need for information about the newfound land, as the whole of Europe seemed to be obsessed with the idea of Utopia, the dream of an earthly paradise. In 1498 Sebastian Brant mentioned the discovery of America in his *Narrenschiff*, which was published in 1509 in English as *The Ship of Fools*, the first English-language publication to refer to the discovery.

The first printed account of the discoveries using the term "New World" appeared in a Latin work published in Augsburg in 1504, *Mundus Novus*. In 1505 a German edition also appeared at Nürnberg, *Von der neu gefundene Region die wol ein welt genennt mag werden.* However, quite soon this New World, which Columbus had thought was Asia, would be named America by means of the publication of a treatise by a German cosmographer in Lorraine, Martin Waldseemüller.

In 1507 Waldseemüller published his *Cosmographiae Introductio*, in which an account was furnished of all the voyages of Amerigo Vespucci. The suggestion of the name "America" appears here for the first time:

> But now that these parts have been more widely explored and another fourth part has been discovered by Americus Vesputius (as will appear in what follows), I do not see why any one may justly forbid it to be named after Americus, its discoverer, a man of sagacious mind, Amerige, that is the land of Americus, or America, since both Europe and Asia derived their names from women.[6]

The credit, therefore, of first advocating in print the use of the name "America," and also of diffusing it widely by means of charts, maps, and globes, belongs to the German cosmographers.

In 1508 Johann Ruysch published the first engraved map showing any portion of the Western continent, before the name of America had widely come into use. In 1519, Jakob Cromberger, a German printer in Seville, printed the first geographic book about America, *Summa de Geographia*. In 1520 Peter Bienewitz produced the earliest map upon which the name of America appeared. In the same year, Johannes Schöner completed the earliest terrestrial globe that bore the name of America. Reference should also be made to Mercator (Gerhard Kremer), who was commissioned by Charles V to produce a terrestrial and a celestial globe, which were said to have been superior to any previous ones. His principal work was a world atlas (1594). Thus, the naming of the continent was due to German cosmographers and cartographers of the period, and that their examples were eventually followed by the geographers and map-makers of all nations.[7]

The First Attempts at Colonization

The earliest German attempts at colonization of the New World occurred in Latin America. Charles V, who was not only emperor of the Holy Roman Empire of the German nation but also king of Spain, granted the German banking house of Welser, located in Augsburg, permission to establish a factory or trading station at Santo Domingo, Venezuela, a city it intended to be a New World metropolis. In 1525 the first Germans arrived there, and in 1528 another group under the direction of Ambrose Dalfinger (Ehinger) landed, which included fifty German miners. They established the first German colony at Santo Domingo, and Dalfinger proclaimed himself governor and captain-general of Welserland. He was followed as expeditionary leader by Georg Hohemuth, Nicolaus Federmann, and Philipp von Hutten.[8]

Many successive German expeditions were sent out to America after the edict was issued by Charles V that granted all of his German subjects the right to emigrate and settle in the West Indies. These expeditions were financed and organized by the German banking houses of the Welser and Fugger families, both located in Augsburg. As these early colonization efforts were confined to Latin America, they shall be followed no further here, although they are significant in that they demonstrate German interest in the New World.

However, there were some books that emerged from these early German contacts with the New World. One of the most interesting was the amazing narrative of Hans Staden, a native of Hessia, which covers his experiences in Brazil from 1547 to 1554 and was published as *Wahrhaftig Historia* (1557), which was published in English as *The Cannibal Book*. The book describes the religion, food, drink, and culture, as well as the cannibalism, that Staden encountered in Brazil. The work became exceptionally popular and was translated not only into English, but into Dutch and Latin as well.[9]

Another work was that of Ulrich Schmidt von Straubingen, a native of Bavaria, whose narrative covers the period from 1534 to 1554. It gives an account of how he participated in an expedition to America in one of the voyages financed by the Welser family. This book was published in Frankfurt am Main as *Wahrhafftige und liebeliche Beschreibung* (1562). Schimdt described the Indians, the landscape, the animals, and the vegetation that he had observed during his sojourn in the New World.[10] Works such as these not only added to the knowledge about America, but also contributed to the growing interest in the New World.

In 1562 and 1564 the French attempted to establish a Huguenot colony at Port Royal, South Carolina. In 1562 the French admiral Gaspard de Coligny commissioned Jean Ribault to establish a colony along the southern coast of North America. In May, a small fort was built at Port Royal, Charlesfort, whereafter Ribault sailed to France for reinforcements and supplies, leaving about thirty volunteers behind. By June they had mutinied, selected a new commander, and sailed home in a vessel they had constructed.

In 1564 an attempt was made to reestablish the colony when Rene de Laudonniere (the leader of the expedition), Lord d'Ottigny, and Theobald d'Erlach commanded an expedition that reached the coast of Florida, where Fort Caroline was built in honor of Charles IX. In the following year, the French fleet fell victim to a hurricane, and the survivors were killed by the Spanish, who had countered the construction of Fort Caroline by establishing St. Augustine in Florida. Apparently there were at Port Royal "a number of Alsatians and Hessians who had served under the Admiral's brother." How many there were, who they were, and when they came is unknown. However, we do know that there was a Swiss-German with the 1564 French expedition, Theobald d'Erlach. He had been third in command of this expedition.[11]

In 1585 Sir Walter Raleigh, Queen Elizabeth's favorite at court, undertook an expedition to explore the eastern coast of North America, which he named Virginia in honor of the unmarried sovereign of England. He settled 108 men at Roanoke Island, located off the coast of North Carolina, but the group remained only a year and then returned home after having faced deprivation, starvation, and the hostility of Indians.[12] Among the group were German miners, most notably Joachim Gans, whose family came from Prague.

The early Spanish predominance in the New World was short-lived, as the defeat of the Spanish Armada in 1588 meant that now Great Britain was clearly established as mistress of the high seas, and this clearly marked Spain's decline as a world power. As a means to further check Spain, Great Britain now began to proceed with its plans for expansion and colonization into the region which eventually became the United States.

Notes

1. Albert B. Faust, *The German Element in the U.S.* (New York: Steuben Society of America, 1927), vol. 1, pp. 6–7.

2. For further information about the Age of Discovery, see Don Heinrich Tolzmann, ed., *Germany and America: 1450–1700: Julius Friedrich Sachse's History of the German Role in the Discovery, Exploration, and Settlement of the New World* (Bowie, Md.: Heritage Books, 1991); Don Heinrich Tolzmann, ed., *In der Neuen Welt: Deutsch-Amerikanische Festschrift zur 500-Jahrfeier der Entdeckung von Amerika, 1492–1992* (New York: Peter Lang, 1992).

3. For a discussion of the work of German cosmographers and cartographers, see Sophus Ruge, "Die deutschen Kosmographen," in: Tolzmann, *In der Neuen Welt*, pp. 66–92.

4. For a survey of the work of German printers in this period, see Ruge, "Die deutschen Buchdrucker," in Tolzmann, ed., *In der Neuen Welt*, pp. 93–103.

5. See Leo Schelbert, "Der Kolumbusbrief," pp. 3–28.

6. Faust, *The German Element*, p. 5.

7. See Tolzmann, *Germany and America*, pp. 43–70.

8. With regard to the colonization efforts of the German banking houses in Latin America, see Tolzmann, *Germany and America*, pp. 81–114, and Hartmut Froeschle, "Lateinamerika: Synthese zweier Kulturkreise—Der deutsche Beitrag zur Erforschung und Erschliessung Lateinamerikas," in Tolzmann, *In der Neuen Welt*, pp. 187–96.

9. Regarding Staden, see Victor W. von Hagen, *Der Ruf der Neuen Welt: Deutsche bauen Amerika* (Munich: Droemersche Verlagsanstalt, 1970), pp. 66, 68, 72–73, 105.

10. With regard to Schmidt, see von Hagen, *Der Ruf der Neuen Welt*, pp. 66–67, 105, 239, 241.

11. Regarding Port Royal, see Tolzmann, *Germany and America*, p. 121, and Faust, *The German Element*, p. 7. For information regarding Theobald d'Erlach, see Leo Schelbert, *Swiss in American Life* (Zürich: Müller, Werder, 1977), pp. 13–16, as well as his article "Le premier Suisse sur sol nord-americain: Theobald d'Erlach (1541–1565)," *Versailles* 38 (1970): 29–42.

12. See Gary C. Grassl, "German Mineral Experts in North America, 1577–1586," paper presented at the eighteenth Annual Symposium of the Society for German-American Studies, Pennsylvania State University, April 1994.

The First
German Settlers

The Jamestown Germans

The first permanent colony in the part of the New World that became the United States was the settlement at Jamestown, Virginia. U.S. history is usually conceived of as beginning there, and this is also where the beginning of German-American history can be found.

On or around October 1, 1608, eight Germans arrived on the ship *Mary and Margaret* at Jamestown, Virginia, the colony which had been established in 1607 by the London Company of Virginia. These first German settlers were glassmakers and carpenters. Altogether there were seventy passengers on board the ship, including an unspecified number of Poles. Both they and the Germans had been contracted by the London Company to produce pitch, tar, glass, milles (paneling), and soap ashes.[1]

The history of these first German settlers is recorded and documented in Captain John Smith's *The Generall Historie of Virginia, New-England, and the Summer Isles with the Names of the Adventurers, Planters, and Governors from their first Beginnings An: 1584 to this Present 1624*.[2] It should be noted that Smith calls the Germans "Dutch," as was commonly done at that time. The confusion of "Dutch" and "German" arose among the English-speaking population from the fact that the Germans called themselves *deutsch*. Also, the Netherlands was part of the Holy Roman Empire of the German nation until the Treaty of Westphalia in 1648, and the Germans of the Lower Rhine and the Dutch were, therefore, similar in background.

Three of the Germans who arrived in 1608 were carpenters; the rest were glassmakers. In addition, there was a Swiss-German settler as well, so the total number of ethnic Germans at Jamestown in 1608 was nine. They were in Jamestown twelve years prior to the arrival of the more well-known English Pilgrims at Plymouth Rock in New England.

As these first settlers were employees of the London Company, the proceeds of their labor went to the company. Glassmakers had been especially sought, as the colony was in need not only of glassware, but also of craftsmen who could teach this craft locally. When the Germans arrived, the conditions were poor, and more than half of the settlers who had arrived in 1607 had perished. With the new arrivals there were now approximately 120 persons. Smith was apparently not overjoyed at the new arrivals and felt that the colony should establish itself before obtaining more new colonists:

> As for the hiring of the Poles and Dutchmen to make Pitch, Tar, Glasse, Milles and Sope Ashes, when the country is replenished with people and necessaries, would have done well, but to send them and seventy more without victualls to work, was not so well advised nor considered of as it should have beene.[3]

As noted, the conditions in the colony were not especially good.

> Things had been going from bad to worse. . . . There had been quarreling among the settlers and they had been harrassed continuously by the Indians. It was evident that most of the leaders, as well as the rank and file of the colonists, were unfitted, both by temperament and training, to deal successfully with the problems of colonization.[4]

The glasshouse, which consisted of three furnaces and a kiln, was constructed on the mainland, about one mile from James Fort, which was located on a peninsula. Together the German and Polish craftsmen successfully began their work, and the products of their craftsmanship were sent to England on board the *Mary and Margaret* when the ship returned in December 1608. The glasshouse at Jamestown marked the foundation of industrial production in colonial America.

Already the Germans had acquired a reputation for their hard work, industriousness, and craftsmanship. Indeed, Captain John Smith compared them favorably in relation to the other colonists whom he described as

> adventurers that never did know what a day's work was, except for the Dutchmen and the Poles and some dozen other. For all the rest were poore Gentlemen, Tradesmen, Serving-Men, libertines, and such like, ten times more fit to spoyle a Commonwealth, than either to begin one or but help to maintaine one.[5]

Again, Smith comments in a statement to the Jamestown authorities in England:

> When you send againe I entreat you rather to send but thirty carpenters, husbandmen, gardiners, fisher men, blacksmiths, masons, and diggers of trees' roots, well provided, then a thousand of such as we have; for except wee be able both to lodge them and feed them, the most will consume with want of necesaries before they can be made good for anything.[6]

However, dissension soon arose regarding the relationship with the local Indians. In December 1608 Smith sent three Germans (Adam, Franz, and Samuel) together with two Englishmen to the Indian chief Powhatan. They were to build a house for the chief, the first European-style home in colonial America. However, the real purpose apparently was Smith's plan to build a house that could be used to either capture or kill the chief and then force the Indians to deliver corn to the colonists. Moreover, one of the Germans was instructed to spy on Powhatan.

What happened next is a matter of conjecture. In Smith's view, the Germans betrayed his plan and deserted to the Indians. He referred to them as "the damned Dutch," thereby creating the first ethnic slur in American history. Smith obviously held the Germans responsible for the failure of his plan. However, German-American historians have interpreted what happened differently. In their view, the Germans preferred the kindly Indians, who supplied them with food, to the bickering and idle English, who treated them with disdain. A more recent interpretation is that "while living with the Indians, the Germans, who were useful to the Indians, cooperated with them out of coercion. They were detained by the Indians. Despite fear of punishment, the Germans tried to return to the English when the opportunity offered itself."[7]

Whether the Germans deserted to the Indians or were actually held by them in a state of coercion is, hence, a matter of contention. However, Smith's plan to capture or slay the Indian chief was thwarted, and the Germans did remain with the Indians for a time, and then they apparently returned to Jamestown. As there is no report of later prosecution, it appears that the Germans were being held by the Indians but that their conditions with them were better than those with the English colonists, as the Indians had greater supplies of food. Perhaps they were being held, but they apparently felt better off for a certain period of time with the Indians than with the colonists.

By 1609 a considerable amount of glass has been produced, all of it the common green-glass variety. As the colony grew, it met with many hardships and privations. The colony was especially hard hit by sickness, famine, and general disorder. The winter of 1609–10 was appropriately called "the starving time," as of the 490 persons at Jamestown, only sixty survived. Now the Indians, no longer afraid, began to harass the settlement. However, more settlers did arrive, including Dutch and Germans. The newly arrived engaged in agricultural pursuits and raised crops, so famine no longer threatened the colony. By 1611 the settlement had grown to a population of two hundred, and the presence of Germans is confirmed in the various reports to the London Company.[8]

In 1621 four German millwrights from Hamburg arrived at Jamestown for the purpose of erecting sawmills. The colony had grown quite concerned with the Indians, especially after the massacre in 1622, which caused great losses. The Jamestowners were now preoccupied with countermeasures against the Indians, so the newly arrived German millwrights got no help with their plan to build a sawmill. Moreover, it was reported that they had become disheartened and impatient with their sojourn in Jamestown. Also, they lacked some of the basic necessities and dietary ingredients, such as beer. Eventually, one or two of them perished, and the rest returned to England.

The Germans who settled in larger numbers by the mid–1600s seem to have been attracted chiefly by the prolific tobacco business. Germans set up a tobacco plantation in Cavalier County, and in 1653 vintners from Heidelberg introduced German wines to the New World. Among the early German settlers of Virginia there were several prominent individuals. The most highly educated citizen of Northhampton County in 1657 undoubtedly was Dr. Georg Nicolaus Hack (Hacke) from Köln, Germany. He practiced medicine and formed a partnership in the tobacco trade with Augustin Herrmann, who is considered the founder of the tobacco trade in Virginia. Hack was one of the framers and signers of the so-called Engagement of Northhampton of 1655. One of his sons, Peter, became a member of the Virginia House of Burgesses.

Dr. Johannes Lederer, a physician from Hamburg, arrived in Jamestown in 1668, and he became the first colonist to explore the Piedmont and Blue Ridge Mountains and the Shenandoah Valley of Virginia in 1669–70. He published what is considered the first report about the region, *The Discoveries of John Lederer.*[9] This work contains valuable information on the Indians, geography, geology, flora, and fauna of the areas he explored. Other prominent early Virginia Germans included Thomas Harmanson from Brandenburg, who was naturalized in October 1684 by an act of the assembly. Johann Sigismund Cluverius, owner of a considerable estate in York County, was also German-born. Because of the growth of the German element, the county records of Richmond appear partially written in German script.

The Jamestown Germans are important for several reasons. First, their arrival marks the beginning of German-American history, as they were the first actual settlers in what became the United States Second, the Jamestown Germans built the first European-style house here. They manufactured the first glass, and by means of their glass production they became the founders of industrial production. Also, a Virginia German produced the first scholarly treatise on the region. And finally, their arrival also denoted that fact that American society from its very beginnings was going to be multiethnic and culturally diverse, rather than uniform.

The scholar Klaus Wust writes of the Jamestown Germans:

The fate of the German glass blowers and carpenters of whom we have record was not dissimilar to that of all the other early emigrants to Jamestown. It was typical of the hardship, confusion, and suffering which went with settling and working in the New World.[10]

The German-American experience has its origins in these humble beginnings.

In 1908 the tricentennial of the Jamestown Germans was commemorated, and in 1958 their 350th anniversary was celebrated. In 2008 the 400th anniversary of the arrival of the first German settlers will take place.[11]

The New York Germans

The largest number of Germans in the pre–1683 period was to be found in New Netherland, the Dutch colony, which eventually would be taken over by the English and renamed New York. New Netherland embraced the Hudson Valley from Manhattan to as far north as Albany. It is estimated that from one-fourth to one-third of the population of the Dutch colony was German.

The first director general of New Netherland was Peter Minuit (Minnewit), who was born in Wesel on the Rhine. He arrived in the colony in May 1626 with nearly absolute ruling powers. The determined Minuit rapidly transformed the colony into a well-organized and prosperous community. He bought the island of Manhattan, some 22,000 acres, from the Indians for sixty Dutch guilders, or about twenty-four dollars in gold. Significantly, no attempt was made at conquest, but rather at negotiations with the Indians. According to Julius Friedrich Sachse, the nineteenth-century scholar, to Minuit belongs the credit for inaugurating the humane policy of "peaceful negotiations and fair dealings with the Indians . . . bargaining with the Indians before he would permit any settlement to be made by his colonists."[12] At the Battery he erected Fort Amsterdam, built of heavy stone. The Indians did not dare attack, and New Amsterdam soon became a thriving town. Cattle and horses were supplied by the Dutch West India Company, good crops were raised, and a profitable fur trade with the Indians soon arose. By 1631 the exportation of furs amounted to a trade volume of 130,000 guilders, and the shipbuilding industry flourished.

Without Minuit's approval, the Dutch West India Company established a patroon system that hindered the development of the colony. Each of the patroons became a manor lord with semifeudal privileges over a large tract of land. Dissension arose, and Minuit was recalled. When he left in 1632, New Netherland was in excellent economic condition. Since Minuit was not exonerated in Holland, he offered his service to the king of Sweden. The Swedes were interested in establishing a colony in the New World, and they listened eagerly to his proposals. At the end of 1637, Minuit returned to America with a warship and a transport carrying fifty immigrants, mainly Dutch and German. He arrived in Delaware Bay in April 1638. With eminent skill, he prevented the English and the Dutch from interfering with his plans for colonization. Near the present site of Wilmington, Delaware, he built Fort Christina, named in honor of the Swedish queen. Under the administration of Minuit, trade and commerce flourished in the new settlement, and immigrants continued to arrive, so the colony from the onset experienced relative tranquility and prosperity.

The Germans, rather than the Swedes, played a leading role in the development of New Sweden (1638–55). Germans were on board Minuit's ship that sailed to establish the Swedish colony on the Delaware, and from the names of the colonists we are assured that many were Germans. It is estimated that 10 percent of the immigrants brought by Sweden to New Sweden were German. Additionally, Germans migrated from New Netherland to New Sweden.[13] Hendrick Huygen, Minuit's brother-in-law from Cleve on the Rhine, was the commissary. From 1640 to 1643 another German, Peter Hollender Ridder, headed the colony. He was followed by Johann Printz, a German nobleman whose real name was Prinz Edler von Buchen. He had brought with him fifty-four German families from Pomerania.[14] This is especially important in German-American history as it represents the first organized immigration of a group of Germans to America.

The last governor of New Sweden was Heinrich von Elswich, a merchant from Lübeck. Consequently, German became the diplomatic language used between New Sweden and New Netherland, and the colony acquired a semi-German character. Also, we know that

> the instructions of the officers were written in Swedish, German, and Dutch. The Dutch and German officers, soldiers, and settlers were able to converse in Swedish, and they gradually became fairly well versed in the language, but all the account books and most of the bills preserved to us are written in Dutch or German.[15]

In 1655 New Sweden became part of New Netherland under the administration of the irascible Peter Stuyvesant.

Stuyvesant, who had been governor of Curacao and had lost a leg in a battle, came to New Amsterdam in 1647. He was an energetic but frequently tactless individual who became easily enraged. Despite the complaints about his administration, the thriving colony continued to grow and develop.

At first the colony was rather cosmopolitan. A Jesuit priest who visited New Amsterdam in 1643 recorded eighteen spoken languages in the settlement with a population that included Germans, French, Swedes, Spaniards, Italians, Turks, and Jews. However, the character of the colony changed as a constant stream of English settlers arrived, settling mainly at Long Island. English was spoken more and more, and this proved to be a vital factor in New Amsterdam's future. Wedged in between New England and the other English colonies, the colony occupied a crucial position geographically. It divided the English possessions both commercially and politically. Charles II solved the problem quite simply. He informed this brother, the Duke of York, that he would give him New Netherland, whereupon his brother inquired as to what the Dutch would think about this, since England and the Netherlands were at peace with one another. Charles II responded that his brother should not worry about this, for the colony really belonged to England.

A fleet was sent across the ocean. It entered the harbor of New Amsterdam on September 6, 1664. Stuyvesant was prepared to fight, and when Colonel Nicholls, the English commander, sent him a conciliatory letter, the fiery Dutchmen tore it up and threw the pieces on the floor. A bystander picked them up, pasted them together, and read the message to a group of citizens. The terms of the English were accepted; they were invited to come in; and thus New Amsterdam became New York. An angry, defeated Stuyvesant retired to his farm, which was on the present site of Union Square, where he spent the remainder of his life.

The second governor of New York was a German, Jacob Leisler.[16] Born in Frankfurt am Main, he had come to New Amsterdam in 1660 as a soldier in the service of the Dutch West India Company. By trading skillfully with the Indians, he became wealthy; through marriage, he entered the Dutch aristocracy. Only three vessels were owned at that time in New York, and one of them belonged to him. When he was captured by the pirates of Tunis in 1678, a ransom of five hundred pounds was paid for him. When a group of Huguenots landed in New York in 1689, he bought them a large tract of land on the site of the present city of New Rochelle. He also saved several Huguenot families from years of servitude by paying the sums they owed as redemptioners for their passage fares.

By that time the Dutch were dissatisfied with British rule, particularly because James II had combined the colonies of New England, New York, and New Jersey under one governor, Edmund Andros. While Governor Andros was in New England, Francis Nicholson acted as lieutenant governor. News arrived that William of Orange had landed in England, and there was much excitement among the Dutch population, who naturally looked to the public-spirited and energetic Leisler as a leader. At that point, Nicholson made the rash remark to a disobedient officer that he would rather see the city on fire than put up with any impudence. Word soon spread that the governor was about to set the city on fire. A mob gathered, formed a small army, and marched to Leisler's home. Leisler refused to assume leadership, but a Lieutenant Stoll led the mob to the fort. Nicholson was captured without offering any resistance. He later fled.

On June 8, 1689, a committee of citizens appointed Leisler commander-in-chief of the city until the arrival of a new governor from England. News soon arrived of the coronation of William and Mary, and Leisler made preparations for an appropriate ceremony. The magistrate and the aldermen, who had refused to join, were dismissed. The Committee of Safety appointed Leisler supreme commander of the colony in August 1689.

Leisler then prepared a careful report of everything that had happened and dispatched Lieutenant Stoll to England with it. Neither Stoll nor the report was favorably received by the king, for Nicholson had prejudiced the king against Leisler and his representative, Stoll. William of England declared that the popular party, which Leisler led, was hostile to the established church as well as disloyal to the new king himself. Meanwhile, the aristocrats in the colony denounced him as a demagogue and a Jacobite.

Albany refused to recognize the government of Leisler, so he sent a company of militia under the command of his son-in-law, Jacob Milborne, to seize the fort at Albany. However, the force was too weak to carry out this order and had to withdraw. The fugitive aristocrats sent complaints to London, accusing Leisler of rebellion against the king.

At the beginning of December 1689, a royal messenger arrived with a letter addressed to Francis Nicholson or to those who were administering the laws in the "Province of New York." The messenger was brought to New York and handed the letter to Leisler, who, on December 11, 1689, assumed the title of lieutenant governor.

His enemies, however, had not given up. After an unsuccessful attempt to capture him on the street one day, the ringleaders were seized, thrown into prison, and charged with high treason. After being sentenced to death, the two men, Bayard and Nicolls, pleaded for mercy, and Governor Leisler magnanimously relented.

Leisler had been lieutenant governor for only a month when the French attacked New York. In January 1690 the fort at Schenectady was taken, burned, and plundered. Albany was then saved by Leisler's quick action in sending troops to its defense. He realized that the French were a formidable foe and that united action was necessary. Hence, in April 1690 he invited the governors of five colonies (Massachusetts, New Jersey, Pennsylvania, Maryland, and Virginia) to meet in New York. This historic conference, held in May 1690, was the first American congress and was followed by a number of others, which eventually led to the Continental Congress.

The six governors decided to equip an army to conquer Canada and to send a fleet to take Quebec, but dissension and misunderstanding ruined the plans for the land expedition. Stormy winds doomed the attack by sea. Despite Leisler's courageous and intelligent action, his efforts were not crowned with success. Huge debts were incurred; taxes were imposed and Leisler's enemies became increasingly truculent. At the end of the year, a new governor, Colonel Henry Sloughter, was appointed by the crown.

During a storm at sea, the new governor's ships became separated, and Major Ingoldsby, second in command, arrived in New York. Leisler refused to yield his office until Colonel Sloughter arrived. Bitter fighting occurred, and Leisler was confined to one of the forts. On March 19, 1691, Sloughter arrived and freed Bayard and Nicolls from prison and incarcerated Leisler and eight of his friends.

Charged with rebellion, illegal taxation, and treason, Leisler was condemned to death by his personal enemies who sat as his judges. They filled Sloughter with wine in order to secure his signature on the death warrant for Leisler and his son-in-law, Milborne. On a cold, wet day on May 16, both men were hanged on a scaffold erected at Pearl and Centre Streets, the site of the Tombs prison.

It soon became apparent that the execution of Leisler had been a grave miscarriage of justice. His son began proceedings in the British courts, and after years of litigation, Parliament finally reversed the charges against Leisler and Milborne in 1695, exonerated both completely, and restored the property that had been confiscated. Three years later, their bodies were removed from under the gallows and interred in the cemetery of the Dutch Church in Exchange Place. Over fifteen hundred persons took part in the ceremonies, and the event attracted attention across the colonies. Increase Mather, one of the prominent figures in colonial politics, declared that Leisler had been "barbarously murdered."

Leisler's calling of the first congress was a milestone in American history. His integrity and zeal were transmitted to a number of descendants, one of whom was Gouverneur Morris, a member of the Continental Congress from New York. A German-American, therefore, was the first great representative of popular government in the colonies.

Elsewhere in the Colonies Before 1683

Although the first German settlers were concentrated in Virginia and New York, there were also Germans to be found scattered throughout the colonies.

In New England, the first Germans arrived with the founders of the Massachusetts Bay Colony in 1630. Some Germans also came to the colony by way of New Netherland and made their way to Connecticut, Rhode Island, and Boston.[17] In 1661, Swiss physician Felix-Christian Spoeri visited Rhode Island, and later published an account of his travels, *Americanische Reisebeschreibung* (Zürich, 1677).[18]

In Maryland, the first Germans came from Virginia, New Netherland, and New Sweden around 1650. In 1660 Augustin Herrmann, born in Prague, promised to produce a map of Maryland, which was completed in 1670, in return for a land grant, and in 1661 he and his family settled at the northern tip of Chesapeake Bay in Maryland. In 1663 he became one of the first citizens of the colony.[19] In 1663 Peter Fabian, a Swiss-German, was a member of the English Carolina Company, which explored the Carolinas. And in 1671 German Lutherans from New York moved to Carolina. The first German in Texas, a Würtemberger by the name of Hiens (or Heinz, Hans), came with the expedition of LaSalle in 1687.[20]

When Franz Daniel Pastorius came to Pennsylvania in 1683, he found "a few High Germans . . . who had already inhabited this country for twenty years, and had become naturalized so to say; these were Silesian, Brandenburgers, Holsteiners, Swiss, etc. Also, one from Nuremberg . . ."[21]

The First Permanent German Settlement

The first permanent German settlement in America was founded in 1683 at Germantown, Pennsylvania, by a group of thirteen German families who had emigrated from Krefeld, Germany. William Penn had been largely instrumental in bringing them to America. Inspired with missionary zeal, the young Englishman visited the Netherlands and Germany in 1671 and 1677 to gain adherents for the Quaker faith. As early as 1655 George Fox, the founder of the Society of the Friends, had sent messengers to the European continent. When Penn arrived on the Rhine River, he found a small community of Quakers located near Worms in a village named Kriegsheim.[22]

The Rhineland was at this time fertile ground for the spreading of Quaker teachings. They stressed the inward life, spirituality as opposed

to dogma, simplicity and purity of living, and opposition to war and violence. In addition to Quakers there were Mennonites, Schwenkfelders,
Dunkards, and Pietists. Since by German law only the Catholic,
Lutheran, and Reformed Churches were officially recognized and established, these various sects were considered illegal.

William Penn, who is said to have preached in German, received a
warm and cordial reception when he spoke along the Rhine and in
Frankfurt am Main. Although he made some converts to Quakerism,
Penn's greatest achievement was not religious, but rather political and
social. It was his appearance on the Rhine that drew attention to the possibility of immigration to America.

In lieu of a payment of sixteen thousand pounds in sterling which the
British government owed Admiral Penn, his son, William, was given a tract
of land that became known as Pennsylvania. Shortly after the issuing of a
royal charter, a brief description of the province was published in 1681 by
William Penn. Among other things, it pointed out the advantages for immigrants in Pennsylvania. It also described the favorable location, the fertile
soil, and the wealth in game and fish available. This book was then translated into German, *Eine Nachricht wegen der Landschaft Pennsylvania
in Amerika* (Amsterdam: Christoph Conraden, 1681), and it came to the
attention of the Pietists in Frankfurt am Main.[23]

The Frankfurters were intrigued by the possibilities of life in the New
World, and they formed a company for the purpose of emigration. Through
Benjamin Furley, Penn's agent, they purchased fifteen thousand acres of
wilderness. Later, the Frankfurt Company, as it was called, extended its
holdings to twenty-five thousand acres, offering a share of five thousand
acres for one hundred pounds. Although there was much enthusiasm
about life in the New World, none of the Frankfurt circle, who apparently
were cultured and well-to-do individuals, came to America.

Only their agent, Franz Daniel Pastorius, came to America.[24] He was
a well-educated and widely traveled lawyer who became so deeply interested in the project that he decided to cast his lot with the immigrants.
According to Pastorius, the discussion of the immigration project "begat
a desire in my soul to continue in their society and with them to lead a
quiet, godly, and honest life in a howling wilderness." He then sailed
from Deal, England, in June 1683, on the ship *America* with a number of

men and women of humble origin. While crossing the ocean, Pastorius won the friendship of Welsh physician and Oxford scholar Thomas Lloyd, who later became the president of the Provincial Council. Since Pastorius knew no English at that time and Lloyd was ignorant of German, they both conversed in Latin. Penn was delighted with Pastorius, who landed on August 20, 1683, and gave him a cordial reception. Twice a week the young lawyer dined at the governor's house. Pastorius wrote, "[A]s I was recently absent from home a week, he [Penn] came himself to visit me and bade me dine with him twice every week, and declared to his counsellors that he loved me and the High Germans very much and wished them to so likewise." Penn characterized Pastorius as "sober, upright, wise and pious—a man everywhere esteemed and of unspotted name."[25]

The cultured Pastorius was amused by the poorly built houses of the city of Philadelphia, which had been laid out only two years before and consisted, as he records in his diary, largely of woods and brushwood. He wrote that this made a striking impression on him, especially after having come from London, Paris, Amsterdam, and Ghent.

The first company of actual immigrants from Krefeld, Germany, set out six weeks later on the *Concord*, considered the *Mayflower* of the German immigration, which was commanded by Captain Jeffreys. The devout group of German Mennonites and Quakers consisted of thirteen families, and on October 6, 1683, the vessel landed safely at the port city of Philadelphia. Their arrival is considered the founding date of the first German settlement in America: Germantown, Pennsylvania, which the newcomers established six miles above the city. Originally called *Deutschstadt*, the name was soon changed to Germantown, which was easier for non-Germans to pronounce. In 1987 October 6 was proclaimed "German-American Day" by congressional and presidential proclamation, and has been celebrated annually ever since.[26]

Pastorius had made the arrangements for the immigrants' departure from Kriegsheim and Krefeld, and he also provided for them when they arrived in Philadelphia. The Frankfurt Company had purchased 25,000 acres of land, and the Krefelder settlers 8,000. In his *Grund und Lager-buch*, Pastorius describes the severe hardships of the early settlers but lauds their "Christian endurance and indefatigable industry." Pastorius shared their difficulties and lived temporarily in a tiny wooden shack with oil-soaked paper for windows, but maintained his humor and his scholarship throughout. Governor Penn laughed heartily when he read the motto the young lawyer had placed over his wretched dwelling: *Parva domus sed amica bonis, procul este profani* (Small is my house, but it welcomes the good people; may the godless ones stay away.) The colonists built small huts, dug cellars, and passed their first winter in much discomfort, but by the next year, better and more permanent dwellings had been constructed, and grain from the first crops (Indian corn and buckwheat) had been stockpiled for the winter.

The industries that the settlers had brought from Krefeld stood them in good stead. There were skillful weavers who produced so much that a store was opened in Philadelphia. They laid out vineyards and raised flax. Within a short time a wide variety of tradesmen, including carpenters, locksmiths, shoemakers, and tailors, appeared in the area. Several of the local products, especially the textiles, soon secured an excellent reputation for the inhabitants of Germantown. The first paper mill in the colonies was established in Germantown by William Rittinghausen (or Rittenhouse) in 1690. Aside from the mill, the Germantowners also built a church, a prison, and a school, where Pastorius held classes.

Germantown grew rapidly and soon incorporated smaller neighboring communities (Crefeld, Krisheim, Sommerhausen), all located along the same road. In Germantown, which was closest to Philadelphia, the road was sixty-five feet wide and lined with peach trees. The modest but comfortable dwellings each stood on three acres of land devoted to trees, flowers, and vegetables. A cross street forty feet wide led to the marketplace, a thriving community of tradesmen, farmers, and gardeners. Pastorius admired the activity around him and deplored the vanity of book learning, remarking, "[N]ever have metaphysics and Aristotelian logic made of a savage a Christian, far less earned a loaf of bread."[27]

Six years after its founding, on August 12, 1689, Germantown was incorporated as a town, and Pastorius had the honor of being the first mayor, an office he held four different times. It was an extremely peaceful and law-abiding community. Crime was practically nonexistent. The court sat every six weeks but frequently adjourned because there was no business. Occasionally, a fine was levied for neglect of fences or a rare case of drunkenness. Two amusing incidents were recorded: A certain Müller was locked up because of trying to smoke a hundred pipes of tobacco in one day as a result of a wager; and Caspar Karsten was incarcerated for calling a policeman a rogue.

Beer was being brewed in the early days of Germantown. Peter Keurlis was in all probability the first beer brewer in America; he was recorded as having been granted the privilege of selling beer at a local fair, and in 1695 was summoned before the court because he had run a saloon on an innkeeper's license.

In 1693 Pastorius and Peter Schuhmacher were commissioned to procure stocks for the public punishment of offenders, yet very little seems to have been made of them. In 1697 Arndt Klincken gave his old house for use as a prison; however, in the same year it was noted in the Germantown minutes that "all crimes that have been committed previous to this date are to be forgiven, but whatever evil happens henceforward shall not be forgiven."[28]

Pastorius complained in 1703 of the difficulty of finding Germantowners to run for public office. Indeed, to some holding office was considered a burden, but others objected on religious grounds. A Mennonite could be excused from public office, but others who refused to participate were fined three pounds for refusal to accept the results of an election. For example, in 1702 Arnold Küster, the ancestor of General George Armstrong Custer, was elected committeeman of Germantown but refused to serve because of conscientious objection. His Mennonite principles, which included not taking an oath, were probably the cause of his refusal. Pastorius expressed the hope that the arrival of new immigrants would alleviate the situation, which apparently it did by the early 1700s.

Pastorius himself set an excellent example in his unselfish and untiring devotion to the community. In fact, the progress and prosperity of the first German settlement in America was largely due to his leadership. He served as burgomaster, town clerk, notary, and member of the Provincial Council. He despised personal gain and asked only for small fees. He was the head of the Quaker School in Philadelphia from 1698 to 1700, and in 1702 he took charge of the school in Germantown, which included a night school for adults.

This must have been highly gratifying to Pastorius, for he was primarily a scholar. In his youth he had studied at the Universities of Altdorf, Strassburg, Basel, and Jena. His learning was clearly encyclopedic, and he had mastered a number of languages. His *Bee Hive* is a neatly written collection of historical, literary, geographical, and poetical works in English, Latin, German, French, Dutch, and Italian. Pastorius published several works dealing with life in the New World, which were influential in encouraging others to immigrate. In 1694 he published a letter to his parents describing America, *Copia eines von einem Sohn an seine Eltern auss America abgelassenen Brieffes, sub data Philadelphia, den 7. Martii, 1684*. In the same year, he published a lengthier letter dealing with Pennsylvania, *Sichere Nachricht auss America*. This was followed up by a major work describing Pennsylvania, *Umständige Beschreibung der zu allerletzt erfundenen Provintz Pennsylvaniae* (Frankfurt am Main: Andreas Otto, 1700).[29]

He was not only a diligent scholar and a conscientious public officer, but also a courageous idealist who sought to apply and realize his ideals. Under his leadership, a group of Germantowners met on April 18, 1688, and issued the first formal protest against slavery—more than 150 years before the Civil War. The document, in the handwriting of Pastorius, was sent to the Quakers, who gracefully avoided the issue.

Faust writes of this historic protest that

> however distinct and valuable the material contributions, such as agriculture, its paper manufacture, its weaving and milling industries, the German settlement in colonial Pennsylvania was still more remarkable for another feature,—a monument built more enduring than brass, erected for the cause of humanity, that will make Germantown forever memorable in the annals of the people of the United States.[30]

The slavery system was repulsive to the Germans from the very beginning, and they were shocked that the Quakers appeared indifferent to the matter. They could not understand how the Quakers could harmonize slavery with their faith. The Germantown protest addressed the monthly meeting of Quakers with the purpose of bringing the matter of slavery before the group for debate and action. The protest stated that the Germantowners were opposed to bringing people "hither or to robb or sell them against their will. . . . Pray what thing in the world can be done worse toward us if men should robb or steal us away and sell us for slaves to strange contries separating husband from their wife and children . . . ?"[31]

At the April 30, 1688, meeting of the Quakers, the issue was held to be of such importance that no action was considered possible, and it was referred to the quarterly meeting, as the content of the protest "was quite in accord with the truth." At the June quarterly meeting of the Quakers similar action was taken, because the matter was deemed so important that a committee was appointed to bring the protest before the annual meeting, the highest tribunal of the Quakers. At the annual meeting the document "protesting against the buying and keeping of negro slaves" was acknowledged but was voted not fit for the association to pass final judgment on, since it stood in intimate relation to other matters. Hence, the protest was in essence tabled, and the matter evaded. It should also be noted with regard to the protest that Pastorius wrote a poem against slavery, "Gegen die Negersklaverei."[32]

Pastorius is also well known for the 1688 poem directed to future generations of German-Americans.[33] This poem, "Hail to Posterity," was widely reprinted and distributed during the 1983 German-American Tricentennial:

Hail to posterity!
Hail, future men of Germanopolis!
Let the young generations yet to be
Look kindly upon this.
Think how your fathers left their native land,—
Dear German-land! O sacred hearths and
homes!—
And, where the wild beast roams,
In patience planned
New forest-homes beyond the mighty sea,
There undisturbed and free
To live as brothers of one family
What pains and cares befell,
What trials and what fears,

Remember, and wherein we have done well
Follow our footsteps, men of coming years!
Where we have failed to do
Aright, or wisely live,
Be warned by us, the better way pursue,
And, knowing we were human, even as you,
Pity us and forgive!
Farewell, Posterity!
Farewell, dear Germany!
Forevermore farewell!

Germantown was not only a German-American settlement, but was also the major destination and distribution center for the colonial German immigration. It also became the major German-American social, cultural, and political center. In 1793, President Washington attended a German service in the Reformed Church there when the epidemic of yellow fever caused him to move from Philadelphia to Germantown, which was an indication of the high regard he had for German-Americans. Germantown itself long remained a cultural center, where books, newspapers, and other publications were printed in German. The industrial activities and the semiannual fairs provided exemplary models that were soon adopted elsewhere.[34]

Notes

1. For further information on the Virginia Germans, see Don Heinrich Tolzmann, ed., *The German Element in Virginia: Herrmann Schuricht's History* (Bowie, Md.: Heritage Books, Inc., 1993).

2. London: Michael Sparkes, 1624.

3. Albert B. Faust, *The German Element in the U.S.*, vol. 1 (New York: Steuben Society of America, 1927), p. 9.

4. J. C. Harrington, *A Tryal of Glasse: The Story of Glassmaking at Jamestown* (Richmond, Va.: Dietz, 1972), p. 8.

5. Faust, *The German Element in the U.S.*, p. 9.

6. Ibid.

7. Gary C. Grassl, "Germans at Jamestown," unpublished paper, pp. 12–13.

8. Don Heinrich Tolzmann, ed., *The First Germans in America, with a Biographical Directory of the New York Germans* (Bowie, Md.: Heritage Books, 1992), p. 4.

9. Klaus Wust, "German Craftsmen in Jamestown," *American-German Review* 23 (1957): 11.

10. London: Samuel Heyrick, 1672. Also, see John Lederer, *The Discoveries of John Lederer, Three Several Marches from Virginia to the West of Carolina, and Other Parts of the Continent: In the Years 1669 and 1670. With an Explanatory Introduction by H. A. Rattermann* (Cincinnati: O. H. Harpel, 1879).

11. For a discussion of my recommendations regarding the celebration of the 400th anniversary of the arrival of the first Germans in colonial America at Jamestown, see Tolzmann, *The First Germans in America*, pp. vii–xiii.

12. See Tolzmann, ed., *Germany and America* (Bowie, Md.: Heritage Books, 1991) p. 134. Also, see Heinrich A. Rattermann, "Peter Minnewit aus Wesel am Rhein," *Der Deutsche Pionier* 1 (1869): 169–81, and Tolzmann, *The First Germans in America*, pp. 6, 9–10, 417.

13. See Don Heinrich Tolzmann, ed., *German Immigration to America: The First Wave* (Bowie, Md.: Heritage Books, 1993), p. 262.

14. Ibid.

15. Tolzmann, *First Germans in America*, p. 7.

16. Regarding Leisler, see Gerard Wilk, *Americans from Germany*, ed. Don Heinrich Tolzmann (Indianapolis: Max Kade German-American Center, Indiana University-Purdue University, 1995), pp. 21–22, and Tolzmann, *The First Germans in America*, pp. 13, 401, 418, 422–24.

17. See Lucy Bittinger, *The Germans in Colonial Times* (Philadelphia: J. B. Lippincott, 1901), pp. 130–42.

18. See Karl Knortz, "Spöri's Reise nach Neu-England im Jahre 1661," *Der Deutsche Pionier* 5 (1873): 301–303.

19. Regarding Herrmann, see Heinrich A. Rattermann, "Augustin Herrmann. Ein Karakterfigur aus der Begründungsgeschichte von New York und Maryland," *Deutsch-Amerikanisches Magazin* 1 (1887): 524–38; "Ein berühmter Pionier," *Der Deutsche Pionier* 18 (1886): 108–109; Dieter Cunz, *The Maryland Germans: A History* (Princeton, N.J.: Princeton University Press, 1948), pp. 12–26, 431–33; and Tolzmann, *The First Germans in America*, pp. 8, 37–39, 414–16. Herrmann's map was entitled "Virginia and Maryland as it was planted an inhabited this present year 1670." See Tolzmann, *The German Element in Virginia*, p. 39.

20. Faust, *The German Element in the U.S.*, p. 28.

21. Tolzmann, *The First Germans in America*, p. 7.

22. Regarding Penn's visits to Germany, see Tolzmann, ed., *Germany and America*, pp. 147–53.

23. A copy of the title page of Penn's book is found in Tolzmann, *Germany and America*, p. 206.

24. For a definitive biography of Pastorius, see Marion Dexter Learned, *The Life of Francis Daniel Pastorius: The Founder of Germantown* (Philadelphia: William J. Campbell, 1908).

25. See Faust, *The German Element in the U.S.*, pp. 35–36, and Wilk, *Americans*, pp. 39–40.

26. Regarding German-American Day, see Don Heinrich Tolzmann, ed., *In der Neuen Welt* (New York: Peter Lang, 1992), pp. 197–209.

27. Faust, *The German Element in the U.S.*, p. 39.

28. Ibid., p. 41.

29. For a discussion of the works by Pastorius and others, which influenced German immigration, see Tolzmann, *Germany and America*, pp. 175–256.

30. Faust, *The German Element in the U.S.*, p. 45.

31. Bittinger, *The Germans*, p. 32

32. Faust, *The German Element in the U.S.*, p. 46.

33. Bittinger, *The Germans*, p. 30.

34. Ibid., pp. 26–35.

Early Immigration and Settlement

In the first century of German-American history, from 1608 to 1708, German immigration was merely a trickle, but one that would become a mighty stream and would bring wave after wave to American shores. There were a number of general and specific reasons for this swelling of the German immigration in the early 1700s, which are referred to as the "push" and "pull" factors of the immigration. The substantial immigration of 1709 and the years before the American Revolution would establish a foundation and framework for the colonial German-American community, which consisted of a wide variety of religious and secular institutions, as well as an influential German-language press.

Causes of the Immigration

By 1708 Germany had undergone several centuries of tumultuous and cataclysmic upheavals, which had brought widescale death and destruction of epic proportions. In the second half of the fourteenth century, the Black Death—*die schwarze Pest*—had swept through Europe, wiping out large sections of its population. Germany lost an estimated 25 percent of its population. Especially hard hit were urban areas.

This disaster was followed in the fifteenth century by the Reformation, revolutions, and the Counter Reformation, all of which threw Germany into turmoil and division. The Reformation brought not only religious, but far-reaching social and political repercussions as well. In the midst of this occurred the Revolt of the Knights in the 1520s, followed by the Peasants' War of 1524–26, in which one-third of the 300,000 peasants involved in this revolution lost their lives. Friedrich II of Saxony wisely observed, "[T]he poor are in many ways oppressed by us, the secular and ecclesiastical authorities. . . ."[1] Rather than seeking a peaceful settlement, as Friedrich had advised, the secular and ecclesiastical princes ruthlessly suppressed the rebellion, thereby causing Martin Luther, who had published a pamphlet condemning the peasants, to be shocked at the tragic outcome. He urged clemency and mercy, and when none was shown, called down judgment on the princes.

As Germany entered the sixteenth century, it had undergone two centuries marked by death, destruction, and disaster, and the new century saw it plunged further into oblivion, and to the gates of Armageddon. It was this general context of disaster that provided the general impetus behind the German immigration, but there were more specific reasons or "push" factors for the German immigration, among them the following:

The Thirty Years' War, 1618–48. Due to Germany's central location in the heart of Europe, it is not surprising that the major wars in European history have usually been fought on German soil. The history of the war itself does not concern us here, but rather the impact of the war on Germany and how this contributed to the deteriorating conditions in the immigrants' homelands. The actual damage is difficult to estimate, as the degree of destruction varied from place to place. For example, Württemberg lost 75 percent of its population of 445,000. Eight cities, 45 villages, 65 churches, and 158 school and parochial institutions had also been burned. In the Palatinate before the war, the population had numbered a half million, but only 10 percent survived the war. Some areas lost one-third or two-thirds of their population, and some no losses at all, depending on where the war was raging. Altogether it is estimated that Germany lost a total of 35 percent of its population. The material and cultural losses are incalculable, but assuredly they were enormous.

Germany itself was invaded by the mercenaries of the contending armies. As Johannes Scherr writes, "The scum of Europe's hirelings spread over Germany's fertile plains, and there perpetrated the most terrible martial tragedy which has ever been recorded. . . ." There were countless cases of arson, robbery, and homicide, as well as "the slaughter of innocent children, the rape of maiden and matron . . . the massacre of entire towns which had been captured . . . the wanton destruction of cattle, grain, crops, and domiciles. . . ."[2] All these and similar trials and tribulations befell Germany during the Thirty Years' War. The economic impact was far-reaching moreover, taking some areas centuries to recover. For example, it is estimated that in some areas the number of family dwellings did not reach their prewar numbers until 1848, a full two centuries after the war.

The Treaty of Westphalia, 1648. The postwar peace treaty dealt a deathblow to German political unity as it had existed via the Holy Roman Empire of the German nation, established in the year 800 by Karl der Grosse, or Charlemagne. From now on, the real political power resided in the individual member states of the empire, which functioned now as sovereign nations and could form alliances with foreign powers. Germany became more of a geographical expression and did not develop into a united nation-state, as did its neighbors such as France. German unity would now be delayed for centuries. Although the Austrian Habsburgs bore the title of kaiser, this was nothing more than a meaningless formality, as the empire had no capital city, no treasury, no courts, and no means of coercing its members. This lack of unity meant that there could be no development of a national economy, no national defense, or, for that matter, anything of national consequence.

In addition to disunity, Germany suffered substantial losses of German territory, especially to France, which took possession of Metz, Toul, and Verdun, and was granted sovereignty over Alsace. Moreover, France was granted representation in the German Parliament, or Reichstag, as was Sweden, an indication of the impotence of that institution. The disappearance of the empire as an entity that could unite the German states rendered Germany a political and economic mess. More important, Germany was now a tempting target and object for conquest.

The History of Warfare. The Thirty Years' War was followed by continued intermittent warfare, as Germany was weak, divided, and vulnerable. France annexed Alsace in 1681, took Burgundy in 1714, and annexed Lorraine in 1766. These were all in accord with the French foreign policy goal of dominion over Alsace to obtain a border on the Rhine. France's second objective was to maintain a weak and divided Germany. It was especially the French king Louis XIV who was regarded as the ceaseless disturber of the peace, as he led France to war for four decades. Again and again, Germany became the battlefield as the armies of France "trampled on her soil and despoiled her people."[3]

The Tyranny of the Princes. As a result of German division into 1,800 states and estates, ranging from large ones such as Prussia and Austria to tiny estates, Germany was governed by numerous princes, each of which ruled their principalities as sovereign, independent states. Some of them patterned their affairs after that of Louis XIV, impoverishing their people through heavy taxes levied to support their extravagant tastes, courts, and lifestyles which included not only hunting, festivities, and revelry, but also the construction of costly castles, theaters, and other stately structures. The peasant classes were the principal sufferers, and their welfare was tyrannically disregarded by the many of these princes. The wretchedness of their condition ultimately convinced many that future improvements were impossible.

Religious Conditions. By means of the Treaty of Westphalia, only three confessions were recognized in Germany: Catholic, Lutheran, and Reformed. Moreover, the treaty provided that the religion of the ruler determined the religion of the ruler's people. Under such conditions, religious problems, intolerance, and persecution arose. This religious situation is significant with regard to the German immigrations, especially for those who found that they were residents of a state whose ruler's beliefs were different.

Weather Conditions. A freak accident of nature also contributed to the first wave of German immigration to America: the severely cold winter of 1708–1709. Hundreds died of cold and hunger throughout the Rhine valley. So intense was the cold that wild animals and birds froze to death. Vineyards were destroyed and fruits trees were ruined.

Chain Migration. The first mass wave of German immigration was a continuation of the trickle of immigrants, which had commenced in 1608 with the movement of individuals, then had included families, and finally had led to the establishment of the first permanent German settlement. This brought more immigrants from similar areas in Germany to certain areas in America, thus coming to be known as chain, or serial, migration.

The Image of America. Since the discovery of America in 1492, the image of America had been extremely positive. This was particularly accentuated by William Penn, who spared no effort to attract German colonists to Pennsylvania. Not only did he write full descriptions of the province, but he proclaimed political and religious toleration as the very cornerstone of the colony. Many of these brochures were spread throughout Germany. The publications of Pastorius also influenced many in Germany to immigrate, especially as it was now known that there was a Germantown in America. Not only these, but numerous other kinds of publications about America began appearing. Tales were told of a land of milk and honey; of a land where the climate was more temperate than in Germany; where the basic conditions of life were more favorable; where all creeds were tolerated, not just the three recognized churches; where secular and ecclesiastical princes were unknown; where universal freedom prevailed; where strife never came; where not only ease and comfort, but also a certain degree of wealth awaited the settler. These descriptions and more were read about and told around many a fireside and enchanted all those who heard about America. With all these positive images coming to their attention, many Germans contrasted them with the grim specter of the continuation of hardships.[4]

Britain's Favorable Naturalization Law. In 1709 England passed the Naturalization Act, which provided for the naturalization of all foreign Protestants. This act not only facilitated the swift naturalization of Germans, but actually encouraged immigration to America. One source indicates that in May 1709, seven thousand Germans "who had been utterly ruined and driven from their habitations by the French" had come to London for the purpose of immigration. The impact of the act was so great that the ruler of the Palatinate published an order making it punishable by death or by confiscation of property for any of his subjects to quite their homeland. All these reasons blended together in various degrees to provide for the general and specific reasons which caused the German immigrations. Each person could cite a particular reason for immigrating, but through them all runs one long, unvarying refrain—"the hope of bettering themselves, of securing religious toleration, and domestic tranquility."[5]

The First Wave: The Palatine Exodus

During the sixteenth century, a large proportion of the inhabitants of the Palatinate on the Rhine joined the Reformed Church. During the Thirty Years' War, the Palatine was repeatedly devastated by the contending armies. The pathetic Frederick V, the Winter King, took over the leadership of the Protestant cause but was badly defeated in Bohemia. General Tily, the Catholic commander, carried the war into his own country and laid it waste. The ruined land did not fare much better when its supposed friends, the Swedes under Gustavus Adolphus, came along. The final blow came with the Spaniards, who exceeded all their predecessors in cruelty and brutality.

The next invaders were the French and the Bavarians in 1639. Their depradations in 1644 were so thorough that they left the land practically a desert. The successor of the Winter King, the Elector Karl Ludwig, was just beginning to make some progress in restoring the land to prosperity when it was invaded by the troops of Louis XIV. The beautiful castle of Heidelberg and the city of Mannheim were burned during the winter of 1688–89. The greed and the cruelty of the invaders reduced the population to complete poverty.

Although Karl Ludwig had been a Catholic, he had treated the Protestants with tolerance. However, his successors ruled with land with an iron fist and mercilessly persecuted the Lutherans and the Reformed. It was no wonder, then, that the impoverished and wretched population looked to emigration as their only salvation. Their thoughts were turned toward America through the words of William Penn and through what seemed like an invitation from Queen Anne of England to settle in her transatlantic colonies. This was due to the bond of a common Protestant faith and to the fact that the royal families were related. Elizabeth, the daughter of James I, had married Frederick V, the Elector of the Palatinate, and had resided with him in Heidelberg Castle.

The idea of a Palatine immigration to America was first raised by the Reverend Joshua Kocherthal, who became known as the Joshua to the Germans in America. As early as 1704, he had visited England to inquire about the possibility of immigration to America. To further the idea, he published an immensely influential brochure in 1706, which was reprinted in 1709. The volume, *Ausführlich und umständlicher Bericht von der berühmten Landschafft Carolina* (Frankfurt am Main: Georg Heinrich Oehrling, 1706), strongly recommended immigration to America, especially to the colony of Carolina.

Kocherthal's book described Carolina geographically, its location to Pennsylvania, and the route from Germany to Holland, and from there to England, and then further to America. He noted that religious freedom prevailed in America, even for the Mennonites. Every head of a family could procure land, and the taxes were minimal. Hunting and fishing were free, and the land fruitful. Among the crops he mentions are Indian corn, rice, grapes, tobacco, apples, pears, and plums. The climate is favorable for the raising of cattle, swine, and other farm animals. Generally, the climate is very good, he writes, and Indians can attain the age of one hundred. He notes that the voyage may take six weeks, and that the fare is 5 to 6 pounds sterling. To his credit, he does not hide any of the dangers and difficulties with regard to immigration. The peril of the long journey and the many hardships are faithfully narrated. Also, his readers are warned against being influenced by the desire for riches, or for an easy life, or by the love of adventure, or mere curiosity. He indicates that the opportunity should be considered only by those for whom all other means of support had failed.

Kocherthal's book became so influential in Germany, especially in the southwestern regions, that in 1711 Wilhelm Hoehn published a book against it, that was supposed to be "a fully description of the unhappy voyage of the pilgrims who recently went from Germany to the English possessions in Carolina and Pennsylvania . . . especially directed against the one-sided, and unfounded report of Kocherthal."[6] Hoehn strongly warns against immigration fever, and points out that everyone going to America must be prepared for troubles, must be ready to die, must have plenty of money, and must be able to support his family for one year out of savings.

Kocherthal's ideas struck fertile ground, especially with the deteriorating conditions in the Palatinate. Throughout the war of Spanish Succession in 1707, a section of the Palatinate was devastated, and thousands were rendered homeless. It was at this point that the Reverend Joshua von Kocherthal applied to an English agency in Frankfurt for permission to take sixty persons with him to England. Since they were without means of support when they reached London, the generous queen provided for them. Kocherthal asked whether they could go to the colonies, whereupon the Lords of Trade decided to send them to New York. On the same ship with Lord Lovelace, the new governor, they set forth after having been naturalized as British subjects. Most of them were carpenters, smiths, and weavers.

They arrived in New York in October 1708 and were delighted with the beauty of the Hudson River, which reminded them of the Rhine. Lord Lovelace gave them a tract of land, apportioning fifty acres to every individual. They founded a settlement named Neuburg, now Newburgh. In 1709, Lord Lovelace, who had helped them, passed away. The Palatines, as they were known, had to appeal to the colonial government for assistance, which was granted to them. Since the soil around Newburgh was not particularly fertile, they sold their holdings to the Dutch and English newcomers and moved north to Schoharie or south to Pennsylvania.

Kocherthal, who served as farmer, minister, and German community leader, sailed to England in 1710 and returned to New York with another company of Palatines. Although he organized a Lutheran Church in West Camp, he was deeply respected by the Reformed. The provincial authorities also valued his judgment and frequently consulted him on temporal matters. The success of Kochterthal in securing the help of the English queen encouraged many others to look to the New World.

Large numbers of Palatines migrated to England. The migratory movement was underway by May 1709; by October there were almost fifteen thousand Palatines in London. Although the city was large and prosperous, it was not at all prepared for such a large influx of foreigners. The authorities and private individuals, however, displayed unusual generosity and provided the Palatines with food and shelter for some months.

An indication of the tragic plight of the Palatines was provided by means of their address to the English people:

We, the poor distressed Palatines, whose utter ruin was occasioned by the merciless cruelty of a bloody enemy, the French, whose prevailing power some years past, like a torrent, rushed into our country and overwhelmed us at once; and being not content with money and food necessary for their occasions, not only dispossessed us of all support but inhumanly burnt our houses to the ground, whereby being deprived of all shelter, we were turned into the open fields, there with our families to seek what shelter we could find, were obliged to make the earth our repository for rest, and the clouds our canopy or covering.[7]

When the Palatines were ready to be moved, a first contingent of five hundred families was sent to the province of Munster in Ireland, where they settled. The second group, which consisted of more than six hundred families, sailed to the Carolinas in 1709. Under the leadership of Baron Chrisopher de Graffenreid and Franz Louis Michel, two natives of Bern, Switzerland, they founded the settlement of Newbern at the mouth of the Neuse River in North Carolina.

The largest contingent, some three thousand persons under the leadership of Colonel Robert Hunter, the new governor of New York, sailed to the colony in 1710. The accommodations were so inadequate that 773 passengers died of fever. One of the ships was lost off the east end of Long Island, an incident that was immortalized by Whittier. Nevertheless, a good many survived the trip, and New York found itself unprepared for such a large number of newcomers. Because of the many deaths, there were children who had lost their parents. These orphans were taken by the authorities and apprenticed to tradesmen. Among these forty-one boys was John Peter Zenger, who later made history by his courageous fight for freedom of the press.

The journey to America, which usually took about six weeks but depending on various conditions could be as short as a month or as long as three months, was rugged. One danger was the large number of pirates along the coasts of the colonies who preyed upon ships at sea. It was estimated that in the 1710s approximately fifteen hundred men were engaged in piracy off the American coast. In 1718 Blackbeard the pirate appeared off the coast of Charleston with four vessels armed with forty guns and four hundred men. They captured all the vessels entering or departing the harbor for a period of four days. There were complaints against the "swarms which every summer infest our coasts, where they not only take vast numbers of our vessels, but have plundered several small towns and villages."[8]

Food and drink on board ships were often not the best quality. Pastorius himself recorded that meat was served four times a week and fish three times a week during his voyage to Pennsylvania. Often the drinking water became depleted so that rain water was stored for the passengers. Also, the captains and sailors could be rough, domineering, and cruel. One immigrant claimed moreover that the immigrants were packed in a ship like herring. Another wrote that his ship had lost 150 passengers due to starvation, and that to satisfy their hunger the survivors had caught rats and mice, with the price of a mouse fixed at half a gulden. Of course, the passengers were especially susceptible should a disease or sickness break out, which could and did spread throughout the ship. Another danger was the stormy and raging sea. One immigrant wrote:

> At noon our third storm began. At four it was more violent than before. Now, indeed, we could say, "The waves of the sea were mighty, and raged horribly. They rose up to the heavens above, and clave down to hell beneath." The winds roared round about us, and . . . whistled as distinctly as if it had been a human voice. This ship not only rocked to and fro with the utmost violence, but shook and jarred with so unequal, grating a motion, that one could not but with great difficulty keep one's hold of anything, nor stand a moment without it. Every ten minutes came a shock against the stern or side of the ship, which one would think should dash the planks in pieces.[9]

After the new immigrants arrived in New York, Governor Hunter thought it would be an excellent idea to send them upstate into the pine forests to have them make pitch and tar. Almost two thousand were then sent forth, some four hundred women and children remaining in New York City. Hunter, a soldier by profession, made a poor manager as far as the manufacture of pitch and tar was concerned, so the enterprise failed. Angered by the failure, the governor refused to allow the Palatines any land for settlement.

Under the leadership of Johann Conrad Weiser and Captain Kneiskern, who had headed a company in an expedition to Canada, the Germans migrated to Schoharie, where the friendly Indians gave them land. There they founded the town of Rhinebeck-on-the-Hudson and also a group of villages on both sides of the Schoharie River. These were named for leaders of the colonists: Weisersdorf, Hartmannsdorf, Brunnendorf, Schmidtsdorf, Fuchsdorf, Gerlachsdorf, Kneiskerndorf.

Weiser was a very capable leader whose son, Conrad, had lived with the Mohawk Indians for a while and had learned their language. He became the mediator between the colonists and the Indians, who traded with one another and shared festivals. Unfortunately the relations between the Palatines and the Netherlanders were not as good. These settlers, generally well-to-do patricians, were very well established and tended to look down upon the plebian newcomers from Germany.

Governor Hunter, too, was still resentful, and Conrad Wesier had to to wage a long fight to maintain the rights of the Palatines to their lands. The next governor, Brunet, was more considerate and persuaded them to move to lands on the Mohawk. About three hundred remained in Schoharie; the others settled in the Mohawk Valley.

This was not only very fertile land, but it was also the frontier of western New York. The Palatines, therefore, made an additional contribution to the colony. In times of peace, the area was a granary for the inhabitants; during the French and Indian War and the American Revolution, it served as a bulwark against the enemy. In the middle of the eighteenth century, there were about three thousand Palatines living in that area.

Still having trouble with their landlords, a number of Palatines decided to migrate. They fixed on Pennsylvania, as its governor, Keith, had given them an invitation that promised freedom and justice. They accepted and moved in two contingents, on in 1723 and a second in 1728. About three hundred persons left Schoharie, paddling canoes down the Susquehanna River. The first settlement they founded was Heidelberg.

In 1728, the second group arrived and settled at Womelsdorf under the direction of Conrad Weiser, who was soon recognized as the leader of the Germans in Berks County. These settlements in the Tulpehocken district prospered and thrived. Their glowing reports to their relatives in the homeland turned the stream of immigration away from New York to

Pennsylvania. Twenty years after the settlement of Tulpehocken, there were almost fifty thousand Germans in the county. Even those Germans who arrived in New York made their way through dense forest to Pennsylvania, to which the main stream of the German immigration flowed. Pennsylvania became the major destination point, as well as a distribution center to surrounding colonies.

The real significance of the Palatine exodus was that it transformed the German immigration into a *Massen-Auswanderung*, a mass migration movement, and once this wave was started, it would be followed by numerous others well into the twentieth century. Even after the 1709 exodus had subsided, the immigration sustained itself. For example, at the port of Philadelphia three thousand Germans arrived in 1732 and another twelve thousand in 1749.

Indentured Servants

Before the American Revolution, thousands of Germans came to America as indentured servants, or redemptionists. Germans who were too poor to pay the ship's captain for the journey to America signed an I.O.U. contract with the captain. Upon arrival in America the captain would sell this contract for a sum of money. The purchaser would then have the service of the immigrant until the debt was paid off. The service time was usually three to seven years. Children served to the age of twenty-one. So many of the indentured servants were Germans that the trade became known as the "German trade."

The indentured servant system began to be used extensively for German immigrants after 1728. Before the ships from Europe were allowed to cast anchor, all the immigrants had to be examined for disease. The next step was to bring them to the city hall to take the oath of allegiance to the king of England. After this, they were brought back to the ship. Those who had paid their ticket fare were released; those who were too poor were to be sold as indentured servants. They were advertised in various newspapers. Buyers would make their choice and bargain for the immigrants. The young, unmarried people were sold quickly, whereas the older immigrants were more difficult to market, unless they had children. The sick were obviously not marketable, and many of them perished. The following advertisements are samples from the German trade:

A 1742 advertisement announces: "To be sold. A likely servant woman having three years and a half to serve. She is a good spinner."

A 1764 advertisement states that hundreds of Germans, including workers, craftsmen, young people, men, women, boys, and girls, were available.

A 1766 advertisement announces a "strong, fresh, and healthy young maiden for five years service."

An advertisement from 1773 announced the sale of a German boy "who has five years and three months to serve; he has been brought up in the tailor's business. Can work well."

A 1774 newspaper advertisement reads "There are still 50–60 German people, which just arrived from Germany, in stock. . . . There are teachers, craftsmen, farmers, etc."

These are just a few examples of the thousands of newspaper advertisements that announced the sale of German indentured servants. Other advertisements next to these announced the sale of bricks, iron, tools, and other items. Heinrich A. Rattermann described the "soul sellers," as the dealers of indentured servants came to be known. They would travel through Germany in elegant carriages, wearing splendid clothes, golden rings, and extravagant attire. They would then entice anyone they could to sign a contract to immigrate to America. One such "soul seller" brought over more than six hundred shiploads of immigrants.

On board, the immigrants were often poorly treated. One shipload of 160 Germans brought only ten live people to the American shore. Heinrich Keppele, the first president of the German Society of Pennsylvania, told of how 250 of his 312 copassengers died on board ship. Other papers reported how Germans were packed in tight like sardines. In 1749, over two thousand Germans died because the quarters in which they had been forced to cross the Atlantic had been packed too tightly.

Finally, in 1764 the German-Americans of Philadelphia established the German Society of Pennsylvania, the oldest German-American society in the United States. It was founded to extend a helping hand to German immigrants. The Pennsylvania Germans succeeded in uniting so that laws were passed rendering impossible the tyrannies and extortions practiced by sea captains and the soul sellers. By 1818, a more effective law was passed by the Pennsylvania legislature. This regulated the importation of German immigrants. However, not until 1820 was the sale of indentured servants banned.

The chief value of indentured servitude was that it gave immigrants who might not otherwise have been able to immigrate the opportunity to come to America. However, in the long run, such a system could not endure, as it was it was not viewed as consistent with the American conception of human rights.[10]

John Peter Zenger, Champion of a Free Press

Among the helpless Palatine orphan boys who had been left behind in New York, one was destined to make one of the most significant contributions to freedom of thought and expression in America—Peter Zenger.

At thirteen years of age he had the good fortune of being apprenticed to William Bradford, a generous, kindly English Quaker who had come to America with William Penn. Bradford was a printer and had the distinction of being the only one in New York. By 1725 he had established the first newspaper, the *New York Gazette*, which did rather well. Bradford soon needed help and hired the young, friendless Palatine.

Zenger was a bright, diligent youth and rose rapidly. Indeed, Bradford was so pleased with his work that he made him his partner. The older man was a liberal, however, and when Bradford offered his unswerving support to the British governor, Zenger left his benefactor and started his own newspaper, the *New York Weekly Journal*, which vigorously attacked the administration and espoused the cause of the opposition.

Zenger soon found an objective for his keen, satiric pen. The new governor, Cosby, was responsible for a number of highhanded actions, which the editor denounced fearlessly in the columns of his newspaper. His Excellency, William Cosby, Captain General and Governor-in-Chief of the Provinces of New York, New Jersey, and Territories thereon depending, was filled with wrath. He directed the grand jury to indict

Zenger for libel. He also requested the assembly to order the public burning of copies of the *Weekly Journal*.

Cosby asserted that Zenger's publication contained

> divers scandalous, virulent, false, and seditious reflections . . . which said reflections seem contrived by the wicked authors of them, not only to create jealousies, discontent, animosities in the minds of His Majesty's liege people of this province . . . but to alienate their affections from the best of kings, and raise factions, tumults and sedition among them.[11]

None of the governor's efforts to silence Zenger met with success. Finally he had the offending editor clapped into jail and held incommunicado. He remained there for ten months. On August 14, 1735, criminal procedures were instituted against Zenger. The defendant's case seemed hopeless until the venerable Andrew Hamilton of Philadelphia came into the courtroom. This able Scotch-Irish lawyer won his case by a very simple argument; he merely pointed out that what Zenger had printed was factual, so there was no case of libel.

Despite the hostile charge by Judge Delancey, the jury returned a verdict of not guilty. The courtroom rang with joy and triumph. Zenger was cheered and acclaimed, and the aged and the infirm Hamilton was escorted down the street by an enthusiastic crowd accompanied by a band.

Zenger possessed not only courage but also exceptional editorial skill. He made a valuable contribution to legal and historical literature by printing a verbatim account of the trial. His bail had been set so high that he had to remain in prison for almost a year. But each day his wife came to see him, so he was able to provide her with the details and the newspaper was able to appear without interruption. Loyal employees took care of the printing.

This dramatic incident is the basis for a novel by Kent Cooper, *Anne Zenger: Mother of Freedom*. He points out that during her husband's ten-month incarceration, Anna Zenger published the *Weekly Journal* and thus became the first woman publisher in the country. She did this with skill and brilliance. According to the accepted versions, Mrs. Zenger was a pious, respectable wife and a devoted mother. Cooper concluded that she was a gifted writer—far superior to her husband. In fact, Zenger's fame is considerably diminished. According to Cooper, he was an uneducated, unimaginative printer. Moreover, he was incapable of writing the incisive articles and vitriolic diatribes that nettled the governor. Apparently it was his wife who was the author.

The question may be argued, but Peter Zenger's fame will rest on his two great achievements: the founding of the first independent newspaper in America and his courageous stand for the principle of freedom of the press.

The New Jersey and Maryland Germans

In 1707 a number of German families belonging to the Reformed Church emigrated from the Braunschweig area and set sail for New York. Driven off its course by adverse winds, their vessel landed in Delaware Bay. From Philadelphia they set out overland for New York. As they journeyed through the beautiful Musconetong Valley in New Jersey, they were so delighted with the region that they decided to go no further. They settled in what is now Morris County and eventually spread to Somerset, Bergen, and Essex Counties. The first German church was opened near Potterstown in 1731.

A considerable number of Germans from the Palatinate also settled in New Jersey around 1710. In fact, in southern New Jersey, some Germans had arrived with Swedish settlers before 1700. The inhabitants in that part of New Jersey, known as German Valley, were chiefly farmers, and through their industry and thrift converted the wilderness into prosperous agricultural areas.

A number of them distinguished themselves during the Revolutionary War: General Frederick Frelinghuysen and Johann Peter Rockefeller, to name only two. The grandson of Theodore J. Frelinghuysen (or Frelinghausen), born in Lingen, Friesland, General Frederick Frelinghuysen took part in the battles of Trenton and Monmouth Courthouse. He later became a member of the Continental Congress, the Convention of 1787, and the U.S. Senate from 1793 to 1796. The Rockefellers are descended from early German settlers in New Jersey. In 1906 John D. Rockefeller erected a monument to the memory of his ancestor,

Johann Peter Rockefeller, "who came from Germany about 1733 and died in 1783."

Although the German settlers were honest and thrifty, there was sometimes serious dissension in the churches. One of these bitter church quarrels was tactfully settled by the Reverend Heinrich Melchior Muehlenberg, the patriarch of the New Jersey German Lutherans from 1757 to 1775.

The church services were, of course, conducted in German. As time went on, however, English made rapid encroachments. Naturally, there was a short transition period during which the two languages mingled. This was the case in the preaching of the Reverend Caspar Wick, who filled the pulpit of Great Swamp Church beginning in 1771. An English army officer interested in hearing a German church service attended the church on Sunday morning. After listening to Wick's preaching, he exclaimed, "I never knew before that German was so much like English; I could understand a great deal of it." He had heard what was supposed to have been an English sermon!

The existence of German settlers in southern New Jersey is confirmed by the diaries of itinerant Moravian preachers who knew practically no English. The Moravian settlements were noted for their cleanliness and neatness, and a model in this respect was Hope Settlement in Warren County, which boasted an unusually fine mill. This is described in detail by an admiring French soldier on Lafayette's staff who visited it in 1788. Later, these Moravians sold their property at Hope and moved to Bethlehem.

A few Germans had settled in Maryland before 1660, having received grants of land in Baltimore County. A curious group of sectarians were the Labadists, a sect of Christian communists who settled in 1684 on the Bohemian River (now in Delaware). The found and leader of the colony was Vorstmann born in Wesel on the Rhine. Before emigrating, he assumed the name of Sluyter (or Schluter). With a coworker, Jasper Danker, he was sent by the mother colony in Westfriesland to found a settlement in America. They chose the land of Augustin Hermann on the Bohemian River. Hermann's son became a convert to the sect. Sluyter became a successful tobacco planter and slave trader and acquired considerable wealth.

Augstin Hermann, the founder of Cecil County, was more distinguished. He had originally lived in New Amsterdam and became prosperous as a dealer in tobacco. Stuyvesant sent him on various diplomatic missions. In fact, he drew a map of Maryland for Lord Baltimore, which was highly praised by the king. Hermann was the representative of Baltimore in the General Assembly.

Although few Germans came to Maryland before 1730, they were active in the settlement of Baltimore. Many came from Pennsylvania. When the city was incorporated in 1796, there were three Germans among the first seven aldermen. During the Revolution, the Baltimore Germans sent several companies of volunteers. Washington's purchasing agent, Keeport (Kuhbord), was a Baltimore German. When the Continental Congress had to flee from Philadelphia, it held its meetings in a hall owned by a German merchant.

The Germans contributed greatly to Baltimore's commercial development. They engaged in the tobacco trade, shipbuilding, leather manufacturing, and foreign trade. Since the city was considered so important, Bremen and Hamburg ship companies established agencies in Baltimore.

The western part of Maryland was settled by Pennsylvania Germans. The first ones, who were on their way to Virginia, arrived at the Monocacy River around 1729. They came by way of an old Indian trail, which had been widened and later became the chief highway from Lancaster County to the South. The Pennsylvania Germans were particularly attracted by Lord Baltimore's generous offer made in 1732. Families might secure two hundred acres at a rental of eight shillings a year, and individuals could rent a hundred acres on the same terms. No rent was paid the first three years.

Monocacy, the first settlement, did not last long. However, nearby Creagerstown, founded by a German named Creager, flourished. Only three miles from Creagerstown another group of Germans founded Frederick Town in 1745, the settlers consisting of a hundred families who had come from the Palatinate. Their leader was Thomas Schley, who assumed the offices of teacher and minister as well as magistrate.

These early settlements were visited by Muehlenberg, the Lutheran patriarch, and Schlatter, the leader of the Reformed Church. The only other Protestant denomination among the Germans were the Moravians, who founded Graceham, some twelve miles northwest of Frederick Town.

Germans from the Palatinate continued to arrive in Maryland. Between 1748 and 1753, about twenty-eight hundred settled in Frederick or in Baltimore Counties. In 1784 John Frederick Amelung from Bremen arrived with over three hundred Germans, largely craftsmen and artisans. Their settlement, called Fleecy Dale, was on Bennett's Creek near the Monocacy. A factory for the manufacture of glass was constructed, and it attained considerable fame—George Washington even mentioned it in a letter to Thomas Jefferson. In fact, Amelung traveled to Mount Vernon to present two goblets made of flint glass to Washington. When he arrived, he found a man in shirtsleeves on a ladder, fixing the grapevines. Amelung continued making punch bowls, wineglasses, decanters, and mirrors of high quality.

Many settlements were founded by Germans in western Maryland. Among them are Middleton, Sharpsburg, Taneytown, Tom's Creek, Point Creek, Owen's Creek, Union Bridge, Emmettsburg, and Woodsboro. The two settlements farthest west were Conogocheague and Hagerstown. Conogocheague was not far from the present town of Clear Spring, eight miles southwest of Hagerstown. Creagerstown, a mile from Monocacy, was founded by a German named Creager.

Hagerstown was founded by Jonathan Hager, who arrived in America before 1739. He secured twenty-five hundred acres and in 1762 laid out a town that he called Elizabeth in honor of his wife. The town, however, came to be known as Hager's Town. It became the county seat and in 1807 contained over four hundred houses. Hager was elected by his district to the assembly of Maryland.

It is interesting to note that Admiral Schley, the commander at the Battle of Santiago in the Spanish-American War, was descended from early Maryland Germans. Thomas Schley, the schoolmaster of Frederick Town, had a son, Jacob, who became a captain in the Revolutionary Army. A grandson, William Schley, was a member of Congress and a governor of Georgia. Several members of the family became judges and legislators.

On the whole, however, the Maryland Germans, like those of Pennsylvania, were farmers; only in Baltimore did they devote themselves to industry and commerce.[12]

The Virginia Germans

It is generally thought that Virginia was settled predominantly by the English. In the Valley of Virginia, however, the English stock was small compared to the German and the Scotch-Irish. There were, in fact, many Pennsylvania Germans settlements in the Shenandoah Valley.

Like a number of other governors, Governor Spotswood of Virginia thought highly of the Germans and encouraged them to settle in his Colony. According to one report, the governor's wife was a German woman from Hannover. At the solicitation of Baron de Graffenried, twelve German families arrived in Virginia in April 1714 to establish and operate iron works. The governor himself founded the town of Germanna. The Germans came from North Germany—that is, from Westphalia. Encouraged by the favorable reports, several other groups followed; twenty families in 1717 and forty families between 1717 and 1720.

The governor pursued his pet project with energy and built homes for the Colonists. Despite these efforts, the mining operations soon ceased. The Colonists and the governor got into a dispute about who was in debt to whom, and the case was finally taken to court. Disappointed and discouraged, all but three of the Gemran families moved away from Germanna in 1748.

This group established two settlements, Germantown in 1721 and Little Fork in 1724. In both villages, schoolhouses and churches were built. The inhabitants belonged to the Reformed faith. The German Lutherans, who had come to Germanna in 1717 and who were chiefly from Wuerttemberg, settled in Madison County.

Eventually a portion of the Shenandoah Valley, sloping to the north, was settled almost entirely by Germans. It is probable that as early as 1726 a number of Pennsylvania Germans founded a village twelve miles above Harpers Ferry, which they named New Mecklenburg. In 1728 a German, Jacob Stauffer, obtained as much land as he could by counting every horse and cow as a member of his family. He settled in the northern end of the Massanutten Range and founded the town of Staufferstadt, later renamed Strasburg. Robert Harper, a German, settled in 1734 at the junction of the Shenandoah and the Potomac Rivers and founded the historic Harpers Ferry.

As soon as the fertility of the valley became generally known, there was a considerable influx of settlers from Pennsylvania, who not only developed prosperous farms, but also took an active part in the life of the community, establishing schools, churches, and shops. They helped defend the frontier. In 1754 five Waggener brothers, German settlers in Culpepper County, joined Colonel Washington when he attacked Fort Duquesne.

Scattered German settlements appeared in various parts of Virginia, and there were individual Germans in almost every town. In Richmond, the oldest stone house is said to have been built by a German in 1737.

Our knowledge of life in the towns and villages inhabited by Germans is based on the diaries of the Moravian missionaries who made annual trips through the frontier settlements. The earliest recorded journey of this type is that of Schnell in 1743. The most extensive trip he made lasted from November 6, 1743, to April 10, 1744. His wanderings took him from Bethlehem, Pennsylvania, through Maryland, Virginia, and the Carolinas to Georgia. In Savannah, he boarded a sloop for New York, arriving in Bethlehem five months after he had left it. The courage and the endurance of these humane and noble Moravians cannot be praised too highly, for their records have become invaluable documents in American history.[13]

The Georgia Germans

In 1731 Archbishop Leopold of Salzburg issued a decree banning all non-Catholics from his bishopric. More than thirty thousand Protestants were driven out of their homes. After enduring many hardships, these pious, hardworking folks were welcomed in a number of countries. About seventeen thousand settled in Prussia.

Their reputation was so good that when King George II of England authorized a number of gentlemen to colonize the southern part of the Carolinas, Scottish Highlanders and German Salzburgers were named as desirable immigrants. General James Edward Ogelthorpe left England with the first group of English colonists and arrived at the mouth of the Savannah River on January 20, 1733. There he founded the city of Savannah.

A number of Lutheran clergymen had espoused the cause of the Salzburgers in London, forming the Society for the Promotion of Christian Knowledge. They agreed to see to it that the Salzburgers were transferred to Rotterdam. The Georgia Land Company was happy to get them and made arrangements for their transportation to America. A group of Salzburgers under the direction of Baron von Reck left Berchtesgaden and reached Rotterdam on November 27, 1733. Two Lutheran clergymen took over the leadership of the emigrants, Bolzius and Gronau, both of whom had been supervisors in Francke's orphanage in Halle.

They left England at the end of December 1733 and arrived in Charleston, South Carolina, in March 1734. When they later reached Savannah they were received with shouts of welcome and booming cannons. General Ogelthorpe was happy to have them in his colony and permitted them to select a site for their settlement. Under the guidance of Baron von Reck, they chose a trace of land on the right bank of the river, some twenty-five miles above Savannah. They named the place Ebenezer, "stone of help," emulating the Old Testament prophet Samuel.

A short time later, fifty-seven more Salzburgers arrived, and the Georgia Land Company generously supplied them with lumber and with tools. Thus, the little settlement took firm root. Von Reck returned to Germany to induce more Salzburgers to join the Colony. A short time thereafter, eighty more came, together with twenty-seven Moravians and a number of English Protestants. They landed in Savannah in February 1736. The Moravians, however, stayed but a brief time. When the neighboring Spaniards began to attack the settlements and armed resistance became necessary, the Moravians, who were pacifists, left Georgia and founded Bethlehem, Pennsylvania, in 1741.

On board ship with the Salzburgers and Moravians were representatives of another religious group: the Wesleys—John, the founder of Methodism, and his brother, Charles. They had come to convert the Indians. John Wesley was much impressed by the humble piety and the strong faith of the Salzburgers and the Moravians. The Moravians especially influenced his religious thinking deeply. The decisive moment in his life came when he attended a meeting of Moravians in London and felt deeply moved.

As a defense against the Spaniards, Governor Ogelthorpe asked some of the Salzburgers to defend a fort on St. Simon Island. Since they were loath to bear arms, most of them decided to stay in Ebenezer. A number of them, however, did go. Under the direction of their captain, Hermsdorf, they founded a settlement known as Frederica. It developed into a charming, attractive village but declined for unknown reasons after 1750.

Ebenezer, meanwhile, was found to be an undesirable site for a colony. The soil was not good, there were swamps, and the area was infested with disease. Two years after the foundation of the settlement, the Salzburgers decided to move. They chose a high ridge, eight miles farther down the river, on which they established a town called New Ebenezer.

New Ebenezer was carefully planned. The streets were laid out at right angles, in checkerboard fashion. Provisions were made for a church, a school, a storehouse, and an orphan asylum. Around the town were pastures and fifty-acre farms. The neighboring Indians did not molest the settlers. On the opposite side of the river was the settlement of Pursburg, which had been founded by Swiss-Germans. Some of them came to New Ebenezer and helped build the silk industry to promote the growing of silk. This industry so prospered that in one year the Salzburgers were able to send a thousand pounds of cocoons to England.

The settlement was a model colony; the inhabitants were thrifty, industrious, and peace loving. There were neither drunkards nor profligates. Since it was a religious community, it is not strange that it was ruled by the two pastors, Johann Martin Bolzius and Israel Christian Gronau. They were responsible to the Society for the Promotion of Christian Knowledge and to the Lutheran Church in Germany. A code was followed that, among other things, required the support of ministers and teachers and made provision for widows and orphans. The two clergymen constituted a court, which seems to have worked out very well, for not a single decision of theirs was ever appealed.

Like the Germans in the other colonies, the Salzburgers were opposed to slavery. Most outspoken on this subject was the Reverend Johann Bolzius. There was, however, strong pressure by the large landowners of the province, who needed slaves to work their plantations. The problem was finally referred to one of the superintendents of the Lutheran parent church in Augsburg. His advice was to yield, adding some pious reflections about taking slaves so as to convert them. Reluctantly, Bolzius withdrew his opposition to the repeal of the law prohibiting slavery.

Bolzius was a very capable leader and an extremely competent manager. When his colleague, Gronau, died, he continued to direct all the affairs of the colony himself, until a successor, the Reverend Hermann Lembke, came over. Bolzius received funds from Europe that he invested in farms and industries. The income from two gristmills, a sawmill, and a rice stamping mill supplied a good income for the payment of ministers and teachers. Bolzius also promoted the silk industry. In 1733 Nicholas Amatis of Piedmont came to Georgia to instruct the colonists in the rearing of silkworms and the manufacture of silk. In 1742 five hundred mulberry trees were sent to New Ebenezer, and a shop was established for the processing of silk.

German settlements continued to spread and grow. Farms owned by Germans were to be found on both sides of a road running from Savannah to Augusta, a distance of one hundred miles. Within a short time there were four churches in the parish, requiring additional teachers and ministers from Europe. Christopher Triebner, one of the ministers, caused dissension; however, the quarrel was tactfully settled by Reverend Muehlenberg, the capable administrator of the Lutheran Church in the colonies (1774).

By this time, New Ebenezer had reached the high point of its importance. It numbered about five hundred inhabitants, who were known for their industry and sober habits. Silk was exported to Europe, and trade was carried on with neighboring towns. From New Ebenezer, Germans soon spread out to other parts of the state.[14]

Germans in New England

Although the German population was heavily concentrated in certain areas of the United States, it was not the case in New England. Nevertheless, there were some who did settle there. The earliest settlements were due to the work of Samuel Waldo, whose father was a Swedish Pomeranian nobleman who came to Boston as the agent of a business located in Hamburg. He became a prosperous merchant who traveled back and forth between Germany and America. His son, Samuel, was born in London of a German mother and was educated at Harvard and in Germany. He was a member of the Hanoverian Elector's bodyguard when he ascended the English throne as George I. On his father's death, Waldo left London in 1724 and came to Boston, where he was made a colonel in the militia.

Waldo was a very successful businessman. In 1732 he acquired a large tract of land on the Muscongus River in Maine, which at that time was part of Massachusetts. In 1736 a colony was established by the Scotch-Irish on St. George's River. Anxious to get more farmers to develop the land, Waldo went to Germany in 1738 to secure colonists. In 1740 he was able to persuade forty families from Brunswick and Saxony to come to Maine. They founded Waldobourg on both sides of the Medomak River. Yet their lot was not very happy, for they were entirely unaccustomed to life in the wilderness.

Having become involved in other business affairs, Waldo turned over his colonial enterprise to an agent named Sebastian Zauberbuehler, who went to Germany and returned with 160 immigrants. Landing in Boston, they set out for Maine. They joined the other German immigrants at Waldobourg (or Waldoboro) and suffered severe hardships. Zauberbuehler stayed with them until December and then disappeared.

The wretched colonists appealed to the governor and the Massachusetts Assembly for assistance. While various committees investigated, debated, and reported, the miserable settlers had to struggle through another winter. In 1744 war broke out between England and France, and the colonists were drawn into this conflict. Samuel Waldo, brigadier-general, was third in command of the New England forces that besieged Louisbourg on Cape Breton Island. Some of the inhabitants of Waldobourg enlisted under Johannes Ulmer, while others sought refuge in nearby forts. When the war was over, they returned to the settlements.

Another disaster to befall Waldobourg was an attack by Indians in May 1746. Surprising the peaceful settlement, they completely destroyed it and massacred many of the inhabitants. Those who survived returned after 1748, the year peace was concluded, to rebuild the village. Waldo, who seems to have taken renewed interest in the settlement, was able to bring twenty-five German families from Philadelphia. This brought new life into the colony: gristmills and sawmills were built, and a church was erected.

In the meantime, the authorities in Boston had become aware of the advantages of settling honest, thrifty, and hardworking immigrants in Massachusetts. They were interested particularly in German Protestants who would introduce useful arts and handicrafts. In 1749, four townships were allotted for the accommodation of the prospective immigrants. Two were located in the extreme western part of Maine.

Joseph Crellius was another interesting person who helped to promote German immigration to Massachusetts. A Bavarian by birth, he migrated to Philadelphia and started the second German newspaper in America, *Das Hochdeutsche Pennsylvania Journal*, in 1743. He became interested in immigration schemes and in 1748 persuaded a shipload of immigrants whom he had brought to Philadelphia to accept Waldo's offer and settle in Maine. Concluding that there were big profits in this field, Crellius notified the General Court of Massachusetts that he would bring over German Protestants, provided there were sufficient inducements. The Court was ready to grant him two hundred acres in each township, if he was able to settle 120 Protestants within each township in three years. Crellius was not able to carry out these conditions, and so the grants were revoked.

Not disheartened, Crellius proceeded to promote his schemes with greater vigor. In his advertisements, he implied that he was the authorized agent of the Massachusetts authorities and that the British government was behind him as well. This caused an uproar, for by this time there were many agents interested in promoting immigration to other parts of the country. In their eagerness to make their undertakings profitable, a number of them had engaged in questionable practices, causing much suffering to unsuspecting immigrants.

However, Crellius, who seems to have been a clever individual, dissociated himself from these disreputable agents by supporting an act—the first its kind—for the protection of immigrants. It was passed by the Massachusetts House of Representatives in 1750. Some of the provisions forbade overcrowding on vessels and set certain minimum standards. This enraged the ship companies so much that they refused to land in Boston.

Again, Crellius was not discouraged. In the spring of 1751 he brought over some twenty-five German families, despite efforts of his enemies to prevent his securing ships. The new arrivals landed in Boston and then proceeded to the Kennebec River. About twenty miles from its mouth they founded a settlement that they named Frankfort—the present Dresden. Among the settlers were French as well as German Protestants.

Immigration agents, or "newlanders," as they were contemptuously called, were responsible for repeatedly deflecting streams of immigration. For example, large numbers of Germans who would have gone to Pennsylvania or the Carolinas were persuaded to go to Nova Scotia by John Dick of Rotterdam. Nova Scotia became a strongly German Protestant community. In 1749 a brigade of Brunswick-Lueneburg troops who had come over in the English service were induced to stay there by liberal offers of land. Lunenburg was settled by them.

From 1750 there was a steady stream of German immigration, and by 1761 more than nine-tenths of the two hundred land grants bore German names. However, in 1753 immigration to Nova Scotia was stopped by the British government because it felt that the country could not support more inhabitants. Waldo took advantage of this by making greater efforts to win the immigrants for his Maine settlements. He advertised in England and Scotland and went to Germany with his son. He collected sixty families, brought them to Massachusetts, and helped them become absorbed in the Broad Bay settlements. Through such activities in recruiting colonists, the Germans spread over a wider area.

When Waldo died, a dispute arose about the ownership of the land. In disgust, a number of German colonists sold their holdings and migrated to the Orangeburg district in South Carolina.

The thrift and industry of the German immigrants won them a good reputation in Boston. A number of promoters decided that it would be advantageous to develop a special area for them, which led to the founding of Germantown, ten miles south of Boston. New arrivals from Germany came in 1750 and in 1757. Some of the families brought over by Crellius in 1751 may have settled there. The town industrialized quickly and distinguished itself particularly through its production of glass. In 1751 Benjamin Franklin was so impressed by the prosperity of the town that he bought eight building lots there. However, by 1760 Germantown had declined. The colony had broken up, and many of its inhabitants headed north for the Broad Bay settlements in Maine.[15]

Notes

1. Hajo Holborn, *A History of Germany: The Reformation* (New York: Knopf, 1964), p. 174.

2. Don Heinrich Tolzmann, ed., *Germany and America* (Bowie, Md.: Heritage Books, 1991), p. 125.

3. Don Heinrich Tolzmann, ed., *German Immigration to America: The First Wave* (Bowie, Md.: Heritage Books, 1993), p. 277.

4. See Tolzmann, *Germany and America*, pp. 175–256.

5. Tolzmann, *German Immigration to America*, p. 292.

6. Ibid., p. 49.

7. Ibid., p. 309.

8. Ibid., p. 92.

9. Ibid., p. 288. For a review of the literature that influenced the German immigration discussed here, see Tolzmann, *Germany and America*, pp. 175–256.

10. Regarding German indentured servants, see Harry W. Pfund, *A History of the German Society of Pennsylvania. Bicentenary Edition 1764–1964* (Philadelphia: German Society of Pennsylvania, 1964), pp. 1–5. Also see Farley Ward Grubb, *German Immigrant Servant Contracts Registered at the Port of Philadelphia, 1817–1831* (Baltimore, Md.: Genealogical Publishing, 1994).

11. Regarding Zenger, see Gerard Wilk, *Americans from Germany*, ed. Don Heinrich Tolzmann (Indianapolis: Max Kade German-American Center, Indiana University–Purdue University, 1995), pp. 78–80.

12. See Lucy Bittinger, *The Germans in Colonial Times* (Philadelphia: J. B. Lippincott, 1901), pp. 114–20, and Don Heinrich Tolzmann, ed., *Maryland's German Heritage: Daniel Wunderlich Nead's History* (Bowie, Md.: Heritage Books, 1994).

13. See Bittinger, *The Germans*, pp. 121–29.

14. George Fenwick Jones, "German Settlements in Colonial Georgia and Their Copius Documentation," in Eberhard Reichmann, LaVern J. Rippley, and Jörg Nagler, eds., *Emigration and Settlement Patterns of German Communities in North America* (Indianapolis: Max Kade German-American Center, Indiana University-Purdue University, 1995), pp. 23–28.

15. Bittinger, *The Germans*, pp. 130–41, and Tolzmann, *The First Germans in America* (Bowie, Md.: Heritage Books, 1992), pp. 5–7.

Beginnings of
Community Life

Settlement Patterns

(O)n the eve of the American Revolution, German-Americans were concentrated in the counties of the following colonies:

- Maine: Lincoln, Knox, and Waldo
- Massachusetts: Franklin
- New York: Dutchess, Ulster, Columbia, Greene, Montgomery, Fulton, Herkimer, Oneida, Saratoga, and Schenectady
- Pennsylvania: Montgomery, Berks, Lancaster, Lehigh, Lebanon, Dauphin, York, Chester, Northampton, Monroe, Cumberland, and Adams
- Maryland: Baltimore, Frederick, Washington, and Carroll
- New Jersey: Hunterton, Somerset, Morris, Sussex, Passaic, Essex, and Salem
- West Virginia: Jefferson, Berkeley, Morgan, Hampshire, Mineral, Hardy, Grant, and Pendleton
- Virginia: Clarke, Frederick, Warren, Shenandoah, Page, Rockingham, Augusta, Rockbridge, Bath, Boteourt, Montgomery, Wythe, Madison, Fauquier, Rappahannock, Loudoun, Prince William, Albemarle, Greene, Louisia, Orange, Isle of Wight, and Henrico

80

- North Carolina: Davidson, Stanly, Cabarrus, Rowan, Iredell, Catawba, Lincoln, Forsyth, Edgefield, Craven, and Brunswick
- South Carolina: Orangeburg, Lexington, Barnwell, Newberry, Abbeville, Fairfield, Edgefield, Beaufort, and Charleston
- Georgia: Effingham, Screven, Burke, and Chatham

German-Americans had settled some of the best land for agricultural purposes, especially the German counties of New York, Pennsylvania, and the Carolinas. Pennsylvania functioned as the granary for all the colonies during the American Revolution. There were German-American settlements along the whole frontier from Maine to Georgia, but although they had settled throughout the colonies, German-Americans were especially concentrated in Pennsylvania and the colonies adjacent to it.

In 1776 the Continental Congress estimated the population of the colonies at 2,243,000. The total number of Germans at that time has been estimated at 225,000. This would break down as follows:

- New England: 1,500
- New York: 25,000
- Pennsylvania: 110,000
- New Jersey: 15,000
- Maryland and Delaware: 20,500
- Virginia/West Virginia: 25,000
- North Carolina: 8,000
- South Carolina: 15,000
- Georgia: 5,000

A Prominent Family

One of the most important families in colonial America was the Rittenhouse family. William Rittenhouse (Rittinghausen) was born in Muehlheim in 1644. Some historians claim he was a descendant of the royal Austrian house of Hapsburg. He served as a minister in the Rhineland and in 1688 immigrated to Germantown, Pennsylvania.

He became the first minister in Germantown and in 1703 Rittenhouse was elected bishop of the first Mennonite Church in America. He formed a company for the purpose of building a paper mill, and among his partners was the famous colonial printer William Bradford. As mentioned earlier, Bradford's assistant printer was a young German, John Peter Zenger. In 1690 Rittenhouse built the first paper mill in America, so now books, journals, and newspapers could be printed with paper made in America. By 1705, Rittenhouse paper was famous and carried a special watermark. Today his paper is a valuable item in antique markets.

William Rittenhouse's great-grandson, David Rittenhouse, is recognized as a genius. Born in 1732 near Germantown, he, like many of his time, did not attend school but was entirely self-educated. At the age of nineteen he opened his own instrument shop, chiefly for the manufacture of clocks. In 1756 he constructed a telescope, the first one made in America, and in 1767 he designed an orrery, a model of the universe. Thomas Jefferson wrote of him that Rittenhouse was an inventor who approached the Creator.

Rittenhouse developed numerous inventions which amazed his contemporaries. One such invention was the metallic thermometer, an item now taken for granted. In 1769 he built the first observatory in America. He experimented with magnetism and electricity, invented barometers and pendulums, devised rain gauges, tested new methods of glassmaking, and devised scores of other inventions.

During the Revolution, Rittenhouse supervised the casting of cannon balls and the making of gunpowder. In 1777 he became president of the Council of Safety. In this position, he was in charge of all civilian affairs for the land. Benjamin Franklin often consulted with him, and he created inventions for Thomas Jefferson and George Washington as well. He helped organize the U.S. Bank and became the first president of the U.S. Mint in 1792.[1]

Religious Leaders and Institutions

Many of the early German settlers had come to America because of deep religious convictions. Johann Jakob Zimmermann was a leader of those with a strong mystical faith. He died in Rotterdam in 1693, on the eve of embarking for America. Nevertheless, his ideas regarding the imminent end of the world were brought to Germantown by Johann Kelpius. He and his followers founded a sort of monastic order on the banks of the Wissahickon Creek, and his successors started the Ephrata Community in Lancaster County.

In addition to a number of individual religious leaders—who often disagreed violently—there were many pietistic sects that were drawn to Pennsylvania. After the first arrivals in Germantown, the next group of immigrants consisted of Swiss Mennonites who came about 1710. They settled on ten thousand acres in what is now Lancaster County. Like the Quakers, they believed in separation of church and state, freedom of conscience, simplicity of dress, and they refused to take oaths or bear arms.

About nine years after the Mennonites came the so-called Dunkards —*Tunker* in German, from *eintunken*, which means "to immerse." They also shared the doctrines of the Quakers and the Mennonites. They founded settlements in Berks County and Conestoga, where the outstanding figure among the Dunkards was Christopher Saur, who published a widely read German newspaper. From his press came the German Bible—the first published in a European language in America.

Despite the meekness and kindness of these small sects, religious differences continually arose. One of the Dunkards, Conrad Beissel, organized a society of Seventh-Day Adventists and founded the Cloister of Ephrata in Cocalico. He too owned a press, and the mystical writings he printed are some of the most beautiful in German-American literature.

These smaller groups were outnumbered by the Lutherans, the German Reformed and the United Brethren. The Lutherans had a very energetic leader in the person of Heinrich Melchior Muehlenberg, who had studied in Goettingen and came to America in 1742. In 1748 he succeeded in bringing unity to the Lutheran Church when the first convention of the Evangelical Lutheran Ministerium of Pennsylvania was held in Philadelphia. He also did most of the editorial work on the *Gesangbuch*, a hymnal published by the Ministerium in 1786. In 1784 the University of Pennsylvania made him a doctor of philosophy.

Under Muehlenberg's ministry, the famous Zion Church was built. Consecrated in 1769, it was for many years the largest church in Philadelphia. Because of its size, it was frequently used for important public gatherings. It was there on December 26, 1799, at the funeral services of George Washington, that Henry Lee pronounced the famous words "First in war, first in peace, first in the hearts of his countrymen."

Muehlenberg led the Lutheran Church with a firm hand and was on friendly terms with the Episcopalian and German Reformed Churches. The latter, which followed the doctrines of Calvin and Zwingli, had a capable leader in Michael Schlatter, who had been sent to the colonies in 1746 by the Dutch Reformed Synod. Despite his success as an organizer, he had difficulties that forced him to give up his pulpit in Philadelphia and become a Revolutionary War chaplain in the Royal American Regiment, which was mainly a German-American unit.

The relations between Muehlenberg and Schlatter were cordial, for both men were of the same character. Although they belonged to different churches, their religious and political views were quite similar. Vigorous fighters, they counteracted the nonresistant attitude of the Quakers, the Mennonites, the Moravians, and other sectarians. In fact, they urged armed resistance against the British.

Although the pietistic groups refused to engage in armed struggle, they made notable contributions to the cultural and spiritual life of Pennsylvania. This was particularly true of the Moravians, or United Brethren. In German they were called Herrnhuter, after Herrnhut, the estate in Saxony to which Count von Zinzendorf had invited them. In fact, it was Count von Zinzendorf who named the settlement on the Lehigh River Bethlehem.

The count was courageous and farsighted. His two great ideals were the conversion of the Indians and the union of the various Protestant sects. The latter proved a failure; the former, a success. The Moravians are credited with being the most effective missionaries among the Indians in American history.[2]

The Colonial German-American Community

The colonial Germans can be described as "church Germans." This is a term used to describe those German-Americans for whom their particular religious affiliation occupied a central place in their life. Various church bodies established churches and schools that utilized the German language in worship services as well as in all printed documents, such as birth and baptismal certificates, and publications, such as prayer and hymn books. From birth to death, one could live within the framework of one's German-language religious community. Ministers occupied an important role since they were often the only persons of education in their community. They also served as linguistic role models, because they usually spoke High German in their services.

Religion and heritage were intertwined. The church was without question the most important factor in the preservation of the German language in America. German heritage was used to ward off heresy, maintain unity, and exclude external influences. Many adhered to the slogan "Language saves faith." The bonds of ethnicity and religion, therefore, contributed to some of the most enduring German communities in America.

The Pennsylvania Germans consisted of several religious subcommunities. It is estimated that in 1752 there were 100,000 Germans in Pennsylvania comprising 60,000 Lutherans, 30,000 Reformed Church members, and 10,000 sectarians.

There were a small number of learned clergymen, teachers, doctors, businessmen, and artisans, but the majority of these colonial German-Americans were the typical German burghers and farmers of the seventeenth and eighteenth centuries who had little or no education. In spite of their humble origins, they had a strong sense of family, a deep religious faith, and a love and pride in their German heritage.

The colonial German farmer usually selected a wooded area for the family home, which was often located on a hillside. A dated stone, or a date painted or carved into the wooden frame, would indicate the name of the owner and the year of construction, as was the custom in Germany. Roofs generally were covered with tile. There was usually an outside bakehouse and a smokehouse where German-style bread and meats could be prepared. Especially important was the barn, constructed with fieldstone and a wooden frame. Much of this construction was patterned after the architectural forms in southwestern Germany, where the immigrants came from. The colonial German-American farmer had a reputation for hard work, industry, and the intensive cultivation of farm lands. Most farms also had a garden, an orchard, and a beehive.

Families were usually large. Children were considered an asset and worked hard; as soon as they could walk, they were assigned a task so that they could contribute to the well-being of the family. Farmers, once settled, generally remained on their farm forever and rarely moved west like the Anglo-American farmer. Hence, many farms in Pennsylvania today have been in the same family since before the American Revolution.

The immigrants also brought with them a mass of fascinating folklore and customs. For example, many of their barns are covered with hex signs to ward off evil spirits. Almanacs were popular and were believed as if they were the Bible. Indeed, to this day most families have farmer's almanacs on the bookshelf. Food customs reflected those of Germany as well. A typical meal consisted of fresh wurst, roast pig, apples, geese, cakes, beer, and molasses candy.

Local gatherings were at fall harvest festivals, hog slaughtering time, apple-butter boilings, and other significant events.

A common custom was bundling, the situation when a Pennsylvania German man and woman would sleep in the same bed with a divider between them. Implicitly, it was a trial engagement and usually occurred when a suitor found it too late to go home for the night. This custom was still in practice in the mid-twentieth century in areas originally settled by Germans in the colonial period.[3]

The German-American Press

There were several German-American printers in the colonies, and the number of German books, almanacs, and tracts published by them is phenomenal. Among the small sects, the Dunkards were the first to make use of the printing press. Chrisopher Saur published a German edition of *Pilgrim's Progress* in 1754. By this time, more than two hundred different publications had been issued by various colonial German presses, most of which were in Pennsylvania.

Although Benjamin Franklin made some negative remarks about the Pennsylvania Germans, he founded the first German-language newspaper in America, *Philadelphische Zeitung*. The editor was a French "language master" whose German was less than sound. The first issue of the paper appeared May 6, 1732, and, not surprisingly, the paper folded after the second issue.

Success, however, greeted the efforts of Saur, who had come to America in 1724. Although trained as a tailor, he was a farmer by trade; he also made button molds, cast stoves, dealt in herbs, repaired clocks, made ink, and sold Franklin stoves. Having built his own press, he began printing books in 1738.

On August 20, 1739, he issued his newspaper, *Der Hoch Deutsche Pennsylvanische Geschichtschreiber*. A few years later, Saur opened his own paper mill and made his own types. His paper, whose name was changed to *Germantauner Zeitung*, appeared quite regularly and was successfully continued by his son upon Saur's death.

A number of other papers and journals made their appearance in German. The only publisher, however, who could compete with the Saurs was Henry Miller, editor of *Der Woechentliche Philadelphische Staatsbote*, founded in 1762. Miller, who was born in Waldeck, had come to America with Count von Zinzendorf, the leader of the Moravians. He was employed by Benjamin Franklin and printed books in German and English. Miller's paper circulated not only in Pennsylvania but also in New York, Maryland, and Virginia. A feud arose between Miller and the Saurs, for the latter were loyalists and Miller supported the Revolution. In fact, he claimed the proud distinction of having been the first to publish the adoption of the Declaration of Independence. He printed the entire document in German type on July 5, 1776.

Saur and Miller were the leading German-American newspaper publishers. There were five successful papers before the Revolution; by 1808 there were fourteen. Between 1732 and the end of the century no fewer than thirty-eight German papers had appeared in Pennsylvania alone.[4]

The German Society of Pennsylvania

Although the Pennsylvania Germans were a church-oriented group, at least one important secular organization was formed by them: the German Society of Pennsylvania. In 1764 this first German-American society was formed in Philadelphia with the motto "Piety, diligence, and courage will enable our German descendants to succeed." The society was formed as a charitable organization to protect the rights of immigrants, to alleviate their suffering, and to assist them in any possible way. Heinrich Muehlenberg wrote that the negative aspects of immigration, especially those related to the redemptionist system, "impelled certain well-intentioned German inhabitants of Pennsylvania . . . to form a society for the purpose of supervising the arrival of those poor immigrants, so that justice and fairness might be practiced."[5] The society gained one hundred members a week after its establishment, an indication that it was fulfilling a genuine need.

In January 1775 the society submitted a resolution to the Pennsylvania Assembly aimed at protecting German immigrants, and it became law in May. Although it did not abolish the indentured servitude system, it stipulated that shipping merchants at least maintain humane conditions on their ships. This is but one early example of direct political action on the part of the Pennsylvania Germans. In the future the lobbying efforts of the society allowed more laws to be passed regarding the immigrant traffic. The German Society was also significant in that it became the model for similar societies established elsewhere.[6]

Political Life

The Pennsylvania Germans were politically a diverse group. The sectarians, for example, were generally conscientious objectors and pacifists as a matter of religious conviction. They refused to participate in anything related to military affairs. As a rule, they also refused participation in politics, such as holding office. Some refused to pay taxes. The sectarians made up 10 percent of the Pennsylvania Germans, so in any conflict, such as the forthcoming Revolution, at least this percentage of the German-Americans would take an antiwar stance.

The majority of the Pennsylvania Germans felt far less loyalty to the British than did the Anglo-Americans, and some nonsectarians were not sympathetic to the movement for independence. For example, the English tea laws did not upset them since they did not drink tea.

Politically, the involvement of the German-Americans was at first limited, since affairs were conducted in English, but they soon became adept at this foreign tongue, especially by the 1760s. An example of their political involvement was their activities with the German Society of Pennsylvania. And, when the Revolution broke out, many of the clergy became politically active, as did the editors of the German-language press.

As noted earlier, the Pennsylvania Germans in 1688 issued the first protest in America against slavery. In prerevolutionary German-American history this is a special point of pride, for it was the first historical protest of its kind. That this took place at Germantown a mere five years after Pastorius and others had arrived is an indication of the early political awareness among colonial German-Americans.[7]

Nativism

Before the American Revolution, Pennsylvania was one-third German, one-third English, and the remaining third consisted of other groups. Some Anglo-Americans, therefore, feared the Germanization of the colony. Although Benjamin Franklin praised the German immigrants at times and even published a German-language newspaper to capitalize on their numbers, his nativist views were most likely held by other Anglo-Americans.

Franklin, for example, referred to the Pennsylvania Germans as "the most stupid of their nation" and described the Palatines as "boors." He accused them of knavery and ignorance, claiming that at election time "they come in droves and carry all before them." Indeed, here is the heart of the anti-Germanism of Franklin—the fear that the English would be outnumbered and the political consequences that would result.

In 1753 he wrote that "measures of great temper are necessary with the Germans and [I] am not without apprehension that . . . great disorder may one day arise among us." He also wrote, "[U]nless the stream of importation could be turned from this to other colonies . . . they will soon outnumber us that all advantages we have will, in my opinion, be not able to preserve our language and even our government will become precarious."

He accused the German "boors" of "herding together" to "establish their language and manners to the exclusion" of English. He feared the colony would become a colony of what he viewed as aliens, who would "shortly be so numerous as to Germanize us instead of our Anglifying them, and will

never adopt our language, any more than they can acquire our complexion."
Sentiments such as these tended to foster the belief in Anglo conformity, the
false notion that equates English ethnicity with Americanism.[8]

Other Anglo-Americans spoke of the "total lack of education" of the
Pennsylvania Germans. And it is true that up to one-fourth of them were
illiterate because there was no compulsory education in the German
states. Governor Gordon had misgivings about the "clannishness and
isolation of the German settlers" also. William Smith, the first provost of
the University of Pennsylvania, considered them "utterly ignorant." He
therefore supported a plan to establish charity schools among the Germans, purportedly to save them for an English version of Christianity.
However, the supporters had a hidden agenda in mind: the Anglicaniza-
tion of German-American children.

At least a dozen of these schools were formed in the 1750s and
1760s, with a peak enrollment of seventy children, but they were dis-
continued in 1763. German schoolchildren won impressive prizes for
delivering orations in the English language or reading English authors
with an English pronunciation. Special importance was placed on edu-
cating German girls, because "as mothers have the principal direction in
bringing up their young children, it will be of little use that the father can
talk English if the mother can speak" nothing but German. The German
communities had nothing to say in the organization of these Anglo
schools. Teachers from Germany were not hired since one "could not be
sure about their principles."[9]

In Easton, Pennsylvania, the Englishman in charge of the school
stated that Germans in the area were "so perverse and quarrelsome in all
their affairs that I am sometimes ready to query with myself whether it
be men or brutes that these most generous benefactors are about to civi-
lize." Christopher Saur, the widely respected newspaper publisher,
denounced the schools as "having only a political purpose and tendency."
The whole scheme was bitterly and successfully opposed by the Pennsylvania Germans and correctly viewed as an attempt to interfere with their
language, culture, and religion. They learned that schools could be used
to destroy their children's heritage, so they made a conscious decision
and effort to establish their own schools to preserve their German heritage, thus leading to the demise of the so-called charity schools.[10]

Educational Influences

The exchange of ideas between Germany and America began in the colonial era. An early example is found in the correspondence between Cotton Mather and August Hermann Francke, head of the pietistic wing of the Lutheran Church at Halle, where he had founded a large orphan asylum. Francke had achieved international fame with his institution, and a number of colleges and orphanages in the colonies were modeled on his concept.

The correspondence between Mather and Francke was astoundingly heavy for an age without airmail or parcel post. The Boston theologian in 1709 sent a collection of 160 books and tracts on pietism to Halle, together with cash contributions for Francke's philanthropies. The German theologian was equally expansive: he replied with a letter of sixty-nine pages, written in Latin, in which he described his various institutions. Cotton Mather was very impressed. He printed an account in Latin of Francke's enterprises and made plans for the establishment of similar institutions in Massachusetts.

The correspondence continued and was primarily concerned with the organization of educational institutions. In those days, schools were almost entirely within the domain of the churches, and the teachers were commonly ministers. Thus, the two professions were almost synonymous. When no pastor could be secured for a smaller community, the teacher usually read the Scriptures and delivered the sermon.

Some of these German teachers were men of considerable learning. The most distinguished among them was Franz Daniel Pastorius, the founder of Germantown and the friend of William Penn. He was the first German teacher in America. He served in the English Quaker School in Philadelphia from 1698 to 1700 and then took charge of the first German school in America, which was established in 1702.

For a beginning educational enterprise in a colonial settlement, this school possessed a number of remarkable features. It was coeducational and maintained a night school for adults and for those who were employed. It was supported not only by the fees paid by the pupils, but also by voluntary contributions.

The basis of education in the colonies was the ability to read, write, and cipher. It was also considered important to be well-grounded in the Bible and to write in a clear, legible hand. In the church schools, German was the language of instruction, and English was frequently not offered.

There were a number of enlightened teachers who introduced some startlingly modern practices to traditional curriculums. For example, Christopher Dock, who taught in a Mennonite school founded in 1706, was a leader in his profession. He substituted the law of love for the birch rod and was the first to use the blackboard for classroom instruction, an important educational innovation. In 1750 he wrote what is undoubtedly the first pedagogical work published in America, his *Schulordnung*. It was printed by Christopher Sauer of Philadelphia. In this book, Dock displayed nobility of character and a keen insight into child psychology. He stressed the development of character as well as the training of the mind, and he placed morality and conduct before scholarship.

The other sectarians, such as the Schwenkfelders and the Moravians, also set up schools. The Moravians established not only schools at Nazareth, Bethlehem, and Lititz, but also academies for young women. These became very popular and were patronized by the non-German population as well as by the Moravians. Their seminary in Bethlehem, founded in 1749, is the oldest school of its type in America.

The schools of the Lutheran and the Reformed Churches were the most numerous, since these were the two dominant religious groups in the German settlements. Heinrich Muehlenberg, the leader of the Lutherans, and Michael Schlatter, the head of the Reformed, paid great attention to their schools. Printer and publisher Christopher Sauer also took a deep interest in the German schools, especially the Germantown Academy, established in 1761.

Although Ben Franklin was Anglocentric with his nativist attitudes, he believed in knowledge of languages. In planning the curriculum for the Public Academy of the City of Philadelphia, which later developed into the University of Pennsylvania, he recommended the study of French and German in addition to English. The Academy grew into a college, and in 1754 the trustees appointed William Creamer (Kraemer) as professor of French and German. He held this position until his retirement in 1775. Incidentally, Ben Franklin was one of the first Americans to attend a German university. While in Göttingen, Hannover, in 1766, he stopped at the university, where the Royal Society of Science awarded him an honorary membership.

Franklin's visit to Göttingen made a deep impression on Benjamin Smith Barton, a young resident of Lancaster. After studying natural science and medicine in Edinburgh and London, he went to the University of Göttingen, where he received a medical degree in 1789. He was the first American to become a Göttingen doctor.

Franklin recommended the teaching of modern languages in the Philadelphia Academy. The ancient languages, however, were not to be neglected. Through the influence of several clergymen on the board of trustees, Latin and Greek were introduced, and Johann Christoph Kunze, a minister and a teacher of the classics, was appointed to teach them through the medium of German.

In 1787, the assembly of Pennsylvania incorporated a German college in the county of Lancaster "for the instruction of youth in German, English, Latin, Greek, and other learned languages, in theology, and in the useful arts, sciences, [and] literature." In honor of the largest contributor and earnest advocate of its founding, it was named Franklin College.[11]

Notes

1. See Edward Ford, *David Rittenhouse: Astronomer-Patriot, 1732–1796* (Philadelphia: University of Pennsylvania Press, 1946), and William Barton, *Memoirs of the Life of David Rittenhouse* (Philadelphia: E. Parker, 1813).

2. See Stephen L. Longenecker, *Piety and Tolerance: Pennsylvania German Religion, 1700–1850* (Metuchen, N.J.: Scarecrow Press, 1994), and John Steven O'Malley, *Early German-American Evangelicalism: Influential Sources on Discipleship and Sanctification* (Metuchen, N.J.: Scarecrow Press, 1994).

3. Regarding community life, see Don Heinrich Tolzmann, ed., *German Pioneer Life: A Social History* (Bowie, Md.: Heritage Books, 1992).

4. For the history of the German-American press see Robert E. Cazden, *A Social History of the German Book Trade in America to the Civil War* (Columbia, S.C.: Camden House, 1984).

5. See Harry W. Pfund, *A History of the German Society of Pennsylvania* (Philadelphia: German Society of Pennsylvania, 1964).

6. Ibid.

7. For sources on German-American political life in the colonial period see Margrit B. Krewson, *German-American Relations: A Selective Bibliography* (Washington, D.C.: Library of Congress, 1995), pp. 83–110.

8. Albert B. Faust, *The German Element in the U.S.* (New York: Steuben Society of America, 1927), p. 111.

9. Ibid.

10. Regarding nativism, see Carl Wittke, *We Who Built America: The Sage of the Immigrant* (Cleveland: Press of Western Reserve University, 1964), pp. 488–97.

11. For a discussion of educational influences, see LaVern J. Rippley, *The German-Americans* (Boston: Twayne, 1976), pp. 116–28.

The American Revolution and Beyond

Since many Germans lived along the frontier and were continuously engaged in skirmishes with the Indians, they were prepared for military activities. The first of these was the French and Indian War, which preceded the American Revolution.

Members of the small nonresistant sects like the Mennonites, Quakers, and Dunkards could not take up arms in the struggle because of their religious views. They were loyal, however, and readily supplied food and clothing. In fact, in some instances, as in North Carolina, they paid a threefold tax because of their exemption from military service. This conscientious objection was not from lack of courage. They had repeatedly demonstrated their willingness to give their lives for what they believed in.

The members of the larger religious denominations, the Lutherans and Reformed, who did not have these scruples against military service, played a leading role in the Revolution. Michael Schlatter, a Reformed Church leader, served in the Revolutionary army despite his age. The Muehlenbergs, father and son, were also distinguished patriots.

The Germans of Pennsylvania formed companies of militia and sharpshooters which were sanctioned by the Lutheran and Reformed churches. In fact, in 1775 both of these church groups in Philadelphia issued a pamphlet of forty pages appealing to the Germans of New York and North Carolina to support the struggle for independence. With Muehlenberg's approval the Germans of all the colonies were urged to resist with arms the oppression and despotism of the English government. Many volunteers responded. In Pennsylvania, they were known as "Associators" and met in the Lutheran schoolhouse in Philadelphia.

German-Americans were overwhelmingly on the side of the Revolution, the major exception being the sectarian groups. John Adams expressed the opinion in a letter to Thomas McKean, the chief justice of Pennsylvania, that at the time of the Revolution, nearly one-third of the population of the colonies were Tories. It was quite natural that the Germans should be against the crown, for many of them had suffered in Europe at the hands of unscrupulous princes. As frontiersmen and farmers who had carved homesteads out of the wilderness, they had developed a spirit of independence, and they certainly felt no national sentiment that bound them to a foreign English sovereign. When Franklin appeared before the British Parliament and was asked whether the Germans were dissatisfied with the Stamp Act, he replied, "Yes, even more, and they are justified, because in many cases they must pay double for their stamp paper and parchments." He pointed out that one-third of Pennsylvania was German.

Although the number of Tories dwindled and the proportion of revolutionaries increased as the war went on, the Germans proved to be ardent revolutionaries from the beginning. There were many Germans among the merchants of Philadelphia who agreed to boycott British goods. Germans were also well represented in the conventions held in Philadelphia in June and July of 1774 and in January of 1775 to provide for closer relations with Massachusetts. The *Staatsbote*, published in Philadelphia by Henry Miller, preached rebellion. In Woodstock, Virginia, on June 16, 1774, under the aegis of Peter Muehlenberg, resolutions were adopted challenging the right of the British government to impose taxes on the colonists. At least half the members on the Committee of Safety and Correspondence that was organized were Germans.

It wasn't only Pennsylvania Germans who were revolutionaries; Germans in the southern colonies also ardently supported the Revolution. In the Carolinas, for example, where the Tories often outnumbered the revolutionaries, the Germans suffered greatly because of their patriotism.

Of course, not all Germans were revolutionaries. In Georgia, for example, two-fifths of the Germans were Tories. However, in that state the Salzburgers lent their weight to the Revolution. One of their number, John Adam Treutlen, was an ardent revolutionary. When the first legislative body of the state met in Savannah in May 1777, he was elected the first governor. When his home was burned to the ground by the British in 1778, he fled and joined the army of General Wayne, serving throughout the war as a quartermaster-general. Many other Salzburgers distinguished themselves similarly.

Outstanding among German revolutionaries is Peter Muehlenberg. His father, Heinrich Melchior Muehlenberg, was the patriarch of the Lutheran Church. He sent his son to Halle, Germany, to study theology. When he returned to the colonies he was sent in 1772 to the Lutheran church at Woodstock, Virginia. A hearty and husky individual, the young man soon made many friends, including Patrick Henry and George Washington.

Muehlenberg was made the chairman of the local Committee of Safety and Correspondence. At the state conventions in Williamsburg and Richmond, he gave his outspoken support to Patrick Henry. At Henry's suggestion, Muehlenberg was made commander of the Eighth Virginia Regiment. This, of course, meant giving up his parish. When he preached his last sermon in January 1776, the little church and the churchyard were filled with eager listeners. He spoke with eloquence of the duties of the citizen toward his country, ending fervently with the words, "There is a time for preaching and praying, but also a time for battle, and that time has now arrived." He dramatically threw off his clerical robe and stood in the uniform of a Continental colonel. Descending from the pulpit, he marched to the open door to the roll of the drums. Wild with enthusiasm, more than three hundred young men joined the regiment, and the next day one hundred more followed.

Muehlenberg's men took part in most of the major engagements of the Revolution, and on February 21, 1777, he was raised to the rank of brigadier-general in command of the First, Fifth, Ninth, and Thirteenth Virginia Regiments. He distinguished himself at Charleston, Brandywine, Germantown, Monmouth, Stony Point, and Yorktown. He was also Steuben's aide in creating an army.

He later held many important public offices. Three times he represented Pennsylvania as a member of the U.S. Congress, in 1789–91, 1793–95, and 1799–1801. When Ben Franklin was president of the state of Pennsylvania, Muehlenberg served as vice president. During 1788 he and his brother Frederick August worked incessantly to have the Constitution adopted.

Frederick Augustus had also been sent to Halle to study theology, but like Peter he had other interests. He entered upon a very successful political career as a member of the Continental Congress from 1779 to 1780. During the next three years he was the speaker of the Pennsylvania State Legislature and a member of the First, Second, Third, and Fourth U.S. Congresses. He also served as the first Speaker of the House of Representatives.

Another brother, Ernest Muehlenberg, who also studied at Halle, became a Lutheran minister in Lancaster, Pennsylvania. Of a scholarly bent, he was a member of the American Philosophical Society in Philadelphia and of several European scholarly associations. His son, Henry August Muehlenberg, however, was a congressman for nine years and was nominated for governor of Pennsylvania by the Democratic Party.

The Muehlenbergs continued to distinguish themselves through several generations. William Augustus Muehlenberg, the great-grandson of the patriarch of the Lutheran Church in the colonies, was the founder of St. Luke's Hospital in New York. Entering the Episcopal Church, he obtained a parish at Lancaster, Pennsylvania. He helped establish the first public schools outside Philadelphia, and in Flushing, New York, he founded a school that later became St. Paul's College. The Muehlenbergs exemplified some of the finest traits of the German-American element.

Of course, most of the colonial Germans were not scholars and intellectuals. Their contributions to the cause of freedom, however, was no less significant. Christopher Ludwig was an excellent example of the devotion of a middle-class burgher to his country. He was poorly educated; his English was halting, but his courage was tremendous. At fifty-seven, he became a volunteer in the military. He served in the army of Frederick the Great, fought against the Turks, and spent seven years at sea.

Although he was only a baker, his tall figure and dignified bearing impressed people. He took an active part in public affairs as a member of the Powder Committee and other Revolutionary groups. In May 1777

Congress appointed him Superintendent and Director of Baking for the entire Continental army. He was instructed to provide one hundred pounds of bread for every hundred pounds of flour. Ludwig, however, remarked: "I do not wish to get rich by the war. I will make 135 pounds of bread out of the 100 pounds of flour." Once he had helpers, he baked six thousand loaves of bread a day. Washington was very fond of him and called him his "honest friend." He frequently closed a toast with the words "Health and long life to Christopher Ludwig and his wife."[1]

When Ludwig died in 1809 at the age of eighty-one, he left his modest estate to charity and education. Sums were to be given to the University of Pennsylvania, to two churches for the benefit of poor children, and to a committee for the founding of a free school.

Muehlenberg and Ludwig were both Pennsylvanians; the Germans in other parts of the colonies were no less patriotic. An excellent example is Nicholas Herkimer. The Germans of the Mohawk Valley had organized four battalions during the summer of 1775. All four colonels were Germans; the supreme commander was Herkimer. He had been a captain during the French and Indian War and had considerable experience in skirmishes with Indians.

In the summer of 1777 General Burgoyne began to march from Canada. His plan was to cut off New England from the rest of the colonies. St. Leger, coming from Montreal, was to join him at Albany. When Herkimer heard of these plans, he immediately drafted all men between sixteen and sixty in Tryon County. With about eight hundred men, he marched toward Fort Stanwix, which was being besieged by St. Leger. Herkimer's militia encamped near the present site of Oriskany and were so eager to fight that they ignored their commander's plea for caution.

St. Leger, noting the situation, decided to prepare an ambuscade for Herkimer's men. He hid his soldiers and Indians on both sides of a thickly wooded ravine. As the colonials made their way through the narrow road, the Tories and the Indians broke forth from the thick brush with loud yells and fell upon them. Despite the surprise attack, Herkimer rallied his men and fought the Indians with knives and rifle butts. He was able to establish some order when his men reached the top of the hill. Unfortunately, at that very moment, his horse was shot from under him and a bullet shattered one of his legs. Seating himself on his saddle under a spreading beech tree, he calmly lit his pipe and directed the battle. The fighting continued until it was interrupted by a violent thunderstorm. In about an hour it was clear again, and the struggle was resumed.

Herkimer, whose keen gaze noted every move of the enemy, noticed that every time one of his men fired a shot from behind a tree, an Indian leapt forward to knife him before he could reload. Herkimer thereupon ordered two men to stand behind a tree so that while the first one was reloading, the second one shot down the approaching enemy. A bloody hand-to-hand struggle ensued, in which the royalists were gradually driven back. Suddenly, the sound of a cannon was heard in the rear. A company of 250 men from Fort Stanwix attacked the British camp, capturing five flags and all the baggage. The royalists beat a hasty retreat.

The Indians were completely demoralized. Their losses were considerable, and because of the capture of the baggage by the Americans, the Indians were not given their promised gifts. From that day on, they were unreliable as allies.

Herkimer's men had also suffered severely. One-fourth of their number, some two hundred men, were killed or severely wounded. However, the greatest loss was that of General Herkimer. Nine days after the battle his leg was unskillfully amputated. He bore the pain, sitting in his bed smoking his pipe. When it was evident that his end was near, he asked to have his Bible brought in, and while his family gathered around his bed he read the Thirty-Eighth Psalm.

The Battle of Oriskany was a decisive battle. George Washington commented: "It was Herkimer who first reversed the gloomy scene . . . [H]e served for love of country, not for reward. He did not want a Continental command or money."[2]

German-American Regiments and Units

On May 22, 1776, Congress decided to raise a German-American regiment consisting of four companies from Pennsylvania and four from Maryland. In a letter dated June 30, 1776, Washington wrote to Congress, stating that this unit "of Germans which Congress has ordered to be raised will be a corps of much service, and I am hopeful that such persons will be appointed officers as will complete their enlistments with all possible expedition." Washington, hence, apparently placed value in the new German-American regiment. In July 1777 a ninth company was added. All of the officers were German-born or of German descent. The colonel of this regiment was Nicholas Hausegger, who was succeeded by Ludwig Weltner. This regiment took part in the Battles of Trenton, Princeton, and Brandywine, and spent the terrible winter of 1777–78 at Valley Forge.

A corps of light cavalry was formed in 1776 by Baron von Ottendorff, who had come from Saxony and who had served under Frederick the Great in the Seven Years' War. In 1780, this corps was merged into another German-American unit, Armand's Legion, which served in the South in the Battle of Yorktown and at the siege of New York.

Other German-American units were also formed. For example, in Berks County, Pennsylvania, Germans served under the command of Captains Nagel and Daudel. They wore Indian leggings and moccasins and a badge with the words "Liberty or Death!" On July 4, 1776, when the delegates of fifty-three Pennsylvania battalions met at Lancaster to choose a brigadier-general, one-third of the delegates were German-American.

One indication of German-American support for the war was the formation in Reading, Pennsylvania, of the Company of Old Men, which consisted of eighty German-Americans. The commander was ninety-seven and the drummer eighty-four years old. Aside from the previously mentioned units, the names of German-Americans can be found in many other army units. The names of hundreds of German-American soldiers are recorded as serving in the First to Thirteenth Continental Regiments of Pennsylvania.

Washington's Bodyguard

One of the most interesting but least known aspects of the German-American role in the American Revolution was that Washington's bodyguard unit consisted of German-Americans. His early bodyguards had been Tories loyal to Great Britain. They plotted to capture Washington and turn him over to the British. On the advice of his adjutant, Washington had a German-American bodyguard formed to protect himself.

The bodyguard was called the Independent Troop of the Horse, and it was placed under the command of Captain Bartholmaeus von Heer, a former soldier in the Prussian army of Frederick the Great. Von Heer recruited most of the men for the unit from the Pennsylvania German counties. They started service in 1778 and continued through the end of the war with outstanding service. Twelve of the German-American body-guards escorted Washington to his home at Mount Vernon after the end of the war. Because of this, they have the distinction of having served longer than any other American soldiers in the Revolution. The body-guard consisted of fifty-three men and fourteen officers who were all, of course, German-speaking. From this, it can be assumed that the first president of the United States was able to converse in German.[3]

Baron von Steuben

The backbone of the colonial army consisted of common people such as the sturdy farmers of Pennsylvania and the Mohawk Valley. But the struggle for liberty also fired the imagination of a number of European aristocrats who came to America in support of the Revolution. The best known of these are Lafayette, Kosciusko, and von Steuben.

The service rendered by von Steuben was invaluable, for it was he who, in the words of Alexander Hamilton, introduced "into the army a regular formation and exact discipline," and he established "a spirit of order and economy."[4] Friedrich von Steuben was born September 17, 1730 in Magdeburg, Prussia, the son of a lieutenant of engineers in the army of Frederick the Great. He spent his early childhood in Russia, where his father had a commission in the army of Czarina Anne. It was customary, then, for officers to serve in the military and at the courts of other countries.

At the age of ten, Friedrich Wilhelm returned to Germany with his father and continued his education at a Jesuit school in Breslau, Silesia. At sixteen he entered the Prussian army and secured a command in the infantry. He displayed such ability that he was soon a member of the general staff. He first saw active service in the War of the Austrian Suc-cession. In the Seven Years' War in which he was a captain, he distinguished himself at the Battle of Rossbach. He became a favorite of Frederick the Great, who made him one of his aides-de-camp in 1762.

At the close of the war, von Steuben resigned and became grand marshal at the court of the prince of Hohenzollern-Hechingen. Financial straits forced the prince to close his court and to live incognito abroad, so von Steuben accompanied him to Montpellier, France. Later on the prince returned to Hechingen. After having served him ten years as court chamberlain, von Steuben accepted a similar position at the court of the Margrave of Baden. It was there that the title of Baron was conferred on him. From now on he was Freiherr von Steuben.

Having been trained for a military career, von Steuben was bored by the monotony of a small provincial court. He looked about for an outlet for his military ability, and his attempts to enter the Austrian army were unsuccessful. Finally, his old friend Count St. Germain, the French minister of war, came to his aid. He suggested that von Steuben offer his services to the American colonies.

Von Steuben was delighted. He met the playwright Beaumarchais who introduced him to Benjamin Franklin and Silas Deane, the American commissioners who were in Paris at that time seeking support for the revolutionary cause. Von Steuben's ability and experience were well known to Franklin and Beaumarchais, but they felt that an obscure baron would not cut much of a figure on his arrival in America. They, hence, decided to build him up. They furnished von Steuben with letters stating that he had been a lieutenant-general in the army of Frederick the Great, they gave him a brilliant uniform with a decoration, and they provided him with a French military secretary and an aide-de-camp.

With his impressive outfit, von Steuben set sail and arrived in Portsmouth, New Hampshire, on December 1, 1777. In February 1778 he was received with the highest honors by the Continental Congress, then sitting in York, Pennsylvania. Von Steuben, who was a cultured European steeped in court etiquette, played his part well. He offered his services as a volunteer, requesting only a guarantee of his expenses and commissions for his two aides. Ultimate compensation would be determined later, depending upon the success or failure of the struggle. His generous offer was gladly accepted.

General Gates, who was intriguing against Washington at that time, tried to gain the baron's favor, but von Steuben's keen insight into human nature prevented his being led astray by flattery. He decided to go directly to Washington at Valley Forge. During his journey through Lancaster County, he received a hearty ovation from the German farmers. On his arrival at Valley Forge on February 23, General Washington gave the baron and his aides a cordial welcome. Washington was impressed by his military appearance and was drawn to him by his personal qualities. The two men became lifelong friends.

The morale of the Continentals was at its lowest point at that time. More than two-thirds of the original force of seventeen thousand men had been lost through death, disease, and desertion. It was a wretched lot of ill-equipped, poorly fed, and badly clothed recruits that the baron beheld at Valley Forge. Undaunted by the depressing spectacle, von Steuben immediately organized a system of inspection, selecting 120 men to form a military school. An able instructor, von Steuben trained his company so well that within two weeks the men knew how to bear arms, march, and perform maneuvers like experienced European soldiers. Within a month, all of the American troops under his inspection executed military commands with the precision of professionals. On May 5, 1778, Congress gratefully appointed von Steuben inspector-general with the rank and pay of major-general.

Von Steuben, accustomed to Prussian discipline, was quite impatient with the laxity, the irregularities, and the inefficiency of the American troops. He insisted on meticulous attention to all details, and when his anger was roused, he swore in French and German. After he had exhausted those languages, he would turn to an officer with the plea, "My dear Jones, swear for me in English!"

The good results of his work were soon evident. His Continentals were the equals of the best British regulars. Von Steuben, however, was not irrevocably attached to Old World tactics. He showed his intelligence by adapting European methods to American conditions. For example, noting the topography of the country, he formed groups of light infantry who fought from behind trees and bushes in Indian fashion.

Because of von Steuben's careful training, many an engagement that might have resulted in a disastrous defeat ended in an orderly retreat. The new spirit of discipline enabled Washington to get his entire army under arms and ready to march in fifteen minutes. At Monmouth, von Steuben's familiar voice rallied the broken columns of General Lee. They wheeled into line under heavy fire as if they were on a parade ground.

During the winter of 1778–79, von Steuben prepared a manual entitled *Regulations for the Order and Discipline of the Troops of the United States* which came to be known as *Steuben's Regulations* or *The Blue Book*. This excellent handbook was not only a guide to the officers in the performance of their military duties, but it also established a definite order in the requisition and management of supplies. Within one year the loss of muskets was reduced from eight thousand to three thousand.

Von Steuben rendered valuable service in Virginia in the winter of 1780–81 and during the siege of Yorktown. He not only established military discipline in a general way, but also created actual armies. That is precisely what he did in Virginia, where he organized an army for General Greene, who had been made the commander of the Southern army. Von Steuben had a big job before him: the men were ignorant of military order, they were demoralized, and they were inclined to plunder, so that on occasion von Steuben lost his temper. However, he was eventually successful, and Arnold's invasion was halted.

At Yorktown, his experience was invaluable, for he was the only officer who had ever participated in a siege. He was in charge of one of the three divisions when the first overtures for peace were made. He, therefore, enjoyed the great privilege of being in command when the enemy's flag was lowered.

Von Steuben was honorably discharged on March 24, 1784, and was given a gold-hilted sword. He continued his services to his country, however, in the field where he had demonstrated the greatest ability. He formulated plans for the founding of a military academy, and in this way he laid the foundations for West Point. In his outline, he showed that he was not merely a soldier, for he stipulated that there should be professors of history, geography, law, and literature, as well as instructors in military science.

After the Revolution, von Steuben, who seems not to have managed his financial affairs very well, despite his organizational skills, lived for several years in difficult circumstances. Finally, in 1786 Congress granted him a tract of land, sixteen thousand acres near Utica, New York, where he took up residence. In 1790 he was voted a pension of $2,500.

Even in his retirement, he occupied himself with matters of public welfare. Among other things, he drew up plans for a system of fortifications for New York. His educational attainments were highly regarded, because he was appointed a regent of the University of New York. He was also the first president of the German Society of New York, which had been organized for the benefit of German immigrants, and he continued to devote himself unsparingly to public service.[5]

Other German Officers in the Revolution

Another German general who served in the colonial army was John Kalb, who is usually referred to as Baron de Kalb but who was not a nobleman. He was born in 1721 in Hüttendorf, Bavaria, the son of a peasant. He was sent abroad by the French government as a secret agent to gather information in the British colonies. Upon his return, he married the daughter of a Dutch millionaire and thereafter lived quite well. In 1777 he came to America with Lafayette and offered his services to the Congress. He was made a major-general and served under Washington. In the South, he was given command of the Delaware and Maryland troops. Having served in the Seven Years' War and having previously visited America, he displayed great skill and acumen. He was particularly adept in matters of engineering and topography.[6]

There were a number of other German generals and barons who fought in the American Revolution. Gerhard von der Wieden, generally known as George Weedon, was born in Hannover. He had served in the War of Austrian Succession, in the French and Indian War, and in Flanders. When the Revolution broke out, he became a lieutenant-colonel of the Third Virginia Militia. In 1777 he was appointed brigadier-general, distinguishing himself at the battles of Brandywine and Germantown.

Baron Friedrich Heinrich von Weissenfels, an officer in the British Army, offered his services to Washington when the Revolution began. He had fought under Wolfe at Quebec and had seen that brave commander die on the Heights of Abraham. After the cessation of hostilities, he settled down as an English officer in New York. There he got married, with General von Steuben as his best man. During the Revolution, he defeated the British at White Plains, accompanied Washington over the Hudson, and took part in the battles of Trenton, Princeton, Saratoga, Monmouth Courthouse, and Newton. He died in 1806 in New Orleans.

A number of other German officers came to America at the inspiration of Benjamin Franklin. Among these was Heinrich Emanual Lutterloh, major of the guard of the Duke of Brunswick, who met Franklin in London. He became a colonel on Washington's staff in 1777, and three years later he was made quartermaster-general of the army. Washington thought very highly of him. It is significant that three of the most important positions in the Continental army were held by Germans: the Inspector-General von Steuben, Superintendent of Baking Ludwig, and Quartermaster-General Lutterloh.

Frequently German officers who were intended for the British army joined the Continental forces. Johann Paul Schott, a well-to-do, cultured young gentleman and a lieutenant of the King of Prussia and Prince Ferdinand of Brunswick, was so impressed by the struggle of the American Colonies to free themselves from the British yoke that he decided to help them. Noting the acute lack of ammunition and military equipment, he organized a supply of the needed materials. He sailed to St. Eustache in the West Indies, a Dutch possession, in the summer of 1776, chartered a schooner, loaded it with war materials at his own expense, and set out for Virginia.

In order to get by the English vessels blockading the entrance to Hampton Roads, Schott hoisted the British flag and had his crew don the uniforms of English sailors. The schooner got through, although it was fired upon by the British when they discovered the ruse. Schott ordered the colonial flag to be raised as they entered the harbor of Norfolk, but the British uniforms, which the sailors had not had time to change, evoked a barrage of shots from the American side. A white flag was quickly displayed, the vessel was anchored, and everything was explained satisfactorily. They received Schott with joy and acclaim, and gratefully accepted the military supplies.

In 1776 Schott was made a captain and served under Washington at New York and White Plains. At a time when many Continentals went home despite the fact that the British forces were being strengthened by fresh mercenaries from Europe, Schott made a great contribution to the army. With Washington's permission, he recruited a German troop of dragoons in Pennsylvania, appointing his own officers, and gave his commands in German. At the Battle of Short Hills he was taken prisoner. Appreciating his military skill, the English commander offered him a commission in the royal forces, but Schott declined. After six months in prison, he was exchanged. He served under General Sullivan, but the wounds he had received at Short Hills incapacitated him for further active service. He was made commandant of the forts in Wyoming Valley, Pennsylvania, a post that he held until the end of the Revolution. Then he settled down in Wilkes-Barre. In 1787 he was elected to the state legislature. Until his death he took an active part in public affairs.

Women in the Revolution and the New Republic

Among the many German-Americans who served in the Revolution, there are a number whose lives were marked by dramatic episodes that have become almost legendary. One of the best known of these is the colorful Molly Pitcher, whose maiden name was Maria Ludwig. She was born October 13, 1754, in Carlisle, Pennsylvania, the daughter of German immigrants. At fifteen she became a maid in the home of Dr. William Irvine, who later served as colonel and brigadier-general in the colonial army.

At the beginning of the Revolution she married John Caspar Hays, a gunner in an artillery company. When she heard that her husband had been severely wounded, she set out to find him. She nursed him back to health and then accompanied him for seven years from one battlefield to another. She helped carry the wounded, served as a nurse, and prepared meals for the soldiers.

During the Battle of Monmouth on June 28, 1778, a very hot day, she supplied the troops with water, carrying it in a pitcher from a nearby well, thus gaining her the name of "Molly Pitcher." When her husband was overcome by heat, she took his place at the cannon, setting it in order and reloading it. By her courageous example she prevented the soldiers around her from retreating. After the battle, Washington personally complimented her when he reviewed the troops.

Another German-American associated with Washington was Barbara

Frietchie. Early American inns take pride in having had General Washington stay at their establishments, and Frietchie made the acquaintance of Washington in a Pennsylvania inn. Frietchie, whose maiden name was Hauser, was born in 1766 in Lancaster, Pennsylvania, and worked in a Pennsylvania German inn. In 1791 Washington spent the night at this inn. Frietchie had the honor of serving him while he stayed there. Hereafter, she became well-known as the person who had been of service to the first president of the United States.

Much later, during the Civil War, in 1862 General Lee's army under the command of Stonewall Jackson entered the town. Frietchie stated, "It will never happen that one short life like mine shall see the beginning and end of a government like this." While the Confederate army was occupying her town, she displayed the American flag and publicly proclaimed her loyalty to the Union cause, thereby becoming a well-known symbol of patriotism. She died in 1862 and is buried in the cemetery of the German Reformed Church in Frederick, Maryland. A restaurant named after her is also located there.[7]

German Troops on Both Sides

In addition to the tens of thousands of colonial Germans who served in the Revolution, there were thousands of Germans among the French troops under Rochambeau; in fact, there were entire German divisions. This was true of the first contingent, the Royal Allemand de Deux Ponts, which was under the command of Prince Christian of Zweibrücken-Birkenfeld. This regiment served in the colonies from 1780 to 1783. One-third of the French troops were German, in the estimate of the author.

There were several divisions of Alsatians and Lothringians and a battalion of grenadiers from the Saar. A number of German officers served in responsible positions in the French army, such as Freiherr Ludwig von Closen-Haudenburg, adjutant of Rochambeau; Captain Gau, commandant of artillery; and Professor Lutz from Strassburg, the marquis's interpreter. There was also a regiment of six hundred men known as Anhalt. At the siege of Yorktown, when Tarleton made a sortie, the English were beaten back by the Legion of Armand and the troops of the Duke of Lauzun, over half of whom were German. It is said that commands on both sides were given in German during the various skirmishes because of the Alsatians among the French troops and the Hessians on the British side.

The Hessians have been undeservedly maligned in American history. Old American history texts pictured them as terrible ogres bent on slaughtering the valiant patriots. Actually, they were a hapless lot of German peasants, mercenaries sold to the British government by luxury-loving princes who needed money to support their palaces and mistresses. It was a dastardly bit of business, which was denounced by the German author Schiller in his play *Kabale und Liebe*. The record of the profits for the various princes in pounds sterling is as follows:

Hesse-Cassell	2,959,800
Brunswick	750,000
Hesse-Hanau	343,130
Anspach-Bayreuth	282,400
Waldeck	140,000
Anhalt-Zerbst	109,120

This barter in human flesh cost the British government over seven million British pounds, or an estimated $150 million. It was a cruel and inefficient business, for the unwilling recruits, who had absolutely no interest in the war, made indifferent soldiers who longed for their homes and families from which they had been torn. Many deserted, therefore, whenever the chance arose. It is said that Washington was able to win the Battle of Trenton and capture the Hessians there because the nostalgic troops had imbibed too much while celebrating Christmas.

In many a battle, Germans were pitted against Germans. In fact, officers who had served under Frederick the Great were on opposite sides, such as von Steuben and Knyphausen. Some of the officers were refined, highly cultured gentlemen. This was the case of Riedesel, who was captured together with his wife at Saratoga. Thomas Jefferson enjoyed both their company and their music.

After they had been captured at Yorktown, the Germans in the British army fraternized with the Germans in the colonial regiments. When they were sent to Lancaster, Pennsylvania, and Frederick, Maryland, they received quite a cordial welcome from the local farmers. They seem to have been honest, sturdy, and thrifty burghers who were only too happy to drop their rifles and return to the paths of peace. Many of them settled permanently in Pennsylvania, Maryland, and Virginia.

The baker Ludwig, himself a Hessian, knew the character of his compatriots when he said: "Bring the captives to Philadelphia, show them our beautiful German churches. They should also see the home in the area and eat a meal with a family."[8] After this, "then send them away again to their people and you will see how many will come over to us." Many of the Hessians did desert for service in the American army. This was encouraged by the German-American press, which printed flyers inviting the Hessians to lay down their arms and join the American cause.

Number of Hessians Who Came to America

	Sent	Returned	Lost
Hesse-Cassell	16,992	10,492	6,500
Brunswick	5,723	2,708	3,015
Hesse-Hanau	2,422	1,441	981
Anspach	2,353	1,183	1,170
Waldeck	1,225	505	720
Anhalt-Zerbst	1,160	984	176
TOTALS:	29,875	17,313	12,562

Of the 12,500 who did not return, it is estimated that at least one-half survived and remained in America.[9]

In the New Republic

In the 1790 U.S. Census, the ethnic stocks of 3.9 million Americans were listed. America was already a multicultural society. Those of English descent, or Anglo-Americans, numbered 2.3 million, or 60 percent. The second largest group were German-Americans, with 350,000, or 9 percent of the total. Two centuries later, German-Americans rose to 25 percent of the population and became the nation's largest ethnic group, a reflection of the great waves of immigration.

Also, certain characteristics were already beginning to take form in terms of the German-American experience. First, by 1790 German-American settlement patterns were becoming apparent. In New England, German-Americans were sparsely settled, with the highest concentration being in Maine (1.3 percent). However, because of the early German involvement in New Amsterdam, the port of New York, and the Palatine immigration, higher concentrations could be found in New York (8.2 percent) and New Jersey (9.2 percent). The real center of the German element was in Pennsylvania (33.3 percent) and neighboring states, especially to the south: Maryland/D.C. (11.7 percent), the Virginias (6.3 percent), North Carolina (4.7 percent), South Carolina (5 percent), and Georgia (7.6 percent). In the west, German-Americans had moved in large numbers into Kentucky/Tennessee (14 percent). They came especially from the Carolinas, the Virginias, Maryland, and, of course, Pennsylvania. Also, the new Northwest Territory already had the beginnings of German settlement (4.3 percent). Therefore, German-Americans were settling in the middle states and in the west but avoiding New England. The beginnings of western settlement could already be noticed. By 1800, taking the 9 percent of 1790 as a rough estimate of the size of the German element, we can estimate German-Americans at about 500,000 out of a total population of 5.3 million, and by 1810 at about 650,000 out of a total of 7.2 million. Again, this population concentrated in the same areas and was moving west.

A second discernible characteristic of German settlement patterns was that a wide range of religious and secular community institutions was being established. German-Americans had not only attained significant population statistics and concentrated in certain geographical areas, but they were also establishing the basic structure of German-American institutions, which were formed to meet the particular social, cultural, religious, political, and economic needs of their group.

Third, German-Americans were actively participating in the political process. As we have seen, German-Americans took an active role in the struggle for independence. Moreover, several German-Americans occupied key positions in the early years of the Republic.

A fourth aspect of German-American life was that German-Americans had already encountered their first contact with anti-German nativism. This would be a recurrent theme in U.S. history and would be repeated again in the nineteenth and twentieth centuries.

After the American Revolution, one of the major issues facing the country was placing the new Republic on a solid foundation, especially with regard to fiscal matters. In this regard, German-Americans played an important role. David Rittenhouse was on the commission that established the U.S. Bank, and he was appointed to serve as director of the U.S. Mint from 1792 to 1795. Another important position was that of U.S. Treasurer, held by Michael Hillegas.

Hillegas was born in 1729 in Philadelphia, the son of German immigrants from Alsace-Lorraine. He acquired a considerable fortune from sugar refining, iron manufacturing, and banking, as well as from family businesses. He first became involved in politics in the 1760s, being appointed a commissioner with the task of selecting a site for a fort to protect Philadelphia. In 1775 he became a member of the Pennsylvania Committee of Safety, and in the same year he was chosen Treasurer of the United Colonies, a position he held until the Treasury Department was created by an act of Congress in 1789. During the Revolution he was referred to as the U.S. Treasurer. Hillegas gave not only of his time and energy, but also a great deal of his own personal fortune to the cause. There is no question that he played a vital role in placing the colonies and the new Republic on a solid financial foundation by having served as Treasurer from 1775 to 1789.

The first years also brought the beginnings of political life and political parties. This was important as it allowed the people to express themselves by means of elected representatives. In the new Congress there were several influential German-Americans. Frederick Augustus Muehlenberg, the second son of Heinrich Melchior Muehlenberg, was born at Trappe, Pennsylvania, in 1750, had studied at the Halle Institution in Germany, and was ordained a minister in 1770. In 1779 he entered politics on the advice of his father and was elected to the Assembly of Pennsylvania, where he also served as speaker for three assemblies. He also presided over the Pennsylvania ratification convention in 1787. From 1789 to 1798, he served as Federalist congressman from Pennsylvania and was the first Speaker of the House in the First Congress. He was displaced in the Second Congress, but then decided to seek the support of the Republicans and abandoned the Federalists in 1799. Altogether, he served in the first four Congresses. His shift from the Federalists to the Republicans (today's Democrats) reflected a general alignment of German-Americans with the position and party that came to be known as the Jeffersonian Democrats. Muehlenberg was clearly recognized as the major German-American political spokesman in these early years.

Among other members of Congress was Simon Driesbach, born in Wittgenstein, Germany, in 1730, who had served in the Constitutional Convention as well as in the Pennsylvania Assembly. He served in the House of Representatives from 1793 to 1794. Charles Shoemaker (Schuhmacher), born in Germantown in 1745, also served in the Constitutional Convention and in the Pennsylvania Assembly before serving in the House of Representatives from 1791 to 1802 and again in 1812 to 1813. Michael Leib, born in Philadelphia in 1760, was elected to Congress in 1798 and served with distinction as a staunch and defiant Jeffersonian (1799–1806) and thereafter served as a U.S. senator (1809–14).

At the state and local levels, German-Americans were also taking an active role. Johann Adam Treutlein served as the first governor of Georgia in 1812. The first governor of German descent in Pennsylvania was Simon Snyder, elected in 1812, and by 1942 twelve of the twenty-seven governors of Pennsylvania had been German. Besides political affairs, German-Americans were actively involved in the commercial life of the new Republic.

In general, German-Americans did not stay affiliated with the Federalist Party, as was reflected in the move of Muehlenberg to the Republican Party. This was because the Federalists favored government for the privileged, the wealthy, and the well-born. Also, they were mainly of English descent and gave expression to their nativist concerns that the Anglo element in America should not be polluted by unrestricted immigration. The 1790s can be viewed as the first nativist period in the history of the new Republic due to the passage of nativist legislation: the Alien and Sedition Acts of 1798. These acts were designed to weaken the influence the immigrants, who were usually Republicans. The Alien Act lengthened the period of residence required for naturalization from five to four-teen years, gave the president the power to deport aliens, and authorized the president to imprison aliens who refused to leave. The Sedition Act aimed to suppress hostile criticism of the Federalists and provided that any conspiracy to oppose the legal measures of government could be punishable by fines and imprisonment. Anyone making a false or malicious statement about the president or Congress could be fined or imprisoned. If enforced, this law could have been used to suppress all those whom the Federalists viewed as dissenters. However, some states, such as Virginia and Kentucky, passed resolutions stating that when Congress exceeded its authority, states could refuse to obey the law, leading to the doctrine of nullification.

The Alien and Sedition Acts so alienated German-Americans that they swung overwhelmingly behind Jefferson for the election of 1800. The acts were seen as not designed against foreign foes, but aimed to deprive the foreign-born of their basic political rights, as well as to suppress dissent. Especially repulsive was the notion of some Federalists that citizenship should be determined by birth in this country. Because of these nativist views, which stood in sharp contrast to the Declaration of Independence and the Constitution, the German-American press supported the Jeffersonians. As early as 1800, the latter issued a document to the "German Citizens of Bucks County and Their Descendants," which called on them to repudiate the militarism and nativism of the Federalists, who were charged with fiscal irresponsibility, hostility to immigrants, and with having a pro-British bias.

Various German-American newspapers became ardent supporters of Jefferson in the early 1800s. In Frederick, Maryland, the press had the motto "To the Republicans I sing, but aristocrats shall feel my sting." The Jeffersonian Republicans laid the foundations for the Democratic Party of the first half of the nineteenth century, and most German-Americans would remain in this camp until the question of slavery caused the old parties to disintegrate, resulting in a new political realignment in the 1850s. Throughout this period, the other major party, the Whigs, had little success in attracting German-Americans due to their nativist outlook.

An important factor in swinging German-Americans into the camp of the Jeffersonian Republicans was the nativist opposition to several resolutions submitted to Congress in the 1790s. This will be discussed in a later chapter dealing with German language influences, but a few points are relevant here. In 1794 resolutions were submitted to print the laws of the land in German. However, Muehlenberg, who at the time was a Federalist, clearly sensed the nativism of the Federalists and feared for his own position as Speaker of the House. He referred the resolution to a committee, which resulted in its being pocket vetoed. The resolution was then submitted a second time but was again tabled. Although Muehlenberg had an influential position, it should be noted that German-Americans, according to the 1790 Census, were only about 10 percent of the population, so they lacked the statistical clout to attempt to enact such legislation. That they did submit such a resolution is indicative of their influence. Also, their political power was limited and concentrated mainly in Pennsylvania as well as neighboring states.

What such opposition to the 1794 resolutions for German printing and the passage of the Alien and Sedition Acts did, however, was to drive German-Americans into the Jeffersonian camp. Also, the German-American congressional leadership was small, being confined to Muehlenberg and a few others. It would be decades before they would obtain a greater degree of political influence in Congress commensurate with their numbers, but the beginnings were seen already.

The Jeffersonian administration was popular with German-Americans not only because of the principles for which Jefferson and his party stood, but also because of Jefferson's appointment of Albert Gallatin as Secretary of the Treasury, a post held during the Revolution and the early years of the Republic by a German-American, Michael Hillegas. To German-Americans it was a vital spot, pertaining as it did to fiscal responsibility. Gallatin, a Swiss-Frenchman born in Geneva, had arrived in America in 1780 and became active in political affairs in Pennsylvania. At the 1789–90 convention to revise the Pennsylvania constitution, he contributed to discussions of suffrage, representation, taxation, and the judiciary. He also served in the Pennsylvania state legislature from 1790 to 1792 and was elected to the U.S. Senate in 1793. However, he was ousted by the Federalists, who challenged him by stating that he had not been a citizen long enough.

In 1794 Gallatin helped bring about a peaceable conclusion to the

Whiskey Rebellion in Pennsylvania, which had been provoked by the excise bill of 1791. He was then elected as a Republican congressman and served from 1795 to 1801. He displayed a deep grasp of constitutional and international law, and became the leader of the minority in the House. He was noted for his fiscal responsibility and insisted on the strict account-ability of the Treasury Department to Congress, which led to the forma-tion of the Ways and Means Committee. He also demanded that no funds be spent except for the purpose for which they were appropriated.

After appointment as Secretary of the Treasury in 1801, he served until 1814 and not only exerted tremendous influence on the fiscal development of the new Republic, but was also interested and involved in a wide variety of political and social issues of the day. Later he served as U.S. Minister to France and then to Britain, and later on in 1831–39 a well-known German-American, John Jacob Astor, convinced him to serve as president of the new National Bank in New York. His outstanding record as well as his position endeared him to German-Americans and further served to solidify as Jeffersonian Democrats.

One event took place in the 1790s that also contributed to the German-Americans parting company with the Federalists—the French Revolution. At first Americans viewed the revolution as a continuation of their struggle for liberty and generally supported it. However, the execu-tion of Louis XVI and the entrance of Britain and Spain into a war against the revolution caused alarm. The Federalists increasingly viewed Britain as the defender of property rights against the disorder of the revolution. Those supporting the revolution opposed Britain and even suggested war against Canada and Spanish Florida. German-Americans clearly sup-ported the revolution, which they viewed as a continuation of the struggle for liberty, and also were opposed to siding with the English.

In a December 1792 meeting of the German Society of Pennsylvania, delegates toasted the republic of France, and expressed hope that tyranny and inequality would be destroyed. In 1793, the French ambas-sador to the United States visited Philadelphia and met with representa-tives of the German Republican Society, who presented him with a letter declaring their adherence to the Republican Party and expressing their warmest wishes to the new republic. The pro-Republican stance in domestic and foreign affairs increasingly came to be expressed in the

1790s and, of course, reflected the undercurrents at work among German-Americans that led to their party shift.

By 1800, the interest in America had reached an all-time high, but due to the Napoleonic wars and the continental blockade, immigration was brought to a halt and would have to wait until the nineteenth century to continue. However, German interest in America was great. By 1800, some fifteen hundred works had been published in German-speaking countries dealing with some aspect of the New World. More than half were published in the last fifteen years of the eighteenth century. Another fourth, or more than 250 works, appeared during the American Revolution, reflecting the great interest in the establishment of the new Republic.

The image of America presented in these works is that of a young land of liberty with great and promising hopes for the future. Many readers, now in the midst of the Napoleonic wars, read these publications with great interest, magnified the news and positive images so that it was not surprising that readers would be left with the impression that it was advisable to immigrate. On the other hand, there were a few works that referred to the rugged conditions to be found in the New World, as well as to what was perceived to be the cultural deficiencies and crass materialism of American society. However, the general view was positive, so much so that by the mid-nineteenth century America was clearly viewed as the El Dorado of the German immigrant.

The War of 1812

The War of 1812 has often been viewed as the second war of independence, as America again found itself at war with England, and the results definitely would confirm that the new Republic was indeed here to stay. The causes of the war do not concern us here, but rather the role German-Americans played in that conflict.

The war itself was unpopular in certain quarters, especially with Anglo-Americans. It was so unpopular that in 1814, Massachusetts called a New England convention at Hartford to discuss "public grievances and concerns" of the New Englanders, as well as to take measures to summon a convention to revise the Constitution. Some of them wished well to the English invasion of New Orleans and to Aaron Burr's secession plot for Louisiana. They hoped that the Hartford Convention would draft a new federal constitution with special clauses protecting the interests of New England. This would then be presented to the original thirteen states, and if they were not accepted, then New England would make a separate peace with England. The *London Times* proclaimed: "New England allied with Old England would form a dignified and manly union well deserving the name of peace." Fortunately, moderates gained control of the convention, and secession was ruled out. Several amendments to the Constitution were suggested, but the very fact that the meeting took place is an indication of the predicament and position of many Anglo-Americans.

A century later, German-Americans would find themselves in a similar situation, although they never took the steps Anglo-Americans did by means of the Hartford Convention. For German-Americans there was no question in 1812—they strongly supported the U.S. in the war. Moreover, they at no time engaged in anti-Anglo hysteria against the New Englanders because of their pro-English stance. Again, this could be contrasted with the way they were treated a century later.

Several German-Americans were prominent in the war. General Walbach, born in Münster, Germany, in 1766, came to America after serving in the Austrian, French, and English armies. He is credited with having saved the U.S. artillery at Chrysler's Field (near the St. Lawrence River) in 1813. For his valor, Walbach was promoted to the rank of brigadier-general and to the commandership of the U.S. Army Fourth Artillery.

The nation's capital has been occupied by a foreign power only once in history. In 1814, the English occupied Washington, D.C., causing President Madison and his wife to flee. The English then enjoyed the dinner that had been prepared for the president's party while the city burned in retaliation for the burning of Toronto in 1813. Now, the nearby city of Baltimore was threatened.

Three thousand soldiers under the command of a German-American general, John Stricker, advanced to meet a much larger English force consisting of seven thousand men. Despite the odds, the English attack was thwarted. General Stricker, born in 1759 in Frederick, Maryland, was the son of a Revolutionary War officer, Colonel George Stricker. He had served in his father's German-American battalion and had participated in the battles of Trenton, Princeton, Brandywine, Germantown, and Monmouth, to name several. In 1783 he was promoted to the rank of captain and moved to Baltimore, where he trained one of the earliest militia units. Thereafter he was promoted to brigadier-general and commander of the state troops.

While Stricker and the militia were halting the English attack against Baltimore, a Virginia German, General George Armistead, withstood the bombardment of sixteen English war vessels for thirty-six hours. Armistead, born in 1780, was the commander of Forty McHenry, which returned the fire coming from the English. The attackers met such a fierce response that they finally withdrew.

Armistead, with a thousand soldiers, also defeated an English force of about the same size that had landed to surprise the fort from the rear. The bombardment, however, continued through the night, and it was during this night that Francis Scott Key, while a prisoner on board an English ship, wrote "The Star Spangled Banner." The next day the English withdrew. Armistead's ancestors had come from Hessen-Darmstadt and had settled in New Market, Virginia. The Armistead family played an important role in Virginia history; they were related to four presidents (James Monroe, William Henry Harrison, John Tyler, and Benjamin Harrison).

The Baltimore Germans placed a full company of *Jaeger*, or infantry, in the field during the War of 1812, while the Pennsylvania Germans were also actively involved. This included participation of the following noteworthy families: Pennypacker, Hambright, and Muehlenberg. In North Carolina, German-Americans were under the command of Colonel George Hambright, the brother of Frederick Hambright, a major-general of a Pennsylvania unit. The War of 1812 came to a conclusion by means of the Treaty of Ghent in 1814, which was accomplished by a Swiss-American, Albert Gallatin. The war itself was significant in that it convinced Europe that the United States was no longer a third-rate power. It also initiated a longer period of peace and decreased the possibilities of foreign intervention in American affairs. For the United States it now meant that the country could concern itself with internal affairs, especially with western settlement.[10]

America's 50th Anniversary

In 1826 German-Americans joined in the national celebration of the 50th anniversary of the Declaration of Independence. The celebration was a time of unbridled rejoicing and marked the half-century point since America had launched its course on the road to independence. In the meantime, the United States had successfully been established, western settlement had begun, and its independence confirmed in the War of 1812. Hence, the festive mood of the time can be readily understood.

A German-American tribute to this event can be found in a work published by a well-known German-American author, Karl Postl, who wrote under the name Charles Sealsfield. In his book *The United States of North America as They Are*, published in 1827, which also appeared in a German edition, he explained the symbolic importance of the jubilee celebration:

> Fifty years have passed since the emancipation of the United States. This lapse of time has solved two great questions. It has exposed the fallacy of human calculations, which anticipated only present anarchy and ultimate dissolution for the new Republic, and it has established the possibility of a people governing themselves, and being prosperous and happy.[11]

Postl observed that the United States had already arrived at that stage in its history when it wanted to preserve its history and celebrate it in the form of public ritual. According to Postl, the reasons for its success were as follows:

> A sea-coast of three thousand miles, excellent harbours, important rivers, rising and emptying themselves into its territory, a rich virgin soil, a temperate climate, a population composed of the descendants of the first nation in the world, the sciences of the ancient, the experience of modern times transplanted into a new and susceptible soil, and both united to the most liberal constitution that ever existed, were certainly elements, which well-employed and well-directed, afforded reasons to anticipate future greatness.[12]

Another reason that Postl alludes to as responsible for the rise of the United States was the good fortune to have had Washington as the first president:

> The Union happily found a genius fully competent to give it this direction in Washington. Ever the same at home, in the field and in the cabinet, he imperceptibly gave to the nation the impress of his character and his politics. A character more firm, more composed, and notwithstanding its simplicity, more dignified, than this statesman's can scarcely be imagined. There never existed a man who knew the true interest of his country better than Washington, or sought it in a simpler or wiser way.

In the writings of Postl is some of the enthusiasm German-Americans felt for the new Republic. As German-Americans did throughout American history, so too did Postl identify Washington's legacy in his famous Farewell Address, which he felt delineated the basic philosophical foundations of the United States for the future.

Postl felt that if America followed the basic precepts of Washington's address, then "unparalleled prosperity" would be guaranteed. If it ever would deviate, however, from Washington's philosophy, then trouble would follow. Progress would come by carefully adhering to American Republican traditions established in the Revolution and enunciated by Washington. Postl provides us with some insight into the nature of the German-American outlook in the early years of the Republic. His writings also would figure in an important way in terms of encouraging German immigration to America.[13]

Locations in 1830

By 1830 German-American settlement patterns had resulted in a German-American triangle with the corners located in New York, Ohio, and Virginia. Most German-Americans of the pre–1830 period had arrived in America before the American Revolution, and few came in the Napoleonic era due to the wars in Europe and the continental blockade, which made emigration difficult, if not impossible. It would only be after 1830 that emigration would substantially increase.

Notes

1. Theodore Huebner, *Germans in America* (Philadelphia: Chilton, 1962), p. 47. For sources dealing with the role German-Americans played in the Revolution, see Margrit B. Krewson, *Von Steuben and the German Contribution to the American Revolution* (Washington, D.C.: Library of Congress, 1987), and Don Heinrich Tolzmann, ed., *German-Americans in the American Revolution: Henry Melchior Richards' History* (Bowie, Md.: Heritage Books, 1992).

2. Ibid.

3. Regarding Washington's bodyguard, see Don Heinrich Tolzmann, ed., *The German-American Soldier in the Wars of the U.S.: J. G. Rosengarten's History* (Bowie, Md.: Heritage Books, 1996).

4. See Krewson, *Von Steuben*, pp. 15–22.

5. Ibid., pp. 23–27.

6. Huebner, *Germans in America*, p. 47.

7. With regard to German-American women, see Martha Kaarsberg Wallach, "German Immigrant Women," *Journal of German-American Studies* 13, no. 3 (1978): 7–13.

8. Huebner, *Germans in America*, p. 47.

9. See Krewson, *Von Steuben*, pp. 29–40, and Don Heinrich Tolzmann, ed., *German Allied Troops in the American Revolution: J. G. Rosengarten's Survey of German Archives and Sources* (Bowie, Md.: Heritage Books, 1993).

10. Regarding the War of 1812 see Tolzmann, *The German-American Soldier*.

11. See Charles Sealsfield, *The United States of North America as They Are*, Sämtliche Werke, vol. 2 (Hildesheim: Olms Presse, 1972).

12. Ibid.

13. Ibid.

Settlement Patterns

On the Frontier

The westward movement on the frontier got underway before the American Revolution. Just as in the settlement of the colonies, the Germans played an important part in the opening of the Midwest and Far West. Many German pioneers were located directly on the frontier that ran from Maine to Georgia. They were accustomed to dealing with the Indians; they knew the topography of the country; and they were ready to trek into the wilderness.

The first German settlers in Kentucky came from the Valley of Virginia and from the western counties of North and South Carolina. In the Valley of Virginia, the Germans were numerous; they even exceeded the Irish. In the Carolinas, too, they appear to have been as plentiful as the Scotch-Irish. Many Germans also came from the midland counties of Pennsylvania.

The German pioneers were a sturdy lot, their women working in the woods and fields together with the men. They were always considered highly desirable settlers by colonial governors. George Washington had plans to settle Germans on his ten thousand acres south of the Ohio River. He even considered sending an agent to Germany to recruit settlers, to whom he would promise free transportation to the Ohio and four years of free rental. However, the Revolutionary War put an end to his plans.

The Ohio Valley

Kentucky occupied a key position with regard to the settlement of the Midwest, as the pioneers entered by way of the Ohio River and from the early settlements in Kentucky and Tennessee. Daniel Boone, a famous Kentuckian, was born in Bucks County, Pennsylvania, and spoke the German dialect of that area, so he has been claimed as a Pennsylvania German, although he was actually of English descent. At age eighteen he went to North Carolina, where he lived as a farmer and hunter.

In 1769, together with several frontiersmen, Boone went on an exploration through the forests between the Ohio and the Tennessee and Cumberland Rivers. After two years, he returned with his wife, children, and relatives, and five other families, only to be driven back by Indians to the Clinch River. In 1775 he brought his family to a stockade on the Kentucky River called Boonesborough. A number of other fortified settlements were established, since the Indians were hostile.

Even before Boone, a schoolmate of his by the name of Steiner and a companion, Harrod, had gone as far as the present site of Nashville. There some forty men, including a number of Germans, founded Harrodsburg in 1774, the earliest settlement in Kentucky. Germans accompanied Boone on his expeditions, and German names can be found in such settlements as Beargrass Creek, Hart's Station, and Lawrenceburg.

The Lincoln family, like the Boones, migrated from Pennsylvania into Kentucky and then further west. This was a pattern that many Pennsylvania, Maryland, and Virginia Germans took, as well as settlers of other backgrounds. Many of these settlers lived in or near German-American settlements and absorbed German influences. Abraham Lincoln's grandfather, for example, spelled his name in the German way as "Linkhorn," because he lived in a region settled predominantly by Virginia Germans. Indeed, his grandfather's tombstone in Long Run Cemetery near Louisville, Kentucky, bears the name "Abraham Linkhorn." The question often arose as to whether or not he was of German descent.

Although he was not, the orthography his name reflects the influence of the German heritage.[1]

A typical frontiersman was Henry Crist (Heinrich Christ), born in 1764 in Virginia of German parents. In 1788 he set forth on a flat-bottom boat on the Ohio River for the purpose of preparing salt. There were twelve armed men and one woman in the company. Arriving in the Salt River, they were attacked by Indians. The lone woman was captured by the Indians but was later exchanged, and all the men were killed except Crist. He was so severely wounded, though, that he could not walk. Crawling on his knees with his clothes and skin torn by briars and thorns, Crist was found and carried to the salt camp. It took him a year to recover from his wounds. Later he became prominent in politics and was elected to the state legislature and afterward to Congress. Despite his hard frontier life, he lived to be eighty.

Some Germans were hunters and trappers, but the great majority of them were farmers. They cultivated the land, built up towns, and took an interest in religion and education. The first college in the Ohio Valley, Transylvania Seminary, actually the first institution of higher learning west of the Alleghenies, received its first charter in 1780. By 1792 it was located at Lexington, and in 1798 it was renamed Transylvania University. Among its first trustees were John Bowman (Baumann), George Muter, and Jacob Froman, all of German origin.

Among the pioneers were also several German Jews who made important contributions. Joseph Simon set up shop in Lancaster, Pennsylvania, before 1740, supplying the backwoodsmen with many necessities. He soon became one of the foremost Indian traders of the time. His boats went down the Ohio River, and his pack trains went across the plains. As one of the largest landholders in the Midwest, he became vitally interested in the promotion of settlements.

The brothers Barnard and Michael Gratz from Langendorf, Silesia, engaged in the import trade after having received a business education in the firm of their uncle, Solomon Henry. Their vessels plied from Mobile to Halifax. Later they became interested in the Virginia western movement and in the attempts at reorganizing the settlements along the Ohio and Mississippi Rivers. They supplied the settlers with provisions and traded for furs with the Indians. Benjamin Gratz, the son of Michael, became a trustee and patron of Transylvania University. He was also one of the promoters, the director, and the second president of the first railroad west of the Alleghenies, the Lexington and Ohio Railroad.

Germans continued to spread into all the settlements of Kentucky. As the name implies, Frankfort was settled by former residents of Frankfurt am Main. It was noted for its *Gemütlichkeit* (good-natured disposition) and had bars with billiard tables and a theater. However, the attempt to establish a library met with failure.

The central and western part of the Bluegrass region were also settled by German farmers. The favorable reports of the fertile soil attracted many German settlers from North Carolina and Virginia. Many Maryland and Pennsylvania Germans also moved into Kentucky. The wave of immigration increased with the Louisiana Purchase in 1803, after which a greater number of settlers entered Tennessee as well as Kentucky.

The territory north of the Ohio River was not settled as early as Kentucky and Tennessee, as it was inaccessible and inhabited by unfriendly Indian tribes. The first two Germans to come to the Ohio country were Conrad Weiser and Christian Post, who were both well acquainted with the Indians. Weiser was the son of the leader of the Palatines, Johann Conrad Weiser, and Post was a Moravian missionary.

Weiser had not only learned the Mohawk language and several dialects, but he had also won the confidence of the Indians. For this reason he was invaluable as an interpreter and an intermediary. In 1737 he undertook a journey to Onondaga in New York at the request of the governors of Pennsylvania and Virginia. He wanted to persuade the chiefs of the Six Nations to make an alliance with the Cherokees and the Catawbas. His mission was successful.

In 1742 Weiser was the interpreter for Governor Thomas of Pennsylvania at a parley with the chiefs of the Six Nations. Weiser was again sent to them in 1745 as an emissary, this time at the behest of Governor Clinton of New York. He managed to regain their friendship.

Three years later he was asked to travel to Ohio. This time he wanted to keep the Indians from an alliance with the French. During this trip he noted the location and strength of the French settlements in the Ohio Valley. Successful at his task, Weiser was able to persuade the Mohawk Indians to form an alliance against the French and the hostile

Indian tribes of the Ohio region in 1745. Weiser died as a lieutenant during the French and Indian War.

Christian Post had married an Indian woman and so maintained very friendly relations with the Indians. This was not approved of, however, by the Bethlehem church fathers, and Post was no longer permitted to serve as an ordained missionary. Nevertheless, he continued his work independently, and in 1761 he became the first settler in the Ohio district in what is now Stark County.

Hopeful of founding a mission for the Indians, Post induced Johann Heckewelder to join him. The young man first learned the Indian language and gave instruction to Indian children. Post began to cultivate the land and to preach to the Indians. This attempt to found a settlement in 1761 failed because of the outbreak of Pontiac's War. Chief Pontiac was a daring and clever leader; he roused the Indians and led them so successfully that all the western frontier forts except Detroit fell into his hands.

However, another Moravian, David Zeisberger, was more successful and founded an Indian congregation on the Allegheny River at Goshocking. By 1770 the congregation had grown, and Zeisberger moved west to Friedensdorf and Schönbrunn. To help the Indians, Zeisberger even prepared a book of the Delaware language, which was published in Philadelphia in 1827.

The Moravians established viable communities together with the Indians, but suddenly, at the instigation of British agents, the Wyandot Indians were induced in 1781 to fall upon and destroy the settlements. The Christianized Indians were entirely unprepared for the murderous attack, for they had been taught nonviolence. The peaceful Indians were first driven from their settlements by the Wyandots under the leadership of the renegade Simon Girty. When they returned, they were barbarously massacred by a group of volunteers under the command of Colonel David Wiliamson in March 1782.

During the Indian wars, a number of Germans acquired fame as scouts and Indian fighters. The most famous of these was Ludwig (Lewis) Wetzel. His father was born in the Palatinate and had settled near Wheeling. One day while he was out hunting with his sons Jacob and Lewis, they were attacked by Indians. Lewis, who was then only thirteen, managed to escape with his brother, but his father was killed and scalped. Both boys swore that they would kill every Indian they laid their eyes on.

Many tales are told of Wetzel's prowess: on one occasion he is said to have killed twenty-seven Indians; on another, fifty. He was an excellent shot and was fearless. His ferocity toward the Indians, however, knew no bounds. Once he killed an Indian who had been granted safe conduct by General Harmar. Held for the crime, Wetzel managed to escape but was recaptured and brought to General Harmar in Cincinnati. Wetzel was so popular, however, that a mob got ready to storm Fort Washington. To prevent bloodshed, the judge set him free on bond.

Enraged at his treatment, Wetzel migrated to Spanish territory. At Natchez, where he regained his popularity, he was arrested as a counterfeiter and sentenced to life imprisonment in New Orleans. After spending four and a half years in a damp cell, Wetzel was released in dramatic fashion. He feigned illness and death, and his body was placed in a coffin and given to friends for burial. In the evening, Wetzel emerged from his tomb, and the coffin was dropped into the river. After the Louisiana Purchase, he migrated to Texas, but the imprisonment had undermined his constitution, and he died in the forest on the banks of the Brazos River in Texas.

The Indians continued their raids until they were subdued in 1794 by General Mad Anthony Wayne of Revolutionary War fame. They signed treaty, and new settlements sprang up on the Ohio, the Muskingum, the Scioto, and the Great Miami Rivers. On the upper Muskingum, Ebenezer Zane (Zahn) from Lancaster, Pennsylvania, founded Zanesville; a descendant of his was Zane Grey. In payment for the land he contracted to establish a packhorse trail from Wheeling to Maysville, Kentucky. U.S. mail was carried over this path for the first time in 1797, and along this path many Germans made their way westward. In the same year, Zane laid out New Lancaster, and in this town the first German newspaper west of the Alleghenies appeared in 1807, *Der Lancaster Adler*, printed in the Pennsylvania German dialect.

On the present site of Wheeling, Zane had built a blockhouse that was attacked during the American Revolution by a company of British soldiers and Indians. The fort was saved largely due to the heroism of Elizabeth Zane, Ebenezer's sister, who at the risk of her life rushed out to get a fresh supply of ammunition.

German settlers gradually spread all over Ohio; nearly every county contained a German township and citizens with such names as Berlin, Winesburg, Saxon, and Hanover. Scriptural names, such as Bethlehem, Salem, Nazareth, Goshen, and Canaan, were given to settlements of German Moravians, Dunkers, or Mennonites. Although Cincinnati did not contain a large number of Germans at first, it would become in the early nineteenth century the major destination point of German immigration in the west and a major distribution center for German immigrants in the Midwest, especially in the Ohio Valley.[2]

The Mississippi Valley

During the nineteenth century, German immigration kept growing until it surpassed all other immigrant groups. The Germans, like other immigrants, migrated to areas where land was plentiful and cheap. Hence, the bulk of the new arrivals went to the Midwest. After the Louisiana Purchase in 1803, the valley of the Mississippi was opened for settlement, but few migrants went to New Orleans. Not until after the Battle of New Orleans in 1815 did the population increase. German settlers had arrived in the Crescent City shortly after its founding in 1718. Speculator John Law, who founded a company in Paris for the settlement of the Lower Mississippi, had sent agents through France, Germany, and Switzerland to attract prospective settlers.

About two thousand immigrants were induced to accept free passage and free land in "the earthly paradise." When they landed at Mobile Bay, they found nothing but an unhealthy wilderness. Decimated by disease, some three hundred of the survivors settled in 1722 in Attakapas, Louisiana, where they prospered. Some Alsatians and Württembergers also settled about twenty miles north of New Orleans. More Germans came to Louisiana in the nineteenth century, and after 1840 there were ten thousand in New Orleans alone. There were also German settlers in St. Peters, Baton Rouge, and along the Red River.

In 1836, sixty families from Rheinhessen arrived in Arkansas and settled near Little Rock. Their leader was the Reverend Klingelhöffer, friend of the German traveler and novelist Friedrich Gerstäcker.

St. Louis became a major distribution center for German immigrants in the Midwest. Settlements extended north and south on the Missouri, as well as the Mississippi, where the Germans had come from Ohio, Kentucky, Tennessee, Maryland, and Virginia. However, no Germans from abroad went there by 1821, when Missouri was admitted as a state.

It was Gottfried Duden, the university graduate, whose enthusiastic descriptions of the beauties of Missouri attracted thousands of Germans to this area. At first peasants from Westfalen and Hannover arrived and were followed by barons, merchants, officers, students, and clergymen, who were unaccustomed to hard work in the open. These "Latin farmers" had a difficult time, and many of them perished miserably.

The next large influx of Germans was due to the efforts of the *Giessener Gesellschaft*, which had been organized to concentrate German emigration in a given area. Under the leadership of Münch and Paul Follenius, thousands of Germans settled on the west bank of the Mississippi in what is now Warren County. From here, Germans spread out to St. Louis, St. Charles, Washington, Hermann, Warrenton, and Boonville, frequently making up more than half of the population. Immigrants of all faiths were involved; they were thrifty and hardworking people, and soon every acre of the country was under cultivation. Trim cottages and neat farm buildings dotted the landscape. The dream of Follenius and Münch of founding a German-American state in the West along the lines of a New England in the East was not realized, but the immigrants did establish many prosperous German-American communities in Missouri and contributed to making that state a destination for German immigrants.

In 1855 this is how German-American settlements of Missouri were described:

> The German settlements in the West are remarkable for their completely German appearance and their purely German atmosphere. While the German farmer in Pennsylvania is more accustomed to Anglo-American ways, and has even sacrificed his native tongue, or half of it at least, the German settlements in the West have preserved their native colouring unmixed. You think you are in a village in Germany when you set foot in one of these settlements. The architecture of the

houses, owing of course to differences in climate is a little different, but
the household furnishings, the family customs, the style and method of
plowing, sowing, and harvesting all remind one of Germany.[3]

A New Germany in America

The idea of founding a German-American state, or a new Germany in
America, was the concept of some of the ardent young Germans in the
old country who felt deeply frustrated by the state of affairs in place after
the Napoleonic Wars. When their many attempts to realize their political
ideals in the Old World failed, they turned their eyes to the New World.

At the beginning of the nineteenth century, immigration was uncon-
trolled and unguided, and because of this there was much suffering
among the immigrants. However, there were idealists who thought that
by concentrating the flow of immigration to a given territory, which had
not yet been admitted to the Union, a German-American state might be
established, just as the English had established New England. There were
also keen-witted theorists who foresaw the possibility of economic development and the advantage of future markets in overseas German
colonies. However, their endeavors were hampered by the absence of a
united Germany, which could have provided moral and economic support to such projects.

Special efforts were made to establish a New Germany in Missouri,
Texas, and Wisconsin. Some felt that the best chances for success were
in Texas, since, for a short period at least, it had been an independent
sovereign state. Moreover, there was an abundance of relatively inex-
pensive or even free land available in Texas. Duden had drawn the attention of prospective emigrants to Missouri; a number of guidebooks and
particularly the fictional accounts by Charles Sealsfield aroused interest
in Texas.

During the first years of the nineteenth century, when Texas was
under the control of Spain, there were numerous plans to settle Germans
in the region, but none of them was successful. Beginning with the
founding of an industrial settlement on land in Austin's colony in 1831
by Friedrich Ernst from Oldenburg, several dozen German farm com-

munities were established in the rich bottom land between the Brazos and the Colorado Rivers. Although they were generally far removed from other settlers, they shared their fate and fortune. When the Texans rebelled against Mexico in 1836, most German men volunteered their services and helped to defeat the Mexican army and General Santa Anna in the famous battle of San Jacinto. To the present day, this agricultural region, a scant hundred miles form Houston, retains many of its German ways, and many can still carry on a conversation in Texas German.

In 1839 a Germania Society was formed in New York for the purpose of reestablishing a German colony in Texas. As a result, a group of 130 persons set sail for Galveston in November. The program, however, was essentially a failure. Because of the fear of yellow fever, which was raging in Galveston when they arrived, the members of the society who had enough money booked return passage to New York on the same boat. Several families, with insufficient funds, however, did remain and were able to settle successfully in Houston. They provided the nucleus for the several German communities that subsequently developed in Houston over the years.

Again and again, ambitious plans were made for promoting settlements in Texas. In the forties, a Frenchman, Henri Castro, founded Castroville in Medina County. Among the settlers he induced to come were Germans, Swiss, and Alsatians. More and more Germans began to arrive in the Republic, motivated by the success of the existing colonies. An extremely positive emigrant letter sent home by Friedrich Ernst and published in the Oldenburg newspaper and in a a popular guidebook contributed to this German immigration to Texas. By 1841, under the leadership of Ernst, the Germans in Austin County had organized a *Teutonia Orden*, which was to preserve German culture, encourage immigration, and carry on correspondence with interested parties in Germany. Through such letters and through printed reports, interest in Texas was aroused in many parts of Germany. During the important formative period of 1815–50, more guidebooks were written about Texas than about any other region in America.

In the early 1840s five sovereign princes and sixteen noblemen formed an organization with a very ambitious plan to establish German settlements in Texas. For this purpose, these minor members of the aristocracy formed the *Verein zum Schutze deutscher Einwandrer in Texas* (Society for the Protection of German Immigrants in Texas). Each member contributed a sum of money to promote the aims of the *Adelsverein* (Society of Nobles), as it was popularly known.

The noblemen were motivated by a mixture of economic, political, and philanthropic reasons. As minor members of the nobility without significant estates at home, they were interested in material gain in the New World. Similarly, they harbored rather naive political and patriotic ideas about the establishment of German colonies at a time when Germany was not yet a nation, let alone an empire. It was, furthermore, in the interest of British diplomacy that Texas be kept independent and that it be maintained as a kind of buffer state. Hence, German relatives of Queen Victoria and Prince Albert eagerly participated in the plans of the *Adelsverein*. Finally, the members of the *Verein* seem to be genuinely interested in the ways immigration could solve some of the economic and social problems of their states.

In May 1842 Counts Joseph von Boos-Waldeck and Victon von Leiningen were sent to Texas to investigate the possibilities for the society's plans. Boos-Waldeck purchased a plantation near Ernst's settlement of Industry, which the society named Nassau Farm in honor of Duke Adolph of Nassau, Protector of the *Adelsverein*. Upon returning to Europe, Leiningen gave a very favorable report about the conditions in Texas for immigration, while Boos-Waldeck was much more cautious and critical. When the society followed Leiningen's recommendations and not Boos-Waldeck's, the latter resigned from the *Adelsverein*.

The society publicized its plans and began to actively recruit immigrants. For a fixed sum the *Verein* agreed to provide transportation and to give each family a log house and 320 acres of land (a single male would receive 160 acres). Cattle and agricultural implements could be purchased at a low price. The society would also provide schools, churches, militia, and other aspects for the new communities.

To obtain the necessary lands, the *Adelsverein* entered into a partnership in Europe with the German-American Henry Fischer, a native of Cassel, who had lived for a number of years in Houston. Fischer had obtained the settlement rights for a three-million-acre grant of land between the Llano-Miller grant. The society members were pleased with the availability of this land and were impressed by its size—ten times that of the Duchy of Hessen Nassau, in which the *Adelsverein* was incorporated. This land, however, which neither Fischer nor any other white person had ever seen, was for the most part unarable, very far from any established civilization, and inhabited by hostile Comanches.

The *Adelsverein* named Prince Carl of Solms-Braunfels as the commissioner-general of its operations in Texas. He arrived in Texas in July 1844. During his stay of nearly a year, Solms made the necessary preparations with the Texas officials and established the city of Carlshafen (later named Indianola) on Matagorda Bay as the port of debarkation for the immigrants. Since the Fischer-Miller grant had not yet been explored and was much too far inland, Solms purchased over eight thousand acres of land on the Comal River near San Antonio, where the first colony, New Braunfels, was established in March 1845 for the first group of several hundred immigrants. These and the subsequent immigrants went by foot and by oxcart on a 150-mile journey from the coast to the colony. This trip was extremely difficult. Because sickness befell many of the immigrants and the adverse weather conditions during the extremely rainy winter of 1845–46, hundred of immigrants died on this route.

Because of organizational, logistical, and financial problems, the *Adelsverein* fell far short of its elaborate colonization plans for Texas. On a strictly numerical basis, however, the society's undertaking was quite successful. Beginning with several hundred society immigrants who came to Texas in the fall of 1844, by 1850, nearly ten thousand German immigrants had come to Texas on ninety ships under the auspices of the *Adelsverein*, and yet another estimated ten thousand were attracted to Texas by the *Adelsverein*'s presence in Texas and by its publicity in Germany. But by 1847 the society was bankrupt, and its operations virtually collapsed within the next few years.

Prince Solms had planned to stay in Texas only long enough to establish the first colony. Neither Solms nor the society officials in Europe were good economic managers. Solms's successor, Baron Ottfried Hans von Meusebach (who Americanized his name in Texas to "John Meusebach"), arrived in 1845. Meusebach struggled heroically and successfully against the mounting debts of the society and angry immigrants who had not been given the promised allotments of land. To provide for the new immigrants now arriving, Meusebach immediately secured a grant of land ninety miles from New Braunfels and founded a second settlement, which he named Friedrichsburg (for Friedrich of Prussia), now called Fredericksburg. In founding Fredericksburg, Meusebach also concluded the only successful peace treaty with the Comanches, thereby opening up West Texas to further settlement. This treaty also allowed German immigrants access to the Fischer-Miller grant, but for reasons stated earlier, German colonization was only minimally successful there.

Because of the impact of the *Adelsverein* settlement, the Texas Hill Country (including the cities of San Antonio and Austin) still retains today an enduring and pervasive German-American heritage. The dramatic history of the *Adelsverein* settlements also became a colorful part of German-Texans' collective memory.[4]

The Homestead and Other Acts

Congress passed several measures, that greatly aided western settlement.

- The Homestead Act of 1862 provided 160 acres to each settler who would farm the land for five years;

- The Morrill Land Grant Act of 1862 gave the states land at the equation of thirty thousand acres for each member of Congress to support state agricultural colleges;

- The Pacific Railway Act of 1862 authorized subsidies in land and money for the construction of a transcontinental railway;

- The National Banking Act of 1863 provided for the establishment of a national currency for the entire country; and

- Various tariffs raised the duties on manufactured goods to an average rate of 47 percent to protect domestic manufacturers.

All of these, especially the Homestead Act, provided great support for western settlement, as well as for the growth and development of a national economy incorporating the West.

The West

The West was settled rapidly after the close of the Civil War. The predominant ethnic groups among the settlers were Germans, Swiss, Scandinavians, and Russians. Among the first were the German Mennonites, who spread out in Kansas and Nebraska between 1876 and 1878. They had migrated from West Prussia to Southern Russia because of the liberal offer made to them by the czarist government. When they heard of the wonderful opportunities in America, they decided to cross the ocean. They became successful farmers in Kansas, raising wheat, corn, rye, and barley. They also raised fruit trees, which they had brought with them from Russia.

Although the Lewis and Clark expedition in 1804–1805 had prepared the way, no settlements were immediately attempted. Three years later, the Missouri Fur Company sent trappers and hunters into Kansas, and in 1811 there arrived from New York one of the most enterprising and successful German-Americans: John Jacob Astor. He became the first of the legendary "self-made men" in American history.

Astor, born in Walldorf near Heidelberg in 1763, migrated to England and then came to America in 1784. While on board ship, a chance acquaintance drew his attention to the opportunities in the fur trade. He had brought along some musical instruments given to him by his brother in England. These he exchanged on his arrival in New York for furs, which he sold in London for a good profit. Nevertheless, he continued importing musical instruments, and he became the first regular dealer in the United States. Successful speculations in real estate and government securities increased his income. In 1809 he organized the American Fur Company through which he acquired immense wealth. Attracted by the West, he moved there and became known as the czar of the fur trade in the Northwest.

At his own expense and at his own risk, Astor founded Astoria at the mouth of the Columbia River. This fur trading post was so successful that it threatened the British fur monopoly. In 1813 English troops seized Astoria and named it St. George. However, it was returned to the United States after the war. In 1834 Astor sold all his fur interests and devoted himself exclusively to real estate speculation, and he was soon known as the "landlord of New York."

From 1837 until 1840 Astor served as president of the German Society of New York, which aided German immigrants. He also presented the society with a handsome endowment. Astor had been extremely successful in his business ventures in addition to fur trading, and at his death in 1848, he left a fortune of more than $20 million. He bequeathed $400,000 to help found the Astor Library on Lafayette Street and also left $50,000 to his native Walldorf for the building of an orphanage.

Histories of New York and the United States usually mention Astor not only because he was the richest man in America at his death, but also because he was largely responsible for the idea of rising from rags to riches as a self-made man.

Around 1839 a stronger current of immigration flowed toward Oregon, although the gold rush of 1848 drew away some of its settlers. By 1853 the territory north of the Columbia River was separated from Oregon and named Washington. That region, as well as Montana and North and South Dakota, did not gain much in population until the opening of the Northern Pacific Railroad, which was the achievement of a German-American, Henry Villard (Heinrich Hilgard). Born in Speyer in 1835, he came to the United States in 1853 after studying at the universities of Munich and Würzburg. Fearing that his father would try to bring him back home, he changed his name. In 1858 the *New Yorker Staats-Zeitung* employed him as a reporter. He wrote on the Lincoln-Douglas debates and established friendly contacts with the future president. Anecdotes told by Lincoln and published by Villard attracted a great deal of attention. For three years during the Civil War he was a prominent war correspondent. His journalism, in addition to a book he published in 1860 entitled *The Past and Present of the Pike's Peak Gold Regions*, attracted attention, and he came to write for various papers, including the *New York Herald*.

In 1866 and 1871 he visited Germany and then returned as the representative of the foreign bondholders of the Oregon and California Railroad. He became the president of this company in 1875. With the aid of German capital, he gained control of the Northern Pacific Railroad, completing the western extension and thereby creating a trunk line from the Great Lakes to the Pacific. This feat made him one of the greatest railroad magnates. Despite reverses in 1883, he regained control of the Northern Pacific. The construction of this railroad more than anything else opened the Northwest for settlement.

In 1889 Villard founded the Edison General Electric Company with Thomas Edison. As early as 1881, Villard had acquired controlling interests in the *New York Evening Post*, and he appointed Carl Schurz as editor-in-chief. Schurz wrote that Villard was a very farsighted man, as well as an enthusiastic idealist, and that he was one of the very few individuals of high ideals to be found in the world of big business. Villard's wife, Helen Villard, was the daughter of the abolitionist William Lloyd Garrison and made important contributions to the women's suffrage movement; she was also an active member of the NAACP and founded the Women's Peace Society in 1919.

Germans took immediate advantage of the opportunities offered in the West. Seattle, the most important city of Washington, was founded by Henry L. Yesler, a Maryland German. Yesler, a carpenter, journeyed to Ohio and settled in Massilon. Diligent and thrifty, he soon became wealthy. Impressed by the news of the boom on the Pacific coast, he decided to go there and sailed from Baltimore to Panama, crossed the Isthmus, and then proceeded by ship to California. The gold of California did not attract him as much as the forests of Washington, in which he saw unlimited possibilities for lumbering. In 1853 he built a sawmill on the present site of Seattle and taught the local Indians about lumbering. As soon as lumber was available, Yesler laid out streets and built homes. In the middle of the settlement, he erected a huge structure of rough-hewn logs called the "cookhouse," which served for years as a town hall, storehouse, hotel, jail, and church. Soon settlers came in great numbers, and Seattle became a thriving community. Yesler, who had acquired considerable wealth, was the mayor and a leading citizen. His foresight and energy laid the foundation for one of the leading industries and one of the most prosperous cities of the West.

Another important person in the west was Friedrich Weyerhaeuser

(1834–1914), who created an empire of lumbering and sawmills. His influence extended to other areas of the economy as well and was continued by his sons and grandsons. Known as the "Timber King," Weyerhaeuser was born in Niedersaulheim, Rhein-Hesse, and came to the United States after the unsuccessful 1848 revolution in Germany.

He moved to Rock Island, Illinois, where he worked on a railroad, and he was soon entrusted with the direction of a sawmill. When the company failed in 1857, he bought the timber yard and the sawmill and was soon purchasing logs from the Mississippi River and acquiring additional sawmills. In the 1860s, he acquired tracts of land in Wisconsin and more still in Minnesota, Idaho, Washington, and Oregon, resulting in millions of acres of the best timber forests. Much of this he acquired from the government for his railroad. At the turn of the century, he owned more timberland than any other American.[5]

The Far West

In California, another German, John A. Sutter, was responsible not only for the development of an enormous area, but also for the development of another typically Western industry—gold mining. Born in Baden, Germany, in 1803, and trained in a Swiss military academy, he arrived in the West in 1834. For many years he maintained a trade route between St. Louis and Santa Fe.

In 1838 he traveled with a party of trappers to Vancouver. From there he went to the Sandwich Islands, Alaska, and then back to the Pacific Coast. Winds drove the vessel into San Francisco Bay, and from there he went to the present site of Sacramento, where he founded a settlement called New Helvetia. The Mexican governor of California, Alvarado, gave him the title to his land and conferred citizenship upon him. So much confidence was placed in him that he was made the governor of the northern frontier territory of Mexico. When California became part of the United States, Sutter was appointed chief justice and Indian agent of his district. He owned vast estates; sleek cattle roamed his pastures, and golden wheat grew in his fields. He was soon the richest man in California.

It was not only wheat that gleamed like gold; the precious metal was in the streams and on the ground. Discovered on January 20, 1848, by John W. Marshall, overseer of one of Sutter's sawmills, the gold proved to be a curse and not a blessing to Sutter. Before he knew it, the news had leaked out and hordes of goldseekers, adventurers, and other unscrupulous elements invaded his property, devastating the land and killing the cattle. As a result, the title to his land was disputed. Although Sutter appealed to Congress for justice, he never regained possession of his property. However, the state of California voted him a pension of $3,000 annually for seven years and made him general of the militia, but he was no longer the proud possessor of a vast domain.

Among the goldseekers were Germans as well as representatives of many other ethnic groups. Largely farmers rather than adventurers, the German-Americans settled down and cultivated the land. They were particularly successful in the production of grapes and wines. The citrus industry, too, was largely developed by German-Americans.

Germans flocked into a number of California cities such as Los Angeles, San Bernardino, San Diego, and Santa Barbara. In San Francisco, an outstanding name of German origin is Lick (Lück). James Lick, born in Pennsylvania of German parents, was the founder of the famous observatory named for him. Among the big industrialists who were German were the following: Claus Spreckels from Hannover, the sugar king; Henry Miller, born in Württemberg, the cattle king; and his partner, Charles Lux, from Baden. The latter began a slaughterhouse in San Francisco in 1857. Since they owned 800,000 acres of land, they were able to drive large herds of cattle from neighboring states onto their own land.

Another well-known German-American had a connection with California: Heinrich Schliemann, the discoverer of the ancient city of Troy. By the time he arrived in San Francisco in 1851, the erstwhile son of a poor Pomeranian parson had traveled all over the world, taught himself a dozen languages and acquired a vast fortune. He took great pride in American citizenship, which he is said to have adopted when California joined the Union.

Within nine months of the gold rush, Schliemann had amassed half a million dollars. He had the precious metal stored in Sacramento in huge safes with armed guards. He had rented an office in the only steel and concrete building in the city because he was afraid of fire. He left for Europe, where he made another fortune during the Crimean War. In 1868 he visited America again to look after his vast holdings.

Despite his business acumen and his fantastic successes in financial operations, Schliemann was a scholar at heart. He studied ancient Greek and learned it so thoroughly that he was able to write the story of his life in Greek for a German university. With passionate devotion he tried to solve the problem of excavating ancient Troy. Overcoming untold difficulties and hardships, his efforts were finally crowned with success. At his death in 1890, kings and queens stood at his bier, and he was buried in a marble tomb fit for a king.[6]

Chain Migration

The process whereby many emigrants came to America has been described as "chain migration." This relates to how immigrants followed the pathways of earlier immigrants from their hometowns, thus establishing a chain-link between the place of origin in the Old World and the place of destination in the New World. Such immigrants were anything but uprooted, but rather were transplanted from one environment to another.

Across the United States, those communities that were based primarily on chain migration were the most successful in maintaining their German heritage, and this was due to the common roots and origins that the immigrants and their descendants shared. In general, that chain migration was the rule rather than the exception, as most immigrants settled where others from their homeland had established themselves.

Indeed, most immigrants arriving by the end of the nineteenth century were joining friends or family. Also, there usually was someone awaiting their arrival at their port of entry. One-third even had their fares paid in advance by friends or family in America, so most emigrants were joining friends and relatives in German-American communities settled by people from their hometown. Under these circumstances, the newcomers would immediately feel at home, because people would speak their dialect and have the same customs and traditions. Also, they would find the same kinds of religious and secular institutions and organizations they had known in their hometowns.

Chain-migration immigrants usually tended to come with families or with groups of families. They often displayed a wide age distribution and were roughly equally divided in terms of men and women. This distinguished them from non-chain-migration immigrants, who were usually young adult males with more education and wealth. Chain-migration immigrants usually were driven by economic reasons and sought a better life for their families and friends in the New World. They came together in groups and desired to stay together in communities where there were Germans from their hometowns. Also chain-migration immigrants and their descendants tended to intermarry in their own ethnic group, often of the same religious background. Individual immigrants, by contrast, were risk takers and tended to migrate to urban areas to seek out opportunity. Thus, it is obvious that chain-migration communities would be more successful in maintaining the German heritage.

All of these factors contributed to the preservation of German heritage and language across America in areas settled by German immigrants. In a study of the German-Bohemians in Brown County, Minnesota, LaVern J. Rippley has shown that this area grew because of chain migration of German-Bohemians and that this region "fostered language retention, religious homogeneity, endogamy, family transplants, retrention of Old World lifestyles," as well as a slower rate of assimilation. This again was the kind of process and pattern that characterized much of the German emigration to America and that is responsible for the strength of the German heritage in communities across the country.[7]

Albert B. Faust in his 1909 German-American history cited some good examples of chain migration with regard to Wisconsin. He noted that

> Lorima, in Dodge County, was settled almost entirely by Prussians from Brandenburg, who belonged to the Evangelical Association. The neighboring towns of Hermann and Theresa, also in Dodge County, were settled principally by natives of Pomerania. In Calumet County there are Oldenburg, Luxemburg, and New Holstein settlements. St. Kilian, in Washington County, is settled by people from Northern Bohemia, just

over the German border. The town of Belgium, Ozaukee County, is populated almost exclusively by Luxemburgers, while Oldenburgers occupy the German settlement at Cedarburg. Three fourths of the population of Farmington, Washington County, are from Saxony. In the same county Jackson is chiefly settled by Pomeranians, while one half of the population of Kewaskum are from the same German province. In Dane County there are several interesting groups of German Catholics. Roxbury is nine tenths German, the people coming mostly from Rhenish Prussia and Bavaria. Germans predominate in Cross Plains, the rest of the population being Irish. The German families of Middleton came from Köln, Rhenish Prussia, and so did those of Berry, a town almost solidly German.[8]

Immigrant Letters

One of the most important links between Germany and America was formed by correspondence sent from immigrants to their families and friends in the old country. These letters not only brought news from loved ones, but also contained informative reports and details about life in the New World. Such immigrant letters contributed to chain migration from one area in Europe to a particular destination point in America where there was a contact person who had written home.

One such letter was written by Josef Riepberger in 1841 from Columbia, located in the eastern section of Cincinnati, to his relatives in Schneeberg in Bavaria. The letter is a good example of the kinds of letters being sent home by immigrants. The letter was directed to Riepberger's brothers, sisters, and brother-in-law:

> I will be happy if this letter reaches you in good health. Thank God we are still healthy. We live 5 miles away from Cincinnati in Kolumpien. We are now leasing a farm. The rent amount[s] to half of the wine we produce. The other half belongs to us. This year we had: 150 bushels of corn, 10 bushels of oats, 50 bushels of wheat, 200 bushels of potatoes, 2,800 cabbage ($4.00 for a hundred). One dollar is worth in your money: 2 1/2 Gulden. One bushel is a Simmer and a half [*Simmer*: an Old German

corn-measure = 20 liters]. We have 6 cows, 2 horses, 13 pigs, and numerous chickens. Our lease is a half dollar and two days of labor for one year.

You want to know how the state supports itself here. It does so from congressional land and every 6 miles we have to pay 11 cents toll. You also want to know how it is in America. If your son would come to America, he could learn a trade which would be of interest to him, and he could also earn some money from this.

Dear Brother, I also want to know how things are with our sister, whether or not she wants to come to America. If she cannot come, she should see to it that her sons come here, as all craftsmen are very much in demand, if they know their trade, especially butchers. And if they are a bit thrifty, they can manage to have their parents come over in two years. If Nannchen from Bremhof should come to America, she would be better off than in Germany.

It is all up to you. I advise all young people to come to America. Their fortunes are ten times better off than in Germany. However, people at the age between 45 and 50 years, who have no children they can rely on, should stay at home in Germany. I thank God a hundred times that I could come to America for I make more money than in Germany and the thought of returning to Germany never comes to mind. My children also do not want to return.

Our oldest daughter is married to a farmer who owns his own land, which is located 4 miles from Cincinnati. His name is Josef Metz from Landau. I have not as yet provided him with means, but only the dowry, and she is more better off than had she married the richest man in Schneeberg, or Weilbach, for in America you don't have to search for wealth.

Dear Brother, I often think what you told me: that I would use up my money and I would eat only two kinds of meat every Sunday. But now in America, I do not only have two kinds of meat but also cheese and butter and coffee and meat as much as I want. My daily meals are far better than your meals are on the whole and I also live well, since I do not see a forester nor a district-policeman, nor a district court, nor a creditor.

The town of Cincinnati has 48,074 inhabitants. 12,000 are Roman Catholics. Johann Baptist Burkel and many other English priests and 3

German Catholic priests: Johann Martin Henni from Switzerland, Franz Ludwig Hubert, a Jesuit from Bavaria, and Klemens Hammer from Bohemia. There are 2 Catholic churches, 1 English and 1 German. The name of the German church is Trinity Church. It is big and majestic. In this year 2 more churches will be built, 1 English and 1 German.

The foundation stone of the second German church was laid on the day of the Annunciation of the Virgin Mary in the afternoon at five P.M. The bishop and all priests and the three German priests were present. There were three sermons, one of which was an English one by the bishop and another one by the German priest Henni. As the foundation stone was laid on the day of the Annunciation of the Virgin Mary, the church, therefore, received the name of St. Mary's. Also on this day 76 people participated in Holy Communion for the first time in this German church.

. . . In America there is a president, 200 congressmen, a court of appellation, and every 8–9 miles there is a justice of [the] peace. This is what you would call a "Landrichter." America has 57 million people. In America everything is reasonably priced at present. A farmhand earns 8–12 dollars a month, a farm girl earns 6–7 dollars. A man working on the channel 11–12 dollars and the meals are far better than in Germany.

All Saint's Day in 1840, Georg Reichert from Schneeberg came to me and was ill and stayed until the 6th of April. His illness was tuberculosis, just as with his sister in Germany. On 7 April I brought him to the hospital. On 20 April I visited him, and he requested that when I write to Germany, I should greet his father, brothers, and sisters. He was in bad condition. He sends money to Germany. In 1839 and 1840, he was very ill and each time he came to me without a cent. The pharmacy and the doctor got everything. Dear brother-in-law, please tell this to Martin Reichert in Schneeberg.

Dear brother-in-law, I always wanted to let you know where Franz Matthaeus Mueller is. He is in the state of Indiana, 42 miles from Cincinnati. There he has bought 120 acres shrub land. He did not stay longer than 8 days in Cincinnati to visit me. He immediately bought land with the money he brought from Germany. I personally have no land of my own, but would not want to trade places with him. Dear brother-in-law, when I write to you again, I will let you know how he is doing.

In the fall, if I remain healthy, I will go to the state of Illinois, which is 1,000 miles from Cincinnati, and there I will buy 140 acres of land for my children. This costs $1.25 per acre. If we should die and not be able to move to there, then at least our children should have some land of their own. If they do not move there, they can sell it in 8–10 years. Then it will be worth 20–30 dollars per acre.

. . . My income in 1840 was: for pigs $54, for cabbage $90, for potatoes $50, for onions $12, for corn $25, for oats $20, and for half of the wine $15. I slaughter every year: 1 cow, 4–5 pigs weighing approximately 170 pounds.

I went to America in order to search for my good fortune and have thus far found it. Now I want to close my letter and greet you all heartily. My regards to brother Johann Dumbacher, and to all our relatives, Peter Eckert, wife, and children, and to the innkeepers in Weilbach, and my Josepha and Genoveva greet all of their comrades who ask about them.[9]

The letter was sent April 27, 1841, and arrived in Germany on June 16 of that year. This meant that to write a letter and get a response back from Germany could take three to four months. Letters were, hence, of great importance and value.

Riepberger paints a very positive picture of America and all that it has to offer. This fits in very well with the positive and glowing image of America in general, which contributed greatly to German immigration. This image stood in stark contrast to the social, political, and economic conditions in the German states.

Not only has Riepberger been successful, but also his fortunes are ten times better off than they would be Germany. However, there was a tendency among immigrants to want to demonstrate to friends and family that they had made it good in America. Although they sometimes overstated the positives, there can be no question that the essence was true.

We see here how chain migration worked between Germany and America—in this case between Schneeberg and Cincinnati. We can also see how there was chain migration internally in the United States. For example, the writer mentions southeast Indiana and Illinois, both of which were destinations for German immigrants who had come to Cincinnati.

Western Settlement

Germans followed the Ohio and Mississippi Rivers in settling—one route leading west and the other leading north into the Midwest. Germans followed these rivers and settled along them as well as the tributaries feeding into the Ohio and Mississippi. These river valleys encompassed huge land areas. For example, the Ohio River Valley embraces an area of 233,000 square miles.

Soon after the rush of settlers, a whole series of states came into being and joined the Union. All of this occurred in a relatively short time. For example, in 1800 the population of Indiana was 4,875, but by 1860 it had mushroomed to 1,350,000. Within a few decades whole areas of land in the river valleys were settled, and states became established. The population of Illinois increased from 600 in 1800 to 1,711,000 in 1860. The Illinois Territory was formed in 1809, and in 1818 Illinois became a state.

How did the settlers get to the West so quickly? Until about 1810, the only way was by keelboat on the river, but this means of transportation was replaced in the 1810s by the rapidly moving steamboat, which could go upstream with ease. By 1830 there were over two hundred of them on the Mississippi.

Of course, German travelers were making their way not only by the river valley network, but farther north they made use of the Great Lakes system, which connected New York, Michigan, Wisconsin, and Minnesota. Moreover, the Great Lakes to the north were connected to the great rivers in the south by an intricate system of canals, such as the Miami-Erie Canal, which connected Lake Erie with the Ohio River.

Further aiding inland traffic were the many roads and turnpikes. The Old National Road, running from Cumberland, Maryland, to Wheeling, Virginia, was completed in 1818 and later extended all the way to Vandalia, Illinois. By 1850 the roadway system assisted the westward flow of settlers to as far west as Minnesota, Wisconsin, Iowa, and Missouri, as well as to Arkansas and Louisiana. Also vital to the immigrants' moving west was a German-American innovation—the Conestoga wagon, or covered wagon. This was a large broad-wheeled covered wagon shaped somewhat like a boat and used by settlers, and it was so named because it was first manufactured by German-Americans at Conestoga in Lancaster County, Pennsylvania.

The next major advance in western settlement came by means of the railway system. By 1840 there were more than three thousand miles of track, and this figure doubled by 1850. A huge spurt of construction took place in the 1850s, bringing the total mileage of tracks to thirty thousand by 1860. The amount of track in the Midwestern states was substantial: in the 1850s Ohio laid more than twenty-three hundred miles of track; Illinois laid twenty-six hundred; and Wisconsin had nine hundred. The impact of this phenomenal growth was profound not only in terms of population movement, but for economic growth and development.

Related to the water- and railway boom of the early nineteenth century was the bridge-building boom. In 1855 Johann August Roebling completed his railroad bridge at Niagara Falls, the first bridge to be suspended from wire cables. Roebling proudly proclaimed that no one would be afraid to cross great divides by means of suspension bridges. In 1869 he completed the great suspension bridge on the Ohio River, connecting Kentucky and Ohio. This served as the model and prototype for Roebling's masterpiece—the Brooklyn Bridge.

Notes

1. Regarding Boone and Lincoln, see Don Heinrich Tolzmann, ed., *Abraham Lincoln's Ancestry: German or English? M. D. Learned's Investigatory History, with an Appendix on Daniel Boone* (Bowie, Md.: Heritage Books, 1992).

2. For further information on the Ohio Valley, see Don Heinrich Tolzmann, ed., *German Achievements in America: Rudolf Cronau's Survey History* (Bowie, Md.: Heritage Books, 1995), pp. 63–69.

3. John A. Hawgood, *The Tragedy of German-America* (New York: G. P. Putnam's Sons, 1940), p. 130.

4. See Glen Lich, *The German Texans* (San Antonio: University of Texas Institute of Texan Cultures at San Antonio, 1981).

5. Albert B. Faust, *The German Element in the U.S.* (New York: Steuben Society of America, 1927), vol. 1, p. 59.

6. Regarding Villard and Weyerhaeuser, see Gerard Wilk, *Americans from Germany*, ed. Don Heinrich Tolzmann (Indianapolis: Max Kade-German-American Center, Indiana University-Purdue University, 1995), pp. 65–67, 75–78.

7. LaVern J. Rippley, *The German-Bohemians: The Quiet Immigrants* (Northfield, Minn.: St. Olaf College Press for the German-Bohemian Heritage Society, 1995).

8. Faust, *The German Element in the U.S.*, pp. 480–81.

9. Don Heinrich Tolzmann, "A German Immigrant Letter from Cincinnati, 1841," *The Palatine Immigrant* 20, no. 4 (1995): 200–205.

Immigration Patterns

Immigration

At the beginning of the nineteenth century, German immigration ranged between two hundred and two thousand persons per year. Not until 1830 did it assume sizeable proportions. In 1832 it was over ten thousand, and in 1837 it was almost twenty-five thousand. These, however, are small figures compared with the numbers that came after 1850. From 1852 to 1854 more than half a million Germans came to America.

The assumption that German immigration was low between 1790 and 1820 cannot be verified, since immigration figures were not kept before 1820. However, the number most likely was small due to the Napoleonic wars and the Continental blockade. The post-Napoleonic period was an era of political reaction in Europe. Metternich had established censorship and espionage in the German states. Liberal student organizations and the Turner societies were suppressed. There were abortive uprisings against the heavy taxation and the extravagance of many of the petty princes.

Political unrest was a contributing factor to the German immigration of the thirties, but economic causes predominated. The rise of the factory system threw tens of thousands of artisans out of work, cities were overpopulated, and agricultural areas were overcrowded.

In contrast to the dreary prospects on the Continent, the United States enjoyed economic prosperity and political freedom. Rich, fertile land could be had for a low price; the West was expanding; trade and industry were thriving. Attractive offers were made by transportation companies, by land speculators, and by officials of new states eager to build up their populations. Land was cheap; taxes were low; workmen were needed. A tide of immigration took off and filled not only the older settlements, but the South and the Midwest too. The great increase came between 1830 and 1840.

Although most of the new arrivals were farmers and tradesmen, there were also many academically trained individuals among them who were known derisively as "Latin farmers." Some of them wrote letters and articles about the new land that were published and circulated in the Old Country. These reports were generally positive and served to stimulate the tide of immigration.

The 1817 Wartburg Fest

When Napoleon had been defeated at Waterloo, Europe was relieved that the tyrant and conqueror was gone; the Continent was again free. The joyful mood, however, was short-lived, for a new despotism replaced the old. The ideals of freedom and fraternity of the French Revolution, which the troops of Napoleon had helped to spread, were swept aside. Medieval thrones were restored and feudal privileges renewed. It was the age of Metternich. Through the skillful diplomacy of the Austrian prime minister and through censorship and repression, the masses were held in check. Year by year, however, the desire for freedom grew stronger. Revolutionaries and radicals—largely of the bourgeoisie—demanded that the privileges of the upper classes be abolished.

German students called for a national convention at the famous Wartburg castle on October 18, 1817, the anniversary of the Battle of Leipzig, which had resulted in the defeat of Napoleonic France. This was also the tricentennial of the Reformation, and Wartburg itself was the castle where Luther had translated the Bible into the German language. About five hundred students gathered, and many of them felt that they belonged to a long tradition of national liberation, including Luther and

Blücher. However, they made no specific political demands. Indeed, the only defiant gesture was an evening bonfire and parade. In honor of Luther's burning of the papal bull, a list of the names of reactionary authors was thrown into the fire and burned, together with other symbols of tyranny, censorship, and oppression.

In 1818 students formed the General German Student Union, which emphasized political action. Many gathered around Karl Follen, a young lecturer at the University of Giessen, who spoke of the necessity of a united German republic and held that the ends justified the means, including tyrannicide. Unfortunately, a confused student, Karl Sand, carried out this philosophy in 1819 against an author who was considered reactionary, August von Kotzebue. This gave Metternich the excuse he was looking for to stamp out everything he saw as opposing the status quo. Many were arrested, such as Ludwig Jahn, while others were placed under surveillance, such as Ernst Moritz Arndt. Then in 1819 the infamous Karlsbad Decrees were railroaded through the German Parliament by Metternich, which made censorship legal. German states could now dismiss any professor charged with the dissemination of the "wrong" ideas. State commissioners were appointed at universities to oversee lectures, and student unions, or *Burschenschaften*, were banned. Following these oppressive decrees, a number of students, professors, and others with education emigrated to America, including Karl Follen.[1]

Karl Follen

According to Dieter Cunz, Follen "was a man who could never stand on the sidelines, who always became involved, who felt responsible for the ills of his time."[2] Born in 1796 in a small village, Follen was the son of a lawyer. As a youth, he observed the Napoleonic armies as they marched across Germany. At the age of eighteen, he joined in the War of Liberation against the French and like many had two goals in mind: to liberate the German states from the French and to unite the German states under a republican form of government. The first goal was attained, but not the second, so Follen emigrated to America.

Follen landed in America in 1824 and later wrote, "I should have liked to kneel and kiss the soil of the new world and cling to it with my hands, so that this last support would not slip away from me."[3] Within two years he became fluent in English and accepted a position at Harvard as the first professor of German in America. He also lectured widely in Boston and interested many in German culture and literature.

Among his friends were Ralph Waldo Emerson and John Quincy Adams, who was quite interested in German literature. Follen, an outspoken individual, abhorred slavery and joined the abolitionist movement, a decision that made him unpopular in certain circles. Follen, however, felt that one must pay the price for one's beliefs. Because of his antislavery stance he lost his position at Harvard, so he entered the ministry. On a ship from New York to Boston he lost his life in a fire. Cunz writes that "very often people with great and lofty ideas try to stand aloof from the affairs of the world. Follen tried to take part in public life, to change it according to his ideas, and to adjust his ideas to the experience of life."[4]

Franz Josef Grund

Often called the Carl Schurz of the first half of the nineteenth century (after the famous immigrant-statesman who will be discussed later in this chapter), Franz Josef Grund emerged as the first national spokesman of German-Americans. Born in 1798 near Vienna, he studied mathematics and philosophy at the University of Vienna before emigrating in 1827. He settled in Boston, where he taught at the Chauncey Hall School. During his time there he published several textbooks on geometry, algebra, chemistry, astronomy, and natural philosophy. In 1837 he published an influential work, *The Americans in Their Moral, Social, and Political Relations*, which was intended to correct misconceptions about America, to "inspire the English with more just conceptions of American worth," and to improve Anglo-American relations in general. This book contains a detailed analysis of American conditions, complete with statistical data, and is still being reprinted and examined for a view of American life in the 1830s.

Grund was a dynamic, flamboyant person who captivated people with his personality. One contemporary remarked that he was "very able and bold. I am quite struck with his conversation. He talks sledgehammers."

In the 1830s a German-American newspaper editor in Cincinnati, Heinrich Roedter, began writing a series of articles calling for the establishment of a German-American university that would attract the best scholars of Germany. The idea gained momentum, and a historic conference was called for October 18, 1837, at Pittsburgh, Pennsylvania.

The Pittsburgh Conference of 1837 was an important event in German-American history as it represented the first national meeting of community leaders. There were thirty-one delegates from seven states: Pennsylvania, Ohio, New York, Virginia, Maryland, Illinois, and Missouri, and the meeting was chaired by Grund. A direct result of the meeting was the creation of a German-American educational institution at Philipsburg, Pennsylvania.

After the conference, Grund came to be viewed as the German-American spokesman. He served for a time in Antwerp as the U.S. consul but soon returned to Philadelphia to edit a newspaper. He then campaigned for Martin Van Buren and General William Henry Harrison for the presidency. His influence outside the German-American community was great.

As a political correspondent, he spent his winters in Washington, D.C., and is credited with being the father of sensational journalism. His articles were filled with hints of the best possible sources and behind-the-scenes information. This also served to increase his influence and reputation. Later he served again as a U.S. consul, this time at The Hague, and returned to the United States in 1861.

Contemporaries described him as an orator of extraordinary power whose influence was surpassed only by that of Carl Schurz. He also spiced his arguments with wit and sarcasm and in debate boldly charged against his opponents. Before he died in 1863, he had traveled widely across the country and published other influential works including *Aristocracy in America* and *From the Sketchbook of a German Nobleman*. In the latter he wrote:

> I trust that the good sense of the people, the intelligence pervading the masses, and, above all, the high degree of morality and virtue, which distinguishes the American above all other nations of the world, will be proof against the temptations of a handful of political skeptics; and that the country, blessed with Nature's richest gifts, and selected by Providence

for the nobelest experiment tried by man, will fulfill its mission,—which is not only the civilization of a new world, but the practical establishment of principles which heretofore only had an ideal existence.[5]

He is the first German-American to attain a national reputation as a spokesman of German-American interests, which reflected the growing importance that was being ascribed to German-Americans.

Francis Lieber

Another significant German immigrant of the early nineteenth century was Francis Lieber, who came to America in 1827. Born in Berlin in 1800, he had taken part in the campaigns against Napoleon, including the Battle of Waterloo. Because of his verse and prose on the subject of political freedom, he was suspended from the University of Berlin, so he went to Jena and obtained his doctorate there in 1820. Filled with enthusiasm for the Greek revolt, he went to Greece to fight for freedom. After many hardships he sailed to Italy. Entirely without funds, he was compelled to make his way on foot to Rome, where penniless and in rags, he appealed to the Prussian ambassador, the famous historian of ancient Rome, Georg Niebuhr. This generous scholar engaged Lieber as a tutor for his son and provided for him for over a year. When Lieber decided to return to Berlin, Niebuhr exerted his influence on his behalf, yet despite this Lieber was still thrown into prison. Upon his release in 1825, he went to London and then to America.

With letters from Niebuhr, he was introduced to scholarly circles in Boston. He wrote articles on history, biography, political science, and penology. His American adaptation and translation of the *Brockhaus Konversations-Lexikon* became the basis for the *Encyclopedia Americana* published later by Appleton. In 1833 he prepared curricula for Girard College in Philadelphia, and two years later Lieber secured the post of professor of history and political economy at South Carolina College, Columbus, South Carolina.

In his leisure moments he devoted himself to international law, producing volumes that gained him worldwide fame. He also became well known through his *Manual of Political Ethics* and *Civil Liberty and Self-Government*. He wrote English as if it were his native tongue. The titles of some of his essays reveal his wide range of interests: *Essays on Property and Labor*; *The Necessity for Continuous Self-Culture*; *Penal Laws and the Penitentiary System*; and *On Questions of the Post Office and Postal Reform*.

In 1856 he was called to the chair of political science at Columbia University. During the Civil War, he was often in Washington to advise Lincoln and Stanton on questions of international law. At the request of the president, he prepared the *Code of War for the Government of the Armies of the United States in the Field*. This treatise was published as General Order Number 100 by the War Department. Lieber, who had warned southerners against secession from the start, felt the tragedy of the war sharply in his own family. Two of his sons were in the Union army, while another son, who had married a southerner, died as a soldier in the Confederacy.

Lieber visited Germany in 1844 and 1848. King Friedrich Wilhelm IV offered the man who had once been lodged in a Prussian jail the supervision of all the prisons in the kingdom. Lieber, however, declined. He was a cheerful, stimulating, and wholesome personality, an ardent gymnast and a scholar. He worked unceasingly for the welfare of humanity and the good of his country. At the time of his death, October 1872, he was in charge of the adjudication of Mexican claims. Throughout his life he exemplified the ideals contained in the Latin verse he had chosen as his motto: "Patria cara, carior libertas, veritas carissima"—"My country is dear to me, liberty is dearer, truth is the dearest of all."[6]

The German Image of America

One of the earliest German writers on America was the distinguished scientist and explorer Alexander von Humboldt. His scientific reports on the conditions in the New World appealed to scholars and intellectuals. His factual descriptions supplemented the vivid and romantic scenes depicted in the novels of François-René de Chateaubriand, who had visited the United States in 1791. It was he who wrote of America as a land of gorgeous forests and splendid streams and influenced German and other European poets.

Humboldt became acquainted with President Jefferson, with whom he maintained a lively correspondence and exchanged books. The German scientist met many other prominent Americans and returned to Europe with favorable impressions of the young Republic. When King Friedrich Wilhelm III asked him what he thought of the U.S. government, he replied: "Your Majesty, it is a government which nobody sees and nobody feels, and yet it is by far mightier than the government of Your Majesty."[7]

The early nineteenth century was a lively period for author-adventurers, particularly in the new Republic. One of these was Friedrich Gerstäcker. Restless by nature, he traveled through the wilds of Australia and America. He was a prolific writer and produced more than 150 volumes. The better-known ones with an American background are *The Regulators in Arkansas*, *The Pirates on the Mississippi*, and *Scouting and Hunting in the United States*. He may have gotten some of his material the from Reverend Klingelhöffer, who arrived in 1836 from Rheinhessen and founded a settlement near Little Rock, Arkansas. He wrote in a lively style, but from a literary point of view his writing cannot compare to that of noted German-American author Charles Sealsfield (discussed later in this chapter).

Another writer who also spent some time in the United States was Otto Ruppius. A number of his adventure novels are set in the Midwest, such as *The Peddler*, *The Devil and the Prairie*, *In the West*, and *A German*. His novels were popular, but not as successful as those of Sealsfield and Gerstäcker.

Because of the unfavorable conditions on the Continent, a number of German intellectuals developed the idea of establishing a model democratic German state in the New World. These reformers had their eye on Texas, Missouri, and Wisconsin. Two ardent young champions of freedom involved in this project were Paul Follenius and Friedrich Münch. The former was the brother of Karl Follen of Harvard. They expressed their plans around 1830:

> We must not go from here without realizing a national idea or at least making the beginnings towards its realization; the foundation of a new

and free Germany in the great North American Republic shall be laid by us; we must therefore gather as many as possible of the best of our people about us when we emigrate, and we must, at the same time, make the necessary arrangements providing for a large body of immigrants to follow us annually, and thus we may be able, at least in one of the American territories, to establish an essentially German state . . . a territory which we shall be able to make a model state in the great American Republic.[8]

Follenius was a born leader; he was tall, impressive, tactful, and courageous. Münch, equally determined and capable, was more cautious and realistic. They formed a society known as the *Giessener Gesellschaft*. It drew its members largely from the grand duchy of Hessen. Arkansas was the first choice for a colony, but unfavorable reports caused the settlers to go to Missouri.

Settlements sprang up rapidly on both sides of the Mississippi around St. Louis. Many settlers of German descent lived in these communities, having come from Ohio, Kentucky, Tennessee, Maryland, and Virginia. By 1817 Missouri had sixty thousand inhabitants; in 1821 it was admitted as a state. No Germans from abroad, however, came directly to settle within its borders.

In 1824 two Germans, Gottfried Duden, a graduate in law and medicine, and Eversmann, an agriculturalist, landed in Baltimore and made their way via Wheeling to St. Louis. There Duden bought 275 acres of land 50 miles above the mouth of the Missouri. This was so-called congressional land, bought at $1.25 per acre. Eversmann bought 130 acres adjoining Duden's property. A wealthy man, Duden had the land cleared and cultivated, and, released from all the hardships of frontier life, he sat down and wrote a romantic description of it. The book entitled *Bericht über eine Reise nach den westlichen Staaten Nordamerikas* was published in Elberfeld in 1829 and has been reprinted often. This work was considered the most influential book in the history of German emigration to America.

Duden's glowing account of life in America with its beautiful scenery, its unrestricted freedom, and its democratic institutions induced many to come to America. Large numbers of farmers arrived from Westphalia and Hannover, followed by scholars, officers, and merchants. Among them were a number of nobles who were entirely unaccustomed to hard work. They settled in the neighborhood of Duden's farm in Warren County, Missouri. The common folk toiled hard and managed to establish successful farms. However, the intellectuals, the "Latin farmers," were in dire straits after their means of support had been exhausted, and some of them were reduced to extreme penury.

Duden's enthusiastic description of conditions in the United States made a deep impression upon his readers in Germany. In fact, it exerted such a powerful influence that Gustav Koerner, a German diplomat who came to America in 1833, felt obliged to publish a critical review of the work. Without deprecating the attractive features of the American scene, he urged readers to accept Duden's highly colored statements with caution.

As the number of immigrants increased and conditions became better known, other critics also attacked Duden. He felt called upon to defend himself, and, in 1837, in a treatise on de Tocqueville's famous work *Democracy in America*, he added a comment on his own book. He expressed regret that so many who were influenced by his description to go to America were eventually disappointed and blamed his enthusiastic portrayal. He said this was not his fault; he claimed he was misunderstood. He rejected all attacks on the America he still admired.

Duden, of course, was not the only one who wrote in glowing terms about the United States. Between 1815 and 1850, more than fifty works were published by Germans who had visited and traveled across America. They were representative of many callings and came from various parts of Germany. Most of these reports were favorable. For example, Tuckerman, in his book *America and Her Commentators* (1864), remarks in comparing the German with the French and English estimates: "Some of the justest views and most candid delineations have emanated from German writers."[9] Among the most valuable descriptions of America are the journals of several German princes who visited America: Duke Paul Wilhelm of Württemberg, Duke Bernhard of Saxe-Weimar, and Prince Maximilian zu Wied. There is hardly any work in the travel literature of the early decades of the nineteenth century that for kindness of tone and comprehensiveness of detail can stand comparison with these friendly and comprehensive presentations of America.

One unfavorable work that aroused attention and that was even read by Goethe was that of Ludwig Gall. It appeared in 1822 and was based on the author's experiences in 1819 and 1820. Gall arrived with an idealistic conception of America and tells how he was disappointed. He was delighted with the scenery; he mentions the trim farmhouses, the neat farms, and the impressiveness of New York harbor and Broadway, which he felt was the finest street in the world. He also praises parts of Pennsylvania and Ohio.

However, Gall becomes bitter when he speaks of the people. He finds them all cold, unsociable, and unkind, and claims that making money is their chief aim in life. Again and again he thinks he has been cheated by the officials and tavern keepers. He felt that in America the worth of a person depends on one's pocketbook. The press is corrupt; the moral and social conditions are deplorable. However, he admits that "the Americans are about a century ahead of the Germans in the efficiency of training for practical life."[10] Many immigrants are homesick, and America has not provided a better way of life, in his view.

It is significant that a number of German writers immediately took issue with Gall and asserted that he had misrepresented conditions. In his work of six hundred pages, Duke Berhard of Sachsen-Weimar-Eisenach summarizes his estimate of the United States as a happy and prosperous country, which was basically the general view in the German states of Europe.[11]

Charles Sealsfield

Of special significance were the numerous novels and publications of Charles Sealsfield. This German-American author was the creator of the ethnographic novel. Sealsfield's writings form part of German, American, and German-American literature, because they were published in English and German. He is, for example, included in the section on "Non-English Writings" in the *Cambridge History of American Literature*. The quality of his work has been considered so high that he is without question the major German-American novelist.

Sealsfield was the pen name of Karl Postl, who was born in 1793 in the little German village of Poppitz in Moravia. At an early age he entered a monastery in Prague and was ordained as a priest. Disappointed with monastic life, he fled in 1822 to the United States. In an attempt to put his past behind him, he pursued an entirely different kind of life and changed his name to Charles Sealsfield. Traveling widely, he journeyed through Louisiana and Texas and finally acquired a farm on the Red River. One day, as he was about to buy some slaves in New Orleans for his farm, his bank failed, and he lost the greater part of his fortune.

Going to New York, he devoted himself to writing. His immediate success encouraged him to attempt more ambitious works. A two-volume descriptive work of the United States preceded a series of fascinating novels. Sealsfield published most of his books in Germany, but they were translated and reached the American public. They were read with great interest; Longfellow referred to Sealsfield as one of his favorites. With consummate skill, Sealsfield described various human and social types and characters that existed between 1820 and 1840 in America. He was a keen observer and an interesting writer. The early pioneer, the fearless frontiersman, the wealthy southern planter, the ruthless millionaire, the bewitching society belle, the desperate outlaw, and the weather-beaten sea captain are presented in vivid colors in his fascinating novels. Sealsfield could be called the German-American James Fenimore Cooper.

Sealsfield's first book, *Die Vereinigten Staaten von Nord-Amerika*, published in 1827 under the pseudonym of C. Sidons in Stuttgart, was such a thorough piece of work that an English version in two volumes, produced by the author himself, appeared the next year. In the first volume the author treats the economic, social, political, and cultural aspects of the United States; in the second, he describes his travels through the Southwest. He gives a detailed account of this region, discussing everything from the quality of the soil to life in the larger towns.

His novels fill out the picture of the New World; in all of them he displays a gift for keen perception, fair judgment, and dramatic presentation. Although he is objective and realistic, his accounts are colored by an enthusiastic appreciation of the magnificent landscape, the courageous, liberty-loving people, and the free institutions of America.

In *Tokeah, or The White Rose*, published anonymously in English in 1828, he pictured the ruthless struggle between the advancing settlers and the retreating Indians in a realistic context, which attracted a great readership. Sealsfield came to America five times. His first visit lasted from 1823 to 1826. After a short stay in Germany, he returned to America in 1827 and remained until 1831. He spent the next year in England and France. By this time his fame had spread, and he was lionized in Europe with no less a person than Louis Napoleon befriending him. He settled in Switzerland but visited the United States in 1837, 1850, and 1853. On his last visit, he stayed five years. He died in 1864 on his estate, *Unter den Tannen* (Under the Fir Trees), near Solothurn in Switzerland. On his tombstone the following words are inscribed: *Bürger der Vereinigten Staaten* (Citizen of the United States).

While in the United States, Sealsfield traveled extensively, especially in the South and Southwest. From 1828 to 1829 he lived in Mexico. His complete mastery of French is evident in the fact that during the next year he was the editor of the *Courrier des Etats-Unis* in New York. He then lived for a while in Kattaninning, Pennsylvania, and in Philadelphia, where he was correspondent for the German publisher Cotta. He made many contacts with individuals in various fields, and this, together with his experiences as a planter and traveler, groomed him well for the task of portraying life in the New World.

He was fond of the historical novel and was deeply influenced by Sir Walter Scott. Sealsfield's keen powers of observation and his reduction of the romantic in his writing led to far more realistic descriptions. His Indian tale, *Tokeah*, was written in English and appeared in America. Of interest are the number of Americanisms that can be found in his German. Sometimes the author did this deliberately, in order to give exotic flair or local color to his writing.

In *Der Virey* (1835) and *Süden und Norden* (1842), he portrays the splendors of the tropical world in Mexico. While in Zürich, he published his *Transatlantische Reiseskizzen*, which contain four novels based on life in Texas and the South. In the same year, he published *Morton oder die grosse Tour*, which deals with high finance, diplomatic intrigues and the aristocracy as a hated institution. In the *Deutschamerikanische Wahlverwandtschaften* (1839), he portrays social life in New York, and in *Kajütenbuch* (1841) he describes the struggle of the Texans for independence from Mexico.

All of these novels are distinguished by a wealth of historical and cultural material, by keen insight into various types of American character, by wonderful descriptions of the grandeur of the American landscape, and by a deep appreciation of democratic institutions. He praises the will power, energy, courage, and adventurous spirit of Americans. He gives them credit for concentrated reasoning and sober judgment. In *Life in the New World* one of his characters says:

> There is something truly practical in our American nature that distinguishes us from other nations of the globe,—a certain straightforwardness, healthy common sense, that unimpressed by external glitter and splendor, appreciates only real values in life; an honest, independent spirit that only pays respect to him who merits it. In the United States, you can adopt it as a rule that so long as you act like a gentleman, you are treated as one.

After his retirement to Switzerland, Sealsfield continued to follow events in the United States with great interest. With his advancing years he became somewhat gloomy; he found the material progress disturbing and, as he states in *The Cabin Book*, "the political development less satisfying." Nevertheless, he praised the vigor and self-reliance of the American people. No European writer has ever given a more detailed, more realistic, and more enthusiastic picture of contemporary life in the United States.[12]

Women Writers and Journalists

Among the German-American women writers and journalists of the early nineteenth century, two names stand out: Theresa von Jakob-Robinson and Anna Ottendörfer. Theresa von Jakob-Robinson was known as Talvj, which stood for her initials: Theresa Albertine Louise von Jakob. Few knew her real identity, as she used Talvj on all her publications. Born in 1797 in Halle, her father was a professor of philosophy at the university, but when the French invaded, her family fled to Russia. In St. Petersburg she studied Slavic languages and literature and as a small girl demonstrated an amazing gift for languages. The family returned to Halle in 1816, where she studied classical literature, and at the age of twenty-six she published a German translation of the work of Sir Walter Scott. After this, she published several short stories and essays, but always under her pen name. In 1825 she wrote another book dealing with folksongs, which attained great success because of Goethe's favorable response to it. Talvj was acquainted with other well-known authors, such as Jakob Grimm. She married Edward Robinson, a professor of philosophy.

In 1830 the newly married couple came to America, where Talvj became a prominent author. She wrote several essays and books dealing with European literature, which received the highest praise from scholars. Grimm stated that her work was based on "thorough knowledge." She, like Karl Follen and others, helped transmit German culture and literature to America. She wrote several important essays, such as "Essay on the History and Characteristics of the Popular Songs of the Germanic Races," and her writings influenced other authors in the United States.

She played a leading role in the early American historical societies and wrote some of the first histories on Captain John Smith and New England. Her novels were adventurous and fascinating to early American readers. Some of her book included: *Life's Discipline: A Tale of the Annals of Hungary* and *The Exiles*. As a major literary scholar and linguist, Talvj was clearly one of the most articulate German-American women in the nineteenth century. Before her death in 1869, she had influenced many writers, including Bayard Taylor, Edward Everett, and William Cullen Bryant.

Anna Ottendörfer had a brilliant career. Born in Bavaria in 1815, she came to the United States in 1837 and helped her husband, Jakob Uhl, edit the *New Yorker Staats-Zeitung* in the 1840s. Together they put out this newspaper three times weekly until 1849, when it became a daily. In 1852 her husband died, leaving her with the care of the children and the paper.

Being acquainted with every detail of the newspaper and endowed with extraordinary executive abilities, she took on the task as sole manager of the publication and consistently refused offers to sell it. By means of her courage, energy, and perseverance she not only made the paper profitable, but also laid the foundation for the most influential and powerful German-American newspaper. Today the *Staats-Zeitung* is the oldest German-American newspaper with a national reputation.

In 1859 she married Oswald Ottendörfer, who became editor of the paper, but she remained business manager until 1884. She came to be widely known for charity and philanthropy. In 1875 she built the Isabella Home for Aged Women in Long Island, New York. In 1882 she spent huge sums of money for the Women's Pavilion in the German Hospital of New York. She gave large amounts of money to other charitable purposes as well. In recognition and in honor of her works of charity, she received a medal from the Empress Augusta of Germany. In her will, she gave $25,000 to the workers at the *Staats-Zeitung*. The German-American branch of the New York Public Library, the Ottendörfer Branch, is named in her honor.[13]

The Hambacher Fest and the Thirtyers

From May 27–30, 1832, tens of thousands of craftsmen, students, farmers, officials, and young intellectuals gathered at the ruins of the castle of Hambach to listen to speeches on liberty, reform, and the tyranny of the German princes. Like the Wartburg Fest of 1817, the Hambacher Fest culminated in arrests, dismissals of professors from their positions, espionage, censorship, and police surveillance. These oppressive measures caused many to emigrate to America. Among the immigrants were numerous intellectuals who made a noticeable impact on German-America, including J. G. Wesselhoeft, Gustav Koerner, and Friedrich Münch. Paul Follenius, brother of Karl Follen, led a group of immigrants to New Orleans in 1834. Georg Bunsen came to Belleville, Illinois, in the same year and opened a school. In 1856 he became superintendent of the public schools and also founded the state normal school.

Many others arrived and contributed to the cultural life of the German-American communities across the country. Karl T. Seidensticker, locked up for life in 1831, was pardoned in 1845 on the condition that he emigrate to America. His son, Oswald Seidensticker, became a professor of German and an important nineteenth-century German-American historian. There were also a number of gifted journalists, such as Heinrich Roedter, who edited the *Cincinnatier Volksblatt*. Other notable immigrants were Karl Ruemelin, elected to the Ohio State Legislature in the 1840s, and Johann B. Stallo, noted for his political writings and influence.[14]

Gustav Koerner

One of the the foremost of the Thirtyers, refugees of the revolution of the 1830s, was Gustav Koerner, born in 1809 in Frankfurt am Main. He studied law at the University of Jena and then joined a patriotic society with the goals of unity and freedom for the German states. He began to practice law after receiving his doctorate in law from the University of Heidelberg. In 1833 he took active part in the revolt in Frankfurt am Main and was forced to flee to France, where he joined other young Germans embarking for America.

In 1833 they arrived in New York and proceeded directly to St. Louis, the destination of many recently arrived immigrants. Koerner, disgusted by the institution of slavery, moved to Illinois, where a number of Germans with education had settled. Their colony became known as the "Latin Settlement," as it was said that one could see farmers plowing the fields while reading the classics. The area soon became a social and cultural center.

Koerner took an active role in politics and was involved in the presidential campaigns of 1840 and 1844. In 1845 he was appointed justice of the Illinois Supreme Court, and in 1853 he was elected lieutenant-governor of Illinois and played an important part in the election of 1856. Koerner was a friend of Lincoln and frequently took over some of Lincoln's cases. He was often consulted by Lincoln on legal matters. In 1862 Lincoln appointed him U.S. Minister to Spain. Later he wrote a book about Spain, revealing his appreciation for Spanish arts, music, and cultural life. He also worked to prevent England and France from influencing Spain to recognize the Confederacy.

After returning to America, the political corruption of the Grant administration caused him to reenter politics. In 1876 he retired and devoted himself to writing. In 1880 he published a history of German-Americans, which is noted for its detail and is arranged according to the various states where Germans resided. Among his works was also a critique of Duden's glowing report of America, in which he urged readers to seek further information and details before emigrating. Koerner was most likely the most prominent of the German-American Thirtyers.[15]

The 1848 Revolution

The first outburst was in Paris on February 24, 1848. Furious mobs surged into the Tuileries palace and displayed such determination that the aged and timid King Louis Philippe fled. The spirited duchess of Orleans brought her young son before the Chamber of Deputies to have him proclaimed king. The republican masses, however, swept into the hall, dispersed the deputies, and set up a republic.

The revolution of 1830 had taken place across Europe, but in Germany the uprisings were mild and were quickly suppressed. By 1848 not only had the areas of popular unrest multiplied, but the republicans and socialists had gathered strength, even in the most reactionary states. For example, one of the first uprisings occurred in Vienna, the citadel of Metternich. On March 13, 1848, the liberals rose and drove the aging despot from the chancellery and from the capital.

In other countries, the desire for freedom was linked with that of national unity. In Austria, it became a cry for decentralization. The Hungarians, Croatians, Czechs, and Italians demanded self-determination. The entire Hapsburg monarchy was in danger of collapse. To save the situation, a parliament was quickly organized.

The news of Metternich's expulsion caused liberals throughout Germany to rejoice, and there were riots in many of the smaller capitals. In Württemberg, Baden, and along the Rhine peasants and tradesmen took up arms. The revolutionary movement was highly idealistic and dramatic. In some instances, it almost took on the color of a comic opera. There was much declaiming, drinking, and singing; there were parades, demonstrations, and festivals, especially along the Rhine and in southern Germany.

In Berlin, the situation was more serious. Even the medieval attitudes of King Friedrich Wilhelm IV had yielded to popular pressure as early as 1847, and a so-called United Diet was convened. It did not accomplish anything, however, and on March 18, mobs gathered before the royal palace. The king withdrew his troops, promised to call an elected parliament, and offered to prepare a constitution. In southwestern Germany, Baden and Württemberg, the radicals attempted to force the issue by the use of armed might. This attempt, in which such idealists as Schurz and Kinkel took part, failed miserably. The efficient Prussian army easily overcame the enthusiastic but untrained insurgents. Franz Sigel—later a general in the Civil War—fled with eight thousand men to Switzerland.

The success of the revolutionaries in Berlin and Vienna, however, made it possible to hold a national assembly. A group of distinguished intellectuals, professors, and poets gathered In Frankfurt am Main at St. Paul's Church on May 18, 1848, to organize a provisional government. The idealists, unfortunately, could not agree and were powerless to overcome several political factors. They wrote a bill of rights and then dispersed. In April 1849 the liberals offered Friedrich Wilhelm IV of Prussia the crown of a united Germany. Being a firm believer in the divine right of kings, he felt he could not accept a crown from a group of citizens. The efforts toward German unity and democracy had failed.

While the idealists were engaged in sophisticated debates in St. Paul's Church, the reactionaries recovered their lost ground. New revolts in Berlin and Vienna were suppressed. Every attempt at democracy was thwarted by military strength, and in Berlin an authoritarian constitution was imposed on the parliament. In Vienna, a number of the radical leaders were executed, and Prince Schwarzenberg, a man of iron, resumed the traditions of Metternich. By the fall of 1848 the revolution was dead. Thousands of exiles swarmed across the borders into Switzerland, Holland, France, and England. Many of them ultimately came to America, where they became known as the "Forty-Eighters."

These freedom fighters cherished a double idea: national unity and political freedom. When they realized that achieving the first was hopeless in Germany, they clung more fervently to the second and looked to the United States as their best possible hope. The young democracy across the ocean exerted an unusual attraction on the Forty-Eighters. Well educated, they had read widely and knew of de Tocqueville, the reports of German writers, and of the Thirtyers. Americans had established free democratic institutions. Their magnificent land was expanding and prospering. Furthermore, many of the Forty-Eighters were poetically and romantically inclined. They were fascinated by the glorious forests and the noble Indian as portrayed by Chateaubriand. America appeared to be the promised land, the land of unlimited possibilities.

It is difficult, if not impossible, to provide accurate figures on the number of Forty-Eighters, but it is estimated that there were from four thousand to ten thousand of them. Some came in 1848, and some in the 1850s. Hence, it is their involvement in the revolution, rather than their date of arrival, that denotes their classification as Forty-Eighters.

What was the reaction of German-Americans to the revolution? Some took little interest, for they had come to America in search of better living conditions and were satisfied with the opportunity to provide a comfortable livelihood for their families, but most did take an interest. German-Americans highly valued democracy and had absolutely no use for the autocratic princes in the German states. Therefore, German-American sentiment, as reflected in the German-American press, was strongly on the side of the Forty-Eighters, and there were demands for the establishment of a republic uniting the German states. The possibility that this might happen raised the level of excitement and interest. There were mass meetings, demonstrations of sympathy, parades, and memorial services. In New York, a great *Revolutionsfest* was held. Thousands of representatives from various ethnic groups marched down Broadway to a park where Jakob Uhl, the publisher of the *Staats-Zeitung*, presided at a huge meeting. Speeches were made in four languages in support of the revolution.

In April 1848 a crowd gathered in Independence Square, Philadelphia, to felicitate the French republic and to gather funds to aid the German revolutionaries. When Friedrich Hecker, one of the most colorful and popular Forty-Eighters, arrived in Philadelphia, they gave him a parade and a banquet. There were demonstrations in Baltimore, Milwaukee, Louisville, Pittsburgh, Detroit, and Cincinnati. Hecker was greeted with tremendous ovations wherever he went. His trip across the country was a veritable triumphal tour. Other ethnic groups joined in these demonstrations, especially the Irish and the Hungarians.

The revolutionaries in Europe realized that, in addition to enthusiasm, they needed money. Noting the favorable reception that the revolution had gotten in the United States, they were determined to capitalize on American support. Louis Kossuth, leader of the Hungarian radicals, toured the country and was quite successful in raising funds. Encouraged by this, the Revolutionary Committee in London sent over professor and poet Gottfried Kinkel, who had been liberated from prison very dramatically by Carl Schurz. He was received everywhere with warmth, and benefits were held for the cause of German freedom.

Unfortunately, by 1852 enthusiasm had waned. Despite Kinkel's winning personality and brilliant oratory, he collected only eight thousand dollars, but he had hoped to float a loan of two million dollars. Kinkel had been sent by the more moderate faction of the Revolutionary Committee in London. There was a more radical branch, however, which decided to send Armand Goegg, a former member of the provisional government of Baden, to America.

Goegg had an idea for raising funds and for creating a worldwide revolution. When he arrived in Philadelphia, he founded the German Revolutionary League, which was to provide leaders for revolutionary committees in various foreign countries. If each German in the United States contributed but one cent per week, they estimated, they could raise the sum of $1,560,000 in one year. Other outstanding revolutionaries such as Karl Heinzen, Gustav Struve, Arnold Ruge, and Franz Sigel supported the plan. However, the plan did fail, as many were repelled by the idea of worldwide revolution.

The startling and significant fact about this grandiose scheme was that these German radicals proposed a magnificent role for America as a world leader and benefactor. Their plan would realize the manifest destiny of the United States of America as not merely a nation, but a community of free peoples where the most diverse races and religions might live in peace and harmony. The ideal of democracy had actually been achieved. Why bother to try and overthrow slow-witted princes and shaky thrones? It would be much simpler for the United States to expand and assimilate other nations.

The first step would be to annex Cuba and Santo Domingo, and then Mexico and Latin America. The suffering peoples of these backward countries would welcome American hegemony. Then would come Europe's turn. England would be "infederate," and thereafter the other European countries. Australia, India, and Africa would follow. Soon a magnificent democratic world would arise.

In September 1852 a meeting was called in Wheeling, West Virginia, to discuss the plan. Only sixteen out of a possible 1,112 appeared, but that did not discourage the revolutionaries. The leader in the discussion was Charles Goepp, technically not a Forty-Eighter. His father had migrated from Silesia in the 1830s and had settled in Bethlehem, Pennsylvania. He had presented his ideas about America's mission in a pamphlet entitled *E Pluribus Unum*. Together with Theodor Poesche, a former German student of philosophy, he wrote a book in 1853 entitled *The New Rome*, and dedicated to President Pierce. Although the work struck some as foolish, parts of the work now appear somewhat prophetic.

In poetic language the two described technical achievements still in the distant future: "And why should our modern steamers not have wings and a motive power to impel them forward? . . . A little alteration of adjustment and these iron ships will leave their native element and ride in mid-air." They wrote:

> We are on the eve of aerial navigation. . . . [T]he balloon, which is a toy, must be discarded and then we shall have the practical navigation of the air. The airplane is fitted for universal navigation. . . . [W]hy should not man fly over the poles[?] Aerial navigation alone will give us the victory over Russian Continentalism.[16]

Comments on Russia are interesting:

> This goal to liberate the world will not be realized before a great World War which is forever seen to hang, like the sword of Damocles, over the passing joys and troubles of the hour. This great World War will break

out between the forming Union and the Russian Empire. . . . No political step can be taken . . . without taking into account the Russian
rulers and their tricky bureaucracy. . . . Europe will be first Cossack,
but then Yankee. . . .

Through this kind of writing Goepp was able to electrify his audiences.
He wrote: "We demand the extension of American freedom! . . . An
Empire, not of conquest and of subjugation, not of inheritance, not of
international frictions and hatreds, but of fraternity, of equality, and of
freedom!"[17]

It was all quite simple. Thrilled with the lofty ideal, the delegates
decided to form a People's League for the Old and New World to found a
political party to further the annexation of Europe. Full of joy, determination, and beer, the delegates left for home. Yet within a short time the
league died a quiet death. All that survived was ridicule of those who met
at Wheeling to advocate the annexation of the world.

Hundreds of thousands of Germans had migrated to America, but no
group made such an impact in the nineteenth century as did the few
thousand Forty-Eighters. Most of the earlier immigrants had been
farmers, tradesmen, and craftsmen, but the Forty-Eighters were well
educated; they were generally teachers, doctors, lawyers, editors, artists,
or musicians. It is no wonder, then, that they were able to contribute to
a German-American cultural renaissance.

There were other characteristics that distinguished the Forty-
Eighters from the earlier immigrants. They usually came alone, unen-
cumbered by family and baggage. If they brought anything, it was a bag
full of books and papers. They didn't come directly from home; sometimes they had fled from an unsuccessful skirmish or had just gotten out
of jail. Before arriving in America they had spent some time in England,
France, or Switzerland. They most likely knew several languages, but
little English. They were well-informed about political and social conditions in the United States, and their chief interest was ideas and not the
practical demands of life on the frontier.

It was natural that these differences caused something of a split
between the older German element and the newcomers. The former
were referred to as the "Grays" (*die Grauen*) and the newcomers as the

"Greens" (*die Grünen*). The Grays admitted that they did not possess a great deal of education, but they had cleared the land and established prosperous farms, factories, and industries. They disliked the Forty-Eighters' radicalism, their criticism of American institutions, and their sarcastic comments on the lack of education among German-Americans. In short, they detested the superior attitude of these European "beer politicians."

In general, the influence of the Forty-Eighters was quite positive. The Forty-Eighters were primarily politically minded, and they actively participated in the political life of their adopted land. They were not interested in patronage, but rather in the maintenance of good government. With a certain degree of tenacity, they adhered to their principles. They refused to "play the game," and they disdained the Anglo tendency to compromise, as they operated on the basis of principles and ideas. They often insisted on absolutes, which, of course, could be an idealistic and impractical position in the real world.

One of their ideals was efficient and honest government, and here the Forty-Eighters made many contributions, such as the civil service reform pioneered by Carl Schurz. Another issue they took a stand against was slavery. They found this completely incompatible with democracy and demanded its abolition. Having fought for the unity of the German states, the Forty-Eighters became staunch defenders of the Union. Freedom and unity went hand in hand.

President James of the University of Chicago stated in a memorial service to Carl Schurz in 1906:

> We who love to compromise, that characteristic of the Anglo-Saxon race might have tried to worry on under some kind of system by which slavery should have increased in power and strength without wekainging the vigor and might of the free states. . . . Or we might have consented to a possible dissolution of the Union. . . . But the men of '48 . . . were men not bound down by any of those traditions. . . . They were men who had suffered in behalf of liberty; they were men who had staked their entire careers on the side of freedom in the great struggle between privilege and democracy. . . . [T]hey saw what was right, and they planted themselves firmly and distinctly on that side with no hes-

itation and wavering. . . . The influence of the Forty-eighters at this great and critical time of our national life was . . . decisive. They turned the balance of power in favor of union and liberty.[18]

The impact of the Forty-Eighters has been documented by Carl Wittke in his work *Refugees of Revolution: The German-Forty-Eighters in America* (1952). He described the diversity of the group as consisting of liberals, republicans, and radicals of every variety; individuals with university education and social standing who were imbued with the writings of Kant, Fichte, and Schiller. There were also the passionate and impractical reformers, the romantic heroes of the revolution, as well as the well-known physicians, inventors, jurists, and journalists. However, there were also many workers, farmers, clerks, and small-business people. In some way they had all been involved in the attempt to establish a united German republic and had emigrated after the failure of the revolution.

According to Wittke, they had a dramatic effect on America in general, and on German-American life in particular. They figured prominently in the debates and conflicts dealing with nativism, foreign policy, slavery, the rise of the labor movement, the rise of the Republican Party, the Civil War, and post–Civil War politics. Their influence in the cultural and intellectual realm was of equal importance.

Although not great in number, the Forty-Eighters exerted a great influence by means of their exceptional abilities, spirit, and principled orientation. They were determined to awaken their contemporaries to an understanding and a realization of true democracy and German culture. As Wittke notes, if they were at times tactless, impatient, impractical, and rejected compromises, it should be said that "their zeal sprang from a genuine devotion to a fixed set of principles for which they were ready to scale the heavens."[19]

Carl Schurz

One of the best known Forty-Eighters was Carl Schurz, who was born March 9, 1829, in Liblar, located near Cologne on the Rhine. He was the eldest son of Christian Schurz, a schoolteacher and farmer. Carl (originally Karl) grew up in pleasant rural surroundings among thrifty, hard-working farmers. He began his schooling in the village, transferring to Brühl, a few miles away, at the age of nine. At ten, he entered the Jesuit school in Cologne.

He was an eager student, fond of the ancient classics and of German literature. His wide reading inspired him to produce original pieces in verse and prose. They were hardly outstanding, but he did display a remarkable gift for oratory. He also became deeply interested in history, and in his earliest youth developed two ideals that motivated his later actions: he wanted to help establish a democratic and united Germany, and he also wanted to go to America. His reading had idealized for him the land of vast forests and huge streams, of political freedom and unlimited opportunities. The desire to emigrate grew stronger with the years.

Schurz was getting along very well at school when financial problems at home compelled him to drop out. He was, however, so thorough a student that he continued studying by himself and passed the rigid final examinations with the highest ratings. He was particularly proficient in Greek. Now ready for the university, he went to Bonn, where one of his teachers, the professor of literature and history Gottfried Kinkel, exerted so great an influence on him that it determined his future career. Kinkel was a poet, an enthusiastic liberal, and a man of great personal charm. He immediately won Schurz's admiration and lifelong friendship. The professor engaged the young man as his assistant in editing the *Bonner Zeitung*, a democratic paper. Schurz wrote vigorously and spoke eloquently. At nineteen, he was the leader of a German student revolutionary movement.

At this time there was political unrest and discontent, which had been brewing for years. Friedrich Wilhelm III, who had ruled from 1797 to 1840, was an autocrat, and his son and successor, Friedrich Wilhelm IV, was no improvement. When the news arrived of the fall of Louis Philippe and the establishment of a new republic in Paris, the more determined revolutionists were galvanized into action. Outbursts and demonstrations took place in various parts of Germany and Austria. Jubilant, Kinkel left his lecture hall and joined the revolutionaries. Schurz followed his example and volunteered his services in the field.

The ardor of the young revolutionists did not, however, make up for the discipline and training of the seasoned troops. A decisive engagement was fought at Rastatt in Baden. When the rebels were defeated, Schurz escaped from the city through a sewer leading to the Rhine. From there he made his way to Switzerland. Franz Sigel—another later immigrant to the United States—escaped with about eight thousand of his men.

Kinkel was captured and condemned to life imprisonment in the fortress of Spandau in Berlin. There he was treated with the utmost severity, even being denied permission to read and write. His wife, a woman of courage and intelligence, was determined to liberate him. With untiring zeal, she collected funds and then wrote Schurz in Switzerland, asking for someone to effect her husband's escape. Schurz immediately replied that he would undertake the daring and dangerous task. He returned secretly to Germany, made careful plans, and succeeded in freeing Kinkel. In November 1850 both were able to board a ship at Rostock, on which they sailed to Leith, Scotland.

The next year Schurz was in Paris. When Louis Napoleon seized power, conditions became uncomfortable for the young German rebel, and the French police expelled him as a dangerous radical. He lived in London for a while, earning his living by teaching German. In July 1852 he married Margarethe Meyer, the daughter of a Hamburg merchant, and in August they set sail for America. Upon arrival in New York, Schurz was like tens of thousands of other immigrants, an unknown, who had no profession and knew very little English. However, because of his remarkable ability and because of the prevailing conditions on the American scene, the unknown youth of twenty-three was destined within the space of sixteen years to rise to the rank of a U.S. senator, a foreign minister, and personal friend and advisor of President Lincoln.

The family first lived in Philadelphia and then spent a year in Europe, after which they settled on a farm in Watertown, Wisconsin. In order to learn English quickly and thoroughly, Schurz read extensively. He went through the works of Goldsmith, Scott, Dickens, Thackeray, Macaulay, and Shakespeare. Since he wanted to prepare for a legal career, he also read the commentaries of Blackstone. He took a deep interest in politics and soon became prominent in the Republican Party. One ideal that stirred him deeply from the beginning was the abolition of slavery. He felt that human bondage was absolutely incompatible with democracy. Mrs. Schurz was active, too, devoting herself to educational activities. In 1855 she established at Watertown what was probably the first kindergarten in the United States.

Schurz studied law, was admitted to the bar, and in 1858 began to practice in Milwaukee. His chief interest, however, was public affairs. In one of the great debates between Lincoln and Douglas, he was introduced to the future president, who immediately took a liking to him. He became a popular orator because his speech on "True Americanism," delivered in Boston on April 18, 1859.

He plunged vigorously into the campaign for Lincoln, addressing large audiences in both German and English. His bilingual abilities made him extremely useful for reaching German-American voters. Indeed, many have claimed that Schurz eloquence was a major factor in bringing about the election of Lincoln in 1860. By the time the campaign of 1864 arrived, Schurz was not only an admirer, but also a close personal friend of Lincoln. As a reward for his work on behalf of the president, he was sent as a minister to Spain in 1861.

Schurz wanted to participate in the Civil War, and in preparation for it he devoted himself to the study of military tactics in Spain. The situation, however, worried him, and he returned to Washington to confer with Lincoln. He was adamant in his stand that slavery must go, and on March 6, 1862, he delivered a powerful speech at Cooper Institute in New York. A few days later, the president sent a message to Congress, recommending the gradual abolition of slavery.

Schurz was so eager, however, to enter the army that he secured from Lincoln a commission as brigadier-general of volunteers. Since he had only slight military experience during the revolution of 1848 in Baden, and since he had only recently studied military science, there was considerable skepticism about the ability of this "civilian." Yet almost from the start he proved his competence. Two months after his first commission, he took command of a division. After the Battle of Bull Run, he was promoted to the rank of major-general. He participated in many of the most significant engagements of the Civil War, such as the Battles of Gettysburg, Bull Run, and Chattanooga, and he was also with Sherman's army in North Carolina. His military service bore the same marks of quality as his political service.

Lincoln's assassination was a severe blow to him, both personally and professionally. It is quite likely that had Lincoln lived, he would have made Schurz a member of his cabinet and would possibly have entrusted with the realization of a generous plan of reconstruction. Although President Johnson's relations with Schurz were not cordial, the new president felt a certain amount of loyalty to Lincoln. He therefore sent Schurz on a very important mission.

Schurz was to visit the South and make a survey of conditions there. With his characteristic conscientiousness, Schurz made a careful study of the situation for three months. Again and again, he was told that black people were lazy, shiftless, unreliable, and improvident. Schurz, however, was not the man to be led astray by deeply ingrained prejudice. He concluded that the success of the former slaves depended not only on the employee, but also on the employer. The carefully prepared report that Schurz turned in was not to Johnson's liking; he even tried to suppress the document. At length, it was furnished to the Senate and became generally known. Schurz recommended readmission of the South into the Union with complete rights and granting of the franchise to blacks. Schurz considered it the best report he had ever written and recorded with satisfaction that it was never refuted.

Schurz also worked actively for the preservation of America's natural resources. His work on behalf of conservation in general, and for the protection of forests in particular, was one of his great interests. He actively opposed what he regarded as the devastation of public forests and was even denounced as applying the land laws of Prussia to America. However, there can be no question that he pioneered the movement toward the conservation of America's woodlands.

It seemed almost as if Schurz's usefulness in Washington had ended. Released from the demands of public activity, he decided to turn to writing. He quickly demonstrated that he had not only oratorical but also journalistic ability. He served under Horace Greeley on the *Tribune* and then became the editor of the *Detroit Post*. In 1867 he took over the large German daily of St. Louis, *Die Westliche Post*. The courage and intelligence with which he handled public issues strengthened his political position. He was proposed as senator, opposing General Ben Loan, who was supported by the other senator, Charles D. Drake. At the crucial moment Drake made the serious mistake of criticizing the Germans of the state. This gave Schurz such a distinct advantage that his opponents left the hall in defeat. Two days after his fortieth birthday, on March 4, 1869, he assumed the office of senator from Missouri.

For the erstwhile immigrant youth it was a moment of great joy and satisfaction; for the idealist and reformer, it was a solemn call to duty. He wondered whether he would be able to justify the honors that had been heaped upon him. He made the solemn vow in his heart

> that I would at least honestly endeavor to fulfill that duty; that I would conscientiously adhere to the principle *salus populi lex*; that I would never be a sycophant of power nor a flatterer of the multitude; that, if need be, I would stand up alone for my conviction of truth and right.[20]

This policy of absolute honesty was, however, entirely too radical for the practical politicians. He was repeatedly attacked and required to defend himself. He could assert fearlessly, "I never betrayed my principles." Dissatisfied with the reactionary policies of the Republican Party, he started the Liberal Republican Movement in Missouri in 1870. He opposed Grant's Santo Domingo policy, his treatment of the South, and the sending of arms to Europe during the Franco-Prussian War. From 1877 to 1881 he was Secretary of the Interior in Hayes's cabinet. Throughout his career he fought for progress, justice, and good government. He sponsored enlightened treatment of the Indians; he installed a merit promotion system; he began the development of a national parks system; and, after the Spanish-American War, he opposed the annexation of the Philippines.

There was hardly an important issue in which Schurz did not participate. Through his uncompromising denunciation of what he considered wrong, he made himself many enemies. Secret agents were hired to follow him and find some irregularity or indiscretion in his life. However, nothing could be found. Aggressive, tireless, and fearless, Schurz never deviated from moral principle. He fought increasingly for the rights of blacks, for a better civil service based on merit, honesty in public office, the maintenance of sound money, the humane treatment of the Indians, the conservation of natural resources, and the promotion of international peace.

He approached every issue with intelligence as well as courage. When he became Secretary of the Interior in 1877, one of the most serious problems was that of Indians being exploited, robbed, and exterminated. A commission appointed by Schurz reported that the Indian Bureau was bursting with "cupidity, inefficiently, and the most bare-faced dishonesty." Schurz immediately reorganized the entire department and set forth a constructive program according to which Indians were to be absorbed into the citizenry of the United States and treated like other people. He also stressed the importance of education. He inaugurated the industrial school, which later became the Carlisle Institute.

Upon his retirement in 1881, Schurz went to New York, where for several years he was editor of the *New York Evening Post*. He also contributed to the *Nation* and to *Harper's Weekly*. He never relaxed his efforts on behalf of social welfare and good government until his death on May 14, 1906. His idealism and patriotism were always tempered by common sense and are best expressed by his motto: "Not my country right or wrong, but, my country: may she always be in the right, and if in the wrong, may I help to set her right." At Schurz's death, Mark Twain wrote that he had the highest opinion of his inborn qualifications for public office: "[H]is blemishless honor, his unassailable patriotism, his high intelligence, his penetration . . . at this time I desire only to offer this brief word of homage and reverence to him, as from a grateful pupil in citizenship to the master who is no more."[21]

Friedrich Hecker

If Carl Schurz became the most prominent Forty-Eighter in America, then Friedrich Hecker was certainly one of the most popular leaders of the revolution. Born in Eichtersheim in Baden on September 28, 1811, Hecker studied law and history and completed a doctorate in law from the University of Munich. After a legal practice, he was drawn into politics. His speech in the Chamber of Baden opposing the incorporation of Schleswig-Holstein into Denmark won him great popularity. In 1845 he was expelled from Prussia due to his growing reputation, in particular as the champion of popular rights. In 1847 he and Gustav Struve drew up a document, "Claims of the People of Baden."

In March 1848 he presented a resolution at the Preliminary Parliament at Frankfurt am Main recommending the establishment of a united German republic. In April he proclaimed the German republic from Konstanz and summoned the people to armed resistance, expecting that tens of thousands would join his march for freedom. However, the poorly armed troops of a few thousand that gathered around him were no match for the combined troops of Baden and Hessen, but he marched on and later stated proudly: "I always went alone, whether someone came along or not." Near Kandern, Hecker's little army was badly routed, and Hecker fled across the border to Switzerland.

When Hecker arrived in New York in December 1848, he was greeted by more than twenty thousand New Yorkers who welcomed him with a sea of black, red, and gold banners. Hecker had come to the United States to collect funds for the continuation of the revolution and later returned to Germany in May 1849, but he got only as far as Strassburg. The course of the revolution had come to an end at Rastatt.

After returning to the United States, Hecker, unlike most Forty-Eighters, did not remain in a city but bought a farm in Summerfield near Belleville, Illinois, and prospered. He remained active intellectually and politically, gave lectures, helped found the first Turner Society in America in Cincinnati, played a significant role in the establishment of the Republican Party and in the election of Lincoln, and was strongly committed to the cause of abolition.

At the outbreak of the Civil War, he and his son volunteered. He first served as a private under General Sigel, who had come from Baden. He was subsequently appointed colonel and commanded the Twenty-Fourth Illinois Infantry regiment, a position he resigned after differences with his superiors. He was then commissioned to recruit the Eighty-Second Illinois Regiment, using his own funds in part for the purpose. He commanded long and successfully, and he was severely wounded at Chancellorsville. In 1873 Hecker paid a visit to his German hometown, where he was welcomed with torchlight processions and shadowed by the police. Although he was asked to remain, he returned home to America, where he died at his farm in 1881.

Hecker's tremendous popularity is reflected in the statues erected in his honor by German-Americans in St. Louis and Cincinnati. The town of Freedom, Illinois, was renamed Hecker in his honor as well. In Singen, Germany, a group has formed—the Hecker Troop of Singen—to commemorate his legacy by means of reenactments, lectures, and presentations. In 1992, the group toured the United States, visiting Hecker memorial programs in St. Louis, Chicago, Cincinnati, and Washington, D.C.

Hecker remained a leader and was often invited to speak at public occasions. He was especially known for his winning personality and his oratory. One of his best-known addresses was presented on July 4, 1871, at Trenton, Illinois, and was included in D. J. Brewer's *World's Best Orations*. He concluded his address as follows:

> . . . [L]et me call up before you a vision, a dream. Heavy night lay over the earth and sky; the sea was dark, filled with black waves, and a proud woman in golden armor, the standard of the Republic undulating in her hand, led me up to a high sea-beaten cliff, that in the ocean afar overtopped the hills of earth! When she raised her hands towards the East, a thousand lights from the Aurora Borealis blazed forth; and like a fire-lit picture before me the Old World lay! In trumpet tones sounded a mighty voice: I am the destiny of the Old World, I am America, and I will plant the banner of the deliverance of humanity on every land!
>
> . . . [T]o protect [America] I hold over it and its future this bright banner of the Stars and Stripes,—an emblem of freedom and human dignity for all,—that beneath it shall be a rendezvous for the free of the earth! And in this sign, I will conquer.[22]

Mathilde Anneke

The most illustrious woman Forty-Eighter was Mathilde Franziska Anneke, one of the pioneers of the women's suffrage movement. Born April 3, 1817, near Blankenstein in Westfalen, she married at nineteen, but the marriage was soon dissolved, and it was in the struggle for rights relating to her daughter that she came to realize the disregard many have for human rights. She also began writing a number of literary and religious works at an early age, such as the *Damenalmanach* (1842).

In 1847 she married a Prussian officer, Fritz Anneke, whose outspoken views led to his dismissal from the army. In Köln, she established and edited the *Neue Kölnische Zeitung*, but it was soon suppressed, and her husband was at the same time imprisoned for eleven months on the charge of treason. She then established a women's journal, *Die Frauenzeitung*, advocating equal rights, but this was also suppressed. Both of the Annekes were involved in the 1848 revolution; he assisted in organizing an artillery unit, and she served as a mounted orderly. Before the surrender of the revolutionists at Rastatt, they fled to Switzerland, then to France, and finally to America.

The Annekes first lived in Milwaukee, where she began public speaking in 1850 on political and literary topics. In 1852 she revived the *Deutsche Frauenzeitung* in Milwaukee, then took it to New York and Newark, New Jersey, where her husband was publishing a German-American paper. Mathilde Anneke traveled widely, speaking on topics such as women's rights, and was especially sought after in German-American communities. She also published a number of literary works, including *Das Geisterhaus in New York*. In 1865 she founded an academy for young women in Milwaukee, which she directed until her death in 1884.

Anneke's influence spread by means of her numerous publications and speaking engagements. An example of her effectiveness is apparent in a speech delivered in 1869, as she admonished:

> . . . [D]on't exclude woman, don't exclude the whole half of the human family. Receive us—begin the work in which a new era shall dawn. In all great events we find that woman has a guiding hand—let us stay near you now, when humanity is concerned. . . . Give us our rights in the state. Honor us as your equal, and allow us to use the rights which belong to us, which reason commands us to use. Whether it is prudent to enfranchise woman, is not the question—only whether it is right. What is positively right, must be prudent, must be wise, and must finally, be useful. . . .[23]

Notes

1. Regarding this period of German history, see Hajo Holborn, *A History of Modern Germany*, 3 vols. (Princeton: Princeton University Press, 1982), especially vol. 3.

2. Dieter Cunz, *They Came from Germany: The Stories of Famous German-Americans* (New York: Dodd, Mead, 1966), p. 60.

3. Ibid.

4. Ibid.

5. Francis J. Grund, *Aristocracy in America: From the Sketch-Book of a German Nobleman* (New York: Harper, 1959), p. xiii.

6. See Frank B. Freidel, *Francis Lieber: Nineteenth Century Liberal* (Baton Rouge: Louisiana State University, 1947). Also see Peter Schafer and Karl Schmitt, eds., *Franz Lieber und die deutsch-amerikanischen Beziehungen im 19. Jahrhundert* (Weimar: Böhlau, 1993).

7. Theodore Heubener, *The Germans in America* (Philadelphia: Chilton, 1962), p. 62.

8. Ibid., p. 63.

9. Ibid., p. 65.

10. Ibid., p. 66.

11. For further references to works dealing with the German image of America see Alexander Ritter, ed., *Deutschlands literarisches Amerikabild: neuere Forschungen zur Amerikarezeption der deutschen Literatur* (Hildesheim: Olms, 1977).

12. Charles Sealsfield, *The Cabin Book, Or, National Characteristics*, trans. Sarah Powell (Austin: Eakin Press/German-Texan Heritage Society, 1985).

13. Regarding women writers, see Dorothea Diver Stuecher, *Twice Removed: The Experience of German-American Women Writers in the Nineteenth Century*. New German-American Studies, vol. 1 (New York: Peter Lang, 1990).

14. A survey of the Thirtyers can be found in Carl Wittke, *Refugees of Revolution: The German Forty-Eighters in America* (Philadelphia: University of Pennsylvania Press, 1952), pp. 6–17.

15. See Gustav Koerner, *Memoirs of Gustav Koerner, 1809–1896: Life-Sketches Written at the Suggestion of His Children* (Cedar Rapids, Iowa: Torch Press, 1909).

16. Huebener, *The Germans in America*, p. 100.

17. Ibid.

18. A. E. Zucker, ed., *The Forty-Eighters: Political Refugees of the German Revolution of 1848* (New York: Columbia University Press, 1950), p. 250.

19. Wittke, *Refugees*, p. 371.

20. Huebener, *The Germans in America*, p. 109.

21. Twain is cited in Zucker, *The Forty-Eighters*, p. 250.

22. Hecker's speech is found in D. J. Brewer, ed., *The World's Best Orations: From the Earliest Period to the Present Time* (St. Louis: F. P. Kaiser, 1899). Also see Alfred G. Frei, ed., *Friedrich Hecker in den USA: Eine deutsch-amerikanische Spurensicherung* (Konstanz: Stadler Verlagsgesellschaft, 1993).

23. Cited in Don Heinrich Tolzmann, ed., *German-American Literature* (Metuchen, N.J.: Scarecrow, 1977), p. 174. Also see Stuecher, *Twice Removed*, pp. 115–58.

Community Life Before the Civil War

The German-American Community

As German-American communities were formed, they displayed some basic and readily discernible groupings, or subdivisions. These have generally been referred to as the *Kirchendeutschen*, or Church Germans, and the *Vereinsdeutschen*, or Club Germans. The former refers to German-Americans for whom their religious affiliation forms a central focal point in their lives, whereas the latter refers to those whose organizational affiliation occupies a central role. These have also been referred to as the religious and the secular camps in the German-American community.

The Church Germans consist of German-Americans who belong to any one of the numerous Protestant, Catholic, or Jewish religious faiths. They formed basically a conservative element in the community. They established a wide variety of religious institutions, including their own hospitals, orphanages, homes for the elderly, seminaries, and societies. Most importantly, they established parochial German-language schools for their youth. Indeed, in some communities, the German parochial school system dwarfed the public school system. Also, many of them maintained German bookstores stocked with books, newspapers, periodicals, and other publications catering to the denomination in question.

Some religious bodies held little in common with each other, as was the case with the various sectarian groups. Hence, in the religious camp, there were further subdivisions. This meant that there was the tendency for each group to grow and develop independently from others. Indeed, sometimes the editors of a group's publications would engage in theological, social, and political debates with the editors of the publications of other religious bodies. For example, some of the most heated debates occurred between German Lutheran and German Methodist editors in the nineteenth century.

Politically, the Church Germans could be characterized as conservative, and some were staunchly antiradical, antisocialists, and anti-Forty-Eighter. However, most did not officially and overtly engage in political affairs and issues except when it was an issue which directly affected their particular church body, e.g., the issue of public laws relating to non-English language instruction.

Religion and heritage were closely intertwined, and it has been often noted that German-American churches have been among the strongest institutional supporters of the German language and heritage in America. The Church Germans used the German language and heritage to ward off heresy, maintain unity, prevent losses, and exclude external influences. This promoted and supported their own identity and religious focus. Also, Church Germans tended to come to America together in groups and families and then settle together, thus promoting a close-knit community structure. Many agreed with the basic notion that "language saves faith," which stressed the importance of the German language in relation to the preservation of one's faith.

Religion thus nurtured and was nurtured by religious identity, and it would be the religious communities that would tend to retain the strongest sense of German ethnicity. Also, it was no accident that in German-American literature, all American-born authors came from a German-American religious community. This reflects the success of such communities in preserving German heritage. The publications of the Church Germans were often youth-oriented and were designed to keep the youth within the fold, as well as to keep them from being unduly affected by Anglo influences in American society.

It should be kept in mind that the concept of Church Germans is designed to cover a diverse array of religious groups, and the only real bond those groups held in common was a strong commitment to religious values and to German language and heritage, both of which were closely interrelated.

The secular camp referred to the *Vereinsdeutschen*, or the Club Germans, was historically viewed as the liberal element in the German-American community. Their commitment to German heritage revolved around secular societies and organizations, *Vereine*. Like the religious element, they were not a homogeneous group either. They consisted of secularized workers recruited usually from the lower ranks of the white-collar class and the higher echelons of the blue-collar class. Financially, many of them were well off. Politically, the entire spectrum was represented, ranging from radicals, free-thinkers, and socialists to conservatives.

The left wing was stamped particularly by three immigrant waves: the Thirtyers, the Forty-Eighters, and the socialists who immigrated in the 1870s and 1880s. Although small in number, these liberals were usually well educated and articulate, so many of them assumed leadership positions in the *Vereine* as well as in the German-American press. Some of them, especially the Forty-Eighters, were noted for their anticlerical views.

The Club Germans formed societies patterned on the models established by the German middle and working class of the mid-nineteenth century. These societies fulfilled a social function, as did the religious institutions for the Church Germans. They built expansive halls and club houses for their members, some complete with beer gardens, bowling alleys, theaters, libraries, and other offices. One of the largest and finest German houses is the *Deutsches Haus* in Indianapolis, designed by Bernard Vonnegut. The profit from the fests, events, and activities of the societies, including the sale of food and drink, kept many a society on sound financial footing.

The early societies, such as mutual and fraternal aid societies, voluntary fire and militia companies, fulfilled practical needs; but many others were formed as well: educational, historical, literary, musical, cultural, social, and political societies. Some were based on the area of origin of the members, such as Swabian, Bavarian, or Pomeranian. The societies were usually organized into regional federations, which in turn affiliated with national organizations. For example, local singing societies were affiliated with district organizations, which were affiliated with either of the two national organizations: *Der Nord-Amerikanische Sängerbund* or *Der Nord-Östliche Sängerbund*. Both of these groups still hold regional and national *Sängerfeste*. The numerous Turner societies, or *Turnvereine*, formed a national organization, *Der Turnerbund*, now known as the American Turner Society. They also sponsored national conventions known as *Turnfeste*.

The societies sponsored numerous kinds of fests, dances, picnics, and other social activities. The Club Germans valued the *Gemütlichkeit* (closeness) of their *Vereine* and their various festivities. Some criticized them for their *Vereinsmeierei*, or devotion to the societies, but this merely reflected the important social, cultural, and political role and function of the societies in the German-American community.

The secular camp became the strongest advocate and supporter of public education and campaigned for the introduction of German instruction, as well as physical education or *Turnunterricht*. Indeed, German-Americans were the first to introduce bilingual education in America in Cincinnati in 1840 and in the 1890s were responsible for the introduction of physical education into the curriculum.

Because of its numerous social, cultural, and political activities and the many public kinds of parades and festivities, the secular camp was without question the most vocal and visible segment of the German-American community and came to define for many both within and without the German-American community what it was that constituted German-Americans. Especially to non-German-Americans, the Club Germans represented and were seen as the German-American community, although in fact they represented only part of the equation. Undoubtedly, the Club Germans shared a commitment to German heritage, which centered on their support and involvement in an array of societies and organizations.

Another discernible segment of the community has been referred to as the elite, which consisted of two groups: the economic and the intellectual elites. The economic elite was made up of those persons who enjoyed social and economic success and were not attracted to the societies. While these persons would often hold membership in some of the organizations, they would not necessarily be active in them. As upwardly mobile people, they were generally just as interested in developing contacts with others of their class as with maintaining ties with those in the secular or religious camps. Nevertheless, they would maintain pride in the German heritage and would often involve themselves in philanthropic and civic activities in the German-American community.

The intellectual elite consisted of three variations: the active, passive, and marginal ethnic intellectuals. The first type remained with the German-American community and focused their interests on German ethnicity and its meaning in the context of American history. Such a person would serve as the cultural historian, the theologian, the community leader, the scholar, and spokesperson for the German-American community. The second type remains within the framework of the community and social class but also has interests besides German heritage. The third type of person becomes a part of the subsociety of intellectuals in American society and does not find ethnicity to be a central focal point.

German heritage was the common denominator among these various groups. Historically, these groups learned to emphasize those elements held in common: a common history, heritage, and cultural background. The German-American community, hence, consisted of a fabric of interwoven strands drawn from these three subcommunities (secular, religious, and elite), all of which contributed to its overall diversity and strength.[1]

Urban Communities

Germans clustered together in urban areas, forming German neighborhoods and districts that flourished as thriving centers of trade and industry. These "little Germanies" became the hubs of German-American social, cultural, business, and political life. Stores stocked German books and specialty foods; theaters staged the plays of Goethe and Schiller; and meeting halls thronged with rifle, athletic, beneficial, choral, and other kinds of societies. People kept abreast of local issues through the German-American press, and beer halls became popular gathering spots for games, celebrations, and community meetings. Churches provided not only German services, but also German parochial schooling for the youth. Open-air markets displayed a variety of German-style *Wurst*, breads, and other foods, and by the mid-nineteenth century the brewing industry was well underway.

Almost every city in the Midwest had a Little Germany, or German-American district or neighborhood. Usually such districts reflected the material impact of the German immigration in terms of the kinds of buildings, statues, and architecture found there. Moreover, by the 1850s the districts carried political clout, which translated into German-Americans getting elected to local, state, and national offices. It also meant that German-American agendas, such as German instruction in the schools, were actively being addressed and achieved. Such German-American districts were not isolated islands but often became highly influential social, cultural, political, and economic centers. By the end of the nineteenth century, German-Americans had synthesized American ideals and manners.

An example of a Little Germany can be found in the German district of Cincinnati, which became known as the Over-the-Rhine district, an area of more than two hundred acres. Its borders were defined by the Miami-Erie Canal, completed in 1832 (now Central Parkway), on the west and south and on the north and east by McMicken Avenue and Reading Road. The old barge canal had been locally dubbed as the "Rhine," since when one crossed over it one entered the German district. Germans began congregating there in the 1830s, and well before the Civil War the canal came to divide the German quarter from the English-speaking areas.

Over-the-Rhine was a social, cultural, economic, and political center for German-Americans. There were numerous German houses, restaurants, churches, bakeries, markets, beer gardens, shops, and stores. Local histories called Over-the-Rhine the district where everything is German and even the American discards his formality and is enveloped by German *Gemütlichkeit*. It was the home of German music, theaters, newspapers, libraries, clubs, societies, and religious institutions. It was filled with little savings and loan societies, or *Bauvereine*, where the thrifty deposited their savings or borrowed funds in this early form of a credit union.

In 1859 the Turners built the *Turnhalle*, which was the central meeting place for the German-American societies. It housed not only meeting-rooms but also a theater, a library, and a gymnasium, and was referred to as "a mighty fortress of German-American culture." Life in the Over-the-Rhine district was portrayed by Carl Wittke:

Cincinnati's German community, in its early years, was concentrated largely in an area north of where the canal entered the city, and was known as "Over-the-Rhine." Here the Germans lived in neat little frame and brick houses built flush with the sidewalk, and with backyards fenced in with lattice work and planted with flower and vegetable gardens. Every Saturday, German housewives scrubbed the front steps of their homes until they were snow white. Here too the German *Hausfrau* nourished her family with German food and delicacies which quickly became part of the American culinary art. After working hours and on Sunday, the men sought recreation in the taverns, played euchre, skat and pinochle, or brought their families to the beer gardens to listen to old familiar German airs.[2]

As the German-American population grew and expanded before the First World War, the population gradually moved beyond Over-the-Rhine to settle throughout the city of Cincinnati, but particularly moved to the west side of the city, so that even today in Cincinnati there is an east-west divide based on ethnocultural factors. This population growth and migration was due to increased German immigration. By the end of the century there were still the old German districts, but usually the entire urban area would range from one-third to over one-half German-American.

Rural Communities

In rural areas, chain migration often led to the development of communities that reflected the origins of the settlers. Today, German-American communities retain traces of their founders' homelands through customs, dialects, and place names. Contacts between these New and Old World communities still exist, often in the form of sister-city relationships.

Examples of such rural communities are the Franconian communities established in central Michigan in the 1840s. They owe their existence to the Reverend Wilhelm Löhe, a Lutheran clergyman in Neuendettelsau near Nürnberg. To achieve the goal of missionary work with the Native Americans, German Lutheran communities in remote areas were to serve as missions. These communities would support their own ministers and would protect one another in the midst of the Anglo environment. Reverend Löhe appealed to German immigrants, admonishing them to preserve their language, as it was important for their history and faith.

The site of the first mission, Frankenmuth, or "Courage of the Franks," was approved, and in 1845 the first settlers arrived. In 1846 one hundred more settlers departed from Franconia for Frankenmuth. After this, chain migration from Franconia, as well as other parts of Germany, especially Württemberg, actively took place. By 1860 the population of Frankenmuth had reached more than one thousand. In addition, several nearby Franconian villages were founded: Frankentrost, Frankenlust, and Frankenhilf. These closely related settlements increased the overall Franconian population and created a powerful base.

In 1847 area churches joined the German Evangelical Lutheran Synod of Missouri, Ohio, and other states, which emphasized doctrinal orthodoxy and the use and preservation of the German language. In their view, revolutions were sinful, so there was little respect for the refugees of the 1848 revolution, who were regarded as radicals, atheists, or socialists. As the Forty-Eighters dominated many of the newspapers, German Lutherans formed their own press so that they could have their own family journals and newspapers, such as *Der Lutheraner*. Although some Forty-Eighters settled in the Frankenmuth area, they appear to have left and moved elsewhere, most likely to an urban area such as Detroit.

In order to govern itself, Frankenmuth used a church and community charter drafted by Löhe, which aimed to preserve the German Lutheran nature of the community. This included stipulations against marriage with non-Lutherans and the exclusion of all those found guilty of apostasy. Hence, the community was held together by ethnoreligious and political criteria.

The aim was for German to be the official community language, as ministers and teachers were to preach and teach in German. The charter stated: "We are founding a community which will remain German forever. Our preachers and teachers are duty bound to support [this goal] as well." The purchase of land in the area was contingent on adherence to Lutheranism. Civil and property disputes were to be adjudicated by the church, which served not only as a central religious institution, but also as the vehicle to preserve and maintain the community.[3]

By way of contrast, another example of a rural community can be found in Brown County, Minnesota, where New Ulm was founded in 1854 by the *Chicagoer Landverein*, led by Ferdinand Beinhorn. The society, centered in Chicago, aimed to locate a townsite somewhere in the Northwest, the only stipulations being that it be located alongside a navigable river and that there be ample timber in the area. The society circulated its resolutions to that effect and published them in the *Illinois Staats-Zeitung*. They soon had a total of eight hundred members who paid $1.20 in annual dues.

After searching for a site in Michigan and Iowa, the society examined places in Minnesota, and the present location of New Ulm finally was agreed on. Pressing financial difficulties in 1856 caused the society to be acquired by the Turner Settlement Society of Cincinnati, led by Wilhelm Pfänder from Heilbronn in Württemberg. An enthusiastic Turner, he and a group of Turners emigrated to America in 1848. Like other Forty-Eighters, they wanted greater political liberty and economic opportunities. After stopping in London, where he met Karl Marx and Friedrich Engels, Pfänder went on to New York and finally to Cincinnati.

After Hecker's visit to Cincinnati in 1848, the first Turner Society in America was founded there, and Pfänder became an active member. He married Catherine Pfau, who came from a Turner family. In March 1855 he published an article in the *Turnzeitung*, stating his belief that in America there was greater security to be found for the individual in a group than for an individual standing alone. This was especially true given the problems emanating from the anti-immigrant Know-Nothing movement, prevalent Anglo Puritanism, and other anti-Forty-Eighter sentiments.

Pfänder wisely stated that the idea of a New Germany was rather utopian, but not that of German-American settlements. After lengthy discussion at the national convention of the Turners in Buffalo, New York, in 1855, the Cincinnati Turners were charged with supervising planning and organizing a Turner settlement. A committee was formed, with Pfänder as its chairman.

The goal was to found a German-American Turner community in the Northwest, where members could establish a home for themselves and future generations. Only members of good character devoted to the principles of reform and over seventeen years old could join. Moreover, the board of the Turner Settlement Society reviewed all applications for membership and could expel members in case of objectionable behavior.

In 1856 the transaction with the *Chicagoer Landverein* was concluded in Chicago, and the new owner was incorporated as the German Land Association of Minnesota. New Ulm has been called an attempt at frontier socialism, but a more accurate description would be that it tried to establish community cooperatives, which meant that certain kinds of services and businesses would be community-owned. The following kinds of cooperatives were established for the benefit of the community: a newspaper, a sawmill, and warehouses. Other community projects discussed were a public sand and clay kiln, a quarry, a cemetery, the municipal sale of liquor, and the community purchase of agricultural machinery.

Although idealistic, the New Ulmers were also frontier pragmatists who worked by the philosophy of trial and error: what didn't work was quickly discarded. After three years, the association was financially unable to undertake any of the projects that had been discussed, so the attempt at community cooperativization was rejected and replaced with frontier free market capitalism. New Ulm thrived, and by means of this flexible kind of pragmatism, the community achieved its basic goals of founding a German settlement on the frontier, avoiding prolonged speculation, and establishing a home with educational opportunities for the children of liberals and freethinkers.

Although initially a Forty-Eighter-oriented settlement, New Ulm later attracted German-American churches of various denominations and became a German Lutheran center for the Wisconsin Synod, as Dr. Martin Luther College was established there. Forty-Eighters practiced and advocated open-mindedness and toleration, and this policy contributed to attracting other German groups to the area.

In 1856 the New Ulm *Turnverein* was established, and this society became a central institution with regard to the preservation and maintenance of community identity. As early as 1858 German theatrical performances were sponsored by the Turners. Other groups were also formed. By 1860 there was a rifle company, a singing society, an agricultural society, a workers society, and a volunteer fire brigade. German instruction as well as physical education were both introduced into the school curriculum and were central to the Turner philosophy of a sound body and a sound mind.

By 1858 the population of New Ulm was 440, and it rose to 635 by 1860. Altogether the population of Brown County at that time was 2,339. Since many of the early settlers had come from the region of Ulm in Württemberg, the new settlement was named New Ulm in honor of their hometown in Germany. This geographical link to a specific region in Germany would provide the basis for future chain migration. Also, the Turner connection worked in favor of internal chain migration from other German-American communities in the United States. Turners from across the United States who were interested in the settlement made their way to New Ulm and were joined by additional groups that came to New Ulm because of its open-minded and cosmopolitan atmosphere, especially German-Bohemians. Thus, the Turners and the German-Bohemians became the two major groups in Brown County, the one secular and the other religious.

The Sioux Uprising of 1862 acted as an agent to solidify the group identity of New Ulm. The town survived two onslaughts, the history of which was recorded by Jacob Nix, a Forty-Eighter. Nix served as commandant in the first battle and saved the town from being wiped out.[4]

Both Frankenmuth and New Ulm exemplify some of the German-American rural communities established in the nineteenth century, before the Civil War, and which would thrive and prosper in the course of the century. They also illuminate the process of chain migration and how various groups formed to establish communities. Although settlers came from various regions and reflected various religious and philosophical beliefs, they shared in common the bonds of their German heritage and the desire for social, political, and economic opportunities.

The Mexican War

When the Mexican War broke out in 1846, German-Americans were among the first to volunteer their services from such diverse areas as Missouri, Kentucky, Illinois, New Orleans, Cincinnati, and Texas. The first regiment organized in Cincinnati was entirely German. James L.

Kemper, the governor of Virginia from 1873 to 1878, was a captain of volunteers in the war.

As in previous wars, German-Americans rendered valuable service. Among these was Captain Henry Koch. Born in Bayreuth, he came to America in 1832 and established a colony in Clayton County, Iowa. A more distinguished officer was General Augustus V. Kautz, who was born in Baden in 1828. He enlisted in the First Iowa Regiment. He also served later in the Civil War, where he distinguished himself through his cavalry raids in southern Virginia in 1864. Another officer who served in both wars was Samuel P. Heintzelmann, a graduate of West Point. He was a captain in the Mexican War, and in the Civil War he participated in the battles of Alexandria, Bull Run, Uniontown, Hamburg, and Fair Oaks. He was retired in 1864 with the rank of major-general.

Outstanding among the German-Americans who took part in the war was John A. Quitmann. His father, Dr. Quitmann, who settled first in Schoharie, was pastor of the Lutheran Church in Rhinebeck, New York, for twenty-five years. John Anthony became a teacher and then studied law. Later he moved to Ohio and in 1821 decided to go to the Southwest. In Natchez, Mississippi, he established a successful law practice and married the daughter of a wealthy planter. As a man of unusually strong physique, he took a keen interest in sports, particularly riflery. One of his townsmen was John Hawkins, a veteran frontiersman and owner of the famous "Brown Bess" rifle. Quitmann challenged him to a shooting match and won three times.

With his reputation as a lawyer and his wealth as a planter, Quitmann easily became president of the Mississippi State Senate. He was also commander of the state militia. When Santa Ana invaded Texas in 1836, Quitmann organized a company of recruits and crossed the Sabine River. At St. Augustine he ran into a crowd of gamblers and criminals whom he had banished from Natchez. While Quitmann was resting on a couch in the hotel, one of the desperadoes was about to attack him with a dagger. Quitmann, however, who had only been feigning sleep, managed to fend him off with his pistol. By this fearless action, Quitmann gained the friendship of the outlaws.

Quitmann proceeded with his company of volunteers, but when they arrived at the camp of General Houston, the Battle of San Jacinto had already been fought, which had ended the invasion. There was nothing for Quitmann to do but to return to Natchez. The adventure had cost him more than ten thousand dollars.

He continued to take an active part in politics. When the Mexican War broke out, he was made a brigadier-general and commanded a brigade at Monterey, where he shared the honors with General Worth. Accompanying the troops who went out to support General Scott, he led the assault on Vera Cruz. He was in command at Alvarado and helped storm Chapultepec. He was one of the most daring of the fighting generals in the war and in active combat at the storming of the Belen Gate at Mexico City. He was the first to enter the Grand Plaza the next morning as the head of the tattered and worn troops.

Quitmann's services had been so outstanding that General Scott appointed him governor of the city of Mexico. However, Quitmann did not like the terms of peace that were proposed, for he favored the annexation of Mexico. He felt so strongly about this that he went to Washington to argue in favor of the measure.

During the Democratic convention of 1846, which was held in Baltimore, Quitmann was proposed as a candidate for the vice presidency of the United States. In 1849 he was elected governor of Mississippi by a large majority. He served from 1850 to 1851, and in 1855 was elected to Congress, where he remained until 1858, the year of his death. An ardent secessionist, he suggested the formation of a Southern Confederacy, one of the few German-American leaders who was on the Confederate side.[5]

Nativism

In the beginning, the U.S. population was two-thirds Anglo-American, but the other third consisted of various ethnic groups, so at its inception the United States was a multicultural nation. However, the majority was Anglo, who by and large viewed Anglo ethnicity as equatable with being American. The view was that becoming an American meant not only the adoption of U.S. citizenship, but also Anglicization. As the nature of the population came to change due to immigration in the nineteenth century, so, too, would the definition of American begin to come into question.

With the arrival of large numbers of immigrants in America, a strong anti-immigrant prejudice seized certain Anglo-American circles between 1852 and 1860. Those who supported the xenophobic trend soon were referred to as Know-Nothings, meaning that members of this movement usually pretended ignorance when asked questions about policies and goals of the organization. The Know-Nothing movement stressed that native-born Americans were legitimate and authentic Americans, as opposed to the recently arrived immigrants. The major strands of nativism were anti-Catholicism, fear of foreign-born radicalism, the belief in Anglo-American supremacy in relation to other groups, and the notion that others should conform to Anglicization.

In the 1850s the main charges against the Germans were that there were so many freethinkers, rationalists, atheists, and desecraters of the Puritan sabbath in the German-American community. Indeed, it was before the Civil War that proponents of the Anglo-American Puritan sabbath fought a losing battle those who advocated the Continental Sunday. The latter held that Sunday was a day of enjoyment for the whole family and a time to celebrate with picnics and festivities. This was contrasted sharply with what German-Americans called the Puritan sabbath, which frowned on all such festive frolic.

Anglo-American evangelicals spoke out, publishing literature against those who advocated "infidelity, Socialism, and other soul-destroying errors." Some attacked the new Christian customs as "foreign"; others called them popish idolatries. German-Americans for their part openly defied and opposed all attempts to legislate their lifestyle, customs, and morality. In Newark, New Jersey, they petitioned the city council to repeal the Sunday "Blue Laws," which caused the *New York Times* to publish an editorial on the topic of "Sunday-keeping." It criticized German-Americans for turning Sunday into a pleasure-seeking "Saturnia." Other newspapers complained about "lager beer loafers" who were transforming Sunday into something it had never been before.

In response to what they perceived as a desecration of the sabbath, nativists formed the Know-Nothing political movement of the 1850s. On several occasions, German-American picnics and festivities were turned into bloody riots in places like Columbus, Cincinnati, and Louisville. Many of the Forty-Eighters came under attack as they were viewed and described as freethinkers and radicals. Their societies were often denounced as alien and threatening to the Republic because of their different ideas and perspectives. The *Boston Pilot* claimed that it would be well if the Know-Nothings could prevent Germans from ever obtaining any kind of political power or representation. Other Know-Nothings concentrated not only on the Forty-Eighters, but also on Catholics, whom they viewed as a threat to Protestantism. Many violently anti-Catholic publications were issued at the time.

In 1855 the Know-Nothings won victories in Kentucky, Tennessee, and Louisiana, and in 1856 they obtained 874,000 votes in the presidential election. They began to appear in Congress and won the governorship of Massachusetts. By 1855 there were governors and legislatures in seven states with elected officials who were Know-Nothings. Also, it was estimated that seventy-five to one hundred members of Congress were openly or secretly attached to the Know-Nothing movement.

As German-American halls, festivities, picnics, and churches came under criticism and attack, many societies formed militias in self-defense. A well-known clash took place in Covington, Kentucky. In the spring of 1856 the Cincinnati Turners held a picnic across the Ohio River in Covington and were followed by a gang of street youths, who began to shout and throw rocks and stones at the Turners. Finally, one of the rowdies grabbed a glass of beer from a Turner, which earned him a slap in the face. The youth then drew a pistol and ran back to Covington, claiming that the Dutch were out to kill him. Unaware of the commotion being caused in town, the Turners prepared to make their way back to Cincinnati at five in the afternoon, conspicuously accompanied by a marching band and displaying the Stars and Stripes.

Outside Covington, the Turners were met by a group who threw stones at them. One of the group members seized a Turner, who, of course, immediately resisted. Others came to the aid of the Turner, and soon a full-scale fight was underway, complete with rocks, stones, and pistol shots flying in all directions. Two marshals received bullet wounds, and the Turners effected a retreat to a ferry on the banks of the Ohio River, where they planned to cross over to the Cincinnati side. In the meantime, fire alarm bells in Covington had summoned an anti-Turner mob. The Turners lined up before the wharf and replied with a volley of pistol shots. The Covington mayor asked U.S. troops to attack the Germans, but the commanding officer refused to comply, as he could act only on direct orders from Washington, D.C. Meanwhile, the disciplined Turners held their ranks and firmly stood their ground, calmly obeying the orders of their commander.

The police strove to quell the disturbance, and the mayor of Covington and nearby Newport demanded that the Turners turn over their weapons to the civil authorities. The mob shouted that they would not desist until this was done. At this time, the ferry arrived, but the Covington mayor would not let the Turners board it. To the renewed demand to turn over their weapons, the commander of the Turners replied that he had no objection to this, if it could be done under safe conditions, but that in the face of a mob, arms were required for self-defense. If an individual was considered to have broken the law, no resistance would be offered to legal arrest. Four Turners were arrested.

However, this did not satisfy the mob, which demanded further action. Local officials were now unable to control the mob, so the Turners decided that since they could not take the ferry, they would retreat to the Turner Hall located in nearby Newport. Judge Johann B. Stallo from Cincinnati, who was also a Thirtyer, arrived at that point and informed the authorities that as long as they could not control the mob, the Turners would not disarm themselves but would remain in the Turner Hall and place themselves under the disposition of the courts in the morning. Thirty-one Turners would be indicted and released on $2,000 bail each; the total sum of $62,000 was paid by two German-American businessmen. The court trial dragged on, but due to the able defense of Judge Stallo, all were eventually acquitted. The clash itself reflected the cultural clash between Anglo- and German-Americans.

Nativism, and along with it the Know-Nothing movement, would fade away in the face of the approaching national crisis that culminated in the Civil War. Indeed, the last meeting of the movement's National Council was in 1857, and it lingered on only shortly thereafter at the state and local levels. The growing national crisis together with the increasing political clout of German-Americans eventually led to the downfall of the Know-Nothings, as German-Americans came to be viewed as essential to victory in the election of 1860.[6]

Politics

Before 1850 German-Americans were mainly aligned with the Democratic Party, as they identified with the traditions of Jacksonian democracy and were also opposed to the anti-immigrant tendencies of the Whigs. Although German-Americans would begin to make their major national political impact after 1850, they had already made their presence known in the pre-1850 period.

The first German-American political leader of national prominence was Frederick Augustus Muehlenberg, the first Speaker of the House. He was followed by a number of other German-Americans in Congress in the early 1800s. The Muehlenbergs played an important role in the eighteenth century and continued to do so into the nineteenth century. By the 1830s Henry Augustus Muehlenberg, son of Gotthilf Muehlenberg, a brother of Frederick Augustus, had risen to national prominence in the political sphere.

Born in 1782 in Lancaster, Pennsylvania, Henry entered the ministry and rose to the presidency of the German Lutheran Ministerium of Pennsylvania. He was clearly viewed as a German-American community spokesman and leader. On the basis of his stature among German-Americans, the Democrats nominated him for Congress in 1829 (21st Congress), and he served until his resignation in 1838. In Congress, he chaired the House Committee on Revolutionary Claims and supported Presidents Jackson and Van Buren. Due to internal dissension, the Democrats ran two Pennsylvania Germans for governor in 1835, Muehlenberg and George Wolf, and Muehlenberg lost, so it was decided that Van Buren would offer him positions of secretary of the navy and minister to Russia, but Muehlenberg declined.

However, when it was decided to send a delegation to Austria, he resigned from Congress and became the first U.S. minister to Austria. As a German-English bilingual he thrived in the position, promoted the use of American cotton in Austria and became acquainted with Prince Metternich. He also traveled extensively in Austria, Germany, Switzerland, and Italy. In 1840 he was again nominated for governor of Pennsylvania, but he died suddenly of a stroke during the campaign. He represents the continued importance of the Muehlenberg family in German-American community affairs, as well as the major German-American political representative nationally in the 1830s and 1840s. Clearly, the Democrats were aware of the German-American presence in Pennsylvania and recognized the need for addressing the needs of German-American voters, thereby nominating and appointing Muehlenberg to office.

After Muehlenberg's death, the next German-American who played a national role as a community spokesman was Franz Josef Grund. In 1836 Grund campaigned for Van Buren, a Democrat, for president, but in 1840 switched to William Henry Harrison, a Whig. This not only diminished his influence, but also alienated him from German-Americans, who were repelled by the nativist tendencies of the Whigs. Grund came to be viewed as a political opportunist looking for an appointment to an office. Yet he was looked on as a German-American spokesman, and political parties by this time were clearly aware of German-Americans as a sizable percentage of the voting population.

By this time, the Thirtyers were asserting their presence and taking an active role in political affairs at the state and local level, especially by electing German-Americans to city councils and school boards. They were beginning to address such issues as prohibition and bilingual education. The stage was now set for an even more active German-American political role in the 1850s.

The passage of the Kansas-Nebraska Bill in 1854, which allowed the two new territories to settle the question of slavery for themselves, caused many to question the issue of states' rights and the more fundamental question of slavery in a so-called democratic republic. Historically, German-Americans had been opposed to slavery and had made the first protest against it in 1688 at Germantown. In 1854 eighty German-American newspapers had opposed the Kansas-Nebraska Bill, and only eight had supported it. Only six days after it was passed, the first German-American protest against the bill was held in Chicago, and others soon followed elsewhere. At a meeting in New York of the American and Foreign Anti-Slavery Society, Abraham Lincoln met the editor of the powerful German-American newspaper *Die Illinois Staats-Zeitung*.

By now, the German-American element was of sufficient size and stature that political parties had taken note of it, especially because of the forceful and articulate German-American spokesmen, many of them

Forty-Eighters. The Whigs made a number of overtures appealing to German-Americans, as did the Democrats, but German-Americans were generally dissatisfied with the status quo and the positions taken by the two major parties.

In 1853 a group known as the League of Free Men, *Der Bund der freien Männer*, met in Louisville and adopted an antislavery platform, which reflected German-American discontent. When the new Republican Party, at first known as the Anti-Nebraska Party, held its convention in 1856 in Philadelphia, many German-Americans were attracted to it. However, the older German papers, financed by the Democrats, opposed the new party, but found it increasingly difficult even to recruit editorial staff.

Still, German-Americans were somewhat reluctant to join the Republicans at first, as Know-Nothings had also joined the new party. Nonetheless, German-Americans generally saw the Republicans as the party holding the greatest promise for the future and felt that it was in their best interest to make a commitment to them. What helped the new party were the endorsements it received from German-American leaders such as Georg Schneider, editor of the *Illinois Staats-Zeitung*; Gustav Koerner, lieutenant-governor of Illinois; F. A. Hoffmann, later lieutenant-governor of Illinois; and other leading representatives such as Friedrich Münch, Franz Sigel, and Emil Pretorius of Missouri; Carl Ruemelin and Friedrich Hassaurek of Ohio; and Friedrich Kapp of New York. Together with Georg Schneider, Abraham Lincoln drafted the anti-Know-Nothing Party plank for the Republican convention. This in itself increased German-American support for the Republicans.

In Illinois and Wisconsin the Republicans passed resolutions against nativism, as the German-American vote would be crucial in those states. Elsewhere, where the German-American vote held the balance of power, the issue of nativism was hushed. Also, in the election of 1856, for the first time German-Americans took an active and highly visible role as their vote was viewed as essential to deciding victory. Friedrich Hecker, who was on the Republican electoral ticket with Lincoln in Illinois, appeared with Honest Abe during the campaign, and banners carried the inscription "Lincoln and Hecker." Hecker also campaigned in several states for the Republicans, as did Reinhold Solger, Friedrich Münch, Gustav Struve, Julius Froebel, Gustav Koerner, Friedrich Kapp, Friedrich Hassaurek, and others.

The Republicans lost the presidential election of 1856, but their party was new, and as Carl Schurz stated, it was only the first battle of a long campaign. German-Americans were not negative but were positive about the future. Schurz was by now well known for his fluency, brilliance, and effectiveness in German and English as a speaker, campaigner, and German-American spokesman. By the time of the 1860 campaign, he was clearly one of the foremost German-Americans in the Republican Party. Although slavery had always been discussed from a constitutional point of view, relating to states' rights, Schurz discussed it from a philosophical perspective, demonstrating that it was inconsistent with the American ideal of liberty. He also spoke of the wrongs that slavery inflicted on the slaves, the country, and the South.

Due to a legislature dominated by nativists, Massachusetts passed legislation adding two years' probation to the five years necessary to become a citizen. This caused some German-Americans to advocate that they leave both the Democrats and Republicans. Others urged the formation of a German-American political party, but Schurz argued strongly against this, as he felt that their best hope was with the Republicans. His position and stature increased when in May 1859 Lincoln sent a letter to Dr. Theodor Canisius, editor of the *Illinois Staats-Zeitung*, stating his opposition to the nativist legislation of Massachusetts. This served to further galvanize support for Lincoln, as well as for Schurz as a German-American spokesman.

In May 1860 a meeting of the German-American Republicans was called at the *Deutsches Haus* in Chicago and scheduled before the Republican National Convention. The meeting's participants read like a "Who's Who" of German-America. The group passed resolutions against slavery, the Massachusetts Amendment, for a liberal homestead act, for a nonslave state of Kansas, and pledged to support the candidates who had not opposed the 1856 platform and who were not identified with the Massachusetts Amendment.

These resolutions were carefully considered at the convention, as the German-American vote was now viewed as holding the balance in Missouri, Iowa, Minnesota, Illinois, Wisconsin, Indiana, Ohio, Michigan, Maryland, Pennsylvania, New York, New Jersey, and Connecticut. As a result, two planks relating to the Massachusetts Amendment and the

Homestead Act were included in the Republican platform and became known as the "Dutch Planks." This task was effectively accomplished by Schurz. Strengthening the German-American position was the presence of fifty-four German-born delegates at the convention.

The adoption of these planks gave a signal to the Republican Party as to where the votes were. Lincoln also made this crystal clear by his firm opposition to the Massachusetts Amendment in his letter to the *Illinois Staats-Zeitung*, which was widely published in the German-American press. Obviously, the Republicans were going all out for German-Americans in 1860.

It was not known publicly at this time, but in May 1859, or soon after he had written to the *Illinois Staats-Zeitung*, Lincoln entered into a secret agreement with the newspaper whereby he purchased it but allowed Canisius to publish it as long as it remained a Republican paper. This meant that Lincoln was now the secret owner of an influential German-American newspaper. Having thus paved the way by his May 1859 letter, as well as through the support he received from this and other German-American newspapers, Lincoln's image among German-Americans was on the rise. By wooing German-Americans and including German-American issues in the Republican platform, Lincoln's path to the nomination was now clear.

In the election of 1860, German-Americans crisscrossed the country for Lincoln. Schurz wrote that a large part of his job was to speak in German, and that this took him into Wisconsin, Illinois, Ohio, Pennsylvania, New York, and elsewhere. Moreover, his speeches, as well as those of other German-American community leaders, were widely published in the press and printed separately as pamphlets for further distribution.

Altogether Schurz was said to have covered twenty-five thousand miles on the campaign trail. Wherever he went huge crowds met him, and when he traveled down the Ohio River, he was received by audiences of several hundred.

Although the extent of German-American influence in the election has been a question of historical debate for some time, there is no question that German-Americans definitely influenced the election in Lincoln's favor. Carl Wittke notes that the debate on the decisiveness of the German-American vote will continue, but all agree that it was without question important.

Lincoln's regard for Schurz was so high that he had him go through his inaugural address line by line. His own personal secretary was John George Nicolay, born near Landau in the Rhenish Palatinate, another indication of Lincoln's appreciation for German-Americans. After taking office in March 1861, Lincoln demonstrated his gratitude for German-American support by appointing German-Americans to various posts.[7]

Notes

1. For a discussion of German-American community structure, see Frederick C. Luebke, *Bonds of Loyalty: German-Americans and World War I* (Dekalb: Northern Illinois University Press, 1974), pp. 27–51.

2. Carl Wittke as cited in Don Heinrich Tolzmann, *Cincinnati's German Heritage* (Bowie, Md.: Heritage Books, 1994), pt. 3, p. 9.

3. For further information and references on Frankenmuth, see Renate Born, *Michigan German in Frankenmuth: Variation and Change in an East Franconian Dialect* (Columbia, S.C.: Camden House, 1994).

4. Regarding New Ulm, see LaVern J. Rippley, *The German-Bohemians: The Quiet Immigrants* (Northfield, Minn.: St. Olaf College Press for the German-Bohemian Heritage Society, 1995), and Don Heinrich Tolzmann, ed., *The Sioux Uprising in Minnesota, 1862: Jacob Nix's Eyewitness History* (Indianapolis: Max Kade German-American Center, Indiana University-Purdue University & Indiana German Heritage Society, 1994).

5. Regarding the Mexican War, see Don Heinrich Tolzmann, ed., *The German-American Soldier in the Wars of the U.S.: J. G. Rosengarten's History* (Bowie, Md.: Heritage Books, 1996).

6. For discussions of nativism, see Carleton Beals, *Brass-Knuckle Crusade: The Great Know-Nothing Conspiracy, 1820–1860* (New York: Hastings House, 1960), and John Higham, *Strangers in the Land: Patterns of American Nativism, 1860–1925* (New York: Atheneum, 1972).

7. This section on the 1860 election is drawn from Carl F. Wittke, *The German-Language Press in America* (Lexington: University of Kentucky Press, 1957), pp. 149–54.

The Civil War
and Beyond

The Civil War

German-Americans represented a remarkably high percentage of the enlisted forces during the Civil War, well exceeding what would have been expected given their percentage of the population. There were several reasons for this rather substantial involvement. First, German-Americans were generally opposed to slavery in a so-called democratic republic. Second, they opposed the concept of secession. Third, military service offered an opportunity to those without the means of a livelihood, especially when bounties were offered for service. Fourth, many immigrants enlisted as a means to facilitate the acquisition of U.S. citizenship. Finally, coming as it did after a nativist-filled decade, the Civil War offered the opportunity for German-Americans to demonstrate their patriotism. Finally, the 1860 election, with the direct appeals made to German-Americans, paved the way for Lincoln's call to arms.

Of the 2.5 million soldiers in the service of the Union, roughly one-third, or more than 750,000, were German-Americans. German-Americans did not constitute one-third of the nation's population, so they clearly surpassed what was expected of them. Of the German-American troops, the German-born alone amounted to 216,000, and the rest were of German descent. Altogether there were five hundred German-born officers in the Union forces. German-Americans were, hence, the largest single ethnic group in the service of the Union, which remains at best a little-known fact.

Wilhelm Kaufmann's history of the German-Americans in the Civil War lists a total of seventy-seven German regiments consisting of the German-born. Kaufmann examined Pennsylvania's rolls and estimated that there were twenty-one regiments consisting of Pennsylvania Germans. Considering that there were seventy-seven German regiments and that German-American regiments in Pennsylvania alone amounted to twenty-one, it would be safe to estimate the total number of regiments consisting of German-born and those of German descent at least in the neighborhood of one hundred regiments. However, it should be noted that German-born and those of German descent were not limited to these regiments, as they were distributed throughout all regiments in the Union forces.[1] There are twenty-nine monuments and markers dedicated to German-American regiments, batteries, and commanders at the Gettysburg National Military Park.

As Germans settled in the South, there were also a number of German-American units in the Confederacy. The number of Germans in the South numbered about 75,000, of whom 15,000 were in New Orleans. Louisiana Germans formed a regiment, as well as eleven companies, and Georgia had some units also. The Virginia Germans placed several units into the field, including the Stonewall Brigade, the German Rifle Company, the Marion Rifles, and the German Home Guard. In Charleston, J. A. Wagener became commander of the first German regiment raised there. Also the Secretary of the Treasury under Jefferson Davis was Karl Gustav Memminger of Charleston.

However, as Germans were concentrated in the German Belt in the North, the relative numbers of German-Americans in the Confederate service were small. Also, not all of them were supportive of the Southern cause. For example, in 1861 a referendum in Gillespie County, Texas, was nearly unanimously against secession, and in 1862 Confederate troops were dispatched there and battled German-American irregular troops at the Battle of Nueces. Even in the North there were voices of protest against the war and were even some antidraft riots, for example, in Ozaukee and Washington Counties.[2]

Military Action

German-American support for the Union was significant from the start. Among the many German regiments, the Eleventh Corps contained two divisions that were entirely German and were under command of Stein-wehr and Schurz. These divisions played a heroic part in the battles of Chancellorsville and Lookout Mountain. General Lee had ordered the famous attack on the center of the Union forces known as Pickett's Ridge. Armistead, a brigade commander, leaped onto a stone wall, waved his sword, and shouted, "Give 'em the cold steel, boys!" One hundred Confederates rushed up and planted battle flags on Cemetery Ridge, but the Union soldiers stood their ground. The defense was carried out chiefly by Steinwehr's and Schurz's divisions.

Another engagement in which Germans distinguished themselves was Missionary Ridge. General Meade had commanded the divisions to move forward. They did, and defying the Confederate artillery, they captured the ridge. A considerable proportion of the Union troops consisted of Germans under the command of General August von Willich.

German participation in the Civil War was not only considerable in numbers, but also distinguished in terms of leadership. Some five hundred German-born officers with the rank of major, colonel, or general served in the Union army, and ninety-six of them were killed in action. Of the nine generals of German birth, seven were major-generals. One of these was Franz Sigel, outstanding for his devoted service, although by no means a military genius. Born in Sinsheim, Baden, in 1824, he received his military training at the Karlsruhe Academy and entered the army of the Duke of Baden, where he rose to the rank of chief adjutant in the artillery. Having killed an adversary in a duel and being a man of pronounced liberal views, he left the army and went to Heidelberg to study law.

Together with Friedrich Hecker, he took part in the revolution in Baden. The Prussians defeated the insurrectionists, and Sigel was forced to retreat to Switzerland. Although he lost the battle, he effected the retreat with such skill that there was practically no loss of men or materiel. In fact, his generalship won him such fame that later on in the

Civil War young German-Americans were eager to serve under him. Also, his swift and ardent espousal of the Union cause evoked great enthusiasm among German-Americans.

Leaving Switzerland in 1851, Sigel went first to England and then to the United States. He supported himself in New York by teaching. In 1857 he went to St. Louis, where he taught at the German-American Institute. At that time Missouri was in a crucial position. Its governor, C. F. Jackson, had strong Southern sympathies and tried to swing the state to the Confederate side. A large part of the native population tried to remain neutral, which was impossible. Governor Jackson sent an appeal to the South for armed forces to seize the U.S. arsenal at St. Louis, but it was saved for the Union largely through the efforts of the Germans. When President Lincoln issued a call for volunteers, Franz Sigel organized one of the first regiments in Missouri, the Third Missouri Volunteers.

In 1860 more than half of the population of 160,000 in St. Louis was German and antislavery. Under the leadership of Congressman Blair, the German volunteers and Home Guards captured one thousand secessionists who were about to take possession of the arsenal. The Germans entered the fort and armed four regiments with the available supplies. On the following morning, May 10, 1861, they surrounded and captured Camp Jackson. The governor was forced to flee for his life, and Missouri was saved for the Union. The first real battle occurred at Cole Camp, where the German Home Guards were successful in forcing the rebels to retreat. The next engagement was at Carthage, where General Sigel was in command of the Union forces. He had only 1,100 men against the enemy's 5,000, and the outcome was indecisive.

On July 25 General Fremont arrived in St. Louis to take command. He left Lyon and Sigel in the vicinity of Springfield with rather small forces. The 5,000 volunteers, attacked by the 12,000 rebels, suffered a defeat. Fortunately, McDowell did not follow up his victory, and Missouri was cleared of the Confederates when General Pope took over. Sigel revived his military reputation by the decisive Union victory at Pea Ridge, which kept Missouri within the Union.

Sigel did not distinguish himself again until the second Battle of Bull Run, where he skillfully covered the retreat. On the eve of the Battle of Chancellorsville, he had to withdraw for a while due to ill health. At New

Market, West Virginia, in 1864, he suffered a humiliating defeat, yet he was instrumental in saving Washington when that city was threatened by the Confederate General Jubal Early. Sigel detained him near Harpers Ferry for four days, making it possible for reserves to be rushed to the capital. Unfortunately, the defeat at New Market brought about his removal. Sigel was immensely popular with German-Americans, although his military achievements were not brilliant. His unswerving support of the ideals of democracy, his unquestioned bravery, and his ardent espousal of the Union cause won him an important place in the history of the Civil War.

Curiously enough, the military successes of the "civilian" Schurz were more notable. Some of the Forty-Eighters, however, were jealous of his commission as a brigadier-general, asserting that he was crowding out the professional soldier Sigel, their favorite. However, for everything he undertook, Schurz made careful preparations. His service in the Baden Revolution and his studies of military science in Spain had not been in vain. According to reports of his superiors and fellow officers, he was an able commander. He showed this at the second Battle of Bull Run, where his division fought in the woods before a railroad embankment for eight hours. At Chancellorsville, he demonstrated his knowledge of military tactics by advising against placing the Eleventh Corps in a vulnerable position. Yet in the Battle of Gettysburg, his division bore the brunt of the attack, but he was able to withdraw skillfully to Cemetery Ridge. At the Battle of Missionary Ridge, he was obliged to stand in reserve during the major part of the engagement.

Because of a bitter quarrel with General Hooker over a military action performed by Colonel Hecker, Schurz left the Eleventh Corps to be put in charge of a training station for recruits at Nashville. He was also active in the campaign to reelect Lincoln. As soon as the election was over, he again entered military service. He was serving as chief of staff under Sherman when the surrender came.

Another significant Forty-Eighter was Major General Peter Joseph Osterhaus, who rose to that post from the rank of private. He had considerable military experience in Germany. After receiving his training in a military academy in Berlin, he served in the Schleswig-Holstein War. Next he took part in the revolutionary skirmishes in Baden, which led to his flight to the United States. When the Civil War broke out, he was in St. Louis. Sympathizing with the Union cause, he immediately enlisted in the Second Missouri Regiment. He displayed such tactical knowledge that he was soon made a major. A few months later he rose to colonel and helped to clear Missouri of the rebels. All of the assignments given to him so far were difficult, yet he carried them out with remarkable competence and precision.

At the Battle of Lookout Mountain, Osterhaus distinguished himself again. After throwing a pontoon bridge across the swollen Tennessee River, he attacked the mountain. The Confederate were put to flight, the mountain was captured by the Union forces, and thousands of prisoners were taken. He was promoted to the rank of major-general and joined Sherman in the march to Savannah. Osterhaus took part in thirty-four battles and never met defeat. Even the Confederates were impressed with his ability and courage.

Another notable Forty-Eighter who rose from the rank of private to that of general was August von Willich. He was of an old noble family with a long military history. His father had served in the light cavalry during the Napoleonic Wars. Willich received his training in Potsdam and at the military academy in Berlin. At thirty, he was a captain of the artillery and could look forward to a successful military career. However, his outlook on life changed and remaining a Prussian officer became impossible.

Despite his noble ancestry, he had become imbued with radical ideas. Because of a refusal to accept an assignment to a distant province, he was court-martialed. His judges were lenient; they permitted him to resign. Dropping all his aristocratic privileges, he became a carpenter. His relatives and former associates were outraged when he walked across the parade ground with an ax on his shoulder and a saw in his hand.

When the 1848 revolution broke out, he hastened to Baden and became a leader of the volunteers. The failure of the uprising forced him, like many, to flee to Switzerland and then on to England. Karl Marx ridiculed him as a "spiritual communist," as he was interested in taking on the life of a worker, but his views were more those of an intellectual interested in the rights of workers and not in line with those of Marx.

In 1853 he landed in New York, where he earned his living as a carpenter. He later became the editor of a workers' paper in Cincinnati.

When Lincoln issued his call for volunteers, Willich joined the Ninth Ohio Regiment, an all-German unit from Cincinnati. He immediately became an adjutant and soon entered the West Virginia campaign. In Indiana, at the request of the governor, he organized the Thirty-second Indiana Regiment, an all-German unit, and taught Prussian maneuvers within a month. At first there was much amusement among the troops over his stilted, literary English and Prussian accent. Very soon, however, his performance on the battlefield and his courage in combat gained him the respect and admiration of all his soldiers. He fought with distinction in more than thirty battles, including Shiloh, Perrville, Murfreesboro, Chickamauga, and Missionary Ridge.

At the Battle of Missionary Ridge, he carried out a spectacular feat. Without waiting for orders, he had his nine regiments storm the summit. He was in the throes of combat when a bullet wound incapacitated him and put an end to his active service. Nevertheless, he was made commander of the Cincinnati district and went to Texas in March 1865 with his corps.

Although a stern disciplinarian, Willich was extremely popular with his troops. He was fundamentally democratic: he never asked a soldier to do what he was not ready to do himself. Among his admirers were the non-German officers who served under him. His radical ideas apparently did not interfere in the least with his effectiveness as an officer in the Union army. Demonstrating ability and courage in all engagements, he ended his military career with the rank of major-general. Despite his many years of service in the camp and on the battlefield, he had a fine character and intellectual aspirations. At the age of sixty, he matriculated as a student of philosophy at the University of Berlin.

Another Forty-Eighter, and one who had cooperated with Willich in the Baden revolution, was Friedrich Hecker. At the outbreak of the 1848 revolution, he joined Willich in Baden and played a prominent role there. After coming to America, he settled in Belleville, Illinois. After the Civil War broke out, Hecker and his son volunteered as privates in St. Louis and entered Sigel's Third Missouri Regiment. Later, Hecker was given the command of the Eighty-second Illinois Regiment. At Chancellorsville, he was shot from his saddle, but he was able to resume active service a few months later. He also participated in the Chattanooga campaign and the Battle of Missionary Ridge. On that occasion, he was accused by General Hooker of having failed to carry out an order. Schurz, his superior officer, took his part and vindicated him, yet the quarrel was quite bitter and resulted in Schurz's transfer and Hecker's resignation. After the war, Hecker returned to his farm but remained a chosen leader of the German element for public events and civic affairs.

A colorful figure was Brigadier-General Louis Blenker. He had seen six years of service in Bavaria and had taken part in the 1848 revolution. Like the other leading Forty-Eighters, he fled to Switzerland and then came to America. In 1861 he joined the Union army as colonel of the Eighth New York Regiment, which he had raised. Largely because of his success at the First Battle of Bull Run, he was later given a brigadier's commission. Blenker was fond of pomp and circumstance. Schurz gives an amusing description of his headquarters, noting that his tent was unique in terms of appointments. Not only officers of the army but civilians from afar came to see it, and he was lavish in his hospitality.

A number of German noblemen had come to America to offer their services during the war. They were attracted to Blenker's division and attached themselves to his staff as "additional aides-de-camp." With these nobleman, he formed what amounted to a semicourt complete with titles. Blenker was often heard to give orders by addressing their royal titles. But Blenker proved that a man can be a perfect staff general and a very efficient soldier at the same time. He was a thoroughly brave man, an excellent organizer, and an efficient commander.

Blenker gave a brilliant reception to General McClellan in camp. In November 1861 Blenker organized an elaborate parade in McClellan's honor in Washington. Riding at the head with fifty-six staff officers in gaudy uniforms and seated on splendid steeds, he was followed by two thousand soldiers carrying torches and marching proudly to the music of twelve bands. Even President Lincoln was there to review the procession, which was a sensation. Blenker was extremely popular, but his extravagance caused his downfall. His expenditures reached such proportions that he was obliged to retire.

One of the ablest German officers was Alexander von Schimmelpfennig, who had settled in Philadelphia after his arrival in America. He had fought as an officer in Schleswig-Holstein and in Baden. Well educated and level-headed, he was free of the crusading spirit that possessed so many of the Forty-Eighters. At the outbreak of the Civil War, he joined the Union forces as colonel of the Seventy-fourth Pennsylvania, a German regiment. He distinguished himself at the Battle of Cross Keys and at the Second Battle of Bull Run. It was there that his men drove Stonewall Jackson's troops back. As a reward for his bravery, he was named a brigadier-general.

At Chancellorsville, he fought in Schurz's Eleventh Corps. As a result of poor placement, the Eleventh Corps was driven back by superior forces on a number of occasions. Generals Hook and Howard seized upon these setbacks and tried to make them scapegoats for their own failures. This happened at Gettysburg, where Howard was in general direction of the field. Schimmelpfennig was in command of Schurz's division. The vastly superior foe drove the two divisions back in confusion down the streets of Gettysburg. At this point, Schimmelpfennig was struck by a blow from the butt of a gun and lay unconscious in the road. Upon regaining consciousness, he crawled into a cellar where he hid for two days, thus eluding capture. Later, he fought in the Carolinas, where he was struck down by another foe: malaria. Again he recovered sufficiently to head his troops when Charleston surrendered. Throughout the war, Schimmelpfennig conducted himself like a gentleman and a well-trained Prussian officer. In the Baden revolution, he had been Schurz's superior officer; in the Civil War he occupied the lower rank. Both were close friends, and Schurz, with his typical frankness, generously acknowledged that he had learned much from Schimmelpfennig.

The first German-American to receive the Congressional Medal of Honor was Private William Bensinger, who received the honor on March 25, 1863. No one has ever disputed the veracity of the remark attributed to Robert E. Lee: "Take the Dutch out of the Union army and we could whip the Yankees easily."[3]

German-Americans felt that nativism was at work in the attempts to minimize or criticize their role during and after the Civil War. Such comments are clearly expressed by Constantin Grebner. He wrote, "Germans were defamed in the Civil War, too. American officers' botches were only too gladly laid on Germans under them. Failures marked time after time against German troops, and charged again and again to German officers, could not be rightly thus assigned." He claimed that research clearly demonstrated that such charges were without foundation.

Grebner forcefully states that "German-Americans return again and again to the warrior ranks, to battle on the field of arms and at the ballot box. In both places, it will be admitted, they almost always strike the blow the nation's true friends want struck: the decisive blow." He claims that they do so in spite of the wrongs suffered and the ingratitude they have dealt with because they are idealistic, and "they strive to be on the side of truth and justice, and to stand for freedom and honor."

Grebner proudly declares:

> We shall not keep mum when it comes to getting their contributions recognized. The bravery, endurance, spirit of sacrifice, and daredeviltry of German-American units have been only too frequently [demonstrated] beyond doubt. In those qualities, no other units could equal and few could surpass the German-Americans.

According to Grebner, "The German soldier in America, with every right to be proud, cannot be too proud." He concludes that German-Americans "are always ready to sacrifice life and property for the freedom and honor of this great land."[4]

Authors such as Grebner obviously felt the need to record and evaluate the role German-Americans played in the Civil War, not only because of the nativist rhetoric and charges of the time, but also because they felt that German-American history was not being reflected in the standard works of American history.

German-Americans were concerned about nativist rhetoric, that assigned battle losses to the German-American troops, yet there were grounds for these concerns. For example, when Schurz's division was driven back at Chancellorsville, much of the blame for the loss was placed on what was referred to as the "cowardice" of the Germans, and the nativist press referred to the German-Americans as "the flying Dutchmen." Horace Greeley even went so far as to demand that the German regiments be disbanded. Hence, nativism clearly was a factor in seeking scapegoats for military losses and setbacks.

A second concern, and one which was clearly felt in the postwar era, was that the role German-Americans had played was not reflected in the standard works of American history. Here again, the concern appears to be justified, as even today the works that make any mention of German-American involvement in the Civil War are the exception rather than the rule. As Richard O'Connor has observed:

> For all their varied endeavors and heroic labors, it cannot be said that the German-Americans won a commensurate share of glory. They did not become known as the fighting Germans.

Indeed, most people believed that the darling of the cavalry, General George Custer, was of Anglo-American stock, and the accomplishments of others did not partake of that quality which attracts legends and make headlines.[5]

The Unification of Germany

After having fought for the preservation of the Union, German-American identity and pride received a tremendous boost. In spite of the nativist remarks and undercurrents, the importance of German-Americans politically and militarily had been recognized by the 1860 election, by the numerous appointments made by Lincoln, and by the heroic role German-Americans played in the Civil War. German-Americans now watched with great interest as the Franco-Prussian War of 1870 unfolded, which resulted in the long overdue unification of Germany, an event that had a dramatic impact on German-American identity in the United States.

A united German republic had, indeed, been the goal of many refugees of 1830 and 1848, and the failure to achieve it had been the cause that brought many of them to America. German-Americans watched with interest as the Prussians attained victory after victory and then captured Paris. The German-American press enthusiastically reported on these events, as it now appeared that after centuries of powerlessness and disunity, the many German states would finally achieve unity.

The events in Europe united German-Americans across the country.

Even the Forty-Eighters by and large were won over, hoping that Germany would make republican-style reforms after unification. However, not all of them joined in the jubilation. For example, Karl Heinzen remained intransigent, strongly stating his disapproval in his journal and noting that he felt the Prussian Junkers, the landed aristocracy, would dominate the military and the police. Others questioned whether the ideals of 1848 would be realized in the new Germany. Some papers were critical of what they viewed as the glorification of Bismarck, while one socialist paper remained antiwar. Several workingmen's associations also protested the war. However, these voices were in the minority, as the pride and joy evoked by the unification was overwhelming. Carl Schurz, then a Missouri senator, accused the secretary of war under President Grant of sending surplus war materiel to Europe and in so doing forced a congressional investigation, which contributed to the German-American disappointment with Grant.

The unification of Germany had the greatest affect on the German-Americans during the nineteenth century, as it created a new sense of identity in being German-American, not merely being from a given region or locality in Germany. There was not only unrestrained joy that the Fatherland had been united, but also a feeling that the status of the German heritage had been elevated. Public displays of elation knew no bounds. There were parades and huge mass meetings in New York, Chicago, Cleveland, St. Louis, and elsewhere. Also, large sums of money were collected and sent to the widows and orphans of soldiers who had lost their lives in the successful struggle for German unity.

The "Grays" and the "Greens," as the Thirtyers and the Forty-Eighters were called, had in past years engaged in crusades for improving government, ameliorating social conditions, and were noted for their radical tendencies. These began to subside, and they became more conservative. German-Americans were now mainly concerned with improving their social and economic status and their involvement in local secular and religious institutions and organizations.

The victory celebrations of 1871 held across America were not only celebrations of German unity, but also celebrations of the German heritage in America. The parade held in New York, for example, aimed to display German-American contributions in the arts, sciences, trades, agriculture, and industry, and included veterans of the Civil War. Every trade was represented in the parade. A reception followed at City Hall, with mass meetings and cultural performances. It was at this time in New York that the idea of a national organization for German-Americans first emerged. Oswald Ottendörfer, editor of the *New Yorker Staats-Zeitung*, proposed the creation of a national organization to promote German-American relations, to increase German-American political clout, and to preserve German heritage.

In Milwaukee, celebrants held a peace parade five miles long. In Cleveland, a huge statue of Germania, the goddess of German culture, was mounted on a five-foot-high pedestal and carried on a triumphal arch to the public square. In Chicago, there was a large parade in which German-Americans marched by trade and profession, with, for example, three hundred German-American shoemakers. Busts of Haydn, Beethoven, Schiller, Goethe, and Humboldt signified the German cultural contribution to the world, and various floats depicted periods in German history from the Peasants' War to the War of Liberation from French oppression to unification.

Through all the celebrations of 1871–72, the general underlying theme was to formulate and display contributions German-Americans had made to the United States. In Louisville, where German-Americans had been the victims of nativist mobs in the 1850s, the German-American press referred to the unification celebration as a symbolic day of honor, which made good for the nativism of the past. A Columbus paper reported that the unification had raised the status of German-Americans 50 percent, and expressed the hope that instead of being called "Dutchmen," they would now be called "German-Americans."

Many poems by German-American authors praised the final unification of Germany and extending greetings from America. Francis Lieber was particularly enthusiastic as he wrote to Germany, wishing peace and prosperity, but not without Alsace and a considerable portion of Lorraine. In 1872 a huge peace parade was held in Philadelphia as part of the end of the Franco-Prussian War and the resulting unification of Germany, and the German Seventy-fifth Pennsylvania Infantry Regiment participated, marching with its Civil War battle flag. Similar celebrations were held elsewhere and included German-American Civil War veterans, Thirtyers, Forty-Eighters, church groups, and others.

German-Americans praised unification but also the fact that decades of peace followed, as well as the phenomenal progress Germany made in the areas of business, industry, trade, the arts and sciences, social legislation, and international prestige. They basked in this reflected glory, which they appreciated after the hard years of the nativist 1850s and the trying years of the Civil War. Germany was now a respected nation, and products bearing the stamp "Made in Germany" translated into quality of the highest order. German-Americans felt they had proved and demonstrated their patriotism and their contributions to America. It had been an uphill struggle, but by 1871 they felt they had earned the right to celebrate that they were now an integral and important part of the nation.[6]

Immigration

The Civil War was followed by half a century of peace, progress, and prosperity. The United States made such tremendous strides that it soon outdistanced the Old World in almost every field of human endeavor. With admiration, amazement, and envy, Europe gazed upon the young giant flexing his muscles. There seemed to be no limit to the growth of America. America was by now well known as *das Land der unbregrenzten Möglichkeiten*, or the land of unlimited possibilities.

The significant factors that brought about this astounding development included the mighty railroad systems spanning the continent, the mechanization of agriculture, the vast growth of industry, the huge waves of immigration, the expansion of world trade, and the organization of workers. In all of these areas, Germans played a vital role. The impact of several million Germans, concentrated in urban as well as in rural areas, contributed greatly to the growth and development of the country in the late nineteenth century.

German immigration in the eighteenth century had numbered in the thousands, but in the nineteenth century it went into the millions, surpassing any other immigrant group.

Germany	5,009,280
Ireland	3,871,253
Great Britain	3,024,222
Scandinavia	1,439,060
Canada	1,049,939
Italy	1,040,457
Austria-Hungary	1,027,195
Russia & Poland	926,902
All other	1,726,913
TOTAL	19,115,221

German immigration by decades, as reported by the U.S. Census, was as follows:

1821–1830	6,761
1831–1840	152,454
1841–1850	434,626
1851–1860	951,667
1861–1870	787,468
1871–1880	718,182
1881–1890	1,452,970
1891–1900	505,152
TOTAL	5,009,280

German immigration after the Civil War continued at an annual rate of 130,000. This was due to the wars of German unification, military conscription, as well as various related pressures on the civilian population, all of which contributed to the desire to immigrate. Moreover, the image of America continued to be quite positive.

Another factor, of course, was the continuation of chain migration, as by now so many Germans had come to America that there were numerous communities with direct connections to places in the Old Country. Immigrants wrote letters and maintained contacts with their friends and families, thus causing more people to come.

Particularly alluring was the Homestead Act of 1862, which granted up to 160 acres without charge so long as the settler lived on the land for five years. Immigrants were also attracted to the rapidly expanding industries of the United States, and immigrants represented a greatly needed labor force. The ups and downs of the economy on both sides of the Atlantic were reflected in the ebb and flow of the immigration—when the economy was doing poorly in Europe, immigration would rise, and when it was doing poorly in America, it would subside. For example, after the financial depression of 1873 in the United States, German immigration fell to 50,000 in 1874.

Another factor contributing to immigration was the organized activities, especially by various states, railroads, and industries, to attract and encourage German immigration. For example, the Northern Pacific Railroad was represented by an agent at the Vienna Exposition in 1873, where the agricultural and industrial products of Minnesota were also displayed. The aim was to attract German immigrants to Minnesota and the upper northwest.

In 1882 the Northern Pacific Railroad alone maintained 124 agents in Europe and distributed well over 600,000 pieces of literature to attract immigrants to settle on its lands. By 1883 about fifteen thousand German Mennonites from Russia had been attracted to settle along the Santa Fe railroad by Carl B. Schmidt, who had served as the commissioner of immigration for several railroads. Shipping companies also specialized in immigration traffic across the country. They too established offices and hired agents in Europe and published massive quantities of German-language pamphlets and brochures promoting America and various states.

Bismarck, North Dakota, was so named to encourage German immigration there, and it was even hoped that Chancellor Bismarck would attend the dedication ceremonies in North Dakota, but he declined. Some states established immigration commissions to attract Germans to settle within their borders. For example, in 1867 Minnesota established a board of immigration to attract immigrants. In many cases, such state boards sent agents to Germany complete with maps and other publications in German designed to entice prospective immigrants. Some of these propaganda items were issued in editions of tens of thousands. Among the states that had such commissions were Minnesota, Iowa, Wisconsin, Nebraska, Kansas, Missouri, Oregon, Montana, and the Dakota Territory.

Congressman Richard Bartholdt (1855–1932), author of the Steuben statue legislation. (From George H. Carter, *Proceedings Upon the Unveiling of the Statue of Baron von Steuben,* 1913?)

John Jacob Astor (1763–1848), fur trader and financier.

Albert Einstein (1879–1955), physicist and winner of the 1921 Nobel Prize for physics.

Unless otherwise specified, all photos are courtesy of the German Information Center.

Dr. Carl Johann Hexamer (1862–1921), president of the National German-American Alliance. (From George H. Carter, *Proceedings Upon the Unveiling of the Statue of Baron von Steuben*, 1913?)

Thomas Mann (1875–1955), novelist and 1929 Nobel Prize winner for literature.

John Augustus Roebling (1806–1869), engineer and industrialist. He suggested and made the preliminary plans for the Brooklyn Bridge; his son Washington Augustus succeeded his father as chief engineer in the bridge's construction.

Carl Schurz (1829–1906), army officer, politician, and reformer.

Henry Engelhard Steinway (1797–1871), piano manufacturer.

Friedrich Wilhelm von Steuben (1730–1794), served as general under George Washington in the Revolutionary War.

An Amish buggy in Pennsylvania-German country.

Levi Strauss (1829?–1902), manufacturer best known for denim trousers called "blue jeans."

The earliest American illustration of a Christmas tree, from H. Bokum, *The Stranger's Gift*, 1836. (Courtesy of German House Research)

It should also be noted that various German-American religious and secular organizations aimed to attract immigrants belonging to their particular background. For example, German Catholics established a branch of the *St. Raphaelsverein zum Schutze katholischer deutscher Auswanderer*, a society for the protection and aid of German Catholic immigrants. Among the Protestants, it was especially German Lutherans who actively engaged in establishing immigration societies to bring immigrants to their communities. Among the secular societies, there were many *Deutsche Gesellschaften*, or German societies, in large urban areas that provided not only promotional literature, but also assistance to recently arrived immigrants.

Another cause for immigration was political, as some groups were dissatisfied with the politics of Bismarck. In 1873 he had begun his anti-clerical policy known as the *Kulturkampf*, which led to the passage of a number of anti-Catholic laws designed to limit the influence of the Catholic Church. This anticlerical policy came to an end by the end of the the 1880s, yet it had caused a number of Catholics, especially from Bavaria, to emigrate.

Bismarck's antisocialist legislation of 1878 also caused Germans to immigrate to the United States. It would remain in place until the new kaiser, Wilhelm II, assumed the throne. He opposed the legislation, thus causing Bismarck to resign, and the legislation was allowed to lapse in 1891. However, this legislation had caused a number of people to emigrate, especially Social Democrats, including Louis Viereck, a former member of the Reichstag, who came to America in 1896.

All of these factors contributed to the great upsurge of immigration in 1880, when the German influx was three times as large as it had been in 1879. In 1881 it was close to 250,000, a record amount for one ethnic group that has never been surpassed. Nevertheless, large numbers did continue to come after 1885. After 1892 the numbers begin to decline, as Germany's *Wirtschaftswunder* began to take hold, resulting in a flourishing and prosperous German economy.

The population growth in Germany together with the traditional form of land distribution led to immigration to America as well. In the southwestern regions of Germany, the custom was to divide the land equally among the sons, which in time resulted in smaller and smaller farms. Those unable to support themselves on small subsistence farms would often emigrate. In the northeastern regions, the right of inheritance was different. There the land was not equally divided, but rather inherited by the eldest son. In such cases, the younger sons would often decide to seek their fortunes in the New World, especially because of the added attraction of the Homestead Act. The alternative was to obtain work as a farmhand in Germany, or migrate to an urban area in search of an industrial job. Those who remained in the country could obtain land, but the cost of renting or buying was high. Farming was undergoing a transformation by becoming increasingly mechanized, so the number of jobs in the agricultural sector was diminished.

German immigration up into the early nineteenth century had mainly come from the southwestern German-speaking regions of Europe, but it slowly declined as immigration began to reach eastward across the German states. In the 1830s immigration was predominantly from the southwest, but by the 1840s it had dropped to 34 percent, and by the 1860s it had fallen to 14 percent. However, from 1870 to 1910 the portion from the southwest averaged at roughly 25 percent of total German immigration. Also, in this period, German-speaking immigrants from other areas such as Austro-Hungary, Switzerland, and Russia were included in the totals.

Who were the immigrants? German immigration drew from all regions, classes, and faiths. All levels and aspects of German society were represented, such as small farmers from the southwest and farm laborers and servants from the north and northeast. Also, families, rather than individuals tended to predominate. These were not the poorest of their hometown communities, but instead those who had enough to invest in immigration, and did not want to lose what they had. Industrial workers seeking better wages and lifestyle came after the Civil War as well. Catholics and Social Democrats came as a result of Bismarck's policies in the latter decades of the century. However, most came for economic reasons and because of the opportunities for advancement in America.

As noted earlier, German immigration came not only from the German states which became the German Empire in 1871, but also from other areas. In the colonial era, about thirty-thousand came from Switzerland, so that the period of greatest Swiss immigration took place from the mid-nineteenth century to the First World War. The Swiss settled in Pennsylvania, Maryland, Virginia, and the Carolinas, and then began to follow the frontier westward after the revolution. By 1900 many Swiss were concentrated in New York, Ohio, Indiana, Wisconsin, Oregon, and California. Of the Swiss immigrants, about 70 percent consisted of German-speakers, and they, of course, became an integral part of German-American communities.

In the nineteenth century, about 60 percent of the Swiss immigrants settled in rural areas, founding communities linked by chain migration to Switzerland. Among their many settlements, New Glarus, Wisconsin, became especially well known. Other noteworthy Swiss settlements were Tell City, Indiana; Bernstadt, Kentucky; Helvetica, West Virginia; and Grutli, Tennessee. Forty percent settled in urban areas, especially New York, Chicago, Cincinnati, and Milwaukee. Among their major occupations were carpenter, tanner, bartender, machinist, plumber, butcher, cook, and mason.[7]

Immigration was already underway from Austro-Hungary, as before the Civil War a number of well-known Thirtyers and Forty-Eighters had come to America. However, the majority came after the Civil War for economic reasons, and many settled in urban areas, which would attract further waves of immigration after the two world wars.[8]

By the late nineteenth century there were more than three thousand German colonies in Russia with a total population of 1.5 million. Migration to the United States on a large scale began in the 1870s and peaked by the First World War. These migrations were prompted by the attempted Russification of German schools and the plan to enforce compulsory military service. The two major groups coming to America were the Volga and the Black Sea Germans. Of the Volga Germans, 65 percent were Evangelical and 35 percent Catholic, while of the Black Sea Germans, 45 percent were Evangelical, 35 percent Catholic, 20 percent Methodist, and a few Baptist.

Most of the Russian Germans settled in the western plain states, especially in Dakotas, Nebraska, Kansas, and Colorado. They founded settlements in America with German names, such as Kassel, New Danzig, and Leipzig. Most of them were farmers, although they eventually entered other professions. Perhaps the most well-known Russian-German-American was the band leader and television star Lawrence Welk, who was born in Strasburg, North Dakota, of Russian-German parents.[9]

The impact of German immigrants on the nation's economy in the nineteenth century was substantial. By 1870 37 percent of Germans had skilled jobs such as butchers, cabinet makers, cigar makers, distillers, machinists, and tailors. German-born women were less likely than other women to join the labor force, but were especially concentrated in the service sectors, such as bakers, domestic help, hotel keepers, janitors, laundry workers, peddlers, nurses, saloon keepers, and tailors. When women were involved in the labor force, the chances were high that they would be working in a business belonging to family or friends. About one-fourth of the German-born immigrants were occupied in agriculture, and they became the predominant ethnic group in that area.

Richard O'Connor comments on the important role German-Americans played in "the part of the machinery that ran the country, an integral and essential part of finance capitalism, of heavy industry, of education and scientific research and agriculture." He notes that "it was possible to imagine that if all persons of German descent were suddenly removed from the United States, the machinery would just as suddenly break down." He also notes how highly desired German immigrants were in the late nineteenth century, citing a survey of the Immigration Restriction League. In response to a questionnaire it sent out to governors of various states, fourteen governors replied that they would prefer more Germans; twelve favored Scandinavians; seven, English or Scotch; six, Irish or other English-speaking people; three, French; two, Swiss; one, Dutch or Belgian.[10]

The German-American Press

Not surprisingly, the German-American press thrived and flourished in the post–Civil War era. By 1872 80 percent of the non-English press was German, and the German-American press was generally considered an influential force socially, politically, and culturally. There were major newspapers in urban areas such as New York, Philadelphia, Chicago, Cincinnati, St. Louis, and Milwaukee, and their editorial stance and endorsements carried great weight and were actively sought.

The German-American press, of course, flourished in the states of the German Belt. In 1880 there were eighty-nine German-American newspapers in Ohio and thirty-two in Indiana. Many of them had substantial circulations, which in some cases dwarfed that of the English-language press. The *Milwaukee Germania*, for example, had a circulation of 92,000 in 1882. Newspapers were found not only in the German Belt states, but everywhere there were German-American settlements. By 1883 there were 488 German-American publications, including eighty-two dailies. By 1900 there was a total of 613 German-American publications. The average subscription rate at that time for a daily newspaper varied from $6.00 to $16.00 annually.

By 1900 German-American newspapers were consolidating at an accelerated pace, resulting in the emergence of huge newspaper chains. Part of this was a national phenomenon, occurring with the English-language press as well, but it also reflected some declining readership due to the language shift of American-born German-Americans, who were now turning to English-language publications. By 1914 German-American publications numbered 537, including fifty-three dailies.

The German-American press was well edited and included some of the foremost journalists in America. Of course, many of the Thirtyers and Forty-Eighters gravitated to the press and deeply influenced and dominated it for the better part of the nineteenth century. The religious press was equally well edited, and its staff included individuals of great learning and scholarship, such as the German Methodist editor Wilhelm Nast.

The German-American book trade flourished as well. By 1860 there were more than two hundred retail dealers or publishers that specialized in German books from coast to coast, and by 1888 there were five hundred German-American bookstores in 208 cities in thirty-two states.

The German-American book trade specialized in reprints, news translations, and original works. Due to the fact that the United States had not signed the international copyright agreement, German-American publishers were free to publish or pirate anything they desired to print, including recent works from abroad. Hence, publishers in America could publish old as well as the most recent works in the German states without any concern about copyright, much to the consternation of European publishers. They also published numerous works in German translation from a wide variety of fields, including history, literature, theology, and philosophy. Providing a special outlet for German-American authors were the many presses that issued original works. Of particular importance were works of German-American literature and history. The latter, especially those dealing with state and local history and biography, were often well done and of exceptional value. The major centers of the book trade were the same as those of the German-American press, and book publishers were often also newspaper publishers. The major book publishers were located in New York, Cincinnati, Milwaukee, and St. Louis.

Not only did the German-American press and book trade thrive in the post–Civil War era, but German-American cultural life and institutions in general flourished as well, and it is in this period that the cultural, musical, and cultural life of America began to experience a great influx from German cultural heritage, a survey of which is the topic of a later chapter.[11]

Notes

1. See Wilhelm Kaufmann, *Die Deutschen im amerikanischen Bürgkrieg: Sezessionskrieg 1861–1865* (Munich: R. Oldenbourg, 1911).

2. LaVern J. Rippley, *The German-Americans* (Boston: Twayne, 1976), p. 9.

3. Insight into the experience of German-Americans in the Civil War can be found in various journals and collections of letters, such as: Henry A. Kircher, *A German in the Yankee Fatherland: The Civil War Letters* . . . ; Bernhard Domschke, *Twenty Months in Captivity: Memoirs of a Union Officer in Confederate Prisons*; Constantin Grebner, *We Were the Ninth: A History of the Ninth Regiment, Ohio Volunteer Infantry* . . . ; and Minetta Altgelt Goyne, *Lone Star and Double Eagle: Civil War Letters of a German-Texan Family*. Most of the source materials pertaining to the role of the German-Americans in the Civil War are in German, and the standard bibliographies, listed at the end of this work, should be consulted for these references.

4. Constantin Grebner, *We Were the Ninth: A History of the Ninth Regiment, Ohio Volunteer Infantry, April 17, 1861, to June 7, 1864* (Kent, Ohio: Kent State University Press, 1987), p. 187.

5. Richard O'Connor, *The German-Americans: An Informal History* (Boston: Little, Brown, 1968), p. 154.

6. See Hans Trefousse, "German-American Immigrants and the Newly Founded Reich," in Frank Trommler and Joseph McVeigh, eds., *America and the Germans: An Assessment of a Three-Hundred-Year History* (Philadelphia: University of Pennsylvania Press, 1985), vol. 1, pp. 160–75.

7. Regarding Swiss immigration, see Leo Schelbert, "On Becoming an Emigrant: A Structural View of Eighteenth- and Nineteenth-Century Swiss Data," *Perspectives in American History* 7 (1973): 441–95.

8. With regard to the Austrian immigration, see Ernest Wilder Spaulding, *The Quiet Invaders: The Story of the Austrian Impact Upon America* (Vienna: Österreichischer Budnesverlag, 1968).

9. For references to works dealing with Russian-Germans, see Michael M. Miller, *Researching the Germans from Russia; Annotated Bibliography of the Germans from Russia Heritage Collection at the North Dakota Institute for Regional Studies, North Dakota State University: With a Listing of the Library Materials at the Germans from Russia Heritage Society* (Fargo: North Dakota State University, Institute for Regional Studies, 1987).

10. O'Connor, *The German-Americans*, p. 366.

11. The German-American press is a veritable gold mine of information on state and local history. See the bibliography at the end of this work for references to relevant bibliographies.

Before the First
World War

Lifestyle

As Germans settled in America, they came to perceive and contrast their lifestyle with that of the Yankees, or Anglo-Americans. They noted that there were a number of differences and that they clearly intended to maintain their own family values and lifestyle. Although a very large and diverse group, German-Americans displayed an ethnocultural lifestyle based on their values, which was uniquely German-American and came to distinguish them as an ethnic group.

German-Americans criticized what they felt was the egalitarian nature of the non-German family, especially in terms of the relationship between children and parents. This they contrasted with the traditional German family, which was clearly patriarchal. They also criticized what they considered to be the social-reform-crusade tendency of Anglo women, and the deference accorded them. It appeared that these women had little to do but cultivate their extensive leisure time or spend it in trying to reform society in terms of Anglo values. By way of contrast, in the German family, the father was the head of the household, and children and other members of the family were not on an equal footing with the father. In American families, women and children did not seem to work together as a family unit, but in German families, children and women worked together with men for the benefit of the family as a whole, whether on the farm or in business and industry.

German-American families tended to be larger than non-German families. Often families in rural areas would have four or more children, all of whom would work together as they grew up. Second, German-Americans tended to marry within their own immediate community and then reside in the region in which they had been raised. It was common that several generations of a family lived together, or in close proximity. Home ownership was high among them as well. Third, children tended to begin to work at an early age and were assigned tasks they could perform on behalf of the family. Also, German-Americans were not necessarily opposed to child labor within the framework of the family and the local community. Fourth, women were more often to be found on the home front in German-American families, as they worked as an integral part of a family business, shop, or farm. Here the family was viewed as an economic unit, and each member had an important role to fulfill in contributing to the financial success of the family. Social activities for women were usually found in the family and in women's groups of the German societies or churches, as contrasted with Anglo women, who formed women's organizations, which, it appeared, were devoted to Anglo reform crusade movements, such as prohibition. German-Americans believed that such groups wanted to impose their values and lifestyle on others, and they were opposed to such proselytism.

In terms of work and business life, German-Americans tended to view work as the basis for economic support for the family, rather than as a means to obtain individual financial wealth. German-Americans were noted for their thriftiness and tended to save their earnings, rather than use it for speculative investment, which they considered reckless. They took pride in their work and believed in doing a job right and carefully. Work's value was in this, rather than in the salary attached to a particular job. They did not approve of speculative business practices and condemned what they viewed as almost an admiration for shady business deals. They did not believe in credit and preferred to pay in cash, if at all possible, but held that credit responsibilities, when made, should be honored.

In terms of politics, German-Americans felt that the candidate and the platform of the party were very important, more so than merely the party, and they disapproved of what they viewed as the tendency to vote according to a particular party. Also, it appeared to them that there was a great deal of corruption in government, and they demanded clean and honest government. Many politicians, it seemed to them, were in politics for personal financial gain, rather than for public service. Also, German-Americans felt that government's main objective should be to guarantee and protect personal liberty. They asked for nothing more and nothing less than this. Law and order should be maintained, but government should not intrude into the life of the individual. This meant, for example, that any attempt to legislate or control morality, or what a person should think, drink, or eat, would be regarded as an invasion of personal liberty.

German-Americans placed a high value on their cultural heritage. Authors such as Goethe, Schiller, and others were, in their view, on an equal footing with English authors and should be equally stressed, as they felt English literature was overemphasized. Church groups maintained their own school system and did not place much stock in public education. Secular Germans, however, did support public institutions, but felt that they should offer German instruction, as well as physical education. Often it seemed that realizing such ideas required a struggle, since nativists would be in opposition. However, German-Americans maintained that they paid taxes, and they insisted on their rights.

In the area of leisure, German-Americans noted that Anglos had a different way of spending their free time. German-Americans felt that non-Germans devoted their leisure time to social reform crusade efforts, which aimed at defining and legislating community values in terms of their lifestyle and which resulted in an invasion of German-American personal liberty. Why did these people spend their leisure time trying to reform society and legislate how others should spend their free time? For example, German-Americans opposed laws against alcohol consumption and Sabbath-breaking. From their perspective, such laws reflected the Puritan Sunday. German-Americans preferred a Continental Sunday, where they would spend an afternoon with the entire family at picnics and festivities. Sunday was the one day of the week they could enjoy a glass of wine or beer with friends and family, perhaps in a local park or at a neighborhood beer garden.[1]

Americanization

By the late nineteenth century, German-Americans had begun to redefine American society to incorporate their notions and concepts of diversity and cultural pluralism, for they rejected the idea of the melting pot as unfeasable and unrealistic. German-Americans maintained that there were patterns of life other than those of the dominant Anglo-Saxon majority, and that each ethnic group had its own vision of happiness. They argued that they could be Americans and still have a unique ethnic identity, as citizenship and ethnicity are two separate entities. Being an American related to one's citizenship in the United States, and the other half of the equation pertained to one's ethnic heritage.

German-American leaders also communicated the message of cultural synthesis, synthesizing the best of the German heritage with the best elements found in the New World. It also implied not only learning, but also mastering English and becoming fully involved in American society. German-Americans were, hence, creating and defining what it means to be American, defining it in terms of what became known as cultural pluralism. They saw and respected cultural diversity and viewed this as completely compatible with U.S. citizenship.

Kathleen Neils Conzen has written that German-Americans "had invented an ethnicity for themselves and, in attempting to win acceptance for the legitimate role of such a group identity, had helped also to create ethnicity itself as a category within American society." This "invention" was something they sought as a means to explain and justify the validity of being and remaining German-American. "To distance themselves from the implications of the melting pot, they groped their way towards justifications for the perpetuation of ethnic differences. Some took the complete step to a principled defense of permanent ethnic diversity."[2] German-Americans were the forerunners for the now-prevalent view that America is a society consisting of various ethnic and racial groups, each contributing unique aspects to American culture.

An ethnic group is defined as an element of the population that is related by common ties of origin and culture. It has a shared history and a shared sense of peoplehood. Ethnicity relates to ancestral origins as something inherited and shared. German-Americans clearly saw themselves in these terms. They were now a major element of the population, and regardless of their diversity shared ties of origin and historical background.

Americanization meant full involvement in an English-speaking society as an American citizen, as well as preservation of the German heritage. Carl Schurz advised:

> As American citizens, we must become Americanized; that is absolutely necessary. I have always been in favor of a sensible Americanization, but this need not mean a complete abandonment of all that is German. It means that we should adopt the best traits of American character and join them to the best traits of German character.[3]

Schurz's description reflected the ways German-Americans viewed themselves after the Civil War. They were German in terms of ethnicity and Americans in terms of citizenship, and both were viewed as separate entities connected by a hyphen. Ethnic Americanization meant that German-Americans were no longer Germans; they were now something unique. They were citizens of the New World, and they had in varying degrees blended and joined together German and American ways, resulting in a uniquely German-American condition. By so doing, they had also redefined the nature of American society as multicultural and diverse. Of course, the degree of cultural maintenance varied from individual to individual, from family to family, and from group to group, but the important point was that one could define oneself as a German-American, or as an American with any other ethnic heritage.

In a work dealing with immigrant letters entitled *America Experienced* (1996), Leo Schelbert discusses ethnic Americanization and describes it as acculturative. An immigrant in this sense genuinely tries to adapt to the New World. Family life tends to reflect the ancestral homeland, but business and work reflect the ways of the new environment. The acculturative immigrant is, therefore, the hyphenated immigrant par excellence. This kind of adaptation to the New World allows for a nearly limitless variety of syntheses of Old and New World ways, which then provide the basis and framework for ethnic heritage and identity for future generations.

In an important work, *Making Their Own America* (1990), Kathleen Neils Conzen has contributed greatly to our understanding of how immigrants adapted to the New World.[4] They did not abandon their heritage, but rather transplanted and adapted it to America by means of the process called "localization." This implies that immigrants established not only themselves, but also their heritage. They did so by means of the family and all the social, cultural, religious, and political institutions they had established. In the case of German immigrants, the heritage of any given community became the German-American heritage established there. German immigrants transplanted their heritage but adapted and evolved it as necessary with the ways of the New World, so a unique synthesis of German-American culture and heritage arose. A key to understanding the German-American experience and identity, as well as that of America in general, can be found in understanding this process. America is a multicultural nation, and this is reflected in communities across the country established by immigrants. German-American heritage viewed in this context becomes an ongoing, living, and evolving heritage, first established by immigrants, and which has continued to grow and develop and evolve as the established way of life of German-Americans and their communities.

The problems encountered during the Know-Nothing era of the 1850s were caused by those who did not share this view, but who viewed Americanism in terms of Anglo conformity. Although German-Americans pioneered the concept of cultural pluralism, it was not until the twentieth century that it finally become accepted as describing the realities of American life. It would take the tragedy of World War I for American society to realize that it was not a melting pot, but a nation consisting of many ethnic elements.

Politics

Some Forty-Eighter newspapers in 1863 proposed a special convention to voice their discontent with what they felt was the conservative manner in which the Civil War was being conducted. The meeting was held in Cleveland, and it proposed the unconditional surrender of the South, a radical program of reconstruction, and the complete equality of blacks. Some urged support for Fremont to replace Lincoln as the Republican candidate. The support for Fremont grew in 1864, and he actually obtained the support of some German-American newspapers, but their influence was limited as they were considered radical publications. In 1864 delegates met in Cleveland and nominated Fremont, and they called for a constitutional amendment against slavery, the confiscation and redistribution of property, and for many other kinds of social and political reforms. Since the Fremonters were viewed as radicals, the German-American press overwhelmingly supported Lincoln for reelection. The radicals were ridiculed, especially as they favored the formation of a separate German-American political party. Many even pointed out that this would divide the Republican vote and ensure a Democratic victory. However, when Fremont withdrew, the radicals threw their support behind Lincoln, so in the end support for Lincoln was almost unanimous.

When Johnson succeeded Lincoln, most German-American newspapers felt that he was too mild and conservative. At the same time, Democrats, aiming to win back German-American votes, campaigned that the Republicans had temperance tendencies. In 1868 Schurz campaigned for Grant and again contributed to another Republican victory at the polls.

In 1869 Schurz was elected to Congress as senator from Missouri. Perhaps no clearer statement of his political philosophy could be found than in the one given after his election:

> And now I was a member of the highest legislative body of the greatest Republic: Would I ever be able to repay my debt of gratitude to this country and justify all the honors heaped upon me? To achieve this, my sense of duty could not be set high enough. Deep in my heart I solemnly swore at least to make a sincere effort to fulfill my obligation to observe the principle of "salus populi suprema lex"; never to resort to base flattery when dealing with powerful individuals or with the masses; to stand alone, when necessary, in defense of my ideas of truth and justice; and to let no personal sacrifice stand in the way of my devotion to the Republic.[5]

This is indicates Schurz's stature and character and the kind of dedication he brought to public service.

Grant's mediocre appointments caused such resentment that the president asked Congress in 1871 to provide that certain offices had to be filled with qualified candidates who would be selected by means of examinations. This was exactly the kind of system used in Europe and had been something that Schurz and others were advocating. Such a law was passed in 1871 but was not actually enforced.

In 1872 there was disgust with the corruption of the Grant administration, and liberal Republicans and Democrats joined together as the Liberal Republican movement, which held a convention in Cincinnati. The meeting consisted of reformers, disgruntled politicians, and high-minded civic activists and was presided over by Schurz. Most German-Americans favored Charles Francis Adams, rather than Greeley, who was considered a temperance man. Also, he was associated with eccentric causes, such as vegetarianism, and had made nativist remarks about the German regiments during the Civil War. Schurz and Hecker tried to galvanize support for the reform ticket, but many German-Americans stayed at home or remained true to the Republicans. Hence, the German-American vote was split by the reformers in 1872. Although many were for reform, they could not accept Greeley. Grant also lost German-Americans because of his sale of surplus arms to France during the Franco-Prussian War. After the election, the Republicans struck back at Schurz in the Republican press for having gone against Grant.

After the election, the Republicans came under continued attack by the Democrats that the Republican Party was filled with prohibitionists, nativists, and Puritans. Therefore, the German-American Republican press raised the question of how German-Americans could ever feel at home in the Democratic Party, which was dominated by Irish Catholics. By 1876 the German-American press was divided, and this was reflected by some supporting Tilden and others supporting Hayes for the presidency. Tilden, a Democrat, had a solid record as a reformer against the Boss Tweed ring of New York, but Hayes had a good record as governor of Ohio, a state with a large German-American population.

The major event of this campaign was that Schurz returned to the Republican fold, and some criticized him, saying the whole reform movement had been a waste of time and energy. Schurz defended his position, stating that Hayes was a reformer and sound on the question of money. After the election, German-Americans took great pride in the appointment of Schurz as the new Secretary of the Interior in the Hayes administration, as this was the first appointment of a German-born citizen to the presidential cabinet.

Schurz aimed to make his department a "demonstration station" for civil service. Indeed, Schurz rendered some of his greatest service to the nation during this period, as he attempted to put principle into practice. He made all of his appointments completely without regard to the political allegiance of the appointees, as he was concerned only with their qualifications. In 1880 when Hayes refused to run for another term, General James A. Garfield of Ohio, a dark horse at the Republican convention, was nominated, with Chester A. Arthur as the vice presidential candidate. After four months, Garfield was assassinated, and Arthur assumed office. He worked for civil service reform, which is an indication of the impact that Schurz had. Unfortunately, however, a Democratic majority of the House blocked the reform efforts.

In 1884 Schurz announced that he would bolt the Republicans if a suitable candidate was not found. The Democrats were encouraged to go with a Reform candidate in the hopes of winning back German-American voters. The Republican nomination of James Blaine proved to be unacceptable, so Schurz jumped ship and endorsed Grover Cleveland for president. Schurz's national influence could readily be seen in the 1884 election. In July he organized a national conference of anti-Blaine Republicans, which drew more than four hundred. They pronounced Blaine an unfit leader unworthy of respect and confidence, and they declared unanimous support for Cleveland.

Schurz went on the campaign trail, speaking to German-Americans across the country. In September he spoke to a group of six thousand in Milwaukee, and was traveling 100 to 150 miles daily. In Ohio alone he delivered twenty-two speeches in German and English. In New York, he addressed a huge German-American gathering, stating that German-Americans would not support any dishonest candidate. Clearly, Schurz again helped mobilize the German-American vote. Schurz's opposition to Blaine was based on an examination of his record, and he felt that electing a person with a questionable record would be a fatal blow to the moral foundations of the republic.

His support was reflected in the Cleveland administration's work on behalf of civil service reform. A total of twelve thousand positions were added to the classified list, but the Democrats pressed him for political appointments, and Cleveland relented to their demands, thus costing him the support of Schurz, German-Americans, and other reformers.

In 1888 most German-Americans went with the Republican candidate, Benjamin Harrison, because of their disappointment with Cleveland, but after the election Harrison ignored all civil service laws and filled offices with party hacks and political appointments, which obviously alienated many who had supported him. By 1892 German-Americans were disgusted with the Republicans, so when Cleveland was nominated to run against Harrison, he attracted their attention. German-Americans were willing to take a second look at Cleveland, as he had long been popular with German-American voters. In 1881 they had supported him in his election as mayor of Buffalo, New York, and again in 1882, when he successfully ran for governor of New York. So, in 1892 German-Americans strongly supported Cleveland.

Schurz was serving as a national spokesman, but he did not focus exclusively on German-American interests, but on national interests for the good of the country. His example and his words were without question influential. In 1896 Schurz rejected the Democratic candidate, William Jennings Bryan, because of his position on silver (the free and unlimited coinage of both gold and silver), whereas the Republican candidate, McKinley, advocated the gold standard.

In 1900 Schurz switched horses again, supporting Bryan and opposing McKinley on the issue of imperialism, as Schurz opposed imperial expansion. This time German-Americans did not heed his call but stuck with the Republicans. Also, knowing Schurz's influence, the Republicans engaged leading German-American Republicans to campaign on behalf of the Republican ticket. For example, Congressman Bartholdt of Missouri spoke throughout the Midwest, thus blunting Schurz's influence. Nor did German-Americans follow Schurz's lead in 1904, when he supported the Democratic candidate, Alton Parker, against Theodore Roosevelt, who was immensely popular. Schurz's leadership had by 1900 clearly run its course, but from the 1850s to the turn of the century, he served as a highly principled and effective leader and spokesman for German-Americans.

The years after the Civil War have been called some of the most drab in American political history because of the lack of quality leadership, the absence of clearly defined programs by the political parties, and their failure to bring about political reform. In this veritable wasteland, Schurz towers as a politician not only of integrity, but also of principle. Following his lead, most German-Americans voted Republican, but some demonstrated their independence and voted Democrat when they felt the other candidate was unacceptable. And in some cases, some migrated back to the Democrats. Schurz not only established the principle as an independent Republican, he also established a pattern and a record of adhering to this principle for more than four decades. Perhaps his greatest political legacy was assuring that German-Americans could not be taken for granted when it came to election time.[6]

This voting trend would hold true until the First World War, which motivated German-Americans against Wilson's Democratic Party. In 1908 Taft was elected and received a good bit of support from German-Americans, as he came from Cincinnati. For German-Americans perhaps the most remarkable aspect was that this was the first presidential election since the 1850s without the influence of Schurz, who had passed away in 1906. In 1912 the Republicans split their vote with the Progressives, so that Roosevelt and Taft both competed with one another, resulting in the victory of Woodrow Wilson.

After Schurz's death, political leadership fell to German-Americans in Congress, including Richard Bartholdt of Missouri, Henry Vollmer of Iowa, Charles Otto Loebeck of Nebraska; Charles Lieb of Indiana; Edward Voigt of Wisconsin; and Julius Kahn of California. Although these were men of integrity and principle, none of them measured up to the stature of Schurz, which placed German-Americans in a difficult situation during the First World War. Albert B. Faust wrote:

> At no time did the German element in this country feel more painfully the want of political leadership than in the period of the great war beginning with 1914. There was a lack of sufficient representation in

both houses of Congress, the newspapers of the country were with the exception of the German-language press in the hands of the Allies' friends. To be sure there were men and women of true courage, not lacking in ability, whose voices rang loud, but they were always in the minority and were loudly shouted down. There was no national figure to advocate their cause, they had no spokesman, no great leader.[7]

Such was the state of German-American political affairs on the eve of the First World War. Since there was no great elected official of Schurz's stature, it fell to the civic association leadership of the National German-American Alliance to try to communicate German-American interests, and after Schurz's death the Alliance increasingly assumed the principal role as the national spokesman. It was supported in this function by the editorials in the German-American press.

At the state and local levels, the political situation in the post–Civil War era demonstrated that German-Americans were successful in attaining election and achieving their agenda. Ethnocultural issues were at the forefront more at the state and local levels than nationally. German-Americans often gained considerable influence in elections for city councils, for mayor, for school boards, and for state and county offices. At the state and local level, issues pertaining to nativism, such as prohibition and bilingual education, were at the forefront.

In 1890, for example, German-Americans united in Wisconsin and Illinois in opposing the dominance of the Republicans when they advocated regulating parochial schools. By 1892 German-Americans in Illinois elected a German-born governor, John Peter Altgeld. His career collapsed, however, after he pardoned the three surviving anarchists who had been convicted after the Haymarket Riot and after he interceded on behalf of the striking workers at the Pullman works. The important accomplishment was that a German-born politician had attained the highest office at the state level.

The Haymarket Riot of 1886 took place in a period of great labor agitation and numerous strikes. The movement for an eight-hour workday had gained tremendous support. Several hundred thousand workers were on strike in various parts of the country. In Chicago, a center of this movement, about eighty thousand workers were involved. German-Americans played a leading role. In Chicago, George Schilling organized the Eight Hour Association, and German-American anarchists emerged as the most articulate spokesmen. When a striker was killed in a fracas at the McCormick Harvesting Machine Company, German-American anarchists called a mass meeting. They printed a German-English handbill and distributed twenty thousand in Chicago. It stated: "Attention Workingmen! Mass Meeting! . . . Achtung, Arbeiter! Grosse Massen-Versammlung!" It advertised: "Good speakers will be present to denounce the latest atrocious act of the police, the shooting of our fellow working-men. . . ."

After the speeches were over and the crowd dispersed, the police attacked those remaining, when suddenly from an adjoining alley, an unidentified person threw a bomb. This caused the death of one policeman and the wounding of many more, triggering an indiscriminate shooting. Seven policeman were killed and sixty more were wounded, while among the workers, four were killed and fifty wounded.

As a result of the riot, public indignation resulted in hysteria directed against the anarchists, and of the ten indicted, eight were German-American, including August Spies, editor of the notable newspaper *Die Arbeiter-Zeitung*, published in Chicago. Of these seven were condemned to death, and four were executed. Public demand for their execution was great and was reflected in the press as well. After a farcical trial at which no proof was offered that the indicted had thrown the bomb, they were found guilty. In November 1887 four of the indicted were hanged.

The trial was considered a travesty of justice. At the trial, Spies said that the death sentence was an attempt to stamp out the labor movement, and at the gallows he proclaimed: "There will be a time when our silence will be more powerful than the voices you hear today." After his election as governor of Illinois in 1892, John P. Altgeld had promised he would correct the trial injustice, and he did by pardoning three of the anarchists on the grounds that "the judge was biased, the jury packed, the defendants not proved guilty," and the trial was illegal.

His eighteen-thousand-word decision condemned the original sentences, but was strongly criticized in the press, in the pulpit, and was a controversy for some time. Also, in the following Pullman Strike, Altgeld strongly opposed the use of federal troops, who crushed the strike and caused the loss of lives. In 1896 when he ran for a second term, he was defeated.

The Haymarket Riot and related events adversely affected German-American affairs in several ways. First, the anarchists were mainly German-American, and some nativists claimed that the evils of socialism and anarchism were brought to the United States by German immigrants and being fomented mainly by German-Americans. Second, this was further complicated, in the view of some nativists, by the fact that the imprisoned individuals were pardoned by a German-American governor.

This nativist reaction translated into support for control and restriction of immigration. As early as 1883, Henry George, author of *Progress and Poverty*, expressed alarm that "human garbage" was coming to America from abroad. Gradually, and especially after the Haymarket Riot, large numbers of social workers, economists, and church leaders began to advocate the restriction of immigration, as did organized labor, which felt threatened by cheap labor.

Nativism flourished again for the first time since the 1850s, as a national hysteria raged against what was considered the refuse of Europe. In 1887, the American Protective League, a secret society, was formed to resist all that it considered threatening to America. And in the 1890s the Immigration Restriction League arose to advocate control and restriction of immigration to the United States.

Such tendencies proved how important it was that the Alliance intervened on behalf of its constituency. It successfully opposed state referendums for prohibition, as happened in Ohio, for example. In state elections, the state branches of the Alliance could usually count on the support of German-American newspapers, as well as that of the local affiliates across the state.

Hence, German-Americans were attaining a relative degree of success in local and regional political arenas. Among the issues they addressed were nativist-driven, such as prohibition and opposition to bilingual education. The power and influence of German-American voters was widely recognized, and German-American festivities and events were usually filled with politicians proclaiming the virtues of German-Americans and praising their enormous contributions to the building of the community and the nation. In 1901 Hugo Muensterberg commented that "for the last three months of every presidential campaign the German voter is praised up and down as a model citizen."[8]

International Relations

After the unification of Germany, U.S.-German relations were cordial, and Bismarck himself had a considerable liking for America. Several issues arose relating to commercial and colonial affairs, however. First, in 1879 Bismarck established a protective tariff that adversely affected lower-priced agricultural goods, especially meat products. Germany claimed this was due to inadequate meat inspection in the United States, and the problem was not settled until 1890, when the United States adopted a comprehensive meat inspection regulatory program. In the 1890s American tariff legislation was harmful to German sugar interests, which led to German restrictions on the import of American meat and livestock. However, in general, trade between Germany and America increased, rather than decreased, in spite of the tariffs.

Germany became united only in 1871 and was viewed as an upstart, somewhat of a "new kid on the block" in the sense of a political unit or nation. In the past there had been no Germany, and now there was, and this proved difficult for some of the great powers. As a newcomer, Germany lacked skill and experience in international diplomacy. Germany by the mid-1890s was little more than two decades old, whereas Great Britain had been a major power since the destruction of the Spanish Armada in the sixteenth century. Germany faced powers ill disposed to the new central European power. France longed for revenge for their defeat in the Franco-Prussian War and had territorial designs on the German-speaking provinces of Alsace-Lorraine. Russia had its eyes on the regions of the Austro-Hungarian Empire. Britain viewed Germany as a threat to its century-old position as the major maritime power.

In issue after issue, British diplomats took positions opposite to those of Germany. Concerns about the German fleet caused Britain to expand its own fleet. Also, by the turn of the century, German goods had acquired an international reputation for quality. Not only that, but German goods of all kind undersold British wares in Europe, as well as in South and North America. The British, hence, viewed Germany as an upstart that did not know its place in the hierarchy of nations. They also saw Germany advancing industrially, while British industrial plants became increasingly obsolete.

Congressman Bartholdt later observed that the objective of British foreign policy was "to discredit everything German in American eyes and to create the impression that German sentiment was distinctly hostile to America." He also noted that an English newspaper had stated, "If Germany were destroyed overnight, every Englishman would find himself richer the next morning. And with the combined power of the new Entente how comparatively easy a task it appeared to be to crush the presumptuous German upstart and thus to rid England forever of an uncomfortable rival." Moreover, he felt that England was very careful "not to divulge its hidden purpose and merely preached Anglo-American solidarity, at the same time employing every means, fair and foul, to poison the American mind against the Huns." He noted that "what British propaganda painted as German lust for world conquest was in truth nothing more but a desire for peaceful commercial growth, a desideratum equally shared by all great nations."[9]

By the 1890s both France and Russia had come to an understanding that emerged as the Franco-Russian detente, and Britain began courting the United States with the goal of an Anglo-American detente. Given this Machiavellian kind of situation, Germany required a gifted and experienced statesman such as Bismarck. Unfortunately, he was relieved from his post by the new young kaiser, Wilhelm II, and none of his successors were his equal.

Wilhelm II set a new course in the post-Bismarck era to establish a *Weltpolitik*, or world policy, which included a navy and colonies. Chancellor Bernhard von Bülow explained: "We do not desire to put anyone else in the shade, but we want our place in the sun."[10] Unfortunately, there were those who could not come to terms with the fact that Germany was now a major power. When they spoke of the balance of power in Europe, they implied a divided Germany. Europe was used to a Germany being divided into numerous states, which had been the status quo since the Thirty Years' War ended in 1648. They resented that suddenly Germany was wanting to establish a navy and colonies, although these were common among the great powers of Europe. In Germany, many were impressed with England and had the "me-too" feeling that what was good for England should also be good for Germany.

In 1898 the first naval expansion bill was passed in the Reichstag, and Germany commenced on the expansion of its "baby fleet," the seventh largest in the world. As a newcomer in terms of being a great power, Germany was certainly justified in establishing itself, but for some, especially Britain, each new expansion or innovation of the German fleet was cause for concern. Hence, friction developed with Britain regarding naval armaments, as well as German colonies. Fears led to the rise of anti-German sentiment in Britain, which in turn fed rumor-mongering about Germany in the press, much of which claimed that Germany was a threat to the British Empire and navy.

Exacerbating the situation was the formation of an ultranationalist organization in Germany in 1891, the Pan-German League. The league had two goals: the union of all Germans in the world into one huge pan-German confederation connected to Germany, and the attainment of the status of world power for Germany. This organization was, of course, separate from the government of Germany, but its ultranationalist propaganda worked against Germany abroad, feeding anti-German sentiment and propaganda in Britain and the United States. In later years, during the First World War, its publications would be scrutinized as proof that Germany was the land of the "Huns."

During the Spanish-American War, when the United States took possession of the Philippines, other warships were there from Britain, France, Japan, and Germany, but the German contingent was the largest, and it was rumored that it was there to pick up any remaining possessions not claimed by the United States. This multinational rivalry became known as the Manila Bay Affair and led to statements by Admiral George Dewey and others that in their view the German navy was cause for concern. Although other navies were present, it was only the British who made it clear that they were wholeheartedly for the American war effort, as they cleverly aimed to cultivate their relations with the United States. In 1899 the United States, Britain, and Germany were drawn together to establish a tripartite agreement on the Samoan Islands. At that time, America was concerned not about German colonial expansion in Africa, but about expansion in the Pacific. Also, there was concern about possible German colonial expansion in Latin America and rumors of a German naval station in the Caribbean.

Much of the concerns was based on hearsay and rumor, but relations were not facilitated by the fact that the American Secretary of State, John Hay, had been the U.S. ambassador to Great Britain and was as ardently pro-English as he was anti-German. This attitude was of concern for German-Americans. Hugo Muensterberg wrote in 1901 that it was not surprising that German-Americans "dislike every approach to England, because they feel instinctively that an Anglo-American union reinforces the feeling that the Americans are an Anglo-Saxon nation in which other Teutonic elements are strangers." German-Americans protested against this possibility in mass demonstrations during the Spanish-American War, when they maintained, as Muensterberg notes, that America "is not a nation of Englishmen" but a multicultural, English-speaking country.[11] One of the major protest demonstrations was held in Chicago in March 1899, where it was stated that the prevalent anti-German sentiment and the idea of an Anglo-American detente should be opposed with all possible means. It was also recommended that there be a national organization among German-Americans to address these issues.

In 1900 the Boxer Rebellion in China was harshly put down by the great powers. However, it was the German military's actions that were condemned, since the kaiser had stated: "Give no quarter, spare nobody, take no prisoners. . . . Be as terrible as Atilla's Huns." His remarks, obviously designed to frighten the opposing forces, created the worst of all possible images and would return with a vengeance during World War I in the form of anti-German propaganda.[12]

After the Boxer Rebellion, the next item on the international agenda marked by Anglo-German tensions was the Boer War. In South Africa, the British had aimed for some time to bring the Dutch under their control, especially after the discovery of gold and the development of the diamond industry. In 1895 they had conducted the "Jameson Raid" into Boer territory, which was defeated by the Boers. The kaiser sent his famous "Kruger Telegram," so named as it was sent to Paul Kruger, president of the Transvaal. His telegram congratulated the Boer, and had the effect of encouraging Boer resistance, which culminated in the British declaration of war against the two Boer republics in 1899. Western opinion in general was with the Boers, who were seen as the underdogs. Not surprisingly, the British won by 1900, but it took them eighteen more months to fight a tough guerrilla war against the Boers. During this war the British introduced a new phenomenon to warfare: internment camps. Here they kept Boers interned for the duration of the war.

German-Americans overwhelmingly supported the Boers in what they viewed as a fight for independence against the British oppressors. On March 1, 1900, a mass meeting was held in Cincinnati in support of the Boers. Heinrich A. Rattermann spoke on "The U.S. and the Boer War in South Africa." He compared the Boer struggle to the American Revolution, warning, "Beware of perfidious Albion!" He pointed out that Britain, with a population of thirty million, was fighting 300,000 Boers and that the latter were outnumbered one hundred to one. He also criticized the McKinley administration for being imperialistically inclined and for its failure to recognize the struggle of the Boers as a struggle for liberty and freedom. In 1901 Schurz wrote a letter condemning the Boer War, describing it as "the evil deed with which the British government is at present defying the judgment of mankind."[13]

In 1902 there were unfounded reports that Germany had pressured Denmark not to sell the Virgin Islands, but rumors about German colonial intentions and her navy were rampant, especially in Britain. These were forwarded through diplomatic channels to the United States. In 1902–1903, Britain and Germany and Italy blockaded Venezuelan ports due to debts owed to them. However, it was mainly the German bombardment that was singled out for condemnation. Rumors were also circulated that the Panama Canal was threatened.

To improve relations, the kaiser sent his brother, Prince Heinrich, to America for a visit and promised a gift of a statue of Frederick the Great for Washington, D.C. President Roosevelt even remarked that the Manila Bay Affair had caused some animosity, and this would take time to subside. However, Prince Heinrich traveled widely across the country, meeting great crowds wherever he went, such as 45,000 in Cincinnati, Ohio. Relations improved in 1904–1905, as Germany supported Roosevelt's mediation efforts during the Russo-Japanese War. However, at the 1906 Algeria Conference to solve the Franco-German crisis over Morocco, Roosevelt appeared to favor France, which was not appreciated in Germany.

Hence, in the early 1900s, there appeared to be a growing Anglo-American rapprochement and U.S.-German estrangement. Germany for its part hoped that German-Americans would act as a counterweight to the Anglo-American detente. It also placed emphasis on the alleged friendship between the kaiser and Roosevelt. In 1908 the latter wrote to the kaiser that he attributed the growing feeling of goodwill between Germany and America to the kaiser. And his successor, Taft, was friendly to Germany as well, so that the German ambassador to the United States could report that from 1909 on, relations were quite good.

Although diplomatic relations had fortunately smoothed out, the public discourse dealing with Germany in the press was still at the level of rumor and innuendo, tending to be pro-England and anti-Germany. For example, in 1909 Lewis Einstein called for Anglo-American collaboration against the domination of Europe by any one single power. Herbert Croly in that same year published a book labeling Germany the major menace to international stability. In 1912 Homer Lee's book, *The Day of the Saxon*, predicted war between the Anglo-Americans and Germany, and in 1913 Roland G. Usher's *Pan-Germanism* claimed that Germany was seeking world domination. Admiral Dewey's autobiography, published that year, again raised the question of the German fleet at Manila Bay. Much of these books was nothing more than yellow journalism and was marked by sensationalism characteristic of propaganda.

Unfortunately, adding fuel to the flames were several works published by German authors. In 1911 Friedrich von Bernhardi published *Germany and the Next War*, which immediately was seized upon as Germany's blueprint for military action. The book also mentioned German-Americans, stating that they and the Irish-Americans constituted a force to be reckoned with. In 1913 Crown Prince Wilhelm wrote a foreword for a book, *Germany in Arms*, which stated that the sword would remain the deciding factor in world affairs, as it had since the beginning of time, and that it was the only factor assuring Germany its place in the sun. Although there was truth to what he said, the remarks of the Crown Prince were better left unsaid, as they gave credence to books such as Bernhardi's. Of course, these remarks lent ammunition to the propaganda writers of pulp literature.[14]

A number of German-American scholars attempted to counteract what they regarded as a negative image of Germany and German culture. Kuno Francke, a professor of German at Harvard, began with a series of works dealing with German literature and culture, but he increasingly came to deal with the image of Germany and German-Americans. In 1898 he published *Glimpses of German Culture* to provide an introduction to German heritage, and he followed this with *German Ideals of Today and Other Essays on German Culture* in 1907. In 1913–14 he edited an impressive multivolume collection, *The German Classics of the Nineteenth and Twentieth Centuries*. In 1915 he dealt specifically with German-American identity in *A German-American's Confession of Faith*, followed in 1916 by *The German Spirit*.

Hugo Muensterberg, a professor of psychology at Harvard, also published a number of works to promote a greater understanding of Germany and German-Americans. In 1909 he published *The Eternal Values*, which discussed the basic values of life, and he followed this in 1913 with *American Patriotism*, which aimed to explain and define what this concept meant to German-Americans. In several other works, he focused on the interest in peace and noninvolvement in the European war, including *The War and America* (1914), *The Peace and America* (1915), and *Tomorrow: Letters to a Friend in Germany* (1916).

Especially bad for German-American relations was the election of Woodrow Wilson in 1912. His few remarks about Germany had all been critical, and he had been decidedly pro-English, as were most of his advisers. For example, Colonel House, who visited Europe in 1914, ranked Germany clearly behind England in terms of preference to an American administration.

In the first few years of the Wilson administration a number of foreign policy characteristics began to take shape. In 1912 Congress passed the Tolls Act, which required non-American ships passing through the Panama Canal to pay more than American vessels. Britain protested this, and Wilson pressured Congress to repeal the act in 1914, which created the impression he had done so on behalf of Britain.

The Wilson administration's foreign policy in the Caribbean and Central America was clearly expansionistic. Beginning in 1916 Wilson intervened in Santo Domingo, Nicaragua, Haiti, and Mexico. The only real interest in the region was the Panama Canal, but other factors now played a role. As U.S. investments grew in the area, the canal received increased importance, as did business interests. Hence, foreign policy to the area came to be known as "dollar diplomacy."

The Wilson administration's anti-German attitude found expression in the rationalization of its intervention in the Caribbean and Central America. Foreign policy in this respect could best be described as "protective imperialism," which meant that imperialism was justified by asserting that the region was in need of protection. But protection from whom? Wilson justified military intervention by claiming that the region was threatened by Germany. However, Germany not only did not pose any threat to the hemisphere, but was not even interested in the region. Moreover, Germany went out of its way to avoid any possible friction with the United States. Indeed, its relations with the Wilson administration have been described as timid and deferential. Hence, the imperialism of the Wilson administration must be described exactly for what it was, namely, imperialism based on military conquest. However, such naked aggression was in need of rationalization, and what better avenue of justification than to claim that the region was in need of protection from Germany.

Another aspect of Wilson's foreign policy could best be described as "missionary diplomacy," which referred to the similarity of his views with those of nineteenth-century Anglo-American missionaries. Wilson's outlook was characterized by a holier-than-thou attitude and by an almost religious belief that his version of the gospel of government should be evangelized to the world.

Given this perspective on foreign affairs, together with Wilson's missionary diplomacy, the likelihood was that if faced with a conflict, the Wilson administration would be more favorably inclined to England, rather than to Germany. When war finally broke out in Europe, Wilson may have said his administration was neutral, but it became quite clear in the first few months of the war on whose side his sympathies were.

The Spanish-American War

After the Civil War the United States played a greater role in international affairs, and by 1900 it had become an imperial power, with colonies scattered around the world. By that time it had annexed the Philippines, Hawaii, Guam, and Puerto Rico. Many authors argued in the 1880s and 1890s that there should be an expansion overseas, especially after the closing of the frontier in 1893. Josiah Strong published *Our Country* in 1895, which preached Anglo-Saxon superiority and the right of extending civilization over "backward" nations. Alfred T. Mahan published *The Influence of Sea Power Upon History* (1895), glorifying a large navy and preaching manifest destiny over the "lesser" peoples of the world. His works became influential throughout the 1890s, and congressmen such as Albert J. Beveridge and Henry Cabot Lodge advanced the belief in the imperialistic mission of the United States. This was supported in the popular press, especially the *New York World* and the *New York Journal*, which made use of sensationalism, atrocity stories, and propaganda to heighten interest and increase circulation.

There were many opposed to the clamoring for war, known as jingoism. Anti-imperialists included Democrats and Republicans and many leading Americans, ranging from writer Mark Twain, industrialist Andrew Carnegie, philosopher William James, social worker Jane Addams, to labor leader Samuel Gompers. They were especially disturbed by the situation in the Philippines, where the people were as opposed to Spanish as to American rule. After three years of guerrilla warfare, which was more costly than the war with Spain, the Filipinos were crushed. During the conflict, Britain had supported the United States and advanced the position that if the United States did not take the Philippines, then Germany would. Clearly, the government in London aimed to curry favor with the United States, as well as inculcate a position against Germany. Hence, some German-Americans felt that the United States had taken the Philippines due to British scare tactics regarding Germany.

Among German-Americans there was now a general mistrust of Britain. German-Americans protested anything that smacked of an Anglo-American alliance and opposed McKinley's policy of annexing the Philippines. In St. Louis, a German-American newspaper called the administration's policy one of imperialism, jingoism, and militarism. Mass meetings were held against any kind of Anglo-American get-together.

Early on, there was sentiment for intervention in Cuba, but Schurz had done his utmost to turn public opinion against such intentions, and he was not alone, as other German-Americans, especially Forty-Eighters, opposed imperialism. After Congress declared war, Schurz stated that "the reckless passions and ambitions of unruly spirits have acquired a sway which bodes ill to the country." He also warned that the American people should heed George Washington's farewell address, and not become entangled in European affairs. Moreover, he opposed the militant imperialism of Theodore Roosevelt, whom he described as having an exceptionally bellicose temperament and whom he considered "dangerously deficient in that patient prudence which is necessary for the peaceable conduct of international relations."[15]

Schurz actively spoke against imperialism and served as vice president of the Anti-Imperialist League. He stated, "History shows that military glory is the most unwholesome food that democracies can feed upon." For the 1900 election, as noted earlier, Schurz spoke out against imperialism and called on voters to repudiate the Republicans as a means of protest. However, the Republicans called German-American congressmen into action to campaign against Schurz, thus dividing the German-American vote. However, as a nationally recognized German-American spokesman, Schurz had again demonstrated his commitment to his principles. He also defended Germany with regard to the question of the Philippines and stated that any attempt to arouse anti-German feelings should be condemned "by every patriotic citizen as peculiarly wicked and abominable." Such statements were provoked by the assertion that the United States must take the Philippines, or else Germany would.[16]

The question of German-American involvement in the Spanish-American War was first raised due to some anti-German remarks made by General Arthur MacArthur, military governor of the Philippines, in 1900–1901. It is important to place his remarks in historical context for the foregoing survey of international relations. He stated that, in his view, a war with Germany was likely in the future and that the Pan-German movement was of such interest to German-Americans that few had chosen to enlist for service during the Spanish-American War. Here MacArthur appears to have succumbed to some of the sentiments and propaganda of the time. More important for German-Americans, the ugly spirit of nativism reared its head, as it had in the Civil War, when defeats and losses were blamed on the German regiments. German-American veterans, resenting the insult, immediately took exception to MacArthur's remarks.

On a motion of the United German Societies of Indianapolis, the German-American National Alliance decided to have the question investigated, and the results were published in the journal *German-American Annals* in 1904. The report was completed by F. König, department commander of the Spanish-American War Veterans. He compiled lists of German-Americans in regiments from Pennsylvania and calculated that roughly 25 percent of these units were German-American. He also established that the crews on several ships were also of the same percentage. German-American naval officers in the U.S. Marine Corps were Majors Lauchheimer and Waller, Captains Meyer and Marix, and Lieutenant Schwalbe. Retired officers placed on the active list were Rear-Admiral Buehler; Commanders Chetkey, Fickbohm, and Hanns; Chief Gunner Sommers; Captains Kindelberger, Schenk, and Hoehling; Colonel Ritter; Lieutenants Ritter and Haggermann; Lieutenant-Commander Eckstein; and Lieutenants Kafer and Kaiser. Long lists of those who served in the war were also provided. König then lists naval officers, including eleven lieutenant-commanders, four ensigns, six commanders, four captains, and four rear-admirals. The latter consisted of Winfield Schley, Louis Kempff, Norman von Heldreich Farghar, and Albert Kautz.[17]

The spark leading to the Spanish-American War was the sinking of the U.S.S. *Maine*, a battleship at the port of Havanna, which caused the death of 260 men, including twenty-one German-Americans. Among the well-known German-Americans who served in the war was Theodor Schwan, who commanded the army that marched against Mayaguez on the west coast of Puerto Rico and fought a bloody battle against the Spanish at Harmigueros. In the Philippines, he would also be in charge of the expeditions in several provinces. General George M. Sternberg served as the commander for the entire medical corps, while John Walter Klaus served as brigadier-general on the staff of General Miles.

Admiral Winfield S. Schley was undoubtedly the best-known German-American in the war. His family came to Maryland before the American Revolution, and he commanded the U.S. fleet at Santiago, Cuba, when the Spanish admiral Cervera tried to break through the American blockade, which led to the destruction of the Spanish fleet and concluded the war, thus ending four centuries of Spanish rule over Cuba.

König's report laid the question of the role of German-American involvement to rest, but a more important point was that internationally negative sentiments were emerging about Germany's place in the world as a colonial power, and this was now being linked to and used as the rationale for anti-German-American sentiments and remarks, which even questioned the patriotism of this segment of the population. The broader concern, therefore, was that the latent and recurrent theme of nativism was brought forth by international tensions. Thus far, such attempts at discrimination and slander had been successfully addressed by the German-American National Alliance.

Seeking a Place in History

If Germany was seeking a place in the sun, and having a tough time of it, so too were German-Americans having an equally tough time in seeking their place on the pages of American historical writing. Until the 1920s, American history was mainly the province of Anglo-American scholars, who largely ignored the role played by the various ethnic groups making up American society. Because of this blatant deficiency in American historiography, German-American pioneer historians in the nineteenth century took up the task of recording and writing German-American history.

These pioneer historians were not full-time academics employed by a university or college. They were, rather, private scholars with amateur status who pursued their research aside from their professions as journalists, politicians, or businessmen. However, they deserve credit for uncovering and preserving valuable primary source materials. It is important to note that they began to write in the mid-nineteenth century, i.e., the nativist period, which found expression in the Know-Nothing movement. The pioneer historians aimed to rectify the absence of references to German-Americans in works written by Anglo-American historians. They also aimed to awaken pride in German-American history and a sense of togetherness in the face of nativism. They saw the ethnic group as a permanent factor in American life, rather than a transient phenomenon confined to the immigrant generation.

The first work of this kind was published in Cincinnati in 1847, *Geschichte und Zustände der Deutschen in Amerika*, by Franz von Loeher. He wrote that the history of German-Americans was a relatively unknown field and that Anglo-Americans provided only a few references to them in their works. He painted a picture of a materialistic and intolerant America that would be enlightened by the German presence. He tried to demonstrate the value of the German-Americans and to awaken ethnic awareness. He also set standards by basing his work on primary German-language sources, and as the first history of the German-American element, his book established a basic framework, or outline, of German-American history that has generally been followed to the present.

Another such early history was *Deutsche Chronik in der Geschichte des Ohio-Thales und seiner Hauptstadt Cincinnati ins Besondere*, published in 1864 by Emil Klauprecht, a Cincinnati German journalist. As the title indicates, it is an account arranged in chronological order, which provides an invaluable collection of facts, details, stories, anecdotes, biographical sketches, correspondence, newspaper articles, and statistics about German pioneers which would otherwise have been lost.

This pioneer period in German-American historical writing receives its name from the well-known society *Der Deutsche Pionier-Verein von Cincinnati*, which published the major nineteenth-century historical journal, *Der Deutsche Pionier*, from 1869 to 1887. The volumes of highest quality (1874–85) were edited by the century's most prolific German-American historian and author, Heinrich A. Rattermann. He aimed to demonstrate that German-Americans had played an important and honorable role in American history.

In order to demonstrate this, he sought out primary source materials and spent months delving in to the archives and libraries of various states. He also claimed that by means of publications on the German element future generations would be informed on past contributions. Indeed, many of his period recognized that their basic task was to collect and preserve information for future generations, and he even stated that his task in the field of history was that of searching, collecting, and investigating the sources of the German-American past.

The pioneer period ran from the mid-nineteenth to the latter decades of the nineteenth century. At that time a filiopietistic period commenced, which lasted until the First World War. This approach was characterized by an overemphasis on the outstanding contributions made by the famous and well known in German-American history. Here again, we see the reaction of German-American historians to the exclusion of their role from standard American history. Filiopietists now saw in German-American achievements an argument for the retention of their own identity, and they viewed history as the means to preserve and further ethnic group pride and solidarity. Also, in this period, the American-born began to write and publish works in English in an attempt to reach beyond the German-American element so that the role of German-Americans would be appreciated and evaluated.

The major work of this period is also a standard work in the field, *The German Element in the United States* (1909, rev. ed., 1927) by Albert B. Faust. However, this was not merely a work praising German-Americans, it was the product of a professional scholar, a Germanist at Cornell University. In his generation the professionalization of the field and the growth of interest in German-American studies on the part of non-German-Americans took shape.

An important representative of this trend was Marion Dexter Learned, a Yankee who had studied at Johns Hopkins and in 1889 commenced work on the study of Pennsylvania German dialects. After joining the German department at the University of Pennsylvania, he became editor of *German-American Annals*, an excellent journal published by the German-American Historical Society. Albert Faust, it should be noted, was a student of Learned's. Another well-known scholar was Julius Goebel, chair of the German department at the University of Illinois-Urbana. A graduate of the universities of Leipzig and Tübingen, he edited the journal of the German-American Historical Society of Illinois, *Deutsch-Amerikanische Geschichtsblätter*, which dealt not only with Illinois German history, but with German-American studies in general.

All of these early scholars were professors of German at American universities who perceived German-American studies as a field in need of research in academia. However, they all maintained ties with the German-American community and, in the cases of Learned and Goebel, edited journals subscribed to and supported by German-Americans.

There was strong interest among German-Americans in their history. Their identity had been strengthened by their involvement in the Civil War, with the formation of all-German regiments and the emergence of articulate ethnic leaders, such as Carl Schurz. This identity was further enhanced as a result of the 1871 unification of Germany, which was widely celebrated. However, the major factor contributing to historical interests was the celebration of the German-American Bicentennial in 1883, which marked the 200th anniversary of the founding of Germantown, Pennsylvania, the first permanent German settlement in America. The main celebration was held in Philadelphia, but similar ones took place across the country.

After the 1883 Bicentennial, many historical societies were formed: the Society for the History of the Germans in Maryland (1886), the Pennsylvania German Society (1891), and the German-American Historical Society (1901), for example. Many of these societies sponsored journals that provided the avenue of publication for some of the early academic scholars in the field, and the German-American Historical Society, under Learned's direction, commenced a series of monographs entitled *Americana Germanica*. The field of German-American studies by the early 1900s was on the threshold of developing into an academic discipline. Yet many of these efforts were brought to an abrupt halt by the advent of the war.[18]

The German-American National Alliance

Amid the unification festivities of 1871, Oswald Ottendörfer, editor of the *New Yorker Staatszeitung*, suggested that a national German-American association be established to promote the preservation of German heritage and German-American relations. Additional impetus in this direction came as a result of the celebration of the German-American Bicentennial in 1883.

The idea of the Bicentennial was developed by Oswald S. Seidensticker (1825–1894), professor of German at the University of Pennsylvania and the son of a Thirtyer. He had long been an active member of the German Society of Pennsylvania in Philadelphia and had been responsible for establishing its German-American Archives, one of the major collections of its kind. In 1880, a German Pioneer Society of Philadelphia had been formed, and Seidensticker was elected president. Seidensticker, an important historian who published a number of significant works, reported at the January 27, 1882, meeting of the German Pioneer Society that the 200th anniversary of Germantown would take place in 1883. The society then appointed a committee to lay plans for the Bicentennial to be held in October 1883, and centered on the sixth of October.

The speakers at the Bicentennial, held in Philadelphia, included Gottfried Kellner, a Forty-Eighter and vice president of the German Pioneer Society; S. W. Pennypacker, later governor of Pennsylvania; and H. A. Rattermann, the well-known German-American historian from Cincinnati. After Rattermann's return to Cincinnati, a similar celebration was held there, with the main address delivered by Rattermann. Due to the efforts of Seidensticker and Rattermann, the celebration was widely publicized throughout the German-American press.

These efforts led to the national awareness and recognition of October 6 as the central commemorative day, henceforth celebrated as "German Day." To celebrate German Day, new organizations, or German Day societies, were formed, or already existing societies merged to sponsor German Day. The first and largest German Day was held in 1893 in Chicago in conjunction with the World Exposition, and it attracted thirty thousand people. Carl Schurz gave the main address. By the mid-1890s, German Day was being celebrated in most urban centers, small towns, and even in rural areas. In 1904 Schurz presented the main address at German Day in St. Louis, held in conjunction with the Louisiana Purchase Exposition.

These annual German Day celebrations led to the formation of numerous local and regional federations of German-American societies, which sponsored the celebration but also began to address questions pertaining to the representation of German-American interests. In 1899 the German-American Central Alliance of Pennsylvania, a federation of societies in the state, was formed. Thereafter other state alliances came into existence. The Pennsylvania Alliance then called for a national meeting to be held on October 6, 1901, in Philadelphia, at which time a national alliance was to be established.

The president of the Pennsylvania Alliance was a former student of Seidensticker's who had been one of the most active assistants for the 1883 Bicentennial, Carl Johann Hexamer (1862–1921). He was the

Philadelphia-born son of a Forty-Eighter family who had received his Ph.D. in 1886 from the University of Pennsylvania and then had become an engineer in Philadelphia. He was unanimously elected president of the new National German-American Alliance and would remain so until 1917. By that date, the Alliance was the umbrella organization of forty-seven state alliances, each of which consisted of local federations of German-American societies. By 1917 the total membership had reached three million members. The Alliance published a journal entitled *Mitteilungen* and took over publication of the journal edited by Marion Dexter Learned, *German-American Annals*. It also claimed every German-American newspaper as its organ and worked closely with the press for the publication of news releases and reports.

The Alliance's platform indicated that it aimed to awaken and strengthen a sense of unity among German-Americans

> for the mutual energetic protection of such legitimate desires and interests not inconsistent with the common good of the country and the rights and duties of good citizens; to check nativist encroachments; to maintain and safeguard the good relations existing between America and the old German fatherland.[19]

With regard to German-American contributions, the Alliance asked for "the full honest recognition of these merits and opposes every attempt to belittle them."[20] It stated that the best way of obtaining goals was by affiliation with the Alliance, so it invited all German-American organizations to affiliate with it, and where there were none it encouraged the formation of such societies. "The Alliance engages to labor firmly and at all times with all the legal means at its command for the maintenance and propagation of its principles, and to defend them energetically wherever and whenever they are in danger."[21]

The Alliance stated that it had the right and obligation to enter the political arena in defense of its principles and that it would inaugurate and support all legislation for the common good of the country. It excluded matters of religion; it recommended the introduction of German instruction in the schools; it supported physical education in the schools; it advocated the attainment of citizenship as soon as possible; it opposed immigration restriction, exclusive of convicted criminals and anarchists; it favored the abolition of antiquated laws that hampered personal liberty; it supported the regulation of the liquor traffic in accordance with good sense; it recommended the formation of educational societies that would foster German language and literature and teach these topics; it recommended the systematic investigation of the role German-Americans had played in the development of the United States; it promoted the protection of American forests; and it stated that it would assist German-Americans with original ideas or inventions that were for the common good of the country. Finally, it stated that the platform "contains nothing whatever that is not in full accord with good citizenship and to the best interests of the country as a whole."[22]

With the assistance of Congressman Bartholdt of Missouri, the Alliance was incorporated by an act of Congress in 1907. One of its first acts was adopting a motion by historian Rudolf Cronau that a monument be erected in honor of Pastorius, for which the Alliance collected $30,000 and to which the U.S. Congress added an additional $25,000. Designed by Cincinnati German Albert Jaegers, the monument was erected in Germantown in Philadelphia and became known as the Founders Monument.

The Alliance also contributed to the erection of other German-American monuments, statues, historical plaques, and the naming of places in honor of German-Americans. For example, the Steuben Monument was set up in Washington, D.C., and the Muehlenberg Monument was placed at Valley Forge. A park bordering on the East River in New York was changed to the Carl Schurz Park, and the New York state legislature passed a bill so that the old homestead of Nicholas Herchheimer was turned into a museum. The widows of Civil War generals Osterhaus and Sigel secured pensions for themselves. Large sums of money were collected for the victims of the San Francisco earthquake, and a substantial amount was given to the needy in Germany and Austro-Hungary during the early years of World War I. The funding raised for philanthropic and cultural purposes was substantial.

In 1908 German Day honored the 300th anniversary of the arrival of the first Germans in America at Jamestown, Virginia, in 1608. Festivities at Vernon Park in Philadelphia attracted more than twenty thousand, with the main address presented by Reverend Georg von Bosse. Even President Roosevelt sent his best wishes for the commemorative event.

At the state level, the Alliance played an important role as a civic association. For example, it effectively defeated attempts at enacting anything that smacked of prohibition and by so doing clearly demonstrated the power of German-American voters. At the local level, it also made itself known through its local branches that reviewed candidates and endorsed those in accord with its principles. In addition, local and state alliances sponsored the annual German Day celebrations, which became an important festivity and one which provided the opportunity for publicly highlighting German heritage.

The Alliance held its national conventions biannually: 1903 in Baltimore; 1905 in Indianapolis; 1907 in New York; 1909 in Cincinnati; 1911 in Washington, D.C.; 1913 in St. Louis; and 1915 in San Francisco. During its convention in Washington, D.C., in 1911, the newspapers were filled with favorable reports regarding the Alliance. One of the editorials stated:

> Throughout American history runs testimony bearing on the value and high character of the Germans who have made the new world their home. . . . The sessions of the National German-American Alliance now in progress in this city are attended by men who command unqualified respect for their character, their progress, their influence in their communities and the constructive work that they have been and are doing in the upbuilding of the nation.

Moreover, it noted, "In statesmanship, in science, in business, in the professions, the trades and the arts, the German-Americans have contributed many leaders and have written a record of great achievements."[23]

The enthusiastic response to the Alliance's formation was reflected in its phenomenal growth and development. Hexamer was a dynamic, enthusiastic, and outstanding leader. Hexamer's biographer compared him to Schurz as one of the two foremost German-American spokesmen, and it was clear that with Schurz's passing, Hexamer had inherited his leading position.[24]

Hexamer had attended the school of the *Freie Gemeinde* in Philadelphia and then the University of Pennsylvania, where he became a student of Seidensticker. He had been one of the most able assistants to the latter in the preparations made in 1883 for the German-American Bicentennial celebration in Philadelphia, and in that year he joined the German Society of Pennsylvania, located in Philadelphia. In 1891 he was elected to the board and entrusted with various responsibilities including the library with its important German-American Archives, established by Seidensticker. In 1898, he presented the main address for German Day in Philadelphia, which proved so popular that it was printed and widely circulated. In 1900 he was elected president of the German Society of Pennsylvania, where a meeting was held in June to lay the groundwork for the formation of a national alliance patterned after the success of the Pennsylvania Alliance.

Hexamer was without question an organizational genius. Although the idea of a national civic association had surfaced in 1871 and then again after the Spanish-American War, it was Hexamer who took these notions and put them together with his experiences of the German-American Bicentennial. Well grounded in German-American history, and with a long record of community involvement, Hexamer was well equipped for his role. An excellent speaker in both English and German, he became a highly sought-after speaker at German-American events. He also published a number of articles and essays which displayed his grounding in history. The Alliance was well served by Hexamer, who was a capable leader and articulate spokesman.

Almost immediately, the Alliance was thrust into the offensive against prohibition. In 1900 the Prohibition Party began an especially militant campaign, and between 1904 and 1906 more prohibition candidates were elected than ever before, causing the Alliance great concern, as their measures were seen as a possible threat to personal liberty. The Anti-Saloon League, an even more active organization, threatened candidates with a hostile vote should they not support prohibition. Hence, the Alliance was quickly forced into taking action due to this sudden outburst of bigotry. The Alliance clearly viewed this as an expression of nativism.[25]

In 1907 Georgia went dry and was soon followed by five other southern states. Although these were areas settled mainly by Anglo-

Americans, it still caused concern. Indeed, when the war broke out in 1914, the Alliance was enmeshed with a campaign to combat prohibition nationwide. During the war, there is no question that some of the anti-German forces were enlisted from the ranks of the prohibition movement, especially the Prohibition Party and the Anti-Saloon League. Almost immediately after its creation the Alliance had its hands full with the issue of prohibition.

Notes

1. This section is based on the essay by Kathleen Neils Conzen, "Patterns of German-American History," in Randall Miller, ed., *Germans in America: Retrospect and Prospect: Tricentennial Lectures Delivered at the German Society of Pennsylvania in 1983* (Philadelphia: German Society of Pennsylvania, 1984), pp. 14–36. Also, see Conzen's article on German-Americans in the *Harvard Encyclopedia of American Ethnic Groups*.

2. See Kathleen Neils Conzen, "German-Americans and the Invention of Ethnicity," in Frank Trommler and Joseph McVeigh, eds., *America and the Germans: An Assessment of a Three-Hundred-Year History* (Philadelphia: University of Pennsylvania Press, 1985), vol. 1, pp. 131–47.

3. Cited in Don Heinrich Tolzmann, *America's German Heritage* (Cleveland: German-American National Congress, 1976), p. 73.

4. Kathleen Neils Conzen, *Making Their Own America: Assimilation Theory and the German Peasant Pioneer* (New York: Berg, 1990).

5. Claude Moore Fuess, *Carl Schurz: Reformer (1829–1906)* (New York: Dodd, Mead & Co., 1932), p. 155.

6. For further information on Schurz, see Hans L. Trefousse, *Carl Schurz: A Biography* (Knoxville: University of Tennessee Press, 1982).

7. Albert B. Faust, *The German Element in the U.S.* (New York: Steuben Society of America, 1927) vol. 2, pp. 668–69.

8. Hugo Muensterberg, *American Traits from the Point of View of a German* (Boston: Houghton Mifflin, 1902), p. 20.

9. Richard Bartholdt, *From Steerage to Congress: Reminiscences and Reflections* (Philadelphia: Dorrance, 1930).

10. Koppel Pinson, *Modern Germany: Its History and Civilization* (New York: Macmillan, 1966), p. 296.

11. Muensterberg, *American Traits*, p. 21.

12. Pinson, *Modern Germany*, p. 306.

13. Fuess, *Carl Schurz*, p. 368.

14. For an interesting account of war propaganda, see George Sylvester Viereck, *Spreading Germans of Hate: With a Foreword by Colonel Edward M. House* (New York: H. Liveright, 1930). Also by the same author, see *The Kaiser on Trial* (New York: Greystone Press, 1937).

15. Fuess, *Carl Schurz*, p. 357.

16. Ibid., p. 362.

17. Regarding the German-American involvement in the Spanish-American War, see Don Heinrich Tolzmann, ed., *The German-American Soldier in the Wars of the U.S.: J. G. Rosengarten's History* (Bowie, Md.: Heritage Books, 1996), pp. 299–324.

18. This chapter is based on my essay on German-American studies found in Don Heinrich Tolzmann, ed., *Germany and America (1450–1700): Julius Friedrich Sachse's History of the German Role in the Discovery, Exploration, and Settlement of the New World* (Bowie, Md.: Heritage Books, Inc., 1991), pp. 16–28.

19. Don Heinrich Tolzmann, ed., *German Achievements in America: Rudolf Cronau's Survey History* (Bowie, Md.: Heritage Books, 1995), pp. 220–21.

20. Ibid.

21. Ibid.

22. Ibid., p. 321.

23. Ibid., p. 224.

24. The only biography available on Hexamer is Georg von Bosse, *Dr. C .J. Hexamer . . . sein Leben und Wirken* (Philadelphia: Graf & Breuninger, 1922). Regarding the Alliance, see Charles Thomas Johnson, *Culture at Twilight: The National German-American Alliance, 1901–1918*, New German-American Studies, vol. 20 (New York: Peter Lang, 1999).

25. See Herman W. Ronnenberg, *The Politics of Assimilation: The Effect of Prohibition on the German-Americans* (New York: Carlton Press, 1975).

The First World War

Before the War

At the turn of the nineteenth century, the population of the United States numbered seventy-five million. Anglo-Americans numbered some twenty million, or 27 percent of the population, and German-Americans some eighteen million, or 25 percent of the population. The Anglo-American element, which had been two-thirds of the population in 1790, was now about one-fourth, whereas the German-American element had risen from 9 percent in 1790 to also one-fourth of the population. In any conflict involving England or Germany, it is understandable that the sympathies of either group would favor their ancestral homeland.

Relations between Germany and America were cordial. When Theodore Roosevelt visited the kaiser in Berlin after his hunting trip in Africa, the two got along quite well. Wilhelm II, later vilified as a warmongering Hun, was acclaimed as one of the best guarantors of peace in Europe. As a result, the German sovereign inaugurated an exchange of professors with America in 1902. The American chair at the University of Berlin, endowed by James Speyer, was named the Theodore Roosevelt Professorship.

Andrew D. White, who twice represented the United States in Germany, praised the Germans for their idealism and their "higher and better development of man." He stated that "in no land has this idea penetrated more deeply than in Germany, and it is this idea which should penetrate more and more American thought and practice."[1] In 1902 Prince Heinrich of Prussia, the kaiser's brother, visited the United States and was welcomed everywhere with parades and banquets.[2]

In 1904 Professor Hugo Muensterberg of Harvard, then one of the foremost scholars in the field of psychology, published a two-volume work, *Die Amerikaner*. It provided a favorable picture of American society and contributed greatly to German-American relations. It was also published in an English-language edition in the United States.

In 1910 the Steuben Monument, located directly across from the White House in Lafayette Park, was dedicated by Congress, with President Taft presenting the dedicatory address. And in 1911 a replica was presented to the kaiser in Berlin. Taft appointed Rep. Richard Bartholdt of Missouri, who had authored the legislation for the Steuben Monument in Congress, to lead a delegation to Germany to present the bronze replica. Speaking to the kaiser at the presentation in Berlin, Bartholdt stated that the gift was "a pledge of peace and amity" and that

> the effect of this ceremony may be to draw more and more closely the bonds of traditional friendship and good will which, strengthened as they are by the ties of blood, have always so happily united the great German Empire with the great Republic of the West, the United States of America.

The kaiser responded, "Now we rejoice to have on German soil, too, a statue, dedicated by America, of that brave German who, with enthusiastic devotion and sublimely simple performance of duty, consecrated his services to the cause of the American people." The semiofficial newspaper, *Die Norddeutsche Allgemeine Zeitung*, expressed the special pride Germany felt that Baron von Steuben had been honored with a monument in the United States and also expressed pride in the German-Americans, stating that in the four generations since the Revolution, America had "received a rich supply of valuable forces through German immigration. On all fields, Germans have contributed to the development of the Union and its present international prestige, not the least on the field of intellectual labor as teachers, scientists, and authors."[3]

In 1910, the population of the United States was ninety-two million, and German-Americans numbered twenty-three million and Anglo-Americans twenty-five million. Although German-Americans would soon suffer greatly, the tragedy of the experience exposed the notion of the melting pot as nothing more than a myth and led to a recognition of the multicultural nature of American society.

The Outbreak of War

Suddenly, during the warm days of July 1914, like a bolt of lightning from a clear blue sky, the First World War broke out in Europe. At first, the reactions of most German-Americans did not differ from those of Americans of other backgrounds: they were surprised, startled, and shocked.

At first, people hoped that the conflict would remain a local struggle, a quarrel between Austria and Serbia. The assassination of Archduke Franz Ferdinand at Sarajevo, June 28, 1914, did not cause great excitement at first. However, when it became clear that a general European conflagration was developing, most felt that it behooved the United States to adhere to its historic policy of neutrality. George Washington and his principle of avoiding entanglements, as enunciated in his farewell address, was frequently quoted in the press. Early on, the press's nearly unanimous attitude was that the United States was not in danger of being drawn into the conflict.

The German-American press expressed views that did not differ sharply from those of other American newspapers. However, as one nation after another was drawn into the war, the English-language press increasingly supported England, while German-Americans defended the position of Germany and Austria. Feelings soon became hostile between the pro-English and the pro-German press, and this was reflected throughout American society, as lines were drawn between the two positions.

German-American newspapers denounced "perfidious Albion" and published the official German versions of the causes of the conflict. Germany was reluctantly obliged to resort to arms since it was being threatened by Russia in the east. In the west France sought revenge for its defeat in 1870, and around the world England enviously eyed the phenomenal growth of the German navy and empire, as well as its industry and worldwide trade. All three powers definitely had something to gain against Germany in terms of territory and possessions, but Germany had little or nothing to gain from a conflict. However, after the Russian mobilization, Germany had little choice but to mobilize to defend itself. Since the German army was well organized, it was hoped that the war would soon be over, but the war quickly developed into a stalemate.

The United States quickly divided into two camps: those supporting and those opposing U.S. involvement. Although President Wilson called for neutrality in word and deed, it soon became clear that he was not only pro-English, but anti-German. Indeed, he angered German-Americans because of his blatant pro-English stance. For example, in September 1914 Wilson received a Belgian delegation but refused to meet with a German-American one, a direct affront to German-Americans. Soon Wilson was seen as the servant of England who got his news from the *London Times*. In December 1915 the U.S. minister to Belgium remarked to Wilson that there was no such thing as neutrality and that he was heart and soul for England, France, and Russia, whereupon Wilson replied, "So am I. No decent man, knowing the situation and Germany, could be anything else."[4]

Wilson's administration was dominated by individuals of Anglo-American descent, so it was not surprising where their sympathies lay, especially when Wilson's were so well known. Walter Hines Page, U.S. ambassador to Russia, was pro-English, as were Wilson's two most trusted advisers, Colonel House and Robert Lansing. The only member of his cabinet who did not have pro-English leanings and who was dedicated to the cause of peace was William Jennings Bryan, who served as secretary of state from 1913 to 1915.

Realizing the importance of having the United States on their side, the belligerents, especially Britain and Germany, did everything possible to win American sympathy. Propaganda missions were organized and much material distributed. The German government sent over Dr. Heinrich Albert and Dr. Bernhard Dernburg and opened an information bureau on Broadway in New York. This office sent out materials and press releases and arranged for interviews, lectures, and films. Programs were planned not only for German-American groups, but also for anti-war, pacifist, and Irish-American organizations, as they all opposed American entrance into the war.

German-Americans aimed to present the German side, as they felt the English-language press was decidedly pro-English, especially after the German news cable to America had been cut by the English. All news related to the war came from England, obviously presented from an English perspective.

In addition, England maintained a highly organized propaganda network in the United States, which not only presented England's case, but also fanned the flames of hatred against Germany and all things German. The German-American press, therefore, strove to present a balanced picture, even going so far as to publish English-language editorials and editions. In 1914 George Sylvester Viereck commenced publication of a journal, *The Fatherland*, in an attempt to obtain "fair play" for Germany and Austria, as well as to counter the well-organized and well-financed English propaganda machine.

Daily editorials were published to prove the righteousness of the German cause and to refute the charge that the kaiser was some kind of inhuman beast. German-American resentment grew toward the English-language press, particularly because of its English point of view on all war-related issues. Inflammatory headlines covered the pages of the newspapers. To offset the avalanche of anti-German propaganda, the German-American press launched an effort to report about the war more accurately, but also began to take on an anti-English position.

Actively supporting the press was the German-American National Alliance and its various state branches. Judge John Schwaab, president of the Ohio branch of the Alliance, stated that he never read English-language papers since they were filled with lies. German-Americans deeply resented the atrocity stories, the propaganda about plots and spies, and the manner in which everything connected to the Allies was sanctified while Germany was demonized. However, German-Americans felt it their duty to defend their beloved ancestral Fatherland where they had so many friends and relatives.

A German Literary Defense League was organized for all authors who were interested in presenting the case of fair play for Germany, and by the fall of 1914 about sixty thousand pamphlets had been issued, such as *The Truth About Germany*. Other organizations came into being, such as the Teutonic Sons of America, dedicated to reasserting American independence.

Especially high on the agenda was humanitarian relief for the Old Country, an important work because of the English blockade of German ports. Organizations, churches, and individuals engaged in a massive labor of love, collecting millions of dollars before 1917 for the starving children of Germany. Funds were sent to churches in Germany, the German Red Cross, the American Hospital in Munich, and other humanitarian programs. Among the special projects was the rebuilding of Ragnit, East Prussia, which had been destroyed by the Russians. German war bonds were also quite popular.

By 1915 President Wilson began to focus on what he called "the hyphenates," a slightly veiled attack on German-Americans. The *Cincinnati Volksblatt* considered this "an infamous insult," and across the country the German-American press condemned Wilson's apparent anti-German prejudice. The *Express und Westbote* of Columbus, Ohio, advised that German-Americans should "quietly and coolly refute all attacks against us" as the best possible policy.[5]

Wilson did not protest the flagrant violations of American neutrality rights by the English. Germany, however, was always held to "strict accountability." German-Americans, hence, concentrated on demands for an embargo of all war-related materiel, but Wilson refused in an unusual twist of logic: he felt that to institute an embargo at that time would be a change of action, which would be construed as unfriendly to the Allies. The basic premise was that current policy was pro-Allied and not neutral. Strongly opposed to an arms embargo, of course, was the burgeoning munitions industry, which was capitalizing with huge profits due to the war. For example, the Bethlehem Steel Company made huge profits by manufacturing submarines for England.

The Alliance organized mass meetings to galvanize support for the embargo, which was especially supported by Irish-Americans and other antiwar groups and individuals. In December 1914 Representative Bartholdt introduced a resolution in Congress prohibiting the export of arms and munitions, and he was supported by Rep. Henry Vollmer of Iowa. Unfortunately, Congress did not act on this resolution, but the promotional efforts on behalf of the embargo continued, and German-Americans gained more support from non-German-Americans.

In August 1915 the American Embargo Conference was held, and later organized 2,500 committees nationally that distributed embargo literature and solicited letters to Congress. The Alliance sent countless petitions to Congress, and delegations of German- and Irish-Americans appeared in Washington, D.C., to deliver them and make their positions known.

The appeal continued as Germany used submarine warfare to break out of the stranglehold of the English blockade. The embargo movement then sought a law prohibiting U.S. citizens from sailing on armed ships. One petition presented to Congress was fifteen miles long! German-Americans were doing their utmost to keep the country out of the war.

The effective English blockade forced Germany to commence submarine warfare not only to break out of the blockade, but also to halt the ever-increasing shipments of munitions being sent to England from America. In self-defense, Germany declared a war zone around England in 1915, and neutrals were warned of the danger of travel in the zone. As the Allies falsely flew the U.S. flag in the zone, it became increasingly difficult for Germany to detect who was who. To German-Americans, the war zone declaration was the appropriate response to the English blockade. Germany had no other choice.

It was not surprising that Woodrow Wilson promptly attacked Germany's position in February 1915. German-Americans naturally protested against this less than neutral president. They felt that Wilson spoke sharply with threats to Germany, but mildly to England. Germany replied to Wilson that it would spare ships with U.S. flags when it could determine they were not in fact English ships.

The embargo was opposed by non-German-American newspapers and journal editors, such as those of *The Nation*, which claimed that it was "a display of partisanship." The journal also questioned the patriotism and loyalty of those supporting the embargo. German-Americans, however, felt the embargo was in the best interest of the United States because it would ensure its neutrality.

Throughout 1916 Congress was sent numerous petitions requesting an embargo. Resolutions were also introduced to warn Americans to stay off armed merchant ships of the nations at war. On February 13 a national meeting was held in Washington, D.C., to demand an embargo and an end to the English blockade. German-American organizations suggested constitutional amendments to curtail the powers of the president, while others recommended the impeaching Wilson for his non-neutral, pro-English foreign policy.

In an attempt to obtain a personal vote of confidence as well as to crush the embargo movement, Wilson demanded a congressional vote on the resolutions to warn Americans about traveling on merchant ships of the nations at war, thereby forcing them to be tabled. German-Americans questioned why Wilson had done this if he was really neutral. Moreover, if he were genuinely in support of neutrality, why did he oppose the embargo?

By now the English blockade was taking its toll on Germany, so that Germany appeared to be justified at long last in seeking some type of retaliation. Moreover, the great amount of munitions flowing to England from America was now definitely prolonging the war. In February 1915 Germany therefore decided it had no other alternative but to fight back by declaring a war zone around England, proclaiming it would sink every merchant vessel in the zone. Neutral countries were hence warned of the danger, so that those entering the zone did so at their own risk.

Allied ships tried to escape the danger by flying American flags. If Germany had had a large enough navy, it could have established a counterblockade around England, but it did not. Thus, it was forced to establish a war zone and to enforce this by with submarines. Due to the widespread use of U.S. flags, Germany declared it could not be held responsible for accidents resulting from this misuse.

Wilson, of course, immediately protested, insisting on the rules of visit and search. This would have required Germany to search each vessel to ascertain whose ship it actually was. By so doing, Wilson was insisting that the United States had the right to go through the German war zone. However, he never demanded the right to go through the English blockade of Germany, and he never protested vociferously against the English blockade of Germany. German-Americans again protested Wilson's flagrant discriminatory treatment.

Germany then promised to spare the U.S. ships until it could be determined if England was still making use of neutral flags. The United States requested of England and Germany that the right of visit and search be observed and that England cease to use American flags on its merchant marine and permit provisions to reach the civilian population of Germany. German-Americans rejoiced at this proposal. Germany agreed to it, but England, unfortunately, rejected it. It was not surprising that Wilson did not protest with a stern response to England.

The crisis came to a head when the English liner *Lusitania*, heavily laden with munitions, was sunk in May 1915, causing the loss of American lives. There had been allegations that the ship was transporting war equipment, which explained the fact that it sank so quickly. The strong suspicion of munitions transport had caused numerous warnings in the press not to travel on this ship and that those who chose to did so at their own risk. Despite this alert, and the fact that it was in a declared war zone, Wilson held Germany to strict accountability. Germany, for its part, felt that its reaction was entirely justified, as the ship was definitely in the war zone and was reportedly filled with arms—a fact that subsequently has been verified.

Wilson's note to Germany was so harsh that it caused Secretary of State Bryan to resign from his office. He felt that the note amounted to an ultimatum, demanding that Germany renounce a major weapon in its arsenal. Germany responded by stating that it would agree to grant immunity to passenger ships if their cargoes could be inspected and certified in the United States and the ships were properly marked. Wilson replied that he was very dissatisfied with this response, since it made undue demands on a neutral power. The German-American press claimed it was not Wilson who was keeping America out of the war, but rather Germany! In the meantime, more ships were sunk, which further complicated the situation. Congress considered a resolution to warn Americans against traveling on armed vessels except at their own risk, but Wilson secured its defeat.

Here again, Wilson clearly demonstrated that in spite of his protests of neutrality in word and deed, his words and deeds indicated that this was not the case. His note after the sinking of the *Sussex* in March 1916 amounted to another ultimatum to Germany, demanding that it "immediately declare and effect an abandonment of its present methods of warfare against passenger and freight-carrying vessels." He was demanding that Germany drop its submarine warfare. At no time did he demand that England drop the blockade of Germany.

This latter ultimatum enraged German-Americans. Judge Schwaab, president of the Ohio branch of the Alliance, telegrammed Wilson, stating that voters opposed a break in diplomatic relations and begged him to work for peace. Numerous organizations and newspapers wrote to Wilson, imploring him to avoid conflict. Dr. H. H. Fick, supervisor of German in the Cincinnati public schools, wrote "in the name of nearly two hundred German teachers of the German Department." The National Alliance was active across the country in numerous letter-writing campaigns to Congress and to Wilson.

Then in May 1916 Germany agreed to stop sinking merchant ships without warning, but indicated that "a new situation" might arise if the United States was not successful in forcing England to respect neutral rights. Again Germany had gone the extra mile. German-Americans, however, knew that the chances of Wilson forcing England to do anything at all were slim. Therefore, Germany reserved its right to act accordingly. Wilson immediately rejected this condition, stating that American rights were not contingent on the conduct of another country. Clearly, the impression was that he was doing his utmost to get the United States into war on the side of England against Germany.

For the remainder of 1916, Germany held to its promises. Such limitations, of course, favored England, as Germany could not fully defend itself by carrying out its policy in the war zone. In the meantime, England's blockade of Germany continued without a word of protest from Wilson. Germany now had to visit and search each ship. Of course, falsely disguised English ships with American flags were now armed and responded accordingly when German vessels tried to visit and search them. This new policy actually became a weapon against Germany.

At the same time, many German-Americans were focusing on the forthcoming 1916 presidential election. Already in 1915 a gathering of close to sixty German-American leaders took place in a conference in Washington, D.C. This included Charles Hexamer, president of the Alliance; Congressmen Batholdt and Vollmer; Professor Albert B. Faust of Columbia University; and George Sylvester Viereck, a well-known publicist. The goals were to strive for genuine neutrality and to support candidates for office who preferred American interests, rather than those of England. The meeting was implicitly an anti-Wilson meeting and clearly reflected German-American feelings of the time. By 1916 the entire German-American press was almost unanimous in its opposition to Wilson and all those who supported him.

In May 1916 another national convention was held in Chicago with representatives of twenty state branches of the Alliance and some sixty German-American newspapers. Among the resolutions agreed on was the call for a return to the principles enunciated in George Washington's farewell address. The convention also denounced all those who had engaged in anti-German rhetoric. Although avoiding an endorsement, the meeting aimed to influence the Republican convention by dispatching a committee to the Republican National Committee to inform its chairman that neither Roosevelt nor Root would obtain the support of German-Americans. However, candidate Charles Evans Hughes was considered acceptable.

Wilson's renomination in St. Louis was viewed as a foregone conclusion. The Democrats, however, adopted a blatantly anti-German plank that was aimed specifically at the German-American National Alliance, as it stated,

> We condemn all alliances and combinations of individuals in this country, of whatever nationality or descent, who agree and conspire together for the purpose of embarrassing or weakening our government of or improperly influencing or coercing our public representatives in dealing or in negotiating with any foreign power.[6]

This was a direct attack on the Alliance and the May meeting in Chicago.

German-Americans bolted the Democratic Party because of their anti-Germanism and flocked to the Republicans. Also joining them were many Irish-Americans who hoped for Irish independence by England's possible defeat. When Charles Evans Hughes acknowledged the support of German- and Irish-Americans, some hostile cartoonists depicted him with a spiked helmet. Wilson, on the other hand, continued his anti-

German political strategy, playing on nativist sympathies, and at every point spoke out against the so-called hyphenates. He stated, "I neither seek the favor nor fear the displeasure of that small alien element which puts loyalty to any foreign power before loyalty to the United States."[7] Such a hate and smear campaign laid the foundation for the outbreak of the anti-German hysteria of the war period. Indeed, it was fomented by Wilson, as he articulated time and time again his opposition to the hyphenates, a euphemistic expression for German-Americans.

During the campaign of 1916, the German-American press stressed Wilson's pro-English bias and campaigned against what they viewed as his attempt to Anglicize America. They emphasized that being American has to do with American citizenship and not with ethnicity; hence, being American should not be equated with Anglo ethnicity. One could and should retain one's own particular ethnicity.

On election night it looked like Hughes had won, but when the rest of the votes arrived from across the country, it sadly turned out that Wilson had won. German-Americans felt that Wilson had won by means of the "big lie" slogan: "He kept us out of war." Deception and the hate-the-hyphen campaign had won.

Now German-Americans viewed their only hope as trying to prevent war. Here they might have been successful had it not been for a major diplomatic blunder known as the Zimmermann affair. In February 1917 the German government announced it would resume unrestricted submarine warfare, which returned relations between the Wilson regime and Berlin to a crisis situation. In March it was learned that German Foreign Secretary Zimmermann had cabled the German minister in Mexico, requesting that he arrange a military alliance with Mexico. As an inducement, the possible recovery of the "lost provinces" of Texas, New Mexico, and Arizona was held out in return for a Mexican declaration of war against the United States. A wave of resentment swept the nation as a result of the Zimmermann telegram. German-Americans were also appalled by this turn of events, but it made their position of trying to keep the United States out of the war impossible.

For Wilson the Zimmermann affair provided him with the necessary excuse and pretext for going to Congress to request a declaration of war. He now had what he needed. On April 2 he asked Congress for the declaration of war. Two days later, the Senate passed the resolution 82 to 6, and the House approved it on April 6 by a vote of 373 to 50. Senators LaFollette of Wisconsin, Norris of Nebraska, and Stone of Missouri courageously spoke out and voted against the war. After the vote, Wilson promptly signed the resolution and issued a proclamation of war. Although the Zimmermann affair had been a colossal blunder, there still was no real need for the United States to go to war. Germany's search for allies could have been protested through diplomatic channels, for example.

Prophetically, Wilson stated on the night he asked for the declaration of war:

> Once lead this people into war, and they'll forget there ever was such a thing as tolerance. To fight you must be brutal and ruthless, and the spirit of ruthless brutality will enter into the very fiber of our national life, infecting Congress, the courts, the policeman on the beat, the man on the street.[8]

Here was a clear statement that there would be a total war involving everyone and everything in an all-out onslaught. War would be waged not only abroad, but also on the home front.

The Anti-German Hysteria

Wilson's declaration of war precipitated a tragic outbreak of hysteria directed against anything and everything German. The stage had been set by Wilson's foreign and domestic policies. According to Carl Wittke, this led to one of the most difficult and humiliating experiences suffered by an ethnic group in American history. He notes that "misunderstanding, suspicion, slander, emotional conflict, bewildered readjustment, and tragedy marked the war years, as excited Americans became convinced that everything of German origin must be treasonable." Everything German was now marked as a target of the anti-German hysteria, with the ultimate goal to stamp out everything that was German.[9]

The president set the tone for the nation. Acting on his endorsement, Attorney General Gregory Thomas organized a massive force of

200,000 voluntary detectives who were to feed information to the Justice Department on anyone suspected of disloyalty. This vigilante force, called the American Protective League (APL), required its detectives to take an oath of office and carry a badge. Although it failed to find a single spy, it conducted investigations. Anyone could be charged and accused and then become a subject of an APL investigation. For example, a German-American minister in Ohio was accused of having said something disloyal during the funeral of a soldier and was indicted. Hearsay was sufficient cause for indictment, and proof was not necessary. Although the minister was cleared of charges, the mere act of being charged resulted in intimidation, since the assumption was that an investigation implied wrongdoing. The APL provided for the creation of a government-endorsed police-state atmosphere.

The APL was supported by the NCD and the CPI, two other organizations that further solidified the war atmosphere. In April 1917 Congress established the NCD, or National Council of Defense. This empowered each state to establish a state council that was granted sweeping legal powers, among them the powers of subpoena and punishment of contempt. State councils were also supported by numerous subcommittees devoted to related tasks, such as "Americanization" (Anglicization) of ethnic groups. These councils led the anti-German crusade at the state level. A study of the Minnesota council, which bore the name Minnesota Commission of Public Safety, determined that it was not only dictatorial, but fascist as well. It aimed to take swift and decisive action toward "suppressing disloyal outbreaks where the German element was predominant." It was empowered to perform "all acts and things necessary or proper so that the military, civil, and industrial resources of the state may be efficiently applied towards the maintenance of the defense of the state and nation, and towards the successful prosecution of the war." The Minnesota Commission had wide-ranging powers, making it in essence a state police force. By July 1917 this Gestapo-like unit had organized its own army, the Home Guard, consisting of twenty-one battalions. One contemporary critic commented that the Commission was Prussianizing Minnesota and establishing "here that military autocracy which we are supposed to be fighting."[10]

Also created in April 1917 on the basis of an executive order from

Wilson was the CPI, or Committee on Public Information. According to Karl J. R. Arndt, "Josef Goebbels found a fiendishly clever forerunner for his efficient and satanic propaganda ministry"[11] in the CPI. Its purpose was to coordinate the national propaganda effort in support of the war. It published and distributed numerous pamphlets and books and distributed thousands of movies, exhibits, posters, and photographs. It also sponsored patriotic pageants and loyalty days for ethnic groups. At its disposal was a force of 75,000 Minute Men, who presented propaganda speeches wherever possible. One of the CPI's booklets was entitled *American Loyalty by Citizens of German Descent*, which was published in English and German editions, and of which over a million copies were distributed. The CPI contributed immensely to the spirit of intolerance, as it "defined patriotism as conformity to a preconceived, idealized pattern of thought; it abetted the oppression of innocent citizens as it agitated against an imagined German spy system." In the name of unity, it "extolled English culture and condemned anything derogatory of Great Britain" while it "cultivated a hatred for everything German."[12]

Aside from the APL, the NCD, and the CPI, there were also a number of national independent organizations that came into being. This included the NSL, the National Security League, and its offshoot, the ADS, American Defense Society. The NSL had 100,000 members. One of its first demands was that all German-American societies be assembled at public meetings to demonstrate their loyalty and to adopt declarations against Germany. Naturally, few societies felt inclined to submit to these self-appointed loyalty judges, which led the NSL to agitate against them. One of its publications provides an indication of the hate literature it published: *The Tentacles of the German Octopus in America*. This was a vicious attack against German-American churches, schools, societies, and newspapers, which were accused of belonging to a worldwide Teutonic conspiracy. It recommended force against German-American institutions that did not respond to their demands and thereby incited violence against German-Americans.

The NSL offshoot, the ADS, was specifically dedicated to the elimination of the German language in America. One of its publications, *Throw Out the German Language and All Disloyal Teachers*, proclaimed that any language that produced such a terrible people "is not a fit language to teach clean and pure American boys and girls." It stated that German instruction must be destroyed so that the kaiser would not be able to gain control of American children. The ADS claimed that Germans "were the most treacherous, brutal, and loathsome" people on earth and that the sound of the German language "reminds us of the murder of a million helpless old men, unarmed men, women, and children . . . the driving of . . . young French, Belgian, and Polish women into compulsory prostitution." In some of the war's most vile anti-German hate literature, it openly advocated the burning of German books and actively campaigned to change the names of cities, streets, parks, and schools that had German names and replace them with English, Belgian, and French names.

There is no question that the establishment of governmental agencies such as the APL, the NCD, and the CPI and nongovernmental organizations such as the NSL and the ADS contributed to a police-state atmosphere enforced by national hysteria and hate against German-Americans. It was these organizations that orchestrated and directed the anti-German measures at the national, state, and local levels.[13]

Tactics and Targets

Anti-German hysteria found expression in a wide variety of crimes, wrongs, and injustices, but some of the major tactics and targets were:

1. Internment. During the Boer War, the English established internment camps in South Africa, and during the First World War they continued their innovation by interning Germans in England, Canada, Australia, and elsewhere in their empire. Following their example, the United States established an internment camp at Fort Oglethorpe, Georgia, where more than six thousand German-Americans were interned. These individuals were U.S. residents but had not yet acquired U.S. citizenship and were classified as "enemy aliens." The camp took on the atmosphere of an artists' colony, as most of the internees were artists and musicians who had been employed at art academies and symphony orchestras across the country. For example, Ernst Kunwald, the concertmeister of the Cincinnati Symphony Orchestra, was interned; he later compared his experi-

ences in the United States to the actions of later totalitarian regimes. Since all the actors in the German Theater of Cincinnati were classified as "enemy aliens" they were interned, thus causing the theater to close. The intelligentsia of the German-American community was deeply affected by internment. Interning this segment of the community amounted to a harsh dose of intimidation to German-Americans.[14]

2. The German Language. An obvious target of the hate campaign was the German language. By the war's end, twenty-six states had passed laws against the use of German. Some of these forbade the use of German on the street, in public meetings, or on the telephone. In Louisiana violators of the ban on German could be fined from $25 to $100, and be imprisoned from ten to ninety days. By January 1921 the number of arrests nationally for those who were guilty of using German in public had reached a total of 17,903. Of these 5,720 were convicted and sentenced. After the war, these laws were declared unconstitutional.[15]

3. The German-American Press. Another obvious target was the press, which struggled for its very existence. In October 1917 the first federal law in U.S. history to control the non-English press was enacted. All war-related news had to be submitted to the local postmaster for censorship. After the loyalty of the publication had been established by the local postmaster, a permit would be granted to the publication exempting it from registering a translation of its news with the postmaster. Hence all German-American publications were at the mercy of their local postmaster. Some postmasters enjoyed their new power and used it to harass the local German-American press. Some post offices even refused to deliver German-American publications, or simply discarded them. Another problem was that their editorial offices were often raided by the Secret Service, although nothing suspicious was ever found. Some municipalities debated whether the German-American press should be banned. Another problem was that newsstands refused to carry and sell such publications. Also, advertising boycotts of the German-American press were organized, and those placing advertisements were threatened with boycotts. Businesses and companies thus withdrew their advertising, depriving the press of much revenue. As a result, the number of German-American publications fell from 537 in 1914 to 278 in 1920.[16]

4. German Instruction. With the anti-German hysteria in full swing,

a movement began to eliminate German instruction in the schools. This was facilitated by state laws against use of the German language. Based on these laws, it was not difficult for local members of the APL, CPI, NSL, or ADS to advocate the elimination of German instruction at the local level. For example, in South Dakota, the State Council of Defense ordered the elimination of German instruction at all levels. At the University of Michigan-Ann Arbor, the entire German department was purged in 1917–18, resulting in the dismissal of five professors. In Cincinnati, the hometown of public-school bilingual instruction, German instruction was banned in 1918, thereby ending a seventy-five-year-old program, one that had served as the model for similar programs elsewhere. In community after community, German instructional programs were banned, so that by war's end, German instruction had been almost completely eliminated from public schools and remained only in some private and parochial schools. However, some states passed laws covering not only public, but also private and parochial schools, such as in Nebraska. As one state legislator there stated, "If these people are Americans, let them speak our language." The law that emerged forbade any teacher in all schools from "teaching any subject in any language but English." In 1923 these laws would be declared unconstitutional, and German instruction would gradually return to the schools.[17]

5. Libraries. After eliminating German from the schools, it was only a logical step to address the problem of German materials in libraries. Numerous libraries decided to burn, destroy, or remove German materials from their holdings. For example, the Iowa State Council of Defense requested that all libraries eliminate books that "laud the Huns." The Public Library of Cincinnati removed its German collection and, fortunately, placed it in storage, so it was not lost, as was the case with many libraries. Not only was German material destroyed, but also materials in English that dealt with German topics. Such eliminations were based on lists of banned books that began to appear in 1918. These were prepared by state councils of defense and related organizations. Also, the U.S. War Department prepared a list of books considered harmful to the morale of the army. It requested libraries voluntarily remove these titles "as being unfit for civilian consumption." On the list, for example, were German-American history titles, such as F. W. Schrader's *German-American Handbook*. The

American Library Association organized its War Service Committee "to act as an agency of patriotic publicity." Library journals were filled with articles such as "Is Your Library a Slacker?" Book lists, exhibits, and other publicity devices joined in the propaganda crusade of the national organizations and their state affiliates. Needless to say, valuable collections of German materials and German-Americana were lost forever.[18]

6. German-American Organizations. Next on the list were German-American organizations, beginning with the major national organization, the Alliance. In January 1918 Sen. William Henry King of Utah introduced a bill in Congress to repeal the Alliance's charter. This signaled an all-out attack on the Alliance, its state and local branches throughout the country as well as on their affiliated societies. State defense councils joined in demanding the repeal of the Alliance's charter and lobbied for the repeal of the state branches as well. Theodore Roosevelt stated that those who tried to be Germans and Americans at the same time were not Americans but rather traitors and that the Alliance served Germany and not America, and that the melting pot should melt all together. "There should be one language in this country—English." The president of the Alliance, Dr. Hexamer, resigned office in November 1917, broken by the anti-German hysteria. His replacement was the Rev. Siegmund von Bosse, a German Lutheran minister. He viewed the congressional hearings of the Alliance as the opportunity to explain and defend the Alliance. The hearings were held from February through April 1918 and bore a striking resemblance to the McCarthy hearings of the 1950s.[19]

German-American witnesses were humiliated, insulted, slandered, smeared, and treated in the most reprehensible and repulsive manner. They were interrupted, misquoted, and accused of all kinds of conspiracies. The principal witness against the Alliance was Gustavus Ohlinger, a rabid anti-German bigot and author of hate literature, including *The German Conspiracy in American Education* and *Their True Faith and Allegiance*. During the hearings, the press referred to members of the Alliance as "spies and suspects" and "the kaiser's best friends," while the Alliance was referred to in one newspaper as a "cancerous growth." Because of the numerous threats on his life, Reverend von Bosse went into hiding. On July 2, 1918, Congress repealed the Alliance's charter, and attacked it as a hyphenated organization which sowed the seeds of disloyalty and fostered German Kultur. However, by April the Alliance had seen the handwriting on the wall and had dissolved in advance of the congressional action. Its final statement was:

> As Americans of German blood, wholeheartedly and without reservation, we say to our fellow citizens that together with them we shall ever stand ready to defend this Government and this country against all foes, internal and external, to the end that the liberty and freedom guaranteed by the Constitution shall forever prevail.[20]

7. Community Leaders. Those who led organizations such as the Alliance became the objects of systematic persecution directed against them and their families. Their places of employment were contacted, as well as those of family members, recommending the termination of their employment. With national leaders, threats were made against their lives. Attempted lynchings, slander, lies, and accusations were common. Children of German-American leaders were harassed in school or at work. Often such leaders were watched by the Secret Service or state councils of defense. This persecution resulted in the demise of many societies, whereas others voted not to meet again until after the war in the hope of avoiding further harassment.

8. Ethnic Harassment, Intimidation, and Violence. Any individual of German descent became a target. Ethnic slurs were a daily matter in public and in the press. Terms like "Hun" and "Hunskunk" were used daily on the front pages of the press when referring to Germans or German-Americans. A common act of harassment was tarring and feathering. Another favorite was dunking German-Americans in syrup. Homes, churches, and German houses were painted with yellow signs on the door or with skulls and crossbones. Sometimes they were burned to the ground. Another popular activity was to march German-Americans through town and then force them to pledge allegiance and sing the national anthem. Refusal resulted in savage beatings by mobs. Being a minister proved no protection. Indeed, the first German-American killed was the Rev. Edmund Kayser, who was shot near Chicago in 1915. Other ministers were stoned, shot at, or had their homes broken into. At Bishop, Texas, a German Lutheran minister was publicly flogged. Even

non-German ministers who were antiwar were in danger. In Cincinnati, a non-German minister opposed to the war was brought to Kentucky, tied to a tree, stripped, and whipped "in the name of the women and children of Belgium."[21]

By 1918 the violence was increasing, with more cases of beatings, tarring and featherings, shootings, and lynchings. At Delphos, Ohio, the Home Defense League organized a vigilante group to hunt down the local editor of a German-American newspaper and chased him through several counties. Searches were conducted from house to house, with flags nailed to the houses after the search was completed. He was finally caught in Fort Wayne, Indiana, and returned to Delphos, where he was forced "trembling for his life" to pledge his loyalty.

The most well-known lynching took place on April 5, 1918, when Robert P. Prager, a coal miner, was seized at Collinsville, Illinois. He was charged with disloyalty, dragged from his home, and led barefoot through town with a flag. Although he was rescued by the police, the jail was stormed by a mob. The police offered no resistance but escorted the mob so that the lynching would not be held within city limits. Before he was murdered, Prager wrote to his parents, "Dear Parents: I must this day, the fourth of April 1918, die. Please pray for me, my dear parents. This is my last letter or testimony of mine. Your dear son and brother, Robert Paul." All of the lynchers were acquitted in a trial even the local newspaper called "a farcical patriotic orgy." This murder and other acts of violence were the most tragic expressions of the anti-German hysteria.[22]

Connected to the public pressures were the public drives on behalf of the sale of Liberty Loan bonds. Such drives were often carried out by threat of violence. The sales were usually advertised with grisly and gory atrocity tales dealing with the "beast of Berlin" and the "ferocious and barbarous Huns." Groups of bigots visited German-American homes, churches, societies, businesses, and especially newspapers and demanded that German-Americans buy the bonds to demonstrate and prove they were 100 percent American. At newspaper offices they ordered that the atrocity propaganda be published under direct threat, and newspaper editors feared to do otherwise, since they knew the consequences could be anything from lynching to tarring and feathering to a beating.

9. Mass Media Propaganda. In the press, war propaganda depicted

England, France, and Russia as heroic and godly nations, while Germany and Austria were presented as the forces of evil. Given the torrent of propaganda being produced by such national agencies as the APL, the NCD, and the CPI, it was not surprising that book publishers soon jumped on the bandwagon by producing a range of books dealing with the war.

Already in 1914, *The German Spy System*, by an ex-intelligence officer, was published, to be followed by works such as John Price Jones's *America Entangled: The Secret Plotting of German Spies in the United States and the Inside Story of the Sinking of the* Lusitania (1917). The spy stories proved to be popular well into the 1920s, with works such as Thomas M. Johnson's *Our Secret Service: True American Spy Stores, 1917–1919* (1929). All of these works created the image of Germans as Huns and of German-Americans as their counterparts in an international conspiracy concocted in Berlin and led by the kaiser.

Soon a new form of media, film, came into use for the purpose of war propaganda and proved to be extremely effective. It was not only the film producers of Hollywood who became involved in the war effort, but also the Wilson administration, as the new Commission on Public Information established a Division of Film to sell the war to the nation.

In 1915 *The Birth of a Nation* demonstrated that film was a propaganda medium without equal, one that could reach a national audience with great impact. In the fall of that year *The Battle Cry of Peace* was filmed at the instigation of Theodore Roosevelt, presenting Germans as Huns and maintaining that the United States should be armed to the teeth to protect itself. However, critics viewed it as a prowar film produced to support the munitions industry.

This was followed in 1916 by *The Fall of a Nation*, a thinly veiled attack on Secretary of State William Jennings Bryan, especially because the actor was made to look almost exactly like Bryan and was characterized as a fool. In April 1917 the film *Civilization* was withdrawn, as it was viewed as an antiwar film. The mere fact that it was withdrawn shows the influence the film had as a propaganda medium. Ironically, the Democratic National Committee had exploited the film in the 1916 campaign for Wilson's reelection under the slogan "He kept us out of war." Now this trick was no longer of use.

At this stage of the war, Hollywood and Washington cranked out hate propaganda against Germany. Atrocity films surpassed the sensationalism of the press and stigmatized the German nation as Huns and the kaiser as a ruthless monarch. The Huns were depicted as brutal, barbaric, bestial savages bent on worldwide conquest. Films such as *The Woman the Germans Shot* depicted Germans as the pillaging Huns, raping, burning, and destroying villages. In *The Little American*, Mary Pickford, the symbol of sweetness and virtue, is saved from the Huns at the last minute. The kaiser was demonized in a whole series of films such as *The Kaiser*, *Beast of Berlin*, and *To Hell with the Kaiser*. He is usually presented as a bestial individual who is either strong or weak but always arrogant, conceited, and outrageous.

Other films sought to inculcate vengeance, such as *Till I Come Back to You* and *Lest We Forget*. Other films urged the audience to stamp out Prussianism. There were many spy movies that created the impression that America was flooded with spies. One of them, *The Evil Eye*, was produced by William J. Flynn, chief of the Secret Service, and gave an official stamp of approval to this kind of propaganda. If anyone came to epitomize visually that the German was a Hun, it was Erich von Stroheim, the well-known Hollywood actor and director. The image presented was that of a fiendish torturer and sadist who raped women, threw babies out of windows, and delighted in destruction.

German-Americans were deeply offended and affected by this onslaught of hate propaganda. Indeed, the hate-the-Hun movies caused problems by means of guilt by association. Being of German descent caused German-Americans to be viewed in a different light. They were now suspected of disloyalty, as possible spies, and as Huns. German-Americans resented films showing their kinfolk as sadistic, arrogant, rowdy, rude, often drunk, beasts bent on rape, plunder, and murder, especially when many of the propaganda films presented the United States being honeycombed with spies working with German-Americans.[23]

The Darkest Hour

Carl Wittke called the First World War "the darkest hour" in German-American history. He summarized the war by noting that it resulted in "a violent, concerted and hysterical effort to eradicate everything of German origin" in America. He noted that the mere use of German on the phone or among neighbors was considered evidence of a conspiracy.

> Teachers were investigated to determine their degree of patriotism, and some were unjustly dismissed; loyalty trials were held in some school systems and institutions of higher learning; and textbooks were scrutinized to eliminate any favorable reference to Germany. . . . Fear of mob violence and race riots haunted millions of law-abiding German-Americans.

Tragically, "a large section of the American population condoned the illegal activities of a minority" that carried out acts of violence. "German music and literature, German church services, the German language, the activities of German societies, and everything even remotely associated with a German origin came under the ban of the superpatriots." German-Americans became the objects of suspicion, hatred, and persecution. The Alliance came under attack, as did German instruction.

> German books were thrown out of libraries as trash, hidden in cellars and attics, or burned in the public square with patriotic ceremonies. The works of German composers disappeared from symphony programs; German artists were denied the use of concert halls; German theaters were closed and German church services interrupted by excited patriots.[24]

There was also the rage to eliminate German names: German place, street, and family names were Americanized and anglicized; German dishes vanished from hotel menus, and sauerkraut was renamed "liberty cabbage." There were occasional street fights. Homes where occupants spoke German, or read a German newspaper, or had failed to respond satisfactorily to the various war drives, were smeared with yellow paint. Public floggings occurred in several communities, and citizens whose patriotism seemed lukewarm were forced to kneel at the public square and kiss the flag to demonstrate their loyalty.

Military Service

In spite of the criminal mistreatment on the home front, German-Americans enlisted in the military in large numbers—an estimated one-third of the armed forces were men of German descent. The list of war dead from Cincinnati reveals a high percentage of German surnames. The Wisconsin Thirty-Second, for example, proved its patriotism in hand-to-hand combat in the Vosges Mountains and on the Marne River.

A German-American general led the American Expeditionary Forces to France in 1917, General John J. Pershing. His forefather, Friedrich Pfoerschin, had arrived in Philadelphia in 1749 as an indentured servant. Pershing placed special trust in units from German-American regions, and the Wisconsin Thirty-Second was one of his favorites. In June 1919 this unit was honored when it paraded down Wisconsin Avenue in Milwaukee. In 1919 "Black Jack" Pershing was made General of the Armies, a position previously held only by George Washington. His book, *My Experiences in the World War*, was awarded the Pulitzer Prize in 1932.

Among the many examples of those who went beyond the call of duty was the two-man team of flyers, Joseph Wehner and Frank Luke, who were considered the greatest fighting team in the U.S. Air Service during the war. Indeed, they shot down so many observation balloons on the front that Luke became known as the "Balloon Buster." He became the first U.S. airman to receive the Congressional Medal of Honor.

Perhaps the greatest airman of the war was Edward V. Rickenbacker, originally Richenbacher, who is credited with having shot down twenty-two planes and four observation balloons. At the age of twenty-six, he was at first considered too old for service, so he accompanied the AEF to Europe as a chauffeur on Pershing's staff, but he later convinced the authorities to admit him to aerial training. He became a member of the Ninety-fourth Aero Squadron, the foremost U.S. flying unit of the war. His book, *Fighting the Flying Circus*, tells the story of his war experiences. After the war, he became the president of Eastern Airlines, a position he held until 1953, when he advanced to chairman of the board, a position he held until 1963.

Antiwar Sentiment

Although the overwhelming majority of German-Americans recognized the difficult situation they were in and made a special effort to go above and beyond the call of duty, there were some who opposed the war on the basis of their beliefs. Members of religious groups, such as the Mennonites and Hutterites, opted for conscientious objector status and refused to serve in active units or to buy Liberty Bonds, but they instead contributed to the Red Cross and war relief projects. Such individuals, however, faced legal action, and some were sent to Alcatraz, Fort Leavenworth, and other federal prisons, where they faced harassment and mistreatment. In 1918, the Hutterites' petition to President Wilson requesting they obtain noncombat service was rejected, thus causing some to emigrate to Canada.

Adolf Dehn, a Minnesota German artist, objected to combat service on the basis of his pacifist views. This caused him to be put in the guardhouse. At his hometown in Waterville, Minnesota, the local newspaper campaigned against him and the Huns, stating that there should be less internment and more executions, which resulted in such hostility that Dehn's father found it necessary to stand guard at his home armed with a shotgun.

In New Ulm, Minnesota, a referendum was held a month before American entrance in the war in April 1917. By more than twenty to one, New Ulmers opposed war. In July more than ten thousand gathered to protest sending draftees to the front. The Minnesota Public Safety Commission investigated the matter and recommended that the mayor, city attorney, and county auditor be removed from office for describing draftees as martyrs of a dictatorial government. Governor Burnquist suspended them, and they all resigned from office, which was then tabled pending further investigation. After reading the testimony, the governor found the mayor and city attorney had been "unpatriotic and un-American" and reinstated only the auditor.

Many privately sympathized with the New Ulm protesters but felt that such actions were ill-advised and would only fuel more anti-German hysteria. Adolph Ackermann, president of the Dr. Martin Luther College in

New Ulm, stated at the protest gathering, "If we are fighting for this country's rights, why did we not declare war against Great Britain, which first violated our rights?"[25]

Ackermann also urged that the United States should place its priorities on domestic issues, noting "there is plenty to do in our own country, without sticking our noses into other people's business, without fighting for Wall Street and John Bull." German-Americans, however, knew that it was their duty to do their duty. The *Christliche Apologete* in Cincinnati stated, "Henceforth, all discussion of the war and its justification must stop. Every American owes his government loyalty and obedience."

Notes

1. Theodore Huebener, *The Germans in America* (Philadelphia: Chilton, 1962), p. 143.

2. Regarding German-American relations before the war, see Hans Gatzke, *Germany and the United States: A Special Relationship* (Cambridge: Harvard University Press, 1980).

3. For the history of the Steuben monument, see George H. Carter, ed., *Proceedings Upon the Unveiling of the Statue of Baron von Steuben* (Washington, D.C.: Government Printing Office, 1913).

4. Joseph Wandel, *German Dimension in American History* (Chicago: Nelson Hall, 1979), p. 185.

5. Carl Wittke, "German-Americans and the World War, with Special Emphasis on Ohio's German-language Press," in Don Heinrich Tolzmann, ed., *German-Americans in the World Wars* (Munich: K. G. Saur, 1995), vol. 1, p. 58. This entire section is based on Wittke's work, vol. 1, pp. 15–123.

6. Frederick C. Luebke, *Bonds of Loyalty: German-Americans and World War I* (DeKalb: Northern Illinois University Press, 1974), p. 173.

7. Ibid., p. 178.

8. For Wilson's comments during the war, see: Woodrow Wilson, *The Public Papers of Woodrow Wilson*, ed. Ray Stannard Baker and William E. Dodd (New York: 1925–1927).

9. Carl Wittke, *The German-Language Press in America* (Lexington: University Press of Kentucky, 1957), p. 235.

10. Regarding the Minnesota Commission, see Carl H. Chrislock, *Watchdog*

of Loyalty: The Minnesota Commission of Public Safety During World War I (St. Paul: Minnesota Historical Society, 1991), pp. 135–36. Chrislock notes that the Commission acquired the image of "a ruthless dictatorship," which perpetrated a reign of terror, p. 326. It was also described as a blatant "example of legalized discrimination." It became "a virtual government in its own right, employing its own agents and constabulary," pp. 335, 367.

11. Karl J. R. Arndt, *The German-Language Press*, vol. 3 (Munich: K. G. Saur, 1980).

12. Luebke, *Bonds of Loyalty*, p. 213.

13. Regarding these organizations, see ibid.

14. For a history of the internment during World War I, see Gerald H. Davis, "Orgelsdorf: A World War I Internment Camp in America," *Yearbook of German-American Studies* 26 (1991): 249–65.

15. See Frederick C. Luebke, *Germans in the New World: Essays in the History of Immigration* (Urbana: University of Illinois Press, 1990), pp. 31–50.

16. See Karl J. R. Arndt and May E. Olson, eds., *The German Language Press of the Americas*, vol. 3, *German-American Press Research from the American Revolution to the Bicentennial* (Munich: K. G. Saur, 1980), pp. 731–75.

17. See Caroln Toth, *German-English Bilingual Schools in America: The Cincinnati Tradition in Historical Context*. New German-American Studies, vol. 2 (New York: Peter Lang, 1990), pp. 81–92.

18. See Wayne Wiegand, *An Active Instrument for Propaganda: The American Public Library During World War I* (New York: Greenwood Press, 1989).

19. For the biography of Hexamer, see Georg von Bosse, *Dr. C. J. Hexamer: Sein Leben und Wirken* (Philadelphia: Graf & Breuninger, 1922).

20. See Tolzmann, *German-Americans in the World Wars*, vols. 1–2.

21. See ibid., vol. 1, pp. 175–208.

22. See Franziska Ott, "The Anti-German Hysteria: The Case of Robert Paul Prager," in ibid., pp. 237–365.

23. See Randall M. Miller, ed., *Ethnic Images in American Film and Television* (Philadelphia: The Balch Institute, 1978), pp. 51–71.

24. Arndt and Olson, *The German Language Press*, vol. 3, p. 766.

25. See Martin A. Schroeder, *A Time to Remember: An Informal History of Dr. Martin Luther College, 1884–1984* (New Ulm: Dr. Martin Luther College, 1984), p. 59.

The Return
to Normalcy

President Harding called for what he referred to as a "return to normalcy" in the 1920s, but to German-Americans the period seemed to be a continuation of the preceding period of "abnormalcy." At the very least, Wilsonism and all that this represented would be rejected in the election of 1920.

A Just Peace

The major issue for German-Americans in the field of foreign affairs after the war was the establishment of a just peace with Germany and Austria based on Wilson's Fourteen Points. Indeed, the German-American press claimed that any peace not based on this plan would be regarded as a violation of the promise to the defeated. However, they soon came to view the Treaty of Versailles as a work of malice and hatred.[1]

The diplomats who gathered at Versailles failed to establish a lasting peace and concluded a treaty that made a mockery of the Fourteen Points. In the German-American press, the treaty was constantly cited without comment to call attention to its glaring inconsistency with Wilson's peace proposals. Ultimately, the German-American press considered the treaties with Germany and Austria as total failures. The

Cincinnatier Volksblatt, for example, first a supporter of the proposed League of Nations, stated that German-Americans did not feel the league was important at all and that the treaties were worthless. Indeed, opposition to them was the basic point everyone agreed on. Wilson vehemently attacked German-American opposition to the Treaty of Versailles. However, many others opposed it as well, and the U.S. Congress failed to approve the treaty.

Trade was finally resumed with Germany in July 1919. Although relations gradually improved, they remained somewhat ambiguous, as the United States did not ratify the Treaty of Versailles. The Armistice remained in effect until August 1921, when the Treaty of Berlin took place. The *Cincinnatier Freie Presse* felt that now normal relations could be resumed. Diplomatic relations were resumed in November 1921, and in May 1922 the German ambassador arrived in the United States, as did the U.S. ambassador in Berlin. In 1923 President Harding ordered the return of the U.S. Army from Europe, and in 1926 Germany was admitted to the League of Nations. Hence, in the field of foreign affairs, "normalcy" was returning by the mid-1920s in terms of U.S.-German relations.

The German-American press strongly protested that in spite of the Armistice, a "hunger blockade" was maintained against Germany until July 1919, when it signed the Treaty of Versailles. German-Americans contributed to postwar relief projects for the sick, starving, and needy in Germany. At the national level, a variety of war relief programs were coordinated by the American Friends Service Committee and Herbert Hoover. With little governmental support, Hoover attracted substantial contributions from German-American financiers and others. He succeeded in unloading huge agricultural surpluses, which helped farm prices in the United States. Later he founded the European Relief Council, which by early 1921 had contributed $29 million to postwar relief. German-American organizations and religious denominations also raised substantial sums in a labor of love for the Old Country.

It is estimated that a total of $120 million was sent by German-Americans to Europe from 1919 to 1921. In many communities, there were local chapters of groups such as the Society of Needy Children in Central Europe. For example, by 1920 the Cincinnati chapter had raised

$52,334.84. German-Americans viewed the postwar relief work as the only positive contribution they could make. Many of them held special benefits to raise funds. German-American farmers even donated milk cows for children in Germany via the American Dairy Cattle Company of Chicago. At least four shiploads of cows reached Germany, where they were distributed across the land. Through the Methodist Episcopal Church, German-American Methodists contributed $500,000 to war relief in Germany, which was coordinated by the Methodist European Relief Office in New York. As Rippley notes, German-Americans "did not forget their ancestral homelands in the hour of greatest need." The total of postwar relief aid raised by German-Americans and the Hoover-led organizations amounted to $150 million.[2]

The Postwar War

Even after the signing of the Armistice in 1918, the anti-Germanism engendered by the war was continued as if the war was still in progress. Again the tone was set by Wilson, whose anti-German rhetoric included references to the dangers of the "hyphen." Following this kind of leadership, the U.S. Senate in 1919 held hearings that reflected this nativist orientation. The Senate Subcommittee on the Judiciary completed its report on *Brewing and Liquor Interests and German and Bolshevik Propaganda*. Here, conveniently lumped together, were all the forces the nativists feared: brewers, Bolsheviks, and Germans.

In the report all segments of the German-American community were charged with disloyalty. Brewers, some of the most affluent members of this community, were described as a "vicious interest" who had been "unpatriotic because it had been pro-German in its sympathies and conduct." Almost all brewers were felt to be of "German birth and sympathy" who had supported German-American societies. All of these were condemned, as most of them had been affiliated with the Alliance.

The Senate report criticized German-American churches, especially Lutherans, who "were particularly active in defending the German cause" during the neutrality period. The report also attacked the German-American press, which it felt discouraged assimilation and had been used on behalf of German propaganda activities. It also felt that non-English publications presented a danger and recommended legislation to control them. It also felt that the preservation of the German language would educate German-Americans "along lines of German thought." The report documented the legitimation of anti-Germanism and provided it with governmental sanction.[3]

It was a logical step from this nativist report of 1919 to another anti-German piece of legislation—the enactment of prohibition. German-Americans viewed this as anti-German, as the liquor industry was predominantly German. Prohibition became associated with the hysterical superpatriotism of the time. To a great extent the Eighteenth Amendment was a legacy of war hysteria, as it identified prohibition with patriotism. Prohibition was linked to an aversion to drunkenness and its attendant problems and was also identified as being distinctly anti-German.

The Volstead Act of 1919 prohibited the manufacture and sale of any beverage with more than 0.5 percent alcohol. Prohibition not only deprived German-Americans of what they regarded as a dietary ingredient, but also deprived German social life of a basic element. Festivities almost became unthinkable now that they were dry. German-Americans regarded Prohibition as but another act against them. Their language and heritage and now their beverage were being forbidden. Judge John Schwaab, who had been vice president of the National Alliance and president of the Cincinnati and Ohio branches, claimed before the war that the prohibition movement was an expression of Anglo-American Puritanism. He felt that Prohibition was being forced on German-Americans by those motivated by anti-German bigotry. According to him, it was the Anglos in Europe and America who wanted to destroy German influences. Moreover, German-Americans felt Prohibition denied them of their personal liberty, as they felt the government had no right to interfere in such matters.

Prohibition was impossible to enforce. In Cincinnati close to five hundred bootleggers were arrested in 1919, and the town was honeycombed with home brew parlors, speakeasies, and private clubs. In March 1933, the production of light wine and 3.2 percent beer was allowed, and states across the land revoked prohibition. Altogether it lasted from January 16, 1920, to December 5, 1933, or twelve years, ten months, and nineteen days. This clearly left its mark on the German-American community.

Gone were the family beer gardens, sitting rooms, and nickel beer, which had brought people together in the community. No longer did they serve as centers of social, civic, and business life. They were replaced by a new institution—the dimly lit tavern, which was not family-oriented as had been the old-style beer gardens. Gone too were many restaurants, concert halls, and gardens. No longer were there family Sunday afternoons in the beer gardens accompanied by little bands playing Strauss and German folk music. Moreover, Prohibition had struck at one of the wealthiest segments of the German-American elite, the brewers, who had strongly supported German-American community institutions. Prohibition not only affected the community as a whole by striking at the elite, but also touched the institutions supported by the elite, the individual and the family.

Another indication of the postwar war against German heritage was that in 1919 laws continued to be passed against the German language. On April 1, 1919, Gov. James M. Cox of Ohio delivered his "Special Message for the Teaching of German in the Elementary Schools." As a result of his address, the Ohio legislature passed the Ake Law, which forbade German in public, private, and parochial schools in Ohio below the eighth grade. Cox's address aimed to find a solution to what he viewed as the evil of German instruction. Cox, who became the Democratic presidential candidate in 1920, was viewed as heir apparent to Wilson. He felt that German instruction was in conflict with Americanism and part of an international conspiracy centered in Berlin.

To support his argument, he offered "three definite accusations." Apparently, proof was not necessary. First, he claimed that the German government maintained agencies in the United States to hold German-Americans together "to preserve Germanism." Implicit in this attack was the notion that German-Americans should not hold together and preserve their heritage. Second, Cox felt that this was being accomplished by means of German instruction. Third, he felt that German textbooks were treasonable. He disliked the idea of communities that, in his opinion, "live and feed on no tradition, historical, or national, except that of the fatherland." He also felt that German teachers were filled with "Prussian poison."[4]

Fortunately, test cases from Ohio, Nebraska, and Iowa were brought to the U.S. Supreme Court, which ruled in June 1923 that all laws against the German language, such as the Ohio Ake Law, were unconstitutional and violated the Fourteenth Amendment, "providing that no state shall deprive any person of liberty without due process."[5] The Court observed that no emergency had arisen "which renders knowledge by a child of some language other than English so clearly harmful as to justify its inhibition with the consequent infringement of rights long freely enjoyed." Anti-German laws, as well as laws against other languages, were reversed. However, until 1923 there were various laws on the books against the German language in more than twenty-six states. Thanks to the Supreme Court, the movement to eliminate non-English instruction was brought to an end.[6]

German-American Intellectuals

Several trends of thought emerged in the 1920s as German-Americans reacted to demoralizing events of World War I. At the forefront of the politics of anger and revenge was George Sylvester Viereck, a publicist who had barely escaped a lynch mob in 1917. He militantly espoused a political strategy with the main vehicle being a national organization, the German-American Citizens League. It was motivated by a spirit of anger over what had been done during the war. Much of its leadership consisted of former Alliance leaders, and their goals and aims were political in nature, and their rhetoric harsh. However, their bitter and demanding tactics often repulsed German-Americans.[7]

Opposed to Viereck's position was Hermann Hagedorn. He was an author, a poet, and biographer of Theodore Roosevelt, whom some regarded as a turncoat. During the war, he had joined the cause of the anti-Germans in castigating and vilifying other German-Americans. He felt it was his duty to expose what he considered as the danger of the German-American press, as he detected a danger because of what he viewed as its "German atmosphere." Hagedorn, a widely published author, strongly identified with the Anglo-American literary culture of New England and represented the German-American intellectual who rejected his heritage and community for that of the Anglo-Americans. He and Viereck presented opposite ends of the scale.

Striking a middle course between these positions were those intellectuals who advocated a cultural course of action. Hugo Muensterberg, a Harvard professor of psychology, was an early proponent of this viewpoint. During the war, he disengaged himself from political activities and moved to a cultural position. He stoically endured the anti-German sentiment. In his last book, *Tomorrow*, he advocated reconciliation and the right of self-expression for German-Americans. He stressed the avoidance of controversial issues but held that one should not forsake ideals. He called the recent attack on German-Americans one of the most deplorable periods in American history. He identified the role of the German-American as one of cultural mediation. The German-American's duty should be to "supply the noblest and most ideal elements of the culture of Germany" to America. The best elements of German heritage should be preserved by the individual and the family.[8]

Another proponent of the cultural approach was Kuno Francke, professor of German at Harvard and director of its Germanic Museum. He regarded it as the paramount duty of German-Americans to be "heirs and guardians of German culture in this country." He felt that this was a cultural task that had nothing to do with group politics. However, he urged an end of "the neglects and injustices" to German-Americans, as well as an end to the abolition of German instruction and "similar outgrowths of war fanaticism." He stressed that it would be harmful to form "a special German-American party." He identified the best and most valuable characteristics that German-Americans could contribute to America were "independence of personality, in depth of conviction, in freedom of prejudice, in earnestness of intellectual effort, in breadth of view, in spiritual striving, in just appreciation of cultural values." He recommended that German-Americans should "take prominent part in all matters concerning the political, intellectual, moral, social, and artistic" life of the country.[9]

If Muensterberg and Francke pointed the way to a cultural course of action, there was another voice that provided a blistering critique of American society—the Baltimore sage H. L. Mencken. He spoke about what he called "the Anglo-Saxon white terror" of the First World War. He admonished that "the facts must be remembered with shame by every

civilized American." To all who persecuted German-Americans he recommended "a nickel-plated eagle of the third class." He attacked the
political process as one controlled by "the mob," those "who have not
got beyond the ideas and emotions of childhood." He viewed American
politicians as demagogues who played on the fears of the masses. By
1917 the American people, in his view, "were in such a state of terror
that they lived in what was substantially a state of siege." The political
process he described as "combat between jackals and jackasses." Wilson
was viewed as "the bogus liberal" and "the perfect Puritan."[10]

By referring to Wilson as a Puritan, Mencken indicated that the real
menace to German-Americans were Anglo-Americans and their Puritan
Weltanschauung. According to Mencken, they were motivated by the
desire "to punish the other fellow for having a better time in the world"
and "to bring the other fellow down to his unhappy level." The Anglo
Puritan was motivated by sadism: "They lust to inflict inconvenience,
discomfort, and, whenever possible, disgrace upon the persons they
hate—which is to say, upon everyone who is having a better time in the
world than they are." He felt that Anglo Puritans were responsible "for
the uneasiness and unhappiness that are so marked in American life."
Regarding the anti-German hysteria, Mencken prophetically and correctly stated "that every other emergency that is likely to arise . . . will
be dealt with in the same adroit and effective manner."[11]

While most German-American intellectuals were specifically concerned with their role in society, one of them focused on the question of
the nature of American society. It was by now obvious that the melting
pot was a myth. Horace M. Kallen, a German-born professor of philosophy and psychology at the New School for Social Research in New York,
published an article in 1915 on "Democracy and the Melting Pot," which
began the series of publications he developed regarding the realities of
cultural pluralism.

Kallen vigorously rejected the myth of the melting pot. The reality
was that each group tended to preserve its own particular language, religion, institutions, and heritage. He viewed English as a common language, but he also felt that people should maintain the language and culture of their heritage.

He saw America as "a great republic consisting of a federation or commonwealth of nationalities." To force Anglo conformity on ethnic groups would violate "the basic law of America itself, and the spirit of American institutions." This would require the complete nationalization of education, the abolition of every form of private school, the elimination of instruction in non-English languages, and the concentration on English history and culture.[12]

As an alternative to this enforced Anglo conformity, Kallen advocated a harmony that would require "concerted public action . . . by way of freeing and strengthening the strong forces actually in operation." This ethnic group harmony would exist within a societal framework that would "seek to provide conditions under which each may attain the perfection that is proper to its kind." This would emphasize mutual respect for all individuals from all ethnic groups in the multicultural fabric of American society. Furthermore, the "provision of such conditions is the primary intent of our fundamental law and the function of our institutions." He defined the ideal of Americanism as self-realization through self-control and self-government. Americanism had nothing to do with ethnicity.[13]

Kallen noted that people can change their clothes, politics, spouses, religions, or philosophies, but they cannot change who their grandparents were. He viewed government as a democratic conception that was an instrument, rather than an end in itself. American would become a multiplicity in one unit. As each instrument in an orchestra has its own timbre and tonality, so too does each ethnic group function as an instrument in society. What Kallen described were the realities of ethnic group life. His was a theory drawn from life. Gradually, it would come to be recognized as foundational to the multicultural definition of American society.

The postwar era was rich in creative social thought among German-American intellectuals. Although there were different perspectives, there was some common ground. They all felt that German-Americans as a major ethnic group had an important role to play. Second, they all began to critically examine the nature of American society and come to the conclusion that America is a multicultural society and that it should be one based on tolerance and mutual respect. No single group should define Americanism in terms of its ethnicity. English should be the common language, but this should not negate or deny individuals and groups their rights to preserve their own heritage.

Community Leadership

Although the German-American National Alliance was now defunct, most of the state and local branches were still intact, and the question arose in the postwar era as to how to address the problem of the lack of a national organization. By 1919 two groups arose to address this question.[14]

On June 9, 1918, the German-American Citizens League was formed in Chicago and called a German-American National Conference for August 1920. Representatives from twenty states attended the meeting, which was chaired by Ferdinand Walther, a prominent Chicago German businessman who had been president of the Chicago branch of the Alliance. However, the driving force behind the meeting was George Sylvester Viereck, the main advocate of an aggressive agenda. It was his hope that the new League would replace the old Alliance. The League circulated questionnaires to congressional and presidential candidates and then issued endorsements. The League was primarily based in the Midwest, with branches in Illinois, Minnesota, Wisconsin, Michigan, Indiana, and Ohio. By means of Viereck's journal, *The American Monthly*, the League reached a national audience.

Primarily based in the East was the Steuben Society of America, established on November 6, 1919, in New York. Former Congressman Richard Bartholdt, who had sponsored prewar legislation for the Steuben Monument and had been part of the embargo and antiwar movement, played a key role in the formation of the new group, which was led by Carl E. Schmidt, a Detroit businessman. Although politically oriented, the Steuben Society adopted a more diplomatic approach than did the League. Its branches, or Steuben Units, were located throughout the country, but mainly in the eastern states. Its journal, *The Steuben News*, provided members and others with information on its platform and endorsements of candidates.

An immediate issue facing the League and the Steuben Society was the 1920 presidential election. Although German-Americans were publicly cautious about expressing political opinions, the national organizations made their positions well known by their endorsements. Of all the presidential elections in the 1920s, none stirred the emotions as much as the 1920 election. German-Americans became some of the strongest supporters of the women's vote at this time as a means to double the German vote.

Governor Cox of Ohio, as sponsor of the anti-German Ake Law, had no chance of German-American support, so the election turned into an anti-Cox vote, which won the election for Harding. The *Cincinnatier Freie Presse* proclaimed, "Down with the Democrats! They are only the exploiters of the people . . . yes, even traitors to the people's cause, but not representatives, not leaders, not servants, of the people."[15] Cox was referred to as "a fanatic Germanophobe . . . a miserable schemer without honor and principles." Both the League and the Steuben Society endorsed Harding, who was also strongly supported by the German-American press. Harding won in a landslide victory, and German-Americans settled scores by expressing their smoldering resentment with the Democrats at the ballot box.

Soon after the election, the League sent a delegation, including Viereck, to visit Harding at Augustine, Florida. The purpose was to urge Harding to appoint German-Americans to the cabinet. However, anti-Germanism was still so rampant that it was ill-advised for Harding to appear to favor the delegation's suggestions. Some in the press criticized Viereck for using pressure tactics, thus alienating some of the moderates in the German-American community.

However, Viereck felt that such demands were entirely appropriate, given the size of the German element and the fact that they had voted overwhelmingly for Harding. Hence, German-Americans may have agreed on goals, but the tactics and strategy were in question. Some preferred a behind-the-scenes approach, rather than Viereck's highly visible approach. However, the latter lambasted his critics and their approach as reflecting the war and an unwillingness to become politically involved. Many church-oriented Germans, including Lutherans and Catholics, did not support the more aggressive position either. Indeed, a German Catholic paper wrote of the League that it consisted of liberal free-thinkers who had little use for church Germans except at election time "to help them attain their particular aims, chief among which at the present time is the defeat of prohibition."[16]

In 1924, both the League and the Steuben Society endorsed LaFolette on the Progressive ticket; the Wisconsin senator was especially popular for his progressive outlook and his opposition to American entrance into the war. However, the German-American press realized that a third party had little or no chance and endorsed Coolidge, the Republican candidate. Charles Nagel, former Secretary of Commerce and Labor, also provided an influential endorsement. Although LaFollette did obtain some of the German vote, most followed the lead of the press in going for Coolidge, thus continuing the vote against the Democrats. In 1928, before Coolidge left office, the Arion Singing Society from Brooklyn, New York, sang at the White House for the president, which reflected Coolidge's popularity among German-Americans.

In 1928, both the League and the Steuben Society, however, endorsed the Democratic candidate Al Smith against Hoover. This proved to be divisive, as some still felt that the Democrats represented Wilsonism. Hoover, on the other hand, was of German descent and had actively been involved in relief work for Germany. However, others said that Hoover was a "dry" and for this reason shouldn't be supported, whereas Smith was a "wet." Some also preferred the latter's Irish Catholic background, his progressivism, and his anti-England position. Sensing the chance for support, the Democrats obtained endorsements for Smith from prominent German-Americans, including Congressman Bartholdt, Babe Ruth, Lou Gehrig, H. L. Mencken, Theodore Hoffmann, and various editors. The German Methodists, however, endorsed Hoover because he was a "dry," but the German Lutherans rejected Smith because he was Catholic. Much of the German-American press went for Hoover, stressing his relief work and Nagel's endorsement, which stressed Hoover's extensive experience, his methodological approach, and his plans for the future.

Hoover's election strengthened the political leadership of the press as opposed to that of the League and the Steuben Society, which had endorsed losers in the last two elections. As a result, they changed direction. The Steuben Society began to concentrate on state and local elections in New York, New Jersey, and Pennsylvania. Also, its journal increasingly focused on German-American heritage topics, rather than politics. Viereck withdrew from active involvement in the League, which thereafter was not active in national politics.

Righting the Wrongs

German-Americans in the 1920s were resentful at their mistreatment during and after the war. This was underscored by the fact that there were no official apologies or condemnations made with regard to the anti-German hysteria. Indeed, at the state level, many laws were passed in the early 1920s against the German language and were overturned by the U.S. Supreme Court only in 1923. German-Americans received no official apologies except for this act of the Court, and much of the Germanophobia continued unabated. Indeed, the last piece of national anti-German legislation, in their view, continued until 1933, when Prohibition finally came to an end. Only then did it seem possible that a real return to normalcy could begin, but unfortunately, troubles again loomed on the horizon.

Notes

1. Regarding the peace settlement, see Don Heinrich Tolzmann, ed., *German-Americans in the World Wars* (Munich: K. G. Saur, 1995), vol. 1, pp. 209–21.

2. LaVern J. Rippley, *The German-Americans* (Lanham, Md.: University Press of America, 1984), pp. 194–95.

3. Senate report on brewers, see ibid., vol. 3, pp. 1248–53.

4. Don Heinrich Tolzmann, *The Cincinnati: Germans After the Great War* (New York: Peter Lang, 1987), p. 179.

5. Ibid., p. 181.

6. Regarding the postwar war, see ibid., vol. 3, pp. 1189–1256.

7. See ibid., vol. 3, pp. 1369–89.

8. Tolzmann, *German-Americans in the World Wars*, vol. 3, p. 1375.

9. Ibid., p. 1377.

10. Ibid., p. 1379.

11. Ibid., pp. 1379–80.

12. Ibid., p. 1381.

13. Ibid.

14. See ibid., pp. 1282–96.

15. Ibid., p. 1286.

16. Ibid., p. 1290.

The Second World War

The German-American Press

Since the German-American press functioned as a mirror of the German-American community, it is helpful to examine the press's outlook on German-Americans before the Second World War. The anti-German hysteria of the First World War had dealt the German-American press a devastating blow. In 1920, there were 278 German-American publications, in 1930 there were 201, and by 1939 there were 181. The war had been hard on the press and had been followed by Prohibition, which had also dealt another blow, since it deprived the press of a major source of advertising revenue, the brewing industry. Adding to this loss were the hard economic times that came with the Great Depression. In spite of these hard times, the press had survived, and approximately one-fourth of German-Americans were reading the German-American press, so it clearly functioned as a mirror of the community and played an important role in community life.

By 1940 there were German-American publications in twenty-six states. The states with the greatest concentrations were: 29 in New York, 22 in Illinois, 16 in Ohio, 16 in Minnesota, 14 in Pennsylvania, and 11 in Texas. The twelve daily newspapers were located in New York, Philadelphia, Baltimore, Rochester, Cincinnati, Cleveland, Detroit, Chicago, and

St. Paul. The rest of the press consisted of weeklies, monthlies, quarter-lies, and annuals. There were also many specialty publications issued by secular and religious organizations and institutions. In the 1930s a number of new newspapers and serial publications were established by the recently arrived immigrants, such as *Aufbau* in New York and the *New Yorker Volkszeitung*.

The German-American press, once noted for its editorial discussions and positions, had been influenced by the First World War to now avoid taking an active political stance or position, especially with regard to controversial issues. It did, however, take a position at election time in terms of endorsing candidates, and would advise German-American voters on various issues. Indeed, the press increasingly took upon itself the responsibility as the institution in the community responsible for making endorsements at the national, state, and local levels.

Besides reticence on controversial issues, there was another dimen-sion which characterized the press at this time—isolationism. Indeed, political scientists have established that isolationism was the strongest in the states where German-Americans predominated. They also tended to more isolationist than other ethnic elements, and this reflected their bitter disillusionment with the World War I experience. They now preferred iso-lationism in international affairs and felt that the United States should maintain an independent position. This isolationism was another under-lying characteristic of the press and reflected German-Americans' desire to remain aloof from European conflicts. It was also an expression of their fear of another outbreak of anti-German hysteria like that of World War I. An expression of this could be found in the journal *Youth Outlook: German-American Monthly*, published in New York by the German-Amer-ican League for Culture. Its December 1939 issue stated:

> It is our interest that America not be led once more into fighting the battles of Europe, for Hitler's oppressive rule can only be abolished by the oppressed themselves. We support the fight of the German people for their liberation and we regard it as our duty to preserve the real German culture and the traditional democracy of the United States. We must prevent a repetition of the chauvinism of the last war. We must not fall again into the trap of war propaganda.[1]

Politics

In 1930 German-Americans numbered roughly 32 million out of a total population of 124 million. Foreign-born German-Americans and their children numbered 6,873,103, with 75 percent of the children being American-born. Obviously, by this time, the majority of German-Americans were American-born.

The German-American National Congress held two meetings of national significance, the first in New York in October 1932 and the second in October 1933. The first meeting took place right before the November 1932 election. A key player was the editor of the *New Yorker Staatszeitung*, Ludwig Oberndorf. Among the items discussed were the formation of a new national organization, the establishment of a German-American research and information center, and the founding of a German-American university. The main concern appeared to be the preservation and maintenance of German heritage by means of addressing the needs for certain kinds of institutions. Unfortunately, the Congress did not meet after 1933, because other issues loomed on the horizon.

After 1928 the Steuben Society and the German-American Citizens League shifted their attention from endorsing candidates for national office to other issues. They had many new issues emerging in the 1930s, as well as a number of items of old business pertaining to the First World War. For example, there had never been anything approaching a public apology by a U.S. president for the wrongs and injustices of the anti-German hysteria. Although candidates and parties actively sought German-American voters, there had never been a plank in any of the political party platforms condemning the anti-German hysteria. This led to a deep and smoldering resentment among German-Americans. Second, there had never been discussion in Congress with regard to a condemnation of the unfair hearings against the German-American National Alliance and the German-American brewing industry. Third, there had never been a bill presented in Congress to provide for an apology and reparations for the internment of 6,500 German-Americans during the First World War. Fourth, although some of the anti-German legislation had been dismantled due to the U.S. Supreme Court's reversal of the laws against the German language, many other laws at the state and local levels still stood in place, so that the new postwar status amounted to a situation that could best be classified as institutional racism in relation to German-Americans. For example, the names of streets, buildings, parks, schools, and the like had been changed by law; after the war, these laws were not revoked, but remained in place. To German-Americans, the anti-German hysteria was still in place. Fifth, in cases where the laws had been revoked, such as laws against German instruction, there had been no action to reinstate German programs, so that the effect was that the impact of the anti-German hysteria in that particular area was still in place. Finally, German-Americans in general protested against what they perceived to be a basic lack of information on German-Americans in the standard works of American history, especially in school textbooks.

These matters were among the specific items of concern that emerged from the World War I experience. Although politicians did not address the German-American agenda, they were keenly aware of the size of the German-American voting public, and both parties went after it. Indeed, attention had been drawn to German-American voters by means of the Congress in October 1932. Also, a recurrent theme in the German-American press in 1932 was the question, "Which candidate will be the most friendly toward German-Americans?"

As the election approached, the German-American press was divided. Hoover continued to be popular due to his German heritage and because he freed Germany from the pressure of war reparations with his declaration of a one-year moratorium in 1931. However, two factors worked strongly against him. First, there was his support of Prohibition, which was anathema to German-Americans, and second, he was being held responsible for the Great Depression. Hence, the press reflected the divided opinions of German-Americans in 1932.

In Cleveland, Otto Fricke, a community leader, advised that German-Americans vote for Hoover, as did Judge A. K. Nippert in Cincinnati. Also, the Republicans heavily advertised in the German-American press with the slogan "Hold Fast to Hoover!" A cartoon in the *Cincinnati Freie Presse* portrayed Roosevelt saying to voters: "I'll promise you anything just so you vote for me." However, Democratic advertising by the

German-American Division of the Democratic National Committee hit hard at the pressing issues of the day. It announced that Roosevelt would repeal the Eighteenth Amendment and noted that this was strongly desired by German-Americans. It also claimed that a vote for Roosevelt would be "a step forward to justice for you and your countrymen." German-Americans, like everyone else, were in the depths of the Depression, and many decided to leave the Republicans and vote for the Democratic candidate in the hope of an improved economic situation, as well as the end of Prohibition. Even in German-American Republican strongholds, such as Cincinnati, Roosevelt won; in the latter case by a vote of 123,109 (Roosevelt) to 118,804 (Hoover).

However, by 1936 German-Americans were disenchanted with Roosevelt, not only because he had not ended the Depression, but also because he was increasingly viewed as pro-British and anti-German in his foreign policy. Therefore, in some areas, especially German Catholic regions, German-Americans voted for William Lemke of the Union Party. He was supported by Father E. Coughlin, the radio priest known for his anti-FDR broadcasts. Lemke, a German-American, polled only 890,000 votes, or about one-fifth of what the 1924 third-party candidate, LaFollette, had received. These votes, however, can be seen as expressions of German-American discontent and protest. Among the cities voting for Lemke (more than 5 percent of the vote) were St. Paul, Dubuque, and Cincinnati. In Wisconsin and Ohio, there were at least thirty German-American precincts that cast a plurality of votes for Lemke, whose father had fought in the Prussian army in the 1870 war with France. These votes were clearly manifestations of a lingering sense of resentment about the war, isolationism, and the suspicion that Roosevelt was leading the country into another war in Europe.

In 1940 German-Americans voted for another German-American candidate, Wendell Willkie, a Republican from Indiana. He followed campaign advisers to "attack Roosevelt as a warmonger . . . with warning that votes for Roosevelt meant wooden crosses for their sons and brothers and sweethearts." With these prophetic words, he struck a responsive chord and received the majority of endorsements from the German-American press. As the tide for Willkie grew in the fall of 1940, Roosevelt continued to assure voters of his sincerity in promises strikingly similar to those of

Wilson in 1916. Willkie predicted that if Roosevelt was elected, he would bring the United States into the war by April 1941. Roosevelt cleverly responded: "I have said this before, but I shall say it again and again and again: Your boys are not going to be sent into any foreign war. . . . The purpose of our defense is defense."[2]

Just as Wilson's promises to keep America out of the war had contributed to his 1916 victory, so too did Roosevelt's promises. However, his victory was smaller than anticipated. He received 27.2 million votes as compared to 22.3 million for Willkie, which reflected German-American dissatisfaction with Roosevelt's policies. In a secret report to FDR, Louis H. Bean noted that German-Americans had shifted away from the Democrats in a much higher percentage than any other group. Also, Samuel Lubell found that Roosevelt's losses among German-Americans averaged from 20 to 30 percent.

Although German-Americans opposed the government of the Third Reich and all it stood for, they were opposed to American involvement in a war against Germany, not only because it was the ancestral homeland, but also because they feared a recurrence of anti-German hysteria. Also, they had no interest in going to war on behalf of Britain or France. They felt that American involvement in the First World War had resulted in the disastrous Treaty of Versailles, which had been dictated to Germany and had made a mockery of Wilson's Fourteen Points. In April 1941 Theodore Hoffmann, head of the Steuben Society, stated that the overwhelming majority of the thirty-two million German-Americans wanted America to keep out of the war, stating that they opposed all isms except Americanism.

International Relations

Isolationism was not just a German-American attitude, but was a view widely held by the American people. An important factor was the Senate investigations in 1934–36 of Sen. Gerald P. Nye of North Dakota, who was convinced that the munitions companies were responsible for American entrance into the First World War. He and his assistants did extensive research and uncovered sensational information about the lobbying activities of banks and munitions companies, as well as their war-based profits. For example, the Du Pont company's profits soared from $5 million in 1914 to $82 million in 1916, an increase of almost twentyfold. Many began to feel that the mistake of 1917 should not occur again.

At the same time, Walter Mills published an influential book, *The Road to War: America, 1914–1919*, which said America had been drawn into the war by British propaganda, the munitions industries, and Wilson's different treatment of Britain and Germany. Charles Warren, a former assistant attorney general, wrote that "under modern conditions there is no reason why the United States government should run the risk of becoming involved in a war simply to preserve and protect . . . excessive profits to be made out of war trading by some citizens."[3] Such publications contributed to the general popularity of isolationism with the American public. A Gallup Poll in 1937 indicated that 94 percent of the American people felt that American policy should aim to keep out of all foreign wars.

These sentiments found expression in the passage of a number of neutrality acts. The 1935 Neutrality Act forbade the sale of munitions to belligerent nations, and Americans who traveled on belligerent ships did so at their own risk. However, Roosevelt opposed this, and fought for a discretionary embargo, but signed the bill due to his fear of the isolationists. The 1937 Neutrality Act continued the previous one but gave the president the discretionary power to sell goods to belligerents on a cash-and-carry basis. This in essence provided a loophole for the United States not to remain neutral.[4]

In 1937 Roosevelt proposed a quarantine of nations that were creating what he called a state of international anarchy, but a storm of isolationist opposition caused him to abandon the idea. To many German-Americans, it was clear which nation he wanted to quarantine. Hence, beginning with the 1936 election Roosevelt was revealing more and more of his interventionist outlook.

In 1938 he spoke of what he called "sister nations," as well as of the "God-fearing democracies." Again, the concern among German-Americans was whether he had Britain in mind as a "sister nation." Then in 1939 he urged Congress to repeal the Neutrality Act so that the United States could sell arms to Britain and France, and the answer became perfectly clear what Roosevelt's thoughts were. In November he pushed through a new law that allowed for the sale of arms and other contraband on a cash-and-carry basis, and short-term loans were also allowed. However, American vessels were forbidden to carry such products to the belligerents. As mainly Britain was in control of the high seas, this legislation favored it and France.

Moreover, by 1939 Roosevelt allowed for the sale of arms to Britain and France, although he had no legal authority to do so. He had in fact abandoned neutrality for nonbelligerent involvement on the side of these two countries. After the fall of France, he arranged to provide fifty destroyers to Britain, although a direct loan or sale would have violated American and international law. This action was performed as a "trade" for American bases in the Caribbean.

After the election of 1940, when he stated that American boys were not going to be sent abroad to war, Roosevelt decided to provide arms to Britain by means of the lend-lease program, after the British had indicated that they could not afford the cash-and-carry program. And in January 1941 he asked Congress for the expenditure of $7 billion for war materials that he could sell, lend, lease, exchange, or transfer to other countries which in his view were vital to U.S. interests. Although not stated, the purpose of the Lend-Lease Act was simply to save Britain.

Although Willkie had predicted that the United States would be involved in the war by April 1941, the Roosevelt administration had involved the country in overt acts of aggression by the summer months. In July the destroyer *Greer* had pursued the German submarine *U652* and had then notified the British of its position. The British then dropped depth charges on it, which provoked the U-boat to attack the destroyer and defend itself. However, Roosevelt stated that the *Greer* had only been delivering mail to Iceland and had not engaged in any hostile acts, so it appeared as if the U-boat had attacked the destroyer without provocation. Roosevelt then used this as an excuse to order the navy to shoot on sight any German craft in the waters south and west of Iceland and to convoy merchant vessels as far as that island.

America was, of course, drawn into the war by Pearl Harbor and Hitler's declaration of war in December 1941. Once again the country was at war with the ancestral homeland of the German-Americans.

Although they favored isolationism, they staunchly opposed the government of the Third Reich and when faced by a declaration of war, they immediately and enthusiastically rose to the defense of the country.

Immigration

The advent of the Third Reich in 1933 led to the emigration of more than a million Germans to escape tyranny and persecution. Altogether, two hundred thousand came to the United States. This immigration was often referred to as an intellectual migration, as it included scientists, artists, musicians, writers, philosophers, doctors, architects, and actors, many of whom were Jewish. Their search for freedom in the New World had been more urgent than for the immigrants of the past, given the barbaric intentions of the Nazi regime. Under these circumstances, the intellectual elite of Germany arrived, ranging from Thomas Mann to Albert Einstein. Indeed, almost anyone who had been considered a representative of German cultural life was in exile after 1933. A biographical guide to this emigration can be found in *The International Biographical Dictionary of Central European Émigrés, 1933–1945* (1983) by Herbert A. Strauss and Werener Röder.

The new arrivals deeply enriched American society from technology to the arts to politics. After Hitler declared war on the United States in 1941, they joined in the effort to liberate Germany from the yoke of National Socialism and later contributed to reestablishing the foundations of German-American friendship, as few of them returned to Germany. A 1944 edition of *American Men and Women of Science* listed 106 refugees of German birth who had already made an impact as physicists, mathematicians, medical researchers, botanists, zoologists, chemists, biologists, geneticists, meteorologists, and students of electrical engineering. A dozen of them went on to win Nobel prizes for their outstanding contributions in their particular fields. Perhaps no name is more well known than that of Albert Einstein, who came to be known as "the pope of physics." Altogether they represented a loss to Germany and a tremendous boost to America's upswing in the sciences.

The extraordinary contributions in the sciences were paralleled by those in the humanities and social sciences. The Frankfurt School for Social Research came to New York with its entire faculty, including Max Horkheimer, Theodor W. Adorno, and Herbert Marcuse. They continued their work at Columbia University. Among the faculty of the New School were immigrants such as economist Hans Staudinger, psychologist Max Wertheimer, and theater director Erwin Piscator.

Among those who became prominent in the film industry were Ernst Lubitsch, Billy Wilder, Douglas Sirk, and Marlene Dietrich. The influence of Walter Gropius and Mies van der Rohe on American architecture continues to this day. In the area of psychoanalysis, Erik H. Erikson and Erich Fromm became well known. The impact on the realm of music, of course, was considerable, with numerous conductors and composers arriving, such as Bruno Walter, Otto Klemperer, Arnold Schönberg, and Kurt Weill.

The new immigrants also exerted a great economic impact on the United States. They opened up new factories, shops, businesses, and industries. In a survey of 158 refugee-owned businesses, sixty-nine were producing goods not previously made in America; fifty had introduced new products; and twenty-two introduced new processes. They also contributed to an appreciation of German literature and culture. Several of them started German publishing houses, such as Schocken, Ungar, and Erga, and the immigrants included Germany's finest authors, such as Herman Broch, Lion Feuchtwanger, Emil Ludwig, and Franz Werfel, who all continued to write in German. The refugees contributed immensely to the material welfare of the communities where they settled, but more significantly, they raised the level of German culture in the United States, just as the Forty-Eighters had done in the nineteenth century.[5]

Anti-German Zeitgeist

As America entered the 1930s, the *Zeitgeist* was "latently, if not overtly, definitely anti-German."[6] As there had been no acknowledgment or recognition of the wrongs and injustices that had been perpetrated against German-Americans, but rather indifference to these matters, the *Zeitgeist* was similar to the country's mood before and during World

War I. This made for a dangerous situation, which contributed to the angst of German-Americans, as well as their support for isolationism. They feared another outbreak of the anti-German hysteria that had happened a little more than a decade ago. This concern was underscored by the general public reaction to several events in the 1930s, which seemed to bring the latent *Zeitgeist* into various kinds of overt expressions.

This was first noticed in the knee-jerk reaction to the emergence of the German-American Bund, a pro-Nazi organization. Although German-Americans made their opposition to this group known, and although the group represented an insignificant number of people, the reaction made it seem as if it were a multimillion-member conspiracy. The Bund attained a total membership of only 6,300, of which 3,900 were German-born or German-American. It represented an extremely small number of individuals. However, what the Bund lacked in numbers it made up for with parades, rallies, and rhetoric.[7]

Originally formed in Chicago in 1924 by one of Hitler's associates who had fled Germany after the failed beerhall *putsch* of 1923, the group was organized as the Society for the Friends of the New Germany, or, as it was simply called, the Bund. It published a weekly, *Das Neue Deutschland*, which contained an English-language supplement. Although it was an insignificant group, the decision was made to hold congressional hearings on it, the Dickstein-McCormack Congressional Investigatory Committee hearings, conducted by the Special Committee on Un-American Activities. The hearings began in April 1934. The committee ignored the wise counsel of Rep. T. M. Carpenter of Nebraska that such investigations would only fan the flames of prejudice, which they did. Although chaired by Congressman McCormack, the committee was actually led by Congressman Dickstein. Thanks to the hearings, the Bund received a great deal of publicity and increased its membership considerably.

What were the facts about the Bund? First, there was a basic misconception about its size. It attained a membership of only 6,500, and its influence was negligible outside of its group. However, it was reputed to have a much larger membership. This was due to the exaggerated claims of its leader, Fritz Kuhn, who asserted it had more than two hundred thousand members. Due to Kuhn's vocal leadership and the congressional hearings, it did grow to some six thousand members. A second misconception was that by being labeled "un-American," the Bund was guilty of wrongdoing. Whatever value judgments are made, the Bund itself "broke no laws, nor did it advocate revolutionary principles, or the forcible overthrow of the government. . . . Under the First Amendment, its activities were legal and protected by the Constitution."[8] Also, there were no financial or organizational links between the Bund and the Third Reich. It was a separate entity on American soil and engaged in nothing but exercising its constitutional rights. However, its very existence had decidedly negative repercussions for German-Americans, as the distinction between them and the Bund was blurred in the public mind, so German-Americans were found guilty by association and were often treated accordingly.

Given the latent, or not so latent, anti-German *Zeitgeist*, the emergence of the Bund did considerable damage to the status of German-Americans. Indeed, its establishment may be likened to striking a match in a room filled with gas fumes. Its mere inception was highly inflammatory, and this was fueled by its repulsive ideology and rhetoric. The situation was not alleviated by the Bund itself.

It held mass meetings and attracted huge crowds due to the publicity as well as the fact that it offered free beverages (beer). In 1936, it held a meeting at Madison Square Garden attended by twenty thousand, and another in 1939 attended by twenty-two thousand. Crowd analyzers later demonstrated that many were simply curiosity seekers, as well as those interested in a free drink.

Kuhn was given to bragging of a relationship with Hitler, as, for example, when he returned from a trip in 1938 and stated he had met with Hitler, although he had had only one audience with him in 1936. In short, the claims, the rhetoric, and the mass meetings inflamed the public and supported the hysterical fear of the Bund.

The manner in which the hearings were conducted confirmed the worst suspicions and fears of German-Americans, who detested the Bund and all it stood for but at the same time vividly recalled the anti-German hysteria of World War I, especially the ruthless manner of the congressional hearings on the German-American National Alliance in 1918. They also remembered that the inquisition of the Alliance had placed a stamp of approval on the persecution of German-Americans during and after the war and that it had never been officially condemned or revoked, but still stood in place as part of the institutionalized anti-Germanism. Hence, German-Americans, who despised the Bund, nevertheless viewed the hearings with grave concern.

The hearings were originally intended to be conducted in an orderly manner, but the atmosphere was raised to an emotional, high-fevered pitch from the start by Dickstein with his persistent baiting and verbal harassment of witnesses. He assailed all those who appeared, assuming the role of prosecutor and judge, rather than that of objective investigator. German-Americans recoiled in anger and horror at the vile manner in which this hearing was conducted, as it violated everything that a democracy stands for. Dickstein was labeled as the number-one German-hater in the United States. Not only were German-American witnesses subjected to insult, abuse, and harassment on the witness stand, but they were victimized in the congressional halls by the mean-spirited intolerance and hostility fostered by the committee. Such intolerance and hostility was reflected in the press, and its reverberations were felt across the country.[9]

The committee invited a wide cross-section of people from German-American communities. The concern was that no distinction was being made whatsoever between those who did and did not belong to the Bund —they were all seen indiscriminately as a whole. Hence, to have been called as a witness was to have been been publicly tried and convicted.

Although the committee was charged with investigating, it soon took on the aura of a court that passed judgment on witnesses as if they were criminals and traitors, assumed guilty of "un-Americanism" merely by being called as a witness. This was clearly reminiscent of the Americanism movement of the First World War, which accused individuals of having "hyphenated loyalty."

Indeed, the new crime was being un-American, a term as all-encompassing as it was vague and indefinable. Indeed, this is specifically what bothered German-Americans: who defined what was American and what was un-American? Were there not federal, state, and local laws and regulations that defined what was legal and illegal? To German-Americans, being an American meant having U.S. citizenship. What further definitions needed to be made, and who would be making these determinations? Would it be the congressional committee which declared one guilty of some undefinable wrong merely by being called as a witness? Was this going to be defined and conducted by those who had been involved in the anti-German hysteria of World War I?

Congressman M. Maverick wisely remarked that the term "un-American" could be defined as "simply doing something that somebody else does not agree with." Since there was no question of anything illegal, the term un-American took an a dimension of extralegality and could be used to smear and destroy those with whom the committee did not agree.

By 1934 German-Americans decided it was time to take a firm stand against the Bund, as well as against the Third Reich, so that the distinction between German-Americans and Bundists was crystal clear. By this time, reports of Nazi terror had reached the United States, including reports of Hitler's seizure of power, his establishment of a police-state dictatorship, his brutal treatment of opponents in the Reichstag, the Roehm purge, and more. German-Americans consequently joined the boycott against German goods that a number of groups had organized. Also, many organizations were taking firm action to make their positions known. The Carl Schurz Foundation, for example, ceased publication of its journal, *Germany Today*, and commenced publication of a new journal with an American focus, *The American-German Review*, which stressed the German heritage of America. In 1936–37 it sponsored a study by Dr. Heinz Kloss, a historian from the Institute for International Relations in Stuttgart, to come to the U.S. and prepare a report on the feasibility of establishing a German-American research center, which would be called the American-German Institute.[10]

A number of anti-Bund organizations arose, including the Loyal Americans of German Descent, the German-American Anti-Nazi League, the German-American Congress for Democracy, the German-American League for Culture, and the Non-Sectarian Anti-Nazi League. In Cincinnati and elsewhere, the Bund was barred from taking part in the annual German Day celebration. In St. Louis, the Bund was banned from using the local German House for its meetings. The Bund was now under heavy attack from the German-American establishment on all fronts, which involved the major organizations and the press. The *New Yorker Staats-Zeitung*, for example, strongly attacked the Bund, and an officer of the Steuben Society stated that some of the Bund members were unfortunately of German stock but were of absolutely no credit to German-Americans. Across the United States, the Bund found only scorn, as German-Americans, their organizations, and their press did their utmost to make clear that the Bund was a tiny fringe group with which they had nothing to do.

In November 1939 the German-American Youth Federation held its conference and an anti-Nazi rally in New York. It aimed to demonstrate that German-Americans were loyal Americans and anti-Nazi. The conference also tried to prevent another outbreak of the anti-German hysteria of the First World War. Its journal, *Youth Outlook: German-American Monthly*, carried the headlines in its December 1939 issue that it wanted "No More Liberty Cabbage," which referred to the fact that during the previous hysteria, sauerkraut had even been renamed as "liberty cabbage." The lead article stated that during the previous war,

> the reactionaries and war-makers in this country deliberately organized a campaign of war-hysteria and chauvinism. They went so far as to demand the destruction of even the language and culture of the "hostile" nation. They condemned words on the basis of their origin. . . . In the course of this war of blind hatred they tried to rechristen "sauerkraut"—"Liberty Cabbage." This is perhaps the lighter side of the problem, but it should serve as a symbol to remind us that such chauvinism is a serious danger to our constitution and to the traditional liberties of our country. It must not be allowed to repeat itself in this war. We do not stand alone in our desire to prevent the return of the pogrom-like atmosphere which, in 1917, made life miserable for loyal and democratic citizens of German descent.[11]

Congress in 1938 authorized the House Committee to Investigate Un-American Activities (HUAC), which was basically a continuation of the 1934 congressional committee investigating the Bund. Again a committee, this time chaired by Martin Dies, would try to investigate what it considered to be un-American. Again Congressman Maverick wisely warned that such a committee could only engender racial hatred and foment unrest while merely earning headlines for the politicians on the committee.

Cabell Phillips in his book *The Truman Presidency* describes the HUAC. He describes Dies as the bull-voiced, xenophobic, fire-eating congressman from Texas who exploited the committee for political purposes, staging a whole series of flamboyant public investigations and seizing the membership lists of various organizations, among them, of course, the Bund.

By July 1939 the committee began to publish its findings, which were basically summaries of its hearings. By this time, the Bund was self-destructing and in rapid decline due to the hearings and public pressure, especially from the German-American establishment. However, the committee credited itself with having destroyed the Nazi movement before it could get underway. To German-Americans, it had been an incredible overreaction to a fringe group that could never become a movement. They felt that what had been destroyed were the reputations and lives of non-Bundists, because no distinction had been made between the Bund and German-Americans who had no connection with it.

Some did recognize the dangers of such committees. Walter Lippmann, for example, compared the committee to a pack of vigilantes, and others called for Dies's resignation. The vigilante committee fed the public hysteria regarding the threat of a Nazi movement. The danger of such a committee is that it "took to defining and categorizing patriotism, thus requiring conformity of a nation founded on divergence of interests and based on freedom." Apparently, the committee forgot that the United States is a democracy and not a dictatorship, even for those one does not agree with. Most important was the fact that the "pursuit of un-Americanism, a convenient catch-all designed to cover any and all prejudice and bias, is inherently un-American itself."[12]

The Bund never made any headway, and it soon became obvious that the majority of German-Americans were utterly out of sympathy with the Nazi regime. Although the failure of the Bund was due to its rejection by German-Americans, its final blow was self-inflicted. In May 1939 Fritz Kuhn, its leader, was indicted and convicted for having embezzled Bund funds for his own personal use. In 1943 he was released from prison and interned to the end of the war. After the war he was extradited to Germany, where he died in Munich in 1951. This illuminates the real function and the purpose of the Bund, a money-making con game designed to make money through the sale of uniforms, badges, flags, and publications. With 6,500 members, there were many such materials to be sold, and Kuhn's embezzlement was an indication that he was living off these funds.

It is alarming that such a small organization could become the focus of a congressional hearing and contribute to public hysteria over a supposed internal Nazi threat. More alarmingly, it led to the formation of the infamous House Un-American Activities Committee, which received notoriety for its witch-hunting of the McCarthy era. Although well known for its work in the 1950s, the committee was taking shape and form in the 1930s and was a continuation of the 1918–19 congressional committees. The HUAC was basically a theatrical spectacle for politicians interested in publicity and "an attempt at ritual purgation by means of public embarrassment and personal ruin." The HUAC took up its work again after the war, and a famous German-American author, Thomas Mann, commented that it was an expression of Know-Nothingism. He was painfully familiar with similar political trends, such as political inquisition which had forced him into exile in the 1930s.[13]

The first indication of problems in the early 1930s was the overreaction to the Bund. A second and related problem was the reaction to the Bund as reflected in the publication of books pertaining to the Bund as a possible *fifth column*, the term used for disloyal elements. An important book was *The Trojan Horse* (1940) by Martin Dies, head of the HUAC. This work listed numerous bona fide German-American organizations and created the impression that there was a German-American "trojan horse" in America. It also recommended that in the case of war individuals from these organizations should be interned.

Other works fanning the flames of public hysteria included Leon G. Turrou's *Nazi Spies in America* (1939), which is highly reminiscent of the genre of spy-conspiracy books published during the First World War. Another well-known work was Richard Rollins's *I Find Treason: The Story of an American Anti-Nazi Agent* (1941). Ralph Bischoff, in an amazingly bizarre work, *Nazi Conquest Through German Culture* (1942), advanced two absurd notions. First, he held that German-American cultural organizations were the vehicles of German nationalism. Second, he cited bona fide German-American establishment organizations as dangerous and threatening, including the old Alliance, the Pennsylvania German Society, the Turners, and German-American schools and churches in general. Here was a full assault on mainline German-American organizations, an indication that the hysteria over the Bund had led to an all-encompassing attack on all German-American associations.

A third area of concern was the flood of books published by a few recently arrived émigrés from the Third Reich. Some of them misread and misevaluated the American—and in particular the German-American—situation by basing their judgment exclusively on their experience gathered under Nazi rule. As much as one would agree with their intention of preventing a Nazi takeover of the United States, one has to admit that these newcomers overlooked the fact that the Bund and their sympathizers by no means represented a threat to American stability and democracy, as the Nazis had to the Weimar Republic. In addition, these well-intentioned yet insufficiently informed writers did not seem to be aware of what had happened on the American homefront during World War I, and they apparently had no idea about the issues that were paramount to German-Americans. They increased the difficulties for decent German-Americans and fed the public misconception of a domestic fifth-column movement. It should be noted that some of these exiled authors were facing the immediate struggle of having to make a living, and the publication of sensational literature provided a livelihood.

An example was the exiled author Kurt Singer, who launched a highly successful career specializing in spy stories. He effectively made the transition from writing books on European topics, such as *White Book of the Church of Norway on Its Persecution by the German Occupation Forces and the Quisling Regime in Norway* (1941) and *Duel for the Northland: The War of Enemy Agents in Scandinavia* (1941), to works dealing with the same kinds of themes but pertaining to American circumstances.[14]

By 1945, he had brought out his magnum opus, *Spies and Traitors of World War II*, a sensational work that went through three printings. Upon his arrival in the United States, he published a number of booklets in the series *Background: The Key to Current Events*, which were widely circulated and capitalized on the Nazi spy theme. These included *Germany's Secret Service in South America* (1941) and *Spies and Saboteurs in Argentina* (1942).

All of these works were damaging, for they painted a picture of the

Western Hemisphere being infested with spies, saboteurs, plots, and intrigues. A direct and vicious attack on German-Americans was Singer's *Confidential Report on 1,036 Pro-Nazi Firms Who Believed You Could Do Business with Hitler* (1942), which listed more than a thousand German-American businesses that did business with Germany before the war. They ranged from shoe stores and meat markets to other common wares and goods. Many companies, of course, had long-standing connections with Germany, especially with friends, family, and relatives, and such a publication was an attempt at blacklisting, as was done in the McCarthy era.

Directly after the war, Singer published *The Revival of the Nazi Bund in the United States of America*, but as the hysteria over phantom Nazis evolved to concerns over Communists, he shifted to works dealing with this topic, such as *Communist Agents in America: A Who's Who of American Communists* (1947). After having exhausted the spy motif, he shifted again to adventure stories, crime stories, and finally to the realm of ghost stories and tales of the supernatural, including his *Gothic Horror Book* (1974).

What is fascinating about Singer is his ability to establish himself in the United States, to sense the climate and interests and to exploit them commercially. He was, of course, not alone, but he was perhaps one of the most successful at his craft. Among others, F. W. Foerster is noteworthy for the publication of works that represent not only gross distortions, but also classic examples of disinformation.

In 1943 Foerster published *Open Letter to the Loyal Americans of German Descent*, and although he claimed his work was not intended to create disunity, his rhetoric was abrasive and hostile to German-Americans. He claimed he wanted to

> expose an intricate chain of organizations in America which have labored for many years to create disunity and ill-feeling. To ignore them is dangerous; to allow them to continue without any protest is not possible to any good American who has been made aware of their existence and their purpose.

What followed was an obvious frontal attack on all German-American organizations.

The author proclaimed that his aim was to expose the threat of pan-Germanism and Germany's plan for aggression against America. He stated that he had done extensive research on fifth-column activities in Latin America and the United States. His work attacked the anti-Nazi German-American organization known as Loyal Americans of German Descent as consisting of people who "spread Pan-German and even undisguised Nazi propaganda in this country up to the day of Pearl Harbor." He claimed that "many German-Americans have been willing, even ardent collaborators in this vicious Pan-German plot." By not melting in the melting pot, he maintained, German-Americans were serving German national interests, rather than America.[15]

Another example of the degree to which some émigrés failed to comprehend the German-American community was their misreading of the German-American press. As discussed earlier, due to their experiences during the First World War, the German-American press was extremely reluctant to take a position on anything that could be construed as controversial, and it confined itself to endorsing candidates at election time. After arriving in America, many exiles expected to find the German-American press engaged in a crusade against the Third Reich. Although the press did take a position against the Nazi Reich, the degree of engagement did not satisfy some of the exiles. They then engaged in the same kinds of smears against the German-American press that Singer and Foerster practiced. For example, the *Aufbau* in New York stated that the Third Reich did not have any better support than the *New Yorker Staats-Zeitung*. It also said that if Hitlerism had taken hold in the German-American societies, then it was in large part due to the *Staats-Zeitung*.[16] Such remarks were unjustified and inadequate polemics that reflected a gross misunderstanding of the German-American press, as well as of the German-American community. For example, the *Staats-Zeitung* employed German Jewish refugees as members of the editorial staff and as freelance writers.

Another area of concern for German-Americans in the early 1930s was the case of Bruno Richard Hauptmann, who was tried and convicted of the Lindbergh baby kidnapping in 1935 and electrocuted in New Jersey in 1936. Before his death, he prophetically remarked: "They think that when I die, the case will die. They think it will be like a book I close. But the book, it will never close."[17] The specific details of the case are not of concern here, but rather the public reaction to the case, especially the reactions of German-Americans.

Immediately after the kidnapping, various publications charged that the baby had been kidnapped by Japanese, Soviet, or German agents. Hauptmann and his wife were German immigrants, and he had served as a machine-gunner in the First World War in the German army. After his arrest, Hauptmann was subjected to twenty-four hours of interrogation, followed by two days of continual physical abuse. His captors tried to beat a confession out of him, and they strapped him to a chair so that they could subject him to repeated beatings. After three days of this treatment, Hauptmann was battered black and blue, but he never confessed to the kidnapping.

In support of Hauptmann, the German-American community in the Bronx collected funds for his defense, and many rallied at the courthouse on his behalf. When Hauptmann spoke, the American press reported that his manner and stance were "typically Germanic," as if this were something negative. The prosecutors stressed that Hauptmann was an immigrant and that such a crime could not have been committed by an American, in fact, not even an American gangster would sink to such a low level. However, Hauptmann was attacked as something worse: he was un-American. As the trial took place in 1935, it almost directly followed the hearings by the Un-American Activities Committee in Congress.

The Hauptmann case was closely followed in the German-American press. The view was that Hauptmann's German origin played a central role in his conviction and execution. Hauptmann had sought out and settled into the German-American community, and during the trial had been strongly supported by the German-Americans from the Bronx. Old newsreels show the courtroom and the crowds outside the courthouse. Many felt that Hauptmann had not been given a fair trial, and reports to that effect continued to appear in the New York German press long after his execution. Coming directly after the congressional hearings, and considering that Hauptmann's ethnicity was taken note of in a negative manner, many German-Americans felt that ethnic bias definitely played a role in the case. The question emerging after the hearings and the Hauptmann case was whether or not a German-American, especially a recent immigrant, could obtain a fair trial.

Films produced in Hollywood and playing up the *Zeitgeist* followed these events. Indeed,

> movie depictions of America's German stock frequently leaned toward the controversial, preferring depictions of Bundists, Nazi spies, and saboteurs in films full of foreign intrigue, in an effort to sell large numbers of tickets and generate substantial profits for film companies.

Such images "fanned flames of prejudice against the German community, without providing a contrasting viewpoint representative of the majority of German-Americans of the day." The precedent had, of course, been set in the First World War. During that war, spy movies were extremely popular, and similar themes were revived in the 1930s, especially by 1938. In that year, Time Incorporated produced a newsreel, *Inside Nazi Germany*, a short film that attempted to report on conditions in Germany, as well as on German propaganda efforts. It claimed that the such propaganda also existed far from "fascist frontiers" and gave special attention to Fritz Kuhn and the Bund. It insisted that German-Americans "believe in Nazi teachings" and "imitate Hitler's mighty military machine." The film aimed to incite the public not only against Nazis, but also against German-Americans.[18]

Perhaps the most well-known film of this genre was *Confessions of a Nazi Spy*, which appeared in 1939. Here an FBI agent investigates Nazi underground activities in America and discovers an organized network of agents and collaborators in defense plants, military branches, and other strategic areas. In the film, German-Americans who oppose the Nazis are either beaten up, kidnapped, or sent to concentration camps in Germany. The film aimed to demonstrate that there was an internal Nazi threat in America:

> [T]he German-American Bund is seen to be the center of a Nazi spy ring, gathering intelligence on the American military and attempting to spread class resentment. The Nazis are predictably stereotyped as sneering, goose-stepping fanatics out to rid America of its Constitution and Bill of Rights. . . . [T]he hysterical tone of the non-fiction sequences tends to overstate the Nazi threat to America itself.

Also, "only two types dominate the American landscape of this film: white Anglo-Saxon Protestants—the good guys, and the Nazis—the bad guys."[19]

Distributors of *Confessions* were warned that Nazi sympathizers might start riots against the film, so squads of detectives were hired at first-run theaters, which was not only a marketing factor, but also a fear-mongering. In September 1941 the Senate held hearings regarding propaganda in American movies, at which time Sen. Charles Tobey asked whether the film industry is bending "its powerful efforts to propagandize the American people into hysteria, so that excitement rather than calm judgment should guide them in the matter of getting into the war," and if so, then it was a matter that should be investigated by the Senate. However, the hearings were overtaken by the events that brought the United States into the war.[20] After American entrance into the war, the Nazi spy film genre continued. Even the ever popular Bowery Boys got into the act. In their 1943 *Ghosts on the Loose*, the Boys discover that their new neighbors are Nazi spies who have a printing press in their basement with which they are producing propaganda.

Major movie studios not only attacked Nazism, but also created the impression that there was an internal threat in the United States, and in the process "German nationals and German-Americans, including those who had voiced opposition to the Nazi regime and its aims, found their reputations tarnished and were cast into suspicion, based on the actions of a miniscule but vocal minority." These films, some of which appeared to be innocuous, "would contribute to the call for action against the German community upon American entry into World War II, and would play a part in bringing about the arrest and internment of over 10,000 German nationals and German-Americans from December 1941 to June 1948."[21]

Just as some of the exiles German and émigrés had contributed to publications dealing with the supposed spy threat, so too did they act in many films dealing with the same topic. Indeed, certain character actors built their reputations on playing villainous Germans, as Erich von Stroheim did in World War I. This was true for Peter Lorre, Konrad Veidt, Walter Slezak, Otto Preminger, William von Brichen, and Martin Koslech to name a few. As much as the political commitment of these refugees and survivors is understandable, the films they participated in were problematic for the German-American population, because no sharp differentiation was offered between regular German-Americans and the dubious Bund members.

The Smear Campaign

The beginnings of the smear campaign emerged in the congressional hearings, where one was in effect guilty by virtue of having been summoned as a witness. Thereafter, the smears became explicit by means of various media. The extent of the smear campaign is clearly demonstrated by an examination of the World War II experience of Sen. Gerald Nye of North Dakota, who, although he was not German-American, represented a state where German-Americans constituted the largest ethnic element. Nye had been a staunch isolationist and had documented in the 1930s the role the munitions makers had played in bringing the United States into the First World War.

In January 1943 Senator Nye placed a lengthy statement in the *Congressional Record* in response to the smear campaign directed against him and, by implication, against his constituency in North Dakota. Drew Pearson had published a column in the *Washington Post* entitled "Hitler's Stooges" in which Nye was viciously smeared as a stooge of Hitler. Nye wrote that he had to respond, as he now faced

> charges which reflect not only upon me but upon my state—North Dakota—and I rise in my place here in the Senate to give answer to those who seemingly are not content with unity, those who will not have unity, if you please, unless unity carries with it the privilege, for them, to deride, berate, and falsely charge those who have not been in agreement with them respecting the conduct of foreign policy and the ways of achieving victory.[22]

Among the various points he addressed were the charge that 5 percent of German-Americans were Nazis, 5 percent were anti-Nazi, and 90 percent were "sitting on the fence." Nye condemned these contentions as "baseless, as foundationless, as any charge could possibly be." He also stated that he was extremely proud of those of German descent in his state, and he also noted that of the casualty lists he had seen thus far, one-third consisted of soldiers with German surnames.

> [D]amned be the man who dares to rise and say that Americans of German origin in the State of North Dakota are not working, sacrificing, bleeding, and dying in the interests of American victory in this war. . . . There are moments when I would like to wring the necks of the agitators and prejudice-builders, who would if they only could, destroy the unity and centralness of purpose which have so long possessed Americans. . . . I for one am quite done with standing idly by while some few go forth in the guise of "patriotism" with programs that are insulting and most destructive in their very nature. . . ." He also spoke out sharply against the "wanton effort . . . to destroy confidence in entire communities of people."[23]

Nye also provides character analysis of those who engaged in the smear campaigns against German-Americans by noting that Pearson "could quote from *Mein Kampf* and make Hitler seem a hero or quote isolated verses from the Bible and make devils out of the Apostles." He stated unequivocally that "there is not the slightest basis for any such charge as Pearson has made and the *Post* has published."

Nye also responded to the charge that he had spread Nazi propaganda by inserting an address by the president of the Steuben Society of America, Theodore Hoffmann, into the *Congressional Record*. Nye noted that Pearson, Walter Winchell, and others had been circulating such stories. Nye aimed to set the record straight by stating that the Steuben Society was a fine organization that detested Nazism. It had demonstrated this in the early days of the Bund when it "put its foot down on this undertaking without mercy, condemned it," and made sure that there were absolutely no connections with the Bund whatsoever. Furthermore, he noted that the society was an American organization and a great credit to the German-Americans who had fought for freedom during the American Revolution.

He also noted that he had inserted an address by Hoffmann in the *Congressional Record* in April 1941, in which the latter stated:

> Ours is a nation composed of citizens of all countries and no one has a place in our ranks whose allegiance is not wholly to the United States of America. . . . Americans of Germanic extraction do not want Communism, fascism, or nazism, and they do not want British imperialism. They want Americanism.

Although this had been clearly anti-Nazi, Pearson and others charged Nye with the dissemination of Nazi propaganda.

Nye then pointedly stated that it was known "how eagerly some forces" had tried to "get something" on Hoffmann and the Steuben Society, strongly declaring that "smearing was rampant to a degree that made the program hysterical." Also, he noted that "once smeared by them one is naturally expected to stay smeared." He concluded his courageous statement:

> I appreciate the privilege which has permitted me to rise in my place and defend myself against the outrageous innuendoes and lies which have been so prominent during many months of seeming effort to smear, smear, smear one and all who dared, prior to Pearl Harbor, to differ with policies which some of us felt were policies which could not lead anywhere other than into war.[24]

Internment

As a result of their political incorrectness during the world wars, German-Americans fell victim a second time to a war-engendered anti-German sentiment. If few today are aware of the anti-Germanism of this period, fewer still are aware of the internment of 6,300 German-Americans during the First World War and 10,905 during the Second World War. The World War II experience was directly related and connected to the experience of the First World War. The anti-German hysteria and sentiment of the world wars is interrelated, two parts of a whole.[25]

Given the public hysteria over the Bund, Nazi spies, trojan-horse elements, the attack on Pearl Harbor, and the anti-German hysteria of World War I, it is not surprising that there was public pressure to take action against what was felt to be the existence of an internal threat to the United States. However, this fear expressed itself differently than in the First World War. What was different in the Second World War was the absence of the widespread vigilante lynch-law spirit of the First World War. However, violence did occur, such as the looting and wrecking of the German Central House in Cleveland, Ohio. However, such cases of violence were sporadic, the exception rather than the rule.

This was due to several factors. First, a World War I–style pogrom would have been politically ill-advised, since FDR had lost German-American votes since the 1936 election, and was well aware and informed of this trend. He also did not speak out publicly against German-Americans, so this vigilante spirit was not encouraged from the top down. Another factor was that German-Americans were enlisting in substantial numbers in the armed forces, so the statistical size of the German-American element was influential. To have taken action against a major ethnic group in a time of crisis would have been disastrous. FDR exercised good judgment in not encouraging a vigilante spirit.

A second factor was that German-Americans were isolationist and neutral in the 1930s. However, before American entrance in the First World War, they had been staunchly in favor of Germany and Austro-Hungary.

Third, a moblike hysteria did not occur because many of the targets had been already abolished, banned, burned, or destroyed during the First World War. For example, German instruction was still banned in most places from the elementary level onward, although it had returned in some places at the high-school level. German books had been removed from libraries and destroyed; streets, buildings, institutions, and monuments with German names had been renamed, and their original German names had not been reinstated. Since many of the targets no longer existed, cases of violence, such as the ransacking of the German House in Cleveland, were isolated incidents.

However, the status of German-Americans had not recovered from the First World War when it received new blows by the congressional hearings and the negative media images. German-Americans and their institutions were still viewed as suspect, even subversive. Given this status, it was not advisable to celebrate German heritage and ethnicity, and most German Day celebrations were postponed until after the war. It also meant that ethnic slurs were common against German-Americans, including such epithets as Huns, Krauts, or Nazis. German-Americans endured these slurs as well as the status loss in the hopes that the anti-German sentiment would not escalate.

Given this kind of hostile situation, it is obvious that those in the most precarious and vulnerable positions would be German-Americans who had not yet obtained their citizenship papers and would be classified as aliens. The Emergency Detention Program begun by FDR in September 1939 ordered the Justice Department to detain persons it considered dangerous in the event of war, invasion, or insurrection. A dangerous person was classified as a person who would engage in or conspire with others to engage in acts of espionage or sabotage. This, together with the Alien Registration Act of 1940, allowed the FBI to compile lists of people thought to be dangerous to the public peace and safety of the United States.

What kind of information was available? It basically consisted of hearsay transmitted to the FBI without the person's knowledge. Such information was obtained from places of employment, neighbors, or so-called confidential informants. In other words, unsubstantiated hearsay was all that was necessary to smear an individual's reputation. This secret-informant system encouraged a climate of spying and informing on coworkers and neighbors. Three categories of suspects were assembled: an "A" category for aliens who were in leadership positions in cultural or assistance organizations; a "B" category for less suspicious aliens; and a "C" category for members of ethnic groups and those who donated money to them. The prime source of such information was the Alien Registration Act, the membership list of the Bund, and lists based on the subscriptions to the German-American press, those who attended German Day celebrations, or leaders and members of German-American organizations. Subsequently, these lists became the basis for internment.

James Rowe, Assistant Attorney General, testified in 1981 that by December 7, 1941, a planning commission at the Department of Justice had been in operation for approximately one year, based on the premise of U.S. entrance into the war, and that lists of names were made on the basis of this premise. An FBI memo dated December 8, 1941, from J. Edgar

Hoover, identified people targeted for internment, including 636 German aliens, 1,393 American citizens sympathetic to Germany, and 1,694 persons of German descent whose citizenship was known. Beginning on December 7, arrests of German-Americans in forty-one states began to take place. Arrests ranged from as few as two in Alaska to as many as 2,200 in New York. The actual number of people arrested was 6,362. As families, including children, often joined in the internment, close to eleven thousand were actually interned. A number of children were born in internment, or concentration camps. Also, more than four thousand Latin American Germans were brought to the United States for internment.

How did an individual get placed on the hit list? Someone had to have reported him or her to the FBI. These unfortunate German-Americans were not informed of the fact that they had been reported on or what had been said about them or who had reported them. Nor were they entitled to legal counsel, a violation of the Sixth Amendment, which provides for the right of the accused to know who their accusers are.

People were turned in for having attended German-American society meetings or a German church; for having received German-American newspapers or having a short-wave radio, speaking German at home. People could be charged with having said something favorable about Germany in the 1930s. Also, if a German-American lived near a port city, factories, government buildings, or railways, this could be reported. Of course, having belonged to or attended a Bund meeting could make one a likely candidate as well.

Many were arrested by means of arrest orders, which tried and convicted the individual in advance, a violation of the Fifth Amendment pertaining to the right of due process. Some did face Local Hearings Boards, which were really kangaroo courts, as sentences were predetermined and often announced in advance in the press. For example, individuals would be interned after a hearing before a so-called Hearings Board. No attempt was made at actually determining the validity of hearsay made against an individual.

One teenager facing a hearing in Cincinnati was asked what his response would be if a German U-boat arrived on the Ohio River in downtown Cincinnati. Such individuals were denied the right to legal defense and could not ask any questions of the hearing board.

German-Americans were concentrated in more than fifty camps, ranging in location from Ellis Island in New York to Tujunga in California to Crystal City in Texas. In most cases, these camps were INS facilities or INS contract facilities, but county and city jails were sometimes used as overnight holding centers. The camps were typically enclosed by barbed wire with armed guards surrounding the perimeter. The last German-Americans were not released until July 1948, or more than three years after the end of the war.

On February 19, 1942, Executive Order 9066 was initiated, which authorized the U.S. War Department to exclude and/or relocate certain people from military areas. Within this group selected for exclusion were so-called enemy aliens (immigrants from countries presently at war with the United States and who were not yet naturalized), as well as American citizens of "alien ancestry," a definition that could, of course, be easily applied to all Americans of German descent.

In addition to internment, forty thousand German- and other European-Americans had been placed on parole with restrictions on their constitutional liberties. In violation of the the Fourth Amendment, that one's home and possessions are secure from unreasonable seizure, thousands were relocated from the coasts, which were considered militarily sensitive.

Since 1948 there have been nine laws enacted to provide for an apology and redress to Japanese-Americans who were interned, but there have been no overtures to German-Americans and others who were interned. In 1980, Public Law 96-317 established the Commission on Wartime Relocation and Internment of Civilians, but when the hearings were held, the testimony of German-Americans was not sought, nor were any attempts made to contact and inform German-American national organizations about the hearings. No scholarly organizations in the field of German-American studies were contacted.

Recently past German-American internees have made some progress in terms of informing the public about the wrongs and injustices against them, as well as the failure of the U.S. government in issuing an apology. For example, Arthur D. Jacobs challenged the constitutionality of the 1988 law that awarded financial compensation only to Japanese-Americans.

Rejecting his claim, the Court based its decision on the aforementioned hearings, which excluded scholars of German-American studies, as well as the internees themselves, thereby, in the view of the latter, victimizing them for a second time. They and their families continue their efforts to set the record straight in the hope of attaining equal treatment before the law, as they regard their case as a tragic example of justice denied. Moreover, scholars have produced a number of valuable studies on the topic, such as Timothy J. Holian's informative *The German-Americans and World War II: An Ethnic Experience*.[26]

Revocation

Internment was not the only action taken against German-Americans during the war. Another tactic was the attempt to undermine German-American organizations by revocation, i.e., the attempt to revoke an organization's tax-exempt status.

During the anti-German hysteria of World War I, the German-American National Alliance had become a major target and was forced to dissolve in the face of congressional hearings in 1918. Although it capitulated as the national umbrella organization, the organizations it represented by and large survived, as did other special-interest umbrella organizations, such as the umbrella organization for the Turner societies, the *Turnerbund*. Certainly one of the largest, if not the largest umbrella group surviving the First World War, was the national federation of German-American singing societies, the *Nord-Amerikanischer Sängerbund*, or NASB. This time the point of origin was not the U.S. Congress, but rather the U.S. Treasury.

In 1944, the Internal Revenue Service informed the NASB that it was suspected of furthering pro-Nazi and pan-German movements, which would deprive it of its tax-exempt status. Faced by the same kind of attack as the Alliance had undergone in the preceding war, the NASB mounted a vigorous and successful campaign to stave off this unwarranted attack on its patriotism and loyalty and that of its affiliates. Having been smeared, the NASB entered into a two-year battle with the goal of regaining its tax-exempt status as a nonprofit organization.

The IRS stated that its investigations had disclosed that a large proportion of German-American societies of various kinds, including singing societies, had been united together under the aegis of umbrella organizations and that they had been utilized to further "un-American" movements. Evidence was, of course, not necessary, as suspicion was sufficient for the NASB to suffer revocation. This meant more than the loss of tax-exempt status; it meant that the organization was under a cloud of suspicion.

To regain its tax-exempt status, as well as its reputation, each local society affiliated with the NASB would now have to sever its ties with the NASB and prove it had purged itself of suspicious elements, as well as provide affidavits from the president and secretary to that effect. Individual societies were, hence, considered guilty and needed to prove their innocence.

In response to this attack, the NASB stated through its lawyers that the societies of the NASB had been in full compliance with the law of the land and that the objectives of these organizations were cultural in nature. Third, they had never engaged in any kind of propaganda activity. Moreover, it was noted that German-Americans had always been loyal, law-abiding, and devoted Americans. It also cited a survey of twenty German-American singing societies that showed that the members held more than one million dollars in Victory Bonds, and had close to six hundred sons and grandsons in the military and more than six hundred wives, daughters, and granddaughters in the Red Cross or related organizations. It also noted that German-Americans should not be judged by different standards due to their ethnic heritage.

By staunchly denying the charges against it and by seeking able legal counsel, the NASB continued its defense. In 1946, at its executive committee meeting, the following policy was decided on as the best means of extricating itself from revocation. Members decided that a resolution should be issued stating that the NASB had purged itself of any pro-Nazi or pan-German members and that it would not join any umbrella organization. Also, sworn affidavits as to the loyalty of its membership were sent to the IRS. The only question now was whether or not the IRS would accept this kind of response from the NASB.

In March 1946 the IRS notified the NASB that its tax-exempt status had been returned. The IRS was not able to prove its slanderous charges against the NASB and dropped them. The NASB had won its case. Had there been any grounds to its charges, they would no doubt have been presented. By taking a strong stand against the smear campaign, the NASB had saved itself and German-American organizations in general. This direct attack by the IRS, however, clearly demonstrated the role the federal government played in the Germanophobia of the Second World War. Charles M. Barber notes in an article in the *Yearbook of German-American Studies* (1995) that the NASB continues to preserve the German heritage to this very day, demonstrating that German-American societies and organizations weathered the storm of Germanophobia for the second time in the twentieth century.

Goethe in Hollywood

The most influential German in America during and after the Second World War was no doubt Thomas Mann, the German author, who became a U.S. citizen, and thereby a German-American. He was looked on as an authority figure not only by German émigrés, but by the American government and by the general public as well. Ludwig Marcuse wrote somewhat sarcastically in his book, *Mein zwanzigstes Jahrhundert*, that during the war Mann "played a role which he had never sought: he was the kaiser of all the German émigrés and the special guardian of the lineage of writers. Everything was expected of him, everything was owed to him, he was made responsible for everything. All devotion was concentrated on him, all rebellion was concentrated against him. . . . Everyone was of the opinion that, without Thomas Mann, nothing in America would have worked out."[27]

When Mann came to America, he already enjoyed a worldwide reputation as the author of *Buddenbrooks*, *Der Zauberberg*, and *Der Tod in Venedig*. Mann, born in 1875, first came to Princeton in 1938 before settling in Pacific Palisades in California, where he resided from 1941 until 1952. Here he came into close contact with other German émigré authors, writers, and artists. In 1933, he had decided to reside in Switzerland due to the new National Socialist regime in Germany, and in 1936 he publicly dissociated himself from this regime in an open letter to Eduard Korrodi, who was on the editorial staff of the *Neue Zuercher Zeitung*. In 1952 he moved from America to Switzerland, where he died three years later.

Without question Thomas Mann was viewed from 1938 to 1952 as the most widely respected German in America. Indeed, he wrote some of his major works in California, including *Lotte in Weimar* (1940), *Joseph der Ernaehrer* (Joseph the Bread-Winner, 1943), *Doktor Faustus* (1947), and *Der Erwaehlte* (The Chosen One, 1951), to mention a few. By the 1940s, Mann was referred to as "Goethe in Hollywood," as well as the kaiser of the German émigrés.

Mann's home in California was located in the hills of Santa Monica Bay, close to the Pacific. Here he lived and worked for more than a decade.[28]

Mann's influence was particularly important with regard to the U.S. image of Germany. In a series of works, Mann dealt with Germany, the issue of a peace settlement, and the future of Germany after the war. Among the works he published dealing with these issues were: *The Coming of Democracy* (1938), *This Peace* (1938), *The Problem of Freedom: An Address to the Undergraduates and Faculty of Rutgers University at Convocation on April the 28th, 1939* (1939), *Order of the Day: Political Essays and Speeches of Two Decades* (1942), *The War and the Future, An Address* (1944), and *Germany and the Germans* (1945). As the most influential and respected German in America, Mann's works, indeed, did play an influential role with regard to the image of Germany in America, and thereby contributed to postwar German-American relations.[29]

Mann was indecisive with regard to a particular resolution to the treatment of postwar Germany, and vacillated on the issue a number of times. However, his strong opposition to the Third Reich found expression in statements such as: "I shall be unmoved by any measures the statesmen of the world deem necessary to render Germany unable to repeat its performance in the foreseeable future." However, he also asked: "But can you blame a German writer for not wishing to stand before his people as agitator for their nemesis?" He helped define the focus on the regime, rather than the German people.[30]

Moreover, he wrote that it was not a case of there being "bad" or "good" Germans, nor of there being an essential difference between Germans and other peoples, as people are people. In this regard, he stated:

"In the end, the German catastrophe is only the paradigm of the tragedy of all mankind. The grace that Germany so badly needs is the need of us all." According to Thomas Prater's *Thomas Mann: A Life*, Mann "believed in a future for Germany in the coming world of social humanism, the awakening of mankind to their essential unity and the dawning of a world state."[31] Mann's views, hence, tended to contribute to an understanding of Germany, as well as its reintegration into the West in the postwar period.

Mann also contributed to the status of German culture in America. Like his German-American predecessor Carl Schurz, he thoroughly believed that U.S. citizenship had to do with political identity and that cultural identity was reflected by the German part of the equation. He stated: "I took my German inheritance with me. . . ." Elsewhere he noted that: "Where I am, there is Germany. I carry my German culture within me. . . ."[32] Such words express the very same thoughts that Schurz and other German-Americans had expressed in earlier generations to indicate that "German-American" meant U.S. citizenship held by one of German heritage.

Not only was Mann of importance for his role in advocating understanding for Germany and for setting an example of cultural pluralism, he also spoke out against maltreatment of recently arrived German immigrants who were in danger of removal and internment. Had he not done so, there is no doubt that many of them would have been endangered.

German immigrants were declared "enemy aliens" on declaration of war. In January 1942 it was announced that enemy aliens were going to be evacuated from coastal areas. Ronald Hayman notes in his *Thomas Mann: A Biography* that: "The refugees had been much worse off since America entered the war. Together with anti-Semitism, prejudice against foreigners—especially Germans—had increased."[33]

Realizing the danger, Mann sent a telegram to President Roosevelt, as well as letters to notables such as Upton Sinclair. Soon thereafter, a congressional Committee on Evacuation of Enemy Aliens under Rep. John H. Tolan was begun, and hearings began in March 1942. Together with Bruno Frank, Mann testified on March 7, 1942. As a result of the hearings, wholesale evacuation of German enemy aliens was abandoned; Mann's personal role here undoubtedly played a role.

Another lasting contribution of Mann, aside from his obvious literary contributions, was that he obtained a position as Consultant in Germanic Languages and Literatures at the Library of Congress, and that this position became the basis for positions at the Library for German specialists, who have continued to build and maintain the Library's German collections to become one of the largest of its kind in the world. A more recent holder of this position, Margrit B. Krewson, moreover organized numerous exhibits to highlight the German collections, sponsored lecture series, and edited a whole series of publications to highlight the holdings of the library such as: *German-American Relations: A Selective Bibliography*. This may be seen as part of the legacy of Thomas Mann.[34]

Peace

The period from 1945 to 1948 was one of extreme hardship for Germany. In addition to the extensive wartime destruction, it now faced the arrival of large numbers of Germans expelled from their homelands in eastern and southeastern Europe. In the greatest expulsion in world history, more than seventeen million Germans were expelled, resulting in the deaths of two million. One-third of German territory in the east, including Pomerania, Silesia, and East Prussia, was placed under Polish and Soviet administration. Moreover, Germans suffered from the lack of basic goods and services, but their primary needs were for food, shelter, and clothing.

Fortunately, America followed the postwar humanitarian policy that Herbert Hoover had established after the First World War. Hoover, a descendant of eighteenth-century immigrants from the Palatinate, had published a work in 1919, *Why We Feed Germany*, explaining that the United States should not kick a man when he is down, but rather provide a lending hand. After the war, Hoover headed the American Relief Administration, which was the model used after the Second World War, and had provided food and provisions for the needy in Europe from 1914 to 1921.

American welfare organizations founded the Cooperative for American Relief Everywhere (CARE Program), through which Americans could send a package with clothing or food to Europe for a mere ten dollars. Besides the basic staples, there were many other gifts for the Old Country, including butter, coffee, cigarettes, cocoa, and candy for the children. Some contained items the children had never seen, such as chewing gum and powdered milk. Altogether more than five million CARE packages arrived in Germany in the postwar years. Also, it is estimated that a total of $260 million worth of merchandise was sent by other organizations and individuals.

Not surprisingly, some of the major donations came from German-Americans. For example, the American Relief for Germany Committee in Cincinnati was organized by the German-American community, and raised a total of forty-four thousand dollars, as well as twenty thousand pounds of clothing for the needy and suffering in Germany. German-Americans gave generously not only through CARE and other relief agencies, but also directly to friends and family in Germany and Austria.

Additional U.S. support for Germany came in 1948, when Soviet forces blockaded Berlin. During the ten-and-a-half-month blockade, the city depended entirely on supplies by air, which meant not only food, but coal, raw materials, and household and industrial products of all kinds. A total of 275,000 Allied missions were flown into Berlin in order to break the Soviet stranglehold and to preserve the independence of West Berlin.

The American war relief programs together with the U.S. Marshall Plan contributed greatly to the postwar recovery of Germany, which became known was the *Wirtschaftswunder*, or Economic Miracle, as Germany completely rebuilt a war-torn country from ground up. In those hard years of reconstruction the foundations were laid for the close friendship between Germany and America. Germany's currency, the *Deutschmark*, soon became the strongest in Europe, and its government one of the strongest democracies in the world. Largely by means of the diplomacy and sagacity of its venerable chancellor, Konrad Adenauer, the Federal Republic of Germany rapidly regained its worldwide respect and became one of the most reliable allies of the United States, as well as one of the strongest members of NATO, which some called the German-American alliance. The close political and military relationship between Germany and America which emerged in the postwar era not only laid the foundations for a strong alliance between the countries, but also significantly raised the stature and improved the image of Germany internationally. It also greatly raised the morale of German-Americans, who justifiably took great pride in the new Federal Republic of Germany. Indeed, their efforts contributed in no small way to the closeness of Germany and America in the postwar era.[35]

Postwar Politics

The presidential election of 1948 surprised some political experts, since Truman received votes in some of the German-American Republican areas of the Midwest. Samuel Lubell studied the vote and found that German-American voters had remained in the Republican camp until 1948 because of their strong dislike of Roosevelt's foreign policy and that their vote switching contributed to Truman's election. For example, German-American precincts in St. Louis that had gone for Dewey in 1944 now went for Truman in 1948. In Wisconsin counties that had voted Republican in 1940 and 1944 now voted for Truman.

German-Americans were attracted to Truman for several reasons. First of all, Truman declared that the U.S. had been fighting not against Germany, but against Hitler, and these words smoothed the way to the beginnings of good relations between Germany and America and were greatly appreciated by German-Americans. Second, Truman had initiated the Marshall Plan and the Berlin Airlift, both of which contributed to the well-being and protection of Germany. Third, Truman appeared to be a down-to-earth, no-nonsense realist who dealt with the facts, rather than the impractical idealist that Roosevelt had seemed to be.

LaVern J. Rippley noted, moreover, "[T]he fact that the Federal Government for once was helping their ethnic brothers—from which British Americans had benefited during two World Wars—could only boost Truman's chances at the polls."[36] Except for Indiana and Michigan, Truman swept through the Midwestern German Belt states to victory.

Notes

1. See "An Editorial: A Tribute to Culture," *Youth Outlook: German-American Monthly*, no. 2 (December 1939): 4.

2. Cited in John A. Garraty, *The American Nation: A History of the United States*, 3d ed. (New York: Harper & Row, 1975), p. 755.

3. Cited in Gerald Nye, "A Personal Statement," *Congressional Record* (January 14, 1943), reprinted in *Steuben News* (January–February 1993): 7.

4. Garraty, *American Nation*, p. 751.

5. Regarding immigration in the 1930s, see Anthony Heilbut, *German Refugees and Intellectuals in America from the 1930s to the Present* (Boston: Beacon Press, 1983).

6. Don Heinrich Tolzmann, *German-Americans in the World Wars* (Munich: K. G. Saur, 1995), vol. 3, p. 1496.

7. Regarding the Bund, see LaVern J. Rippley, *The German-Americans* (Boston: Twayne, 1976), pp. 203–206.

8. Susan Canedy, *America's Nazis: A History of the German-American Bund* (Menlo Park, Calif.: Markgraf, 1990), p. 223.

9. Information on the hearings can be found in ibid.

10. See the report by Heinz Kloss, *Research Possibilities in the German-American Field*, edited with Introduction and Bibliography by LaVern J. Rippley (Hamburg: Helmut Buske Verlag, 1980).

11. *Youth Outlook: German-American Monthly* (November 1939): 1.

12. Canedy, *America's Nazis*, p. 222.

13. Heilbut, *German Refugees*, p. 386.

14. For further information on Singer, see John M. Spalek and Sandra H. Hawrylchak, eds., *Guide to the Archival Materials of the German-Speaking Emigration to the United States After 1933* (Bern: Francke, 1992), vol. 2, pp. 649–50, and John M. Spalek, Konrad Feilchenfeldt, and Sandra H. Hawrylchak, eds., *Deutschsprachige Exilliteratur seit 1932* (Munich: Saur, 1994), vol. 4, pp. 1706–10.

15. The title by Foerster will be reprinted in Don Heinrich Tolzmann, *German-Americans in the World Wars: Supplement* (in preparation).

16. See Gerhard Reich, "The German Exile Writer in New York City 1933–1945: A Case Study," *Focus on Literature* 2, no. 2 (1995): 155–62.

17. Edward Oxford, "The Other Trial of the Century," *American History* 30, no. 3 (1995): 27.

18. Timothy Holian, "Confessions of a Nazi Spy: Hollywood Film Portrayals of America's German Element During World War II," unpublished paper presented at the nineteenth annual meeting and symposium of the Society for German-American Studies, Louisville, Kentucky, April 1995. Also see Randall M. Miller, ed., *Ethnic Images in American Film and Television* (Philadelphia: The Balch Institute, 1978).

19. Ibid.

20. Ibid.

20. Ibid.

22. Nye, "A Personal Statement."

23. Ibid.

24. For further information, see Tolzmann, *German-Americans in the World Wars*.

25. See ibid., vol. 4, p. 2647.

26. See Timothy J. Holian, *The German-Americans and World War II: An Ethnic Experience* (New York: Peter Lang, 1996).

27. Cornelius Schnauber, *German-Speaking Artists in Hollywood: Emigration Between 1910 and 1945* (Bonn: Inter Nationes, 1996), p. 96.

28. Ibid., pp. 96–97.

29. For full bibliographical information on Mann's works, see Georg Potempa, *Thomas Mann—Bibliographie: das Werk* (Morsum/Sylt: Cicero, 1992).

30. Donald Prater, *Thomas Mann: A Life* (Oxford: Oxford University Press, 1995), p. 366.

31. Ibid., p. 373.

32. Ibid., p. 385.

33. Ronald Hayman, *Thomas Mann: A Biography* (New York: Scribner, 1995), p. 476.

34. See Margrit B. Krewson, *German-American Relations: A Selective Bibliography* (Washington, D.C.: Library of Congress, 1995).

35. Regarding the period of the peace, references can be found in Don Heinrich Tolzmann, ed., *Catalog of the German-American Collection* (Munich: K. G. Saur, 1990), vol. 1, pp. 185–90.

36. Rippley, *The German-Americans*, p. 212.

The Second Renaissance

Immigration

From 1941 to 1950 one quarter of a million German-speaking immigrants arrived in the United States. Many of them were admitted under the Displaced Persons Act, which included ethnic Germans, or *Volksdeutsche*, who had been brutally expelled from their homelands in eastern and southeastern Europe as well as in the Soviet Union. In addition, Germans had been forced from their homes in the old eastern German provinces of Pomerania, Silesia, and East Prussia. Altogether, a total of seventeen million Germans were driven from their homes in the greatest expulsion in human history. Some of these came to America in the late 1940s and 1950s.

A small but significant number of postwar immigrants were war brides who had married American soldiers stationed in Germany. Another interesting group of postwar immigrants were former POWs who returned to America. An estimated five thousand out of a total of 426,000 German POWs who were kept at 623 camps (112 main camps and 511 branch camps) scattered throughout the United States immigrated to America after the war.

In the 1950s and 1960s German immigration soared to three quarters of a million, and then dropped to a little under one hundred thousand in the 1970s, remaining roughly at this level in the 1980s. This decline in German immigration was no doubt due to the *Wirtschafts- wunder*, or economic miracle of the Federal Republic of Germany. This great economic upswing created jobs, high rates of employment, and a strong German currency, which reduced general interest in leaving the country. However, from 1941 through 1970 approximately one million German-speaking immigrants had come to America.[1]

The Eisenhower Era

In the 1940s and 1950s German-Americans adopted a strategy of low-key, subdued ethnicity because of the anti-German *Zeitgeist* engendered by the two world wars. Nevertheless, a permanent case of submerged eth- nicity could not endure for a number of reasons. First, there was sub- stantial postwar German-speaking immigration to America. Many of these immigrants were from areas outside Germany, such as the Russian-Ger- mans and the Danube-Swabians from the former provinces of the old Austro-Hungarian Empire. These ethnic Germans had maintained their German heritage for centuries outside Germany, and this adherence, strengthened by adverse circumstances, contributed to the rebirth of ethnic pride among German-Americans. The strong sense of ethnicity, community, and family had a rejuvenating and invigorating impact on German-Americans, who had been demoralized by the events of the first half of the century. Indeed, many of the new immigrants provided not only enthusiasm, but also leadership to many of the older German-Amer- ican organizations and societies, breathing new life into them.

The postwar immigration brought many German immigrants who made substantial contributions to their adopted country. Perhaps most prominent was Dr. Wernher von Braun, who has been called the greatest human element behind the rocketry success of the United States. Under the codeword "Operation Paperclip," numerous German scientists came to the United States after the war. One hundred twenty scientists accepted a contract with the United States to come to America and work on the rocket program. Von Braun and others came to Huntsville, Alabama, now called Rocket City USA. Their work brought quick results.

In 1953 the U.S. Army launched the Redstone missile at Cape Canaveral, Florida, and in 1958 launched *Explorer I*, America's first space satellite. This German-American space team also contributed to the development of the Saturn V rocket, which took the Apollo spacecraft to the moon in 1969. Von Braun and his predominantly German space team had ushered the United States into the space age. He explained that: "It makes us feel that we paid back part of a debt of gratitude we owed to our adopted country."[2] In the succeeding two decades an estimated eighteen hundred scientists and five thousand technicians came from Germany to America.

A second reason for the ethnic revival relates to the simple fact that German-Americans were the nation's largest ethnic element and it would be only a matter of time before they would take their rightful place alongside America's other ethnic groups in their awareness of their history and heritage. German-Americans, moreover, were interested in restoring and maintaining good relations between the United States and the new Federal Republic of Germany.

A third reason contributing to the revival of German-American ethnicity was the swift turnaround in German-American relations. Germany soon became one of America's strongest allies. In 1955 the Federal Republic of Germany became a member of NATO, which led to extensive military and political cooperation. Indeed, not only were U.S. forces stationed in Germany, but German troops were trained in the United States, mainly in Texas, Arizona, and California. Moreover, Germany was blessed with the venerable Konrad Adenauer as its chancellor, who wisely coordinated the postwar recovery of Germany and the integration of the Federal Republic into the Western alliance. His statesmanship and wisdom contributed not only to the high regard in which he was held, but also to that of the new Republic. The two allies found that they had much more in common than diplomatic relations. When Chancellor Ludwig Erhard visited President Johnson's ranch in the Texas hill country, he was pleased to be able to speak German with some of the German-Texans in the area.

Many other contacts contributed to improving German-American relations. In 1952 the Atlantic Bridge was formed in Hamburg to promote these relations by means of conferences and seminars. The Atlantic Bridge corresponded to its counterpart in the United States: the

American Council on Germany. In the same year, the German-American Culture Agreement was signed. It provided for German involvement with the Fulbright Program, which is responsible for the exchange of students and faculty between the United States and other countries. Also, the German Academic Exchange Service contributed greatly by supporting students and faculty from the United States so that they could engage in research and study in Germany. Numerous other types of exchange programs and partnerships began, especially between educational institutions. Also, more than fifty American and German cities contributed to German-American relations by establishing sister-city relationships.

A fourth reason for a return to normalcy was that the major American leader of the period was of German descent: Dwight D. Eisenhower, who had served as Supreme Commander of Allied Forces in Europe during the war. He was elected as the thirty-fourth president of the United States in 1952 and served two terms until 1960. German-Americans recognized him as one of their own and voted for him in great numbers. Indeed, a central part of the Republican campaign strategy had been the work of the Ethnic Origins Division of the Republican National Committee, which made detailed studies in regard to ethnic groups. Truman campaigned for Adlai Stevenson and complained bitterly that the Republicans were playing politics by stirring up "our citizens who have ties of blood" with the peoples of Europe.[3] In spite of his complaints, Eisenhower was swept into office with a huge landslide vote. This vote marked an increasing return to the Republican fold by German-Americans, a trend evident since 1920. Political parties were well aware of the size and importance of the population of German descent, as far as presidential elections were concerned.

A final reason for the transition to the ethnic revival period was that German-American organizations and the German-American press devoted a great deal of energy to restoring a positive image of Germany and an awareness and pride in German heritage. In the 1950s German Day celebrations were again held across the country, and Steuben Day parades were introduced in New York, Philadelphia, and Chicago, where they became major displays of German-American heritage and U.S.-German relations.

Older German-American organizations, such as the Steuben Society of America, continued their valuable programs and activities. In 1958 the German-American National Congress was founded in Chicago and began to play a major role in representing German-American interests, particularly in the Midwest. German-American newspapers, such as the *New Yorker Staats-Zeitung* and *Der Deutsch-Amerikaner*, continued to represent and reflect German-American interests as well. Also, in the 1950s German-American radio programs emerged in communities across the United States, broadcasting not only music, but also news and items of general interest.

By the 1960s the stage was set for the ethnic heritage revival among German-Americans, which could perhaps best be described as the second German-American renaissance, as it represented the first nation-wide expression of renewal and reemergence of German-American identity and pride since before the wars.

The Ethnic Heritage Revival

The 1970s were marked by what became known as the ethnic heritage revival. At that time, there was not only an increased interest in and appreciation of ethnicity, but also a long-overdue recognition of it as a permanent factor and dimension in American society. In 1964 President John F. Kennedy's book *A Nation of Immigrants* was published, which not only recognized this basic fact of life, but also praised the many contributions German-Americans had made to building the nation. This was quite a dramatic change from Woodrow Wilson, who polemicized against what he called "hyphenates," and from Roosevelt, who spoke of what he called "sinister nations." The political leadership at the presidential level had finally come to the realization that America is a nation consisting of various ethnic groups and that the melting pot was nothing more than a myth. In its place, a recognition of the pluralistic nature of American society emerged. A new paradigm based on reality, rather than myth, emphasized America's cultural diversity. Each culture within American society is valuable in its own right and deserves recognition, preservation, as well as study and respect.

Two examples of this recognition were the Elementary and Secondary Act (1965) and the Ethnic Heritage Studies Act (1972). The former referred to America as a multiethnic society, stating, "[A] greater understanding of the contributions of one's own heritage and those of one's fellow citizens can contribute to a more harmonious, patriotic and committed populace. . . ."[4] The 1972 Act provided federal support to the legitimization of ethnicity and pluralism in the United States.

The 1970s were also the time of increased interest in family history, which became known as the "roots revival" and related to the concurrent ethnic heritage revival. For German-Americans, both phenomena had special significance. German heritage has often been referred to as a "heritage deferred" because of anti-German hysteria and sentiment, but the second half of the century has been called the period of "heritage fulfilled," as German-Americans began to reassert themselves and celebrate their traditions.

Aside from the ethnic heritage revival, a number of special events occurred that helped the German-American cause. In 1976 the American Bicentennial took place with numerous conferences, symposia, publications, and celebrations, many of which investigated and illuminated the role German-Americans had played not only in the American Revolution, but in American history in general. In 1976 President Ford sponsored a White House Conference on Ethnicity and the 1980 Census, which included German-American representatives from across the country. This was the first time they had been included since before the world wars.

The 1976 conference formulated questions about ethnic identity that would be asked in the 1980 U.S. Census. Previously the Census had asked whether one was an immigrant or the child of an immigrant, but now it asked about people's ethnic identity. For the first time the statistical tabulation of American ethnic groups was discovered. Many were surprised to learn that the German element equalled the Anglo-American element, and that with the addition of other German heritage groups (Austrians, Swiss-Germans, Alsatians, and Luxemburgers), the German element was the nation's largest ethnic group. In the two centuries since the American Revolution, German-Americans had grown from approximately 10 percent of the population to 25 percent. It was further discovered that in twenty-three states, German-Americans constituted the major ethnic element, with at least 20 percent of the population. In five states, German-Americans numbered more than 50 percent!

The long-overdue public recognition of and pride in German heritage during the beginning of the ethnic heritage revival, the emphasis on German-American achievements during the American Bicentennial, and the awareness that German-Americans constituted the largest ethnic group led to a great number of German heritage celebrations. One widespread manifestation of this was what can be called the "Oktoberfest phenomenon." German-American festivities, especially Oktoberfest, came to be celebrated across the country in German-American areas. During this time as well German bilingual programs were reintroduced in the curricula of public schools in some of the old German-American centers, such as Cincinnati and Milwaukee.

There was also increased interest in the history, literature, and culture of German-Americans, which led to the establishment of the Society for German-American Studies in 1968. The SGAS commenced publication of the *Journal of German-American Studies*, which was succeeded by the *Yearbook of German-American Studies*, and it also began to sponsor annual meetings and symposia. It created guidelines for the introduction of German-American studies into the curricula at all educational levels and initiated the successful campaign for establishing German-American Day.

The establishment of centers, institutes, and collections dealing with German-Americana also occurred in this period, reflecting the academic interest in the field of German-American studies. Among those established were the Max Kade German-American Document and Research Center at the University of Kansas; the German-Americana Collection and the German-American studies program at the University of Cincinnati; the Max Kade Institute for German-American Studies at the University of Wisconsin-Madison; the Center for Pennsylvania German Studies at Millersville University; and the Max Kade German-American Center at Indiana University-Indianapolis.

There is much interest in German-American historical and heritage societies. Many of them hold annual meetings, lecture series, programs, and sponsor regional publications. Among these groups are the Indiana German Heritage Society, the German Texan Heritage Society, and the

German Heritage Society of Greater Washington, D.C. Also, there are a number of organizations formed in the nineteenth century that still maintain an active publication program, such as the Society for the History of the Germans in Maryland and the Pennsylvania German Society. Moreover, many German-Americans have formed regionally based organizations, such as the German-Russian Heritage Society and the Swiss-American Historical Society. The activities of these state, regional, local, and special-interest organizations reflect the diversity of the German heritage.

It was also at this time that German-American national and regional civic organizations began to call for the cessation of anti-German stereotypes in film and other media. Politicians again began to attend German-American activities and functions and sought the support of German-American communities. German-American organizations also took an active role in the programs and celebrations for the American Bicentennial in 1976 at the national, state, and local levels, which paved the way for the 1983 German-American Tricentennial Celebration.

Presidential Elections

German-American ethnicity continues to be a factor in terms of voting behavior. The upset victory of Truman in 1948 can partly be explained by the fact that German-Americans voted Democrat, now that FDR was not on the ballot. In 1952 Eisenhower benefited not only from his German surname and war record, but also from the widespread discontent with the Truman administration's policies at home and abroad. German-Americans were particularly resentful at the handling of the Korean War and the failure of the Truman administration to go for an all-out victory. They did not understand the point of fighting a stalemate war against Communism when the United States had previously engaged in world wars aimed at victory.

The Truman administration's policies had seemed to support the charges of "soft on Communism" by the Republican senator Joseph McCarthy, who was of German descent on his mother's side and from the state of Wisconsin. In their view, McCarthy was pointing out that Communism was the major threat in the world, and he was going to make use of the House Committee on Un-American Activities and turn it against the Communists. At the same time, Republicans charged the Democrats with having "sold out" to Stalin at Yalta and charged the State Department with having contributed to the Communist victory in China. Eisenhower launched a "great crusade" for honest and efficient government at home and for "freedom in the world," and he pledged "an early and honorable end" to the disastrous Korean War. The 1952 election was a time for German-Americans to register their protest at the ballot box. On election day, Eisenhower swept into office with thirty-nine states, and in 1956 he attained another landslide victory with forty-one states.

In 1960 the Irish-American Catholic John Fitzgerald Kennedy faced the Republican cold warrior Richard M. Nixon, which divided German-Americans. Some Catholics voted for JFK, while Protestants mainly opted for Nixon. President Kennedy proved especially popular among German-Americans, particularly after his speech in Berlin in 1963. On June 26, 1963, he addressed a crowd of 400,000 Berliners, declaring: "*Ich bin ein Berliner.*" In his address, he stated:

> There are many people in the world who really don't understated, or say they don't, what is the great issue between the free world and the Communist world. Let them come to Berlin. There are some who say that communism is the wave of the future. Let them come to Berlin. And there are some who say in Europe and elsewhere we can work with the Communists. Let them come to Berlin. And there are even a few who say that it is true that communism is an evil system, but it permits us to make economic progress. *Lasst sie nach Berlin kommen.*
>
> Freedom has many difficulties and democracy is not perfect, but we have never had to put a wall up to keep our people in, to prevent them from leaving us. I want to say, on behalf of my countrymen, who live many miles away on the other side of the Atlantic, who are far distant from you, that they take the greatest pride that they have been able to share with you, even from a distance, the story of the last eighteen years. I know of no town, no city, that has been besieged for eighteen years that still lives with the vitality and the force, and the hope and the determination of the city of West Berlin. While the wall is the most obvious and vivid demonstration of the failure of the Communist system, for all the

world to see, we take no satisfaction in it for it is, as your Mayor has said, an offense not only against history, but an offense against humanity, separating families, dividing husbands and wives and brothers and sisters, and dividing a people who wish to be joined together.

What is true of this city is true of Germany—real, lasting peace in Europe can never be assured as long as one German out of four is denied the elementary right of free men, and that is to make a free choice. In eighteen years of peace and good faith, this generation of Germans has earned the right to be free, including the right to unite their families and their nation in lasting peace, with good will to all people. You live in a defended island of freedom, but your life is part of the main. So let me ask you, as I close, to lift your eyes beyond the dangers of today, to the hopes of tomorrow, beyond the freedom merely of this city of Berlin, or your country of Germany, to the advance of freedom everywhere, beyond the wall to the day of peace with justice, beyond yourselves and ourselves to all mankind. Freedom is indivisible, and when one man is enslaved, all are not free. When all are free, then we can look forward to that day when this city will be joined as one and this country, and this great continent of Europe in a peaceful and hopeful glow. When that day finally comes, as it will, the people of West Berlin can take sober satisfaction in the fact that they were in the front lines for almost two decades.

All free men, wherever they may live, are citizens of Berlin, and, therefore, as a free man, I take pride in the words: *Ich bin ein Berliner.*[5]

JFK also increased in stature among German-Americans due to his posthumously published book, *A Nation of Immigrants*, which included, as noted earlier, a chapter on German-Americans. As an heir apparent, Lyndon Baines Johnson easily came into office in 1964, but in 1968 Richard Nixon returned, this time not facing a Catholic, and German-Americans voted heavily for him. Indeed, his major gains in this election were in German Catholic regions of the country. German-Americans agreed with his positions on domestic and foreign affairs, especially when he claimed to represent the interests of the "silent majority," which German-Americans felt they had been since before the First World War.

German-Americans also appreciated the many German-Americans

in the Nixon administration: Ron Ziegler, press secretary; Walter Hickel, secretary of agriculture; George Schultz, secretary of labor; Henry Kissinger, special advisor on foreign policy; John Ehrlichmann, special advisor on domestic policy; H. R. Haldeman, White House chief of staff; Richard Kleindienst, attorney general; and Herbert Kalmbach, Nixon's private attorney—a total of eight appointments.

After the Watergate affair, anti-German rhetoric surfaced because of the preponderance of German-Americans in the Nixon administration. H. R. Haldeman, for example, wrote in his book *The Ends of Power* that he was referred to as the "keystone of a Berlin Wall around Mr. Nixon" and as "the Prussian guard who keeps Nixon's door," who was known for his "legendary arrogance, efficiency and power." He was also called "a Nazi chief of staff. . . . That German name. Those German eyes that would freeze Medusa." Others wrote of his so-called rigid Nazi-type activities.[6] Clearly, critics of Nixon administration, and of Haldeman in particular, made use of ethnic slurs based on World War II stereotypes. Although the central focus was the Watergate affair, the anti-German rhetoric that surfaced provides insight into the ethnic prejudice in general and anti-Germanism in particular that German-Americans were subjected to in the post–World War II period.

The Democratic candidate in 1972, George McGovern, received little sympathy from German-Americans, who voted solidly for Nixon. In 1976 only Ohio, Missouri, Minnesota, and Wisconsin went for Ford, while all other states went for Carter. Ford did campaign in some German-American areas. For example, he went to Cincinnati and addressed a gathering at which German-American dance groups performed. However, in 1976 the German-American vote split, with most of it going to Ford.

In 1980 and 1984 another Irish-American, Ronald Reagan, was on the Republican ticket, and German-Americans strongly supported him due to his position on domestic and foreign affairs. Major German-American organizations, such as the German-American National Congress, endorsed Reagan for president. In various states, German-Americans for Reagan Committees were formed in 1980 and 1984, yet another indication of the reemergence of German-Americans in public affairs.

Reagan strongly opposed Communism, supported the Federal Republic of Germany, and specifically supported and recognized German-

Americans. In 1983, when German-Americans celebrated the German-American Tricentennial, the Reagan administration officially endorsed and supported this anniversary. In 1985 Reagan went to Germany as part of the ceremonies commemorating the 40th anniversary of the end of World War II. In the summer of 1987 German-Americans enthusiastically supported Reagan's courageous speech in Berlin in which he demanded that Gorbachev tear down the infamous wall. In 1987 he also held a special White House Rose Garden signing ceremony during which the first national German-American Day was proclaimed for the October 6, 1987. Here was a consistent pattern of support and recognition for German-American interests and positions.

In 1988 George Bush, regarded Reagan's heir apparent, also received German-American endorsements and support. Bush's first campaign stop after the Republican convention was to deliver an address at the Danube Swabian German-American Cultural Center in Cleveland. However, by 1992 German-Americans had dramatically lost enthusiasm for Bush due to the perception that he had not held firmly to his principles, especially in the area of domestic affairs and the economy.

Military Service

German-Americans have continually served in numbers larger than their percentage of the population. In the nineteenth century one-fourth of American forces were German-American, and in the twentieth century one-third were German-American. It is no understatement that their service was not only invaluable, but indispensable, given such high statistics.

In the Korean, Vietnam, and Gulf Wars, German-Americans numbered one-third of the American forces. A recent examination of the names listed on the Vietnam War Memorial in Washington, D.C., indicated that one-third of the 58,000 names were German surnames, for example. The extent of German-American military service is a little known, almost unpublicized fact.

Commanding the armed forces in the Gulf War was General "Stormin'" Norman Schwarzkopf, whose grandfather, Christian Schwarzkopf, arrived in New York in 1855 from his home in Untersteinbach near Heilbronn, Germany. On his grandfather's gravestone in Newark, New Jersey, the German inscription reads: *"Ich weiss, dass mein Erlöser lebt"* ("I know that my Redeemer lives"). In Cincinnati, a local newspaper carried a cartoon depicting General Schwarzkopf and Hussein of Iraq with the caption: "Schwarzkopf und Dummkopf," which according to Schwarzkopf was his favorite. German-Americans were proud of Schwarzkopf, who received many invitations to German-American festivities, such as the Steuben Parade in New York City.[7]

The German-American Tricentennial

After celebrating the American Bicentennial in 1976, German-Americans made plans for the German-American Tricentennial.[8] In October 1982, Sen. John Heinz of Pennsylvania introduced a resolution proclaiming 1983 as the "Tricentennial Anniversary Year of German Settlement in America," which was sent to the House of Representatives. The resolution was passed by the House and the Senate and was signed in early 1983. President Reagan appointed a Tricentennial Commission, and an office was established in Washington, D.C. In the course of the year, several thousand events commemorating the German-American Tricentennial took place, and the total attendance was estimated at several million.

Tricentennial themes were included at German-American festivities, such as Maifest and Oktoberfest celebrations. Local symphonies presented special programs with music of Beethoven, Brahms, Bach, Mozart, Schumann, and others. The Steuben Parades promoted the tricentennial in New York, Chicago, and Philadelphia. There were numerous exhibits, conferences, symposia, programs, and publications dealing with the German-American dimension of American history. Special commemorative stamps were also issued in honor of the German-American Tricentennial by the U.S. Postal Service and the German Bundespost.

The U.S. Park Service provided land near the Washington Monument for a German-American Friendship Garden, with groundbreaking ceremonies taking place on October 5, 1983. President Karl Carstens of the Federal Republic of Germany participated in these ceremonies, stating that Germany was gratified that the American people remember what German immigrants contributed to the development of the United States. It is quite right to commemorate in this way. However, it is also right to mention at the same time that other nations furnished other equally important contributions to American civilization. America has many roots. Together, they make up and nourish the American tree.[9]

Noting that one-fourth of the American population is of German descent, Vice President Bush remarked in an address in Krefeld that German-Americans inhabit a country made prosperous and free largely by the work of German-Americans. He noted that the immigrants had brought with them "a belief in God, the family, and the goodness of the earth as solid as the Alps and as steady as the Rhine. And they brought another belief, a belief in work—hard, honest work." And in an address during the tricentennial year, Reagan stated: "Germans and Americans of German descent have benefitted from the contributions which German-Americans have made to our country—and we should all participate in honoring this heritage."[10]

As a result of the enthusiasm engendered by the tricentennial, a German-American Memorial Association was founded, which raised funds for the the erection of a German Immigrant Monument in Bremerhaven, which was officially dedicated on July 5, 1986.

German-American Relations

Two anniversaries took place in 1985. First, it was the 200th anniversary of the signing of the Treaty of Amity and Commerce between Prussia and the newly established United States of America. Prussia was one of the first European powers to undertake such relations with the new republic, and the treaty itself became an outstanding example for many international treaties signed since that time. The treaty was edited for publication by Karl J. R. Arndt in a bilingual edition published in 1977. The treaty was signed by Thomas Jefferson, Benjamin Franklin, and John Adams, and ratified by Congress on May 17, 1786.[11]

The 40th anniversary of the end of the Second World War was

another landmark of 1985. In a truly eloquent speech, Richard von Weizäcker, president of the Federal Republic of Germany, spoke of the meaning of the end of the war and closed with words of admonition: "Let us honor freedom. Let us work for peace. Let us respect the rule of law. Let us be true to our own conception of justice. . . . Let us face up to the truth as well as we can."[12]

It was in this spirit of peace and friendship that President Reagan agreed to go to Germany and participate in ceremonies commemorating the end of the war. Plans called for the American guest to speak at the historic Hambach Castle and at the military cemetery at Bitburg. However, the Bitburg ceremony had been accompanied by a much-publicized controversy because some of those buried there had belonged to the Waffen-SS, or the military units of the SS. Despite the discussion about the site, Reagan held on to his schedule.

Perhaps more important was Reagan's address at Hambach, in which he connected with the nineteenth-century traditions of the Thirtyers, stressing their relevance and meaning for a vision of the future in touch with the imperishable values of the past—which the Thirtyers were striving to attain—namely, freedom and democracy. In so doing, he illuminated an important dimension of German-American history and pointed the way to a constructive future.

At Hambach Castle, which had been the site of a protest in 1832, Reagan referred to the Thirtyers' noble visions of a democratic and united Germany, and he praised the success of the Federal Republic of Germany in rebuilding itself in the postwar era. He stated, "Germany's success showed that our future must not depend on experts or on government plans, but on the treasures of the human mind and spirit—imagination, intellect, courage, and faith." He closed by stating:

> Your future will be a way station further along that same journey in time begun by the great patriots at Hambach 153 years ago—a journey that began in a dream of the human heart; a journey that will not be complete until the dream is real; until the feat of a political torture is no more; until the pain of poverty has been lifted from every person in the world. . . . This is freedom's vision, and it is good. And you must go out from here and help make it come true. . . . My young friends, believe

me, this is a wonderful time to be alive and to be free. Remember that in your hearts there are the stars of your fate; remember that everything depends on you; and remember not to let one moment slip away, for as Schiller has told us: "He who has done his best for his own time, has lived for all times."[13]

In 1987, only a few months before the establishment of German-American Day, another important event occurred that was important for German-American relations and ultimately for the unification of Germany. On Friday, June 12, 1987, Reagan went to West Berlin and stood at the columns of the Brandenburg Gate, a past monument to German unity. Visible behind him through a bulletproof window was the Berlin Wall. Speaking before a crowd of thousands, Reagan stated that there was in fact only one Berlin, and he declared that if Soviet leader Mikhail Gorbachev was really serious about his celebrated new openness, or *glasnost*, he should demonstrate this by means of a singular act. He then courageously stated: "Mr. Gorbachev, open this gate. Mr. Gorbachev, tear down this wall."[14]

Reagan's address, which clearly echoed that of JFK's famous "Ich bin ein Berliner" speech of 1962, underlined the strong U.S. political and military support for West Germany on the occasion of the 750th anniversary of Berlin. There is no question that his open defiance of Soviet tyranny in general and the criminal Berlin Wall in particular helped to prepare for the fall of the wall a few years later. The events of the 1980s, hence, proved that the United States stood by Germany, the ancestral homeland of more Americans than any other element in the population, and which had become the strongest ally of the United States.

German-American Day

After the celebration of the German-American Tricentennial in 1983, many felt that October 6 should be reestablished as an annual national celebration of German-American heritage, just as it had been in the nineteenth century. In 1986, at the annual meeting and symposium of the Society for German-American Studies, Ruth Reichmann, president of the Indiana German Heritage Society, submitted a resolution that October 6 be declared German-American Day, and this motion was unanimously approved. The SGAS German-American Day Committee, chaired by SGAS president Don Heinrich Tolzmann, then launched a national campaign in support of German-American Day, which proved successful.

Due to a limited amount of time, the resolution did not pass in 1986, but in 1987 the drive began anew and passed through Congress. National organizations such as the German-American National Congress, the Steuben Society of America, and the United German-American Committee played a key role in enlisting the support of German-Americans across the country. Also, the German-American press strongly supported the resolution and encouraged German-Americans to contact their congressional representatives in support.

This overwhelming national grassroots enthusiasm for German-American Day further reflected the reemergence of German-Americans on the national scene. Based on the passage of Public Law 100–104, President Reagan issued a proclamation declaring October 6 as German-American Day. In a special White House Rose Garden Ceremony, he issued the following proclamation, which provides a concise summary and overview of the role German-Americans have played in American history:

More Americans trace their heritage back to German ancestry than to any other nationality. More than seven million Germans have come to our shores through the years, and today some sixty million Americans—one in four—are of German descent. Few people have blended so completely into the multicultural tapestry of American society and yet have made such singular economic, political, social, scientific, and cultural contributions to the growth and success of these United States of America as have Americans of German extraction.

The United States has embraced a vast array of German traditions, institutions, and influences. Many of these have become so accepted as parts of our way of life that their ethnic origin has been obscured. For instance, Christmas trees and Broadway musicals are familiar features of American society. Our kindergartens, graduate schools, the social security system, and labor unions are all based on models derived from Germany.

German teachers, musicians, and enthusiastic amateurs have left an indelible imprint on classical music, hymns, choral singing, and marching bands in our country. In architecture and design, German contributions include the modern suspension bridge, Bauhaus, and Jugendstil. German-American scientists have helped make the United States the world's pioneer in research and technology. The American work ethic, a major factor in the rapid rise of the United Staes to pre-eminence in agriculture and industry, owes much to German-Americans' commitment to excellence. For more than three centuries, Germans have helped build, invigorate, and strengthen this country. But the United States has given as well as received. Just a generation ago, America conceived of and swiftly demonstrated the American commitment to the defense of freedom when, still recovering from war, Berlin was threatened by strangulation form the Soviets.

Today, the Federal Republic of Germany is a bulwark of democracy in the heart of a divided Europe. Germans and Americans are rightfully proud of our common values as well as our shared heritage. For more than three decades the German-American partnership has been a linchpin in the Western Alliance. Thanks to it, a whole generation of Americans and Europeans has grown up free to enjoy the fruits of liberty.

Out histories are thus intertwined. We now contribute to each other's trade, enjoy each other's cultures, and learn from each other's experiences. The German-American Friendship Garden, which will be dedicated in the District of Columbia in the near future, is symbolic of the close and amicable relationships between West Germany and the United States.[15]

Since 1987, German-American Day has been widely celebrated across the United States and has become a genuinely national day of commemoration. Since 1995 the German-American Joint Action Committee, which consists of the German-American National Congress, the Steuben Society of America, and the United German-American Committee, have sponsored German-American Heritage Month, which takes place from mid-September to mid-October and is centered on October 6, German-American Day.

The Unification of Germany

October 3 has been celebrated annually as German Unification Day, since it was on this day in 1990 that unification of the two German postwar states officially took place. This brings it into close proximity with German-American Day, and in many places both are celebrated and commemorated together, one in honor of the ancestral homeland, and the other in honor of German-American contributions to the United States.

On the fourth annual German-American Day in 1990, President George Bush stated in his proclamation that:

> German-American Day, 1990, is like none before it, for this year's commemoration coincides with the achievement of the goal Americans and Germans have long shared: a united, democratic, and sovereign Germany. During the past year, the German people have torn down the artificial barriers that, for too long, cruelly divided their country. The Berlin Wall, which once stood as a bleak and even deadly symbol of division, now lies in ruin—a fitting reminder of the discredited regime that had directed its construction twenty-nine years ago. . . . Since the end of World War II, the American people have stood shoulder to shoulder with the people of the Federal Republic of Germany in efforts to secure our freedom and to advance our common interests. The spirit of friendship and cooperation between the people of the United States and the FRG is reflected in the wide range of exchange programs and other contacts we have developed over the years. . . . Now, from this day forward, a new, united Germany will be our partner in leadership. We Americans, and above all, those of German descent, are proud of the role we have played in support of German unity. We rejoice with the German people on this day and celebrate the centuries-old relationship between the American and the German peoples.[16]

An article in a German newspaper entitled "Unification Was a Boost for German-Americans" noted that "German unification triggered a wave of sympathy in the USA and fostered a new self-awareness among German-Americans." The article noted that coming soon after the establishment of German-American Day, "there is a noticeable sense of relief at again being able after decades to openly admit their roots."[17]

Reunification was the best possible advertisement for Germany.

The years after the German unification in the nineteenth century were known as the *Gründerzeit*, or age of the founders, which saw the transformation of Germany from an agrarian society of many states into a unified, modern industrial state in a relatively short period of time. This foundational period was, therefore, a time of great economic and industrial upswing, as well as a time of blossoming and flowering of German cultural life. The *Zeitgeist* of that time was noted for its spirit of optimism and and its progress-oriented *Weltanschauung*. In like manner, the post-unification period of the twentieth century has witnessed the beginnings of similar growth and development in the same areas as the former East and West grow together after decades of disunity.

The 1990 Census

Like the 1980 U.S. Census, the 1990 Census again confirmed that German-Americans are the largest ethnic element in the country. There are seven categories in the U.S. Census for German heritage groups, which reflects the background and diversity of the German heritage: German: 57,985,585; Alsatian: 16,465; Austrian: 870,531; Luxemburger: 49,061; Swiss-German: 700,000; German-Russian: 10,153; and Pennsylvania-German: 305,841. Altogether, the German ethnic groups total 59,937,646, or one-fourth of the population of 248,709,873. What is especially noteworthy is that the German element, which was roughly 10 percent of the population in 1790, had grown to 25 percent of the population two hundred years later in 1990 and became the nation's largest ethnic group.[18]

A listing of the top twenty groups in the United States in 1990 was as follows (in millions): German: 59.9; Irish: 38.7; English: 32.7; Afro-American: 23.8; Italian: 14.7; American: 12.4; Mexican: 11.6; French: 10.3; Polish: 9.4; Native American: 8.7; Dutch: 6.2; Scottish-Irish: 5.6; Scottish: 4.7; Swedish: 4.7; Norwegian: 3.9; Russian: 3; French-Canadian: 2.2; Welsh: 2; Spanish: 2; Puerto Rican: 2; and Slovak: 1.9.

The Beer and Bratwurst Summit

The congeniality of U.S.-German relations by the close of the twentieth century was best reflected in the May 1996 summit meeting between Chancellor Helmut Kohl and President Clinton, which took place in the city historically known for its German-American population—Milwaukee—which, according to the Census, is 54 percent German-American. The meeting was described as the "Beer and Bratwurst Summit," since Clinton claimed that the best bratwurst in the United States could be found in Milwaukee. The city was adorned with American and German flags welcoming Clinton and Kohl, and a billboard announced: "In Milwaukee wird auch deutsch gesprochen" (In Milwaukee German is spoken). Addressing a crowd of sixteen thousand, Clinton and Kohl spoke of the indivisible friendship between the United States and Germany. The mayor of the city greeted them in German, and the *Milwaukee Journal* extended greetings by means of a six-column headline proclaiming: "Wilkommen."

The meeting was a reflection of the closeness of German-American relations. There was also an indication of the importance placed on the votes of German-Americans, as the meeting was scheduled in a presidential election year in a strategic Midwestern state. Indeed, some claimed that Clinton needed Kohl and his Midwest visit to ensure his position in the election. Both aspects reflected not only the international significance of U.S.-German relations, but also the stature and regard German-Americans enjoyed by the last decade of the twentieth century.[19]

The German-American Quadricentennial

The year 2008 will mark the 400th anniversary of the arrival of the first permanent German settlers in America. Given the numerous celebrations, conferences, symposia, and publications associated with the Germantown Tricentennial in 1983, as well as with the German-American Heritage Month, it is likely that the German-American Quadricentennial in 2008 will become the focal point of interest with regard to the German-American dimension in history.[20]

Clearly, to understand American history, it is necessary to understand German-American history. German immigrants came to America at various times for a wide range of social, economic, political, and religious reasons. They were attracted to America by letters, reports, books, and other publications which extolled the beauty and grandeur of the land and the freedoms available in the United States. They became successful and devoted citizens of the United States and helped build the nation and made notable contributions in every field of human endeavor. Hundreds of thousands of them fought and died on the battlefields to secure independence, to preserve the Union, and to protect America's democratic institutions. They truly helped to build, preserve, and protect America. Rightfully proud of their heritage, German-Americans are an integral part of the fabric of American society. The German dimension in American life is so fundamental and ever-present that it is often taken for granted and overlooked, so much so that it brings to mind the question first asked by the nineteenth-century German-American author Konrad Krez: "Ever wonder then, what kind of land, 't'would be if ne'er a German came!"

Notes

1. Regarding recent German-American history, see Dorothy and Thomas Hoobler, *The German-American Family Album* (New York: Oxford University Press, 1996), pp. 109–22.

2. Cited in Don Heinrich Tolzmann, *America's German Heritage* (Cleveland: German-American National Congress, 1976), p. 98.

3. LaVern J. Rippley, *The German-Americans* (Boston: Twayne, 1976), p. 212.

4. Cited in Tolzmann, "The Survival of an Ethnic Community" (University of Cincinnati, Ph.D. diss., 1983), p. 13.

5. Cited in Juergen Eichhoff, "Ich bin ein Berliner: A History and A Linguistic Clarification," *Monatshefte* 85, no. 1 (1993): 74.

6. H. R. Haldeman, *The Ends of Power* (New York: Dell, 1978, p. 87.

7. See Don Heinrich Tolzmann, ed., *The German-American Soldier in the Wars of the U.S.* (Bowie, Md.: Heritage Books, 1996), pp. 330–34.

8. In 1980, at the Annual Meeting and Symposium of the Society for German-American Studies at the University of Missouri-Columbia, Don Heinrich Tolzmann issued the first national call for the celebration of the German-American Tricentennial in 1983. The idea swiftly caught on across the country. See Don Heinrich Tolzmann, "Celebrating the German Heritage," *Yearbook of German-American Studies* 18 (1983): 1–6. The celebration of the tricentennial led to interest in reestablishing October 6 as German-American Day. See footnote 14, below.

9. Cited in *German-American Tricentennial: Three Hundred Years of German Immigration to America 1683–1983: Final Report of the Presidential Commission for the German-American Tricentennial to the President and the Congress of the U.S.* (Washington, D.C.: U.S. German-American Tricentennial Commission, 1985), p. 40.

10. Ibid., p. 99.

11. See Karl J. R. Arndt, ed., *Der Freundschafts und Handelsvertrag von 1785* (Munich: Moos, 1977).

12. Cited in Wolfgang Glaser, *Americans and Germans: A Handy Reader and Reference Book* (Gräfeling vor Munich: Moos, 1986), p. 88.

13. See "An Open Letter to Ronald Reagan," in *Der Deutsch-Amerikaner* (June 1985): 1.

14. Ronald Reagan, "Text of Reagan Speech at Hambach Castle, May 6, 1985," in ibid., pp. 1–2.

15. Cited in Don Heinrich Tolzmann, ed., *In der Neuen Welt* (New York: Peter Lang, 1992), pp. 206–208. After the celebration of the German-American Tricentennial in 1983, the interest arose in placing October 6 on the calendar as a national day of commemorating German-American Day. At the 1986 annual meeting and symposium of the Society for German-American Studies in Cincinnati, Ruth Reichmann proposed a resolution in this regard, which was unanimously endorsed. Thereafter, Don Heinrich Tolzmann, SGAS president, led a national campaign as chair of the SGAS German-American Day Committee, which culminated in the proclamation in 1987 by President Ronald Reagan of October 6 as German-American Day.

16. Proclamation in possession of the author.

17. See the article on German unification by Karin Walz, published in *Kieler Nachrichten* (October 6, 1992).

18. See Don Heinrich Tolzmann, "1990 Census Statistics," *Society for German-American Studies Newsletter* 13 (1992): 27.

19. See Elsbeth M. Seewald, "President Clinton and Chancellor Kohl in Milwaukee," *German-American Journal* 37, no. 6 (1996): 1, 3.

20. Regarding the quadricentennial, see Don Heinrich Tolzmann, ed., *The First Germans in America* (Bowie, Md.: Heritage Books, 1992), especially the introduction.

German-American Influences

Agriculture

Ask a German-American farmer about the importance of agriculture, and he no doubt will respond that farmers of German descent are the backbone of the nation. The value of German-American farmers was recognized early in American history. Dr. Benjamin Rush, an eminent American physician and cosigner of the Declaration of Independence, wrote an essay on the manners and customs of the Pennsylvania Germans in 1789, in which he illuminates the particular contributions of the German-American farmer.

Rush concluded that German-American farmers were experts in their occupation; that they were industrious and economical; that they knew good land when they saw it and maintained possession of it in their family after they obtained it; that they rotated crops; that they took good care of their stock; that their neat farmsteads were immediately recognizable; and that, most important, they were noted for their hard work. Dr. Rush emphasizes the importance of their success to the economic foundations of the Commonwealth of Pennsylvania, which made possible the operation of the Bank of North America, the original financial backbone of the nation.[1]

There are some unique characteristics of the German-American farm families that distinguish them from non-German farming families.

Non-German-American farmers have been motivated more by the idea of becoming financially secure, while German-American farmers have historically been more interested in attaining success within the framework of close-knit farming communities. Also, German-American farmers were more interested in residing within such a community, whereas non-German farmers did not have this sense of community but tended to operate and see themselves as individuals unrelated to the community at large.

Moreover, German-American farmers were not particularly interested in establishing bigger farms and were less likely to go into debt. They seemed to operate with a definite ceiling in mind as to how much they wanted to spend and how large they wanted to expand their farms. For them, the main goal was to have enough land for their children and family. On the other hand, non-German farmers were more motivated toward expansion, investment, and ever larger farms, as their central goal was not directed at the family and the community but at individual profit.

Also, with German-American farms there is the tendency to turn the farm over to one's children, and then live nearby, whereas non-German farmers tend to postpone retirement and then are most likely to retire to Florida or Arizona. The end result is that land ownership is high among farmers of German stock, and there is an implicit emphasis on community and family. Indeed, in many German areas, farms have signs indicating that the farm has been in the family for one or more centuries.

There are many characteristics of the German-American farmer:

1. The German-American farmer looked for good land, preferring that which was already slightly improved. He selected land of rich forest growth and by paying cash for it frequently displaced even the native-born settlers from the best lands.

2. His methods of farming were thorough and patient. He would clear the land carefully of stumps and stones and aim at producing the largest possible yield per acre. He believed in rotating crops, so as not to exhaust the land, for he planned for the future, with a view to permanent possession.

3. The German-American farmer was not wasteful, but economical. He saved even wood, which seemed so abundant, using stoves instead of huge fireplaces, constructing fences of a kind that did not squander

wood. He was frugal, his diet was simple, his furniture plain but substantial, and his clothing of the best material calculated to last a long time. If his standard of living was lower than that of the native population, it was best suited to ensure success in farming.

4. He was very considerate of his livestock, feeding his horses and cattle well and housing them instead of letting them run wild. In the winter he kept them warm in barns or stables. He kept them hard at work, but never overworked them.

5. Everything about his place was in good order, fences, houses, gardens, and agricultural implements. He first built a great barn to keep his grain. The barn was more imposing than the house, and the particular architectural style of German barns, first built in Pennsylvania, made its way through the Ohio Valley and can be seen in Wisconsin and wherever else German-American farmers are located. Before the days of the train, German farmers used a wagon equally inconspicuous and serviceable. The "Conestoga wagon" was a familiar sight from the Mohawk to the Carolinas, and in the latter days of westward progress, its descendants, "prairie schooners,"crossed the plains. A German farmer's house was constructed of stone for permanent occupancy, though for reasons of economy it generally took a second generation to build it. This characteristic is noticeable in many areas, where the farmer's dwellings are built of light-colored brick.

6. The German-American farmer did most of his work with his own hands and was assisted by his wife and children. Large families were therefore a source of prosperity. Children were welcomed as a joy, as well as an asset. Hired labor was used only in harvest time and usually consisted of nearby friends and family.

7. German-American farmers made it a matter of pride to keep farms in their own families, generation after generation. This was true in the colonial period as well as in the present. They kept their own land and bought that of their neighbors.

8. German-American farmers have consistently proved themselves to be the most successful ethnic group in the field of agriculture in American history.[2]

Finally, 36 percent of the American rural farm population is German-American. In the twelve states of the Midwest, the percentage is even higher—49 percent. So, in the central agricultural region of the United States, half of the farmers are German-American.

Business and Industry

German-Americans have played a major role in the industrial history of the United States, especially in areas that required vocational training and education. This is likely due to the presence of schools in Germany for training in technical fields. The German element predominates in engineering; chemical industries; the manufacture of musical and optical instruments; the preparation of food products, as sugar, salt, cereals, flour, starch, and in canning, preserving, milling, and brewing.

German-Americans have been prominent in inventing agricultural machinery, such as the manufacture of wagons, electric and railway cars. From the eighteenth century on they have been identified with the growth of the iron and steel industries and glass manufacture; they have been prominent in printing and have made a monopoly of the art of lithography. German-Americans have also been prominent in the clothing trade and department stores, and their organizational skill has been evident in banking and finance.

There were first-class engineering colleges in Germany long before any were founded in the United States, so many of the greatest bridges in this country were built by Germans. Johann A. Roebling established the suspension bridge as the leading type for great spans over large rivers. The Roeblings completed the famous Brooklyn Bridge in 1883; an earlier prototype had been completed across the Ohio River connecting Cincinnati, Ohio, and Covington, Kentucky. The wire cables of Roebling bridges were always manufactured in the Roebling family factory. Charles C. Schneider demonstrated with his cantilever bridge over the Niagara River that the cantilever type was the better for railway traffic, and the beautiful George Washington Bridge over the Hudson was designed by Ammann, a Swiss-German.

German-Americans have played a significant role in the building trades and construction. After the Second World War, for example, many recently arrived immigrants brought with them skills from the building trades and formed construction companies, which contributed immensely to the huge building spurt in the postwar era. They built a large number of the homes, apartments, commercial buildings, and subdivisions, that were necessary for the baby-boom generation. German-Americans continue to play a large role in this field.

The only peer of Thomas Edison in electrical engineering is Charles P. Steinmetz, who was born in Breslau. In his laboratory at Schenectady he made brilliant discoveries and inventions and became the consulting engineer of the General Electric Company. Called "The Wizard of Schenectady," he was responsible for more than one hundred electrical inventions.

Another German-American wizard was Edward Kleinschmidt, who invented or played a major role in the invention of the teletype, the high-speed stock ticker tape, the stock quotation system, the facsimile telegraph and a similar machine for radio circuits, a railroad block signal, and a telephone signal system. Altogether he held 117 patents and in 1930 sold his Teletype Corporation to AT&T.

Adolf Sutro was the constructor of the great tunnel under Virginia City in Nevada. Herman Haupt, general superintendent, chief engineer and director of the Pennsylvania Railroad, built the Hoosac Tunnel. Albert Fink, expert railway engineer, was the originator of through traffic in freight and passenger service, and Count Zeppelin made his first experiments in military aviation in this country during the Civil War. William Boeing, the son of a German immigrants, founded the aircraft industry that produces commercial aircraft such as the Boeing 727 and 747. The American space program was a creation of Wernher von Braun and his predominantly German-American scientific team.

In industrial pursuits as well as in professions, Germans of the nineteenth century advocated training, preparation, or education for a particular profession. In the pioneering days, an individual might build his house with his own hands, be a successful farmer and cattle raiser, as well as be his own physician, lawyer, and legislator. With the increase in population, competition brought about improvement. Higher effort was crowned with success, and this depended on training. In this emphasis on training, the German-American has stood in opposition to the notion of the jack-of-all-trades or the adventurer in business who seeks to make quick money rather than to develop the industry in which he is engaged.

The manufacture of agricultural machinery was begun by Germans. The Buckeye mower was developed by Autelmann in Canton, Ohio. Blickensderfer, a Moravian, invented the typewriter. The first glass was produced at Jamestown in 1608. A glass factory was established near Salem, New Jersey, in 1738 by Caspar Wistar from Baden. Baron Stigel set up a glass plant at Mannheim, Pennsylvania, before the Revolution.

In the steel industry, German-Americans stand forth. The earliest known iron works, those of Governor Spotswood at Germanna, Virginia, were operated from 1714 to 1740 by Germans from Siegen. In Pittsburgh, the first iron was made in 1792 by Georg Anschuetz from Strassburg. Other Germans developed the steel industry in various parts of Pennsylvania. John Fritz originated the steel mill in Bethlehem. His product was so good that he was awarded the Besemer gold medal by the Iron and Steel Institute of Britain. With regard to steel we think of Andrew Carnegie, whose two ablest lieutenants were German-Americans: Henry C. Frick and Charles M. Schwab. German specialists in chemistry helped in the development of the steel industry. A useful contribution by Charles T. Schoen was the invention of the pressed steel coal and freight railroad car in 1897.

In other industries, such as textiles, tanning, and leather-making, German-Americans were also active. John G. Brill of Kassel stands out as the founder of one of the largest electric car and truck firms. During the nineteenth century, the largest vehicle factory was that of the Studebaker brothers in South Bend, Indiana. Of course, an earlier German-American contribution to vehicles was the Conestoga wagon, designed in Pennsylvania by German-Americans.

Henry Villard was responsible for establishing the Northern Pacific Railroad, which connected the country to the Pacific northwest. In 1858 the first railroad sleeping car was built by Webster Wagner from the Mohawk Valley of New York, and in 1867 he built the first drawing-room car; he was also responsible for other inventions and was elected to the state senate several times. Ship-building also engaged the inventiveness of German-American engineers—Charles H. Cramp designed the *New Ironsides* used in the Civil War.

German-Americans were predominant in lithography, with most of the firms engaged in this field founded by Germans. One of them, F. A.

Ringler from Hesse-Kassel, invented a galvanoplastic process that proved very helpful in reproducing pictures. The great contribution to newspaper production was the linotype machine, invented by Ottmar Mergenthaler from Württemberg. The *New York Tribune* was the first daily to introduce this machine in its typesetting room.

German-Americans also played a major role in the manufacture of musical instruments. Some of the finest violins were produced by Georg Gemuender of Würtemberg. At the London Exposition of 1851, they took first prize. In the area of piano manufacturing, German-Americans have been predominant: Playel, Erhardt, Behrent, Steinway, Weber, Steck, Kranich & Bach, Sohmer, Behr, Schnabel, and Knabe. The first piano made in the colonies was in 1775 in Philadelphia by Georg Behrent. Henry Steinway and his four sons arrived in New York in the mid-nineteenth century and began manufacturing pianos, which became a tremendous success. Wurlitzer is another well-known name in this area.

Other German-American products are the pencils of Eberhard Faber and the Welsbach lamp, the latter of which revolutionized street-lighting in larger cities. In the East, two large department stores were Wanamaker and Siegel-Cooper. John Wanamaker, a Pennsylvania German, established his first store in Philadelphia in 1876. In 1899 Sebastian Kresge opened his first general store in Detroit and went on to become the "Dime Store King," and his stores today form the K-Mart chain.

German-Americans also became well known in the food processing and packing industries. The Heinz brand name belongs to a company founded by Henry J. Heinz. The manufacture of oatmeal, or rolled oats, was originated in 1856 by Ferdinand Schumacher of Hannover. Claus Spreckels, also of Hannover, became a success in California as the so-called sugar king of the Pacific Coast. Later he organized the sugar-beet industry, which competed with the sugar refineries of the East. Spreckels was also involved in banking, railroad building, and constructing gas and electric plants. Another prominent family in the sugar industry was the Havemeyers, who came from Germany in 1799. The Hershey family of Pennsylvania is also connected with the food industry. There is much German influence on American foods. For example, two items that carry the names of the German cities they came from are some of the most popular food items in the United States: frankfurters and hamburgers.

Also, bratwurst has gained tremendous popularity in recent years. In the area of brewing, of course, German-Americans have always predominated, with such names as Anheuser-Busch, Stroh, Schell, and Hudepohl.

The German-American work ethic provided the basic elements, building blocks, and ingenuity essential to the birth, growth, and development of business and industry in America.[3] Historically, German-Americans viewed work as the basis for family, rather than as the means of obtaining wealth for the individual. They stressed careful investment and high rates of savings, rather than speculative business practices. They believed in the careful accomplishment of a well-defined task and appreciated the value of work for its own sake, rather than for the monetary value placed on it.

The German-American philosophy of success also goes a long way in explaining their impact on American business and industry in general. An expression of this can be found in J. H. Strasser's history of New Ulm, Minnesota, *New Ulm in Wort und Bild* (1892). Although the author was writing about New Ulm, what he was saying was really part of the German-American *Weltanschauung*. Strasser wrote:

> If we should now chance a look into the future . . . we do so feeling absolutely justified in having a great deal of hope that the success . . . attained thus far, will continue in the future. Everything points in that direction. This is as definite as anything regarding the future can be. . . . By means of hard work and thriftiness, you can make it here . . . and attain a relative degree of success . . . and there is definitely always room for those who are hard-working and industrious, who have a spirit of enterprise, and also possess the necessary capital. For such newcomers there is plenty of opportunity.[4]

Strasser also stressed that the German heritage was an integral part of this philosophy of success, which implied that all the values were identified as virtues inherent to the German-American heritage. In other words, values and virtues such as hard work, diligence, and thriftiness were part of what it meant to be a German-American and were the underlying factors in the success that New Ulm had attained.

Social Life

European travelers in the eighteenth and early nineteenth centuries were appalled by the gravity, melancholy, and monotony of American social life. For example, a Mrs. Trollope, returning from her residence in America from 1827 to 1831, wrote that she had never seen a population so totally divested of gaiety, and she quotes a German woman as saying: "They do not love music; and they never amuse themselves; and their hearts are not warm, at least they seem so to strangers; and they have no ease, no forgetfulness of business and of care, no not for a moment."[5]

The importance of social life is underscored in a nineteenth-century German-American guidebook, *Der Goldne Wegweiser* (The Golden Signpost), which expressed the German-American viewpoint on a wide variety of topics. With regard to social life, it indicated that "hospitality and cheerful social relations should actually be just an extension of family life, and if friendship is only possible between a few, we can still associate with many."[6]

It noted that social life "becomes a real refreshment of everyday existence" and that "truly noble and cheering pleasures change the fleeting hours to unforgettable ones, they make them an enduring monument, so to speak, and are a means of education that should not be underestimated." Germans, hence, brought with them a large capacity for the enjoyment of life; they had agricultural fairs and frolics in the eighteenth century and expanded them to large-scale festivals as time went on. A word commonly used to describe German-American social life is *Gemütlichkeit*, which is defined as the quality of a good-natured, sanguine, easygoing disposition. To German-Americans, the word signifies all that and more, for it refers to a basic outlook on life and way of living. The word *Gemütlichkeit* is derived from *Gemüt*, which refers to the human soul, specifically to an emotional level of comfort and pleasant warmth.

Susan Stern, a recent commentator on German social life, noted in her book *These Strange German Ways* (1995) that "in some parts of the United States, German customs and traditions are more religiously clung to and practiced than they are in Europe. From *Fasching* through the

Oktoberfest to *Advent*, the celebrations are marked on the German-American calendar." She also noted that "if you want to see traditional German costumes, feast on sausages and sauerkraut, sway arm in arm at a beer table—you might have an easier time in Indianapolis than in Berlin or Düsseldorf."[7] Indeed, German-American social life and all the festivities connected with it provides the most visible display of a wide variety of German customs and traditions, some of which are not even practiced in the Old Country.

Aside from the numerous German-American festivities, German-Americans also Germanized American ones. The Fourth of July, for example, reflects the German impact, as German-Americans turned it into a festive occasion with not only fireworks, but cannons and rifle-shooting societies participating as well. In Cincinnati, children went trick-or-treating on Halloween, but when they came to the door, they asked for *Küchele*, which is German for donut.

German-Americans introduced numerous customs and traditions, from the Easter Bunny to the Christmas tree. Indeed, they made Christmas the principal festivity of the year and gave delight to the young with a flood of toys designed with consummate skill and fascinating workmanship, from the indestructible picture book to the doll with movable joints, from the tin soldiers to the self-propelling man-of-war, from Noah's ark to the Teddy bear (an invention of Margarete Steiff of Würtemberg).

The American celebration of Christmas was largely influenced by German-Americans. In 1776 Hessian soldiers set up the first Christmas trees in America. The first record of the traditional custom of going out to cut down or buy a tree was established in 1821, when the Pennsylvania German family Hensel cut down a tree in Lancaster and brought it home. The *Saturday Evening Post* reported about Pennsylvania German homes where the trees were visible through the windows and the green boughs were laden with fruit and candles that sparkled in the night.

It was not until the 1830s that the Christmas tree came to be used on a wide scale, however. In 1832 Karl Follen, the first professor of German in America, set up a tree in his home in Boston. He spared no expense at adorning the tree and made it as beautiful as possible with candles, ornaments, fruit, and various decorations. The story of his tree was published in Boston and this became widely known throughout New England, where no one had heard of Christmas trees before. Soon the custom of the Follen tree took hold.

In 1833 Gustav Koerner of Illinois, who had recently arrived from Germany, set up his tree. With no decorations available, Koerner adorned the tree with apples, bits of ribbon, nuts, and brightly colored paper. In 1834 Constantin Hering introduced Christmas trees to Philadelphia. Born in Leipzig, he longed for a German-style tree, so he and his friends cut down several trees and carried them through the streets of the city. It caused great excitement among the children, who had never seen Christmas trees before. Hering set the tree up in his home, and people from all over the city came to see it. He maintained the custom for fifty years and by the time of his death in the 1880s, Christmas trees were used throughout Philadelphia.

In Cincinnati, the first Christmas tree was set up by Ludwig Rehfuss in 1836. The first illustration of a Christmas tree appeared in a book by Hermann Bokum, published in the same year. This picture helped make the Christmas tree more popular, because now people could see what it should look like and how it should be decorated. The idea of a community Christmas tree was established in 1841 by Karl Minnegerode in Williamsburg, Virginia. Each year when the president lights the national tree or the mayor of a city does, they are carrying on a tradition started by German-Americans.

In 1845 the most famous Christmas book in American history appeared: *Kriss Kringle's Christmas*, which told how to celebrate Christmas with German-style customs. The name Kriss Kringle came from the German word *Christkind*, or Christ child. The first Christmas tree set up in an American church was in Cleveland, Ohio, in 1851, when the Rev. Heinrich Schwan set the tradition, which is now followed by nearly all churches in America. The first picture of Santa Claus was drawn by Thomas Nast, a prominent German-American illustrator. So many of the customs and traditions in America were influenced or established by German-Americans, but Christmas is the one most deeply influenced by them. An overview of German customs and traditions can be found in LaVern J. Rippley, *Of German Ways*.[8]

Family Life

In German-American families there is a great deal of preparation when it comes to celebrating birthdays, betrothals, and weddings. Annual family reunions have proved to be popular recently.

German-Americans historically celebrated the patriarchal family, one in which women and children all worked together for the common good of the family. Families not only worked together, they also enjoyed their social life together. They recognized lifelong obligations between parent and child. Historically, German-American families were larger than the average family. German-Americans more often married and resided in areas near their extended family and enjoyed high rates of home ownership. Children began to work at an earlier age and contributed their earnings to the welfare of the family. And women assisted the family enterprise either at home or by working. Each member of the family had a contribution to make.

Religion

Albert F. Faust noted in his history *The German Element in the U.S.* that

> for the large majority of the German immigrants, their history has shown them to be eminently a religious folk. They brought their preachers with them at the beginning and held to their religious doctrines until merged in the stronger currents of American life, or until they gained strength enough to found lasting religious institutions of their own, as the Lutheran Church, the German Reformed, and many others.[9]

German-American communities have been defined in terms of their religious or secular institutions, so historians have spoken of the religious and secular parts of the community.

The religious element consisted of German-Americans who belonged to Protestant, Catholic, and Jewish religious institutions and organizations, which formed a central focal point of their religious and social lives. As a group, they have often been referred to as the church Germans, or *Kirchdendeutsche*. They established a wide variety of religious institutions, including hospitals, old peoples' homes, schools, seminaries, societies, and, of course, places of worship. Many of them maintained German bookstores, where the publications of their own presses were available.

In religious educational institutions, German was an academic subject as well as the language of instruction. Some of these religious bodies held little in common with one another and went their own way in accordance with their own denomination, so they developed their own unique, religiously oriented social, educational, and sometimes even economic and political institutions. At times, the representatives of a particular religious denomination or the editor of the group's publications would engage in theological and doctrinal debates and disputes with other denominational publications.

Politically, the church Germans were conservative. Historically, some of them were staunchly antiradical, antisocialist, and especially anti-Forty-Eighter. Indeed, the latter were often viewed as divisive. However, most did not officially and overtly engage in political affairs and issues, except when there was an issue that directly affected their particular denomination, such as the issue of language instruction in parochial schools or abortion.

Religion and heritage were closely intertwined. Perhaps the most important institution for the preservation of the German language in America was the church. The church Germans used the German language and heritage to ward off heresy, maintain unity, prevent losses, and exclude external influences. This promoted a sense of a denomination's unique identity and religious particularity. Also, religiously oriented immigrants tended to come together in groups and stay together, and in such communities the church was the most important institution outside the family. Often in rural areas there would not even be a public school, for the only school in the area would be the parochial school.

Church Germans believed that language and faith were interrelated, so German was well maintained by the various religious denominations. Religion nurtured and was nurtured by religious consciousness. The least Anglicized communities were usually those with the strongest religious ties. Also, it is interesting to note that in German-American literature, every author who was American-born and wrote in German came from a church-centered community. In fact, it is quite common for German-Americans of four or more generations to speak German, particularly if they are from such a church-oriented background.

Such religious denominations were always youth oriented in terms of their educational programs and publications. Although a quite diverse group, their common bond was a commitment to the German heritage. It is estimated that there are still about two thousand congregations in the United States that hold German services, weekly, monthly, or annually. However, by the 1950s most German-American churches had made the language shift to English, mainly because of the desire to keep the youth within the fold. Although German-American denominations in the main have made the language shift, they clearly maintain a strong sense of identity as German-American religious denominations, and many of them continue to sponsor occasional German services and hold German-style dinners as well as church festivals. Also, German-American church records are highly important for the study of German immigration and settlement history, as well as for the family history of congregational members.

It is beyond the scope of this work to provide a detailed discussion of individual denominations founded by German-Americans, but references to works dealing with them can be found in the bibliographical sources listed at the end of this volume.[10]

Education

German thought and practice have exerted a great deal of influence on American education. These influences were transmitted not only by German-Americans, but also by non-German-Americans who had studied in Germany, had traveled there, or who had maintained correspondence with leading German educators and intellectuals. The entire educational system from kindergarten to university was deeply influenced by and patterned after German educational models.

These influences began early in American history. Cotton Mather, the famous New England divine, corresponded in Latin with August Hermann

Francke, the noted philanthropist who established the first model orphanage in Halle, Germany. This was an example of the Anglo-German intellectual exchange that took place between leading thinkers in both countries and contributed to the flow of ideas to the New World from Germany.

In Pennsylvania, Germans maintained their own schools that used German as the language of instruction. Their most distinguished teacher was Franz Daniel Pastorius, the founder of Germantown. He served as burgomaster and leading educator. The school he established in 1702 even had an evening program for those who worked during the day. Another German-American who distinguished himself in the classroom was Christopher Dock, a Mennonite. He introduced the blackboard into the American classroom, which became a basic instrument of instruction. In 1750 he published the first pedagogic work in America, and in 1764 he published his well-known *One Hundred Necessary Rules of Conduct for Children*, which provided some basic rules and guidelines for how children should behave.

A number of colonial educators went to Germany and became acquainted with the German educational system. One of the earliest to visit a German university was Benjamin Franklin. In 1776 he attended a meeting of the Royal Society of Science in Göttingen and became a member. Another American who visited Göttingen was Benjamin Smith Barton, who obtained his M.D. in 1789 at the university. Upon his return to Philadelphia he became a well-known physician. He was among the first of many Americans who would obtain their education at a German university.

In the nineteenth century, many more began to attend German universities, and upon their return they exerted a strong influence in terms of introducing German educational ideas, methods, and practices. Ticknor and Longfellow used the German university model in organizing their language department at Harvard. Among the teachers that Longfellow hired, the most outstanding was Carl Follen, a cultured political refugee and later a Unitarian minister who became the first professor of German in the United States at Harvard (1831–36).

Interest in German educational methods was greatly enhanced by a French brochure, *Report on the State of Public Education in Prussia*, published in 1832 by the well-known philosopher Victor Cousin. "The

Prussian system" came to be a phrase describing a plan of education based upon freedom of access to schools operated at public expense, with state supervision, and with three gradations of scholastic teaching: the common school, the high school or academy, and the university.

When the Michigan constitution of 1835 was in the process of being written, the Prussian system was incorporated into that fundamental law due to the work of individuals familiar with Cousin's report. All of the elements of the Prussian system were put in place in Michigan: primary schools, secondary schools, and a university, all supported by public taxation and under state supervision. Due to Cousin's report, the school board of Ohio was induced to send the Rev. Calvin E. Stowe, the husband of Harriet Beecher Stowe, abroad to make a closer study of German education. His enthusiastic report published in 1836 gave a detailed account of what he had observed.

Another American educator who gave high praise to German schools was Horace Mann of Massachusetts. His unbounded admiration of the preparation of teachers inspired him to organize the first American normal school in 1839. In his book on Mann, Burke Hinsdale noted, "It is Germany that in this century has exerted upon our country the most protracted, the deepest and the most salutary educational influence."[11] Mann's famous *Seventh Annual Report* (1843) praised the Prussian schools. Mann was especially impressed with the teacher training, their kindness, and the absence of corporal punishment.

One of the most profound educational influences came through the works and writings of Johann Friedrich Herbart, a professor at Göttingen. He introduced psychology into teaching, and enthusiastic American educators founded the first Herbartian Club in 1892. The German educator's ideas and methods were widely adopted throughout the nation. Bancroft, who had been impressed with German methods of teaching, aimed to introduce them in New England. Together with Cogswell, he founded the Round Hill School in 1823 near Northhampton, Massachusetts. Another American educator who observed schools abroad was John Griscom, who visited Pestalozzi in Switzerland. Thomas Jefferson said that Griscom's report gave him valuable ideas in organizing the University of Virginia.

Efforts to use the German university as a model were particularly pronounced in Michigan. Several of the early university presidents were tireless in their endeavors to follow the German model. A university in the East that reflected the German model was Cornell, founded in 1868. Its first president, Andrew D. White, had served as U.S. minister to Germany from 1879 to 1881 and was impressed with what he saw. He was guided by the German university model as he helped establish Cornell University. White was especially interested in building up technical education, and it is no doubt due to this influence that the first school of forestry in the United States was established at Cornell. German influences were also strong at Johns Hopkins University, which was founded in 1876. Almost all of the faculty members had obtained their doctoral degrees in Germany. The idea of establishing university libraries with separate departmental libraries was patterned after German universities, as was the concept of a seminar, in which students and professors gathered in small groups.

American education was influenced not only at the upper levels, but also at the lower levels. The kindergarten—a German term—which had been founded in Germany by Friedrich Froebel, was introduced into this country by Carl Schurz's wife at Watertown, Wisconsin, in 1855.

In most areas where German-Americans were settled, German instruction could be found. Although private and parochial schools offered German instruction in the colonial era, it was not until 1840 in Cincinnati that the first German bilingual public-school programs were established. Thereafter, similar public-school programs spread throughout the country. They were based on the model in Ohio, where the legislature had directed all boards of education to introduce German instruction whenever it was requested by at least seventy-five citizens. German-Americans, hence, created and established bilingual education in America, something that today is quite common across the country.

German was taught in elementary schools across the country well into the twentieth century. Until 1918, there was a German department in the Cincinnati public schools under the direction of Dr. H. H. Fick, who published a series of textbooks that were used in German bilingual programs across the country. Before the First World War the program consisted of 250 German teachers, and there were more than 15,000 German students. A typical book used in the program was Fick's *Neu und Alt: Ein Buch für die Jugend* (1911).

During the latter quarter of the nineteenth century a new German educational influence was introduced, which had a marked effect on the American school system: vocational education. Germany had had great success with its trade schools, and they were eagerly imitated by other European nations. Americans, too, became interested, and German practices were soon introduced here. Today, vocational education is commonplace. In Germany, a dual track system of education has developed, which provides equal opportunities for students to enter the vocational education track or the track leading to university education. This kind of dual track system with equal possibilities for vocational and academic education has not been developed in the United States, unfortunately. Indeed, vocational education is highly underrated and underdeveloped. However, there are some exceptions in some areas, especially where German-Americans settled. Here vocational high schools were developed so that students could prepare themselves for various trades, crafts, and occupations. Also, German-Americans introduced what became known as the "co-operative" form of education, which would allow for students to gain on-the-job training while enrolled in high school. This concept was also introduced at the University of Cincinnati in the early 1900s by Herman Schneider, where co-op education thrives today.

In the early 1900s, Schneider began to ponder the question of how theoretical knowledge in the classroom could be combined with firsthand experience on the job. As a professor of engineering, he felt that engineers could be trained concurrently in theory and practice by having students begin part-time employment during their college years and having this work recognized as a part of their educational program. He proposed that a school be established and have students co-op with industrial plants. These plans were developed while Schneider was at Lehigh University in Pennsylvania. In 1903 he came to the University of Cincinnati as an assistant professor of civil engineering. In 1904 he presented a paper entitled "A Communication on Technical Education," which displayed his thoughts on the need to integrate practical work experience into education. He was granted the opportunity of trying his plan for one year, and the plan was introduced in 1906. It became a great success at the University of Cincinnati and is still utilized today not only in the college of engineering, but also in the colleges of business, design, architecture, art, and planning.

Another feature of German education that has greatly influenced American schools is physical education. In 1811 Friedrich Jahn had started what was known as "Turnerei," a movement to make young Germans vigorous in body and mind. In fact, the motto was "a sound body and a sound mind." Through Carl Beck and Carl Follen it spread to New England and was introduced at the Round Hill School in Northhampton, Massachusetts. Francis Lieber set up the first swimming pool in Boston.

The Turner movement spread swiftly in the United States, especially after the arrival of several thousand refugees of the failed German 1848 Revolution. In Cincinnati, the first Turnverein, or Turner society, was established in 1848, and thereafter many more were established across the country. Almost every German-American community had its own Turnverein. German-Americans strongly recommended that physical education become a part of the curriculum of the schools, and they influenced their school boards to institute courses in physical education. By 1914 gymnastics had been introduced into seventy-six cities due to the direct efforts of the German-American Turner societies. Every school building had to have a gymnasium, and physical training became a basic element of the program of the YMCA. Many colleges and universities, as well as the Military Academy at West Point and the Naval Academy at Annapolis, joined the movement, engaging mostly teachers who had received their education at the Turner training school in Indianapolis, located in the beautiful *Deutsches Haus*.

Finally, there are various centers, collections, and institutes at colleges and universities that deal with the field of German-American studies, including the Max Kade Institutes at the University of Wisconsin-Madison, the University of Kansas, Indiana University-Purdue University at Indianapolis, and Pennsylvania State University; the University of Cincinnati's German-Americana Collection; and the Germans from Russian Heritage Collection at North Dakota State University.

An excellent survey of German educational influences before World War I can be found in Henry Geitz et al., *German Influences on Education in the United States to 1917* (1995). For references to sources of information dealing with influences since that time, see the bibliographies listed at the end of this volume.

From the top to the bottom of the scale, German educational influences can be found and have come to be widely accepted as American. This is perhaps but one more indication of how deep and widespread German influences are, that they are accepted as American and as a part of the way things are in America. Yet here, as in other areas, when the origins are examined, they are found to be German.[12]

Music

German-Americans brought to America an appreciation for music. Indeed, they contributed to the inclusion of numerous German composers into the basic orchestral repertoire, such as Bach, Mozart, Haydn, Beethoven, Schubert, Schumann, Brahms, Wagner, and others. It has been said that if German-Americans had done nothing more than bring music to America, that would have been a major contribution to American life. *Der Goldne Wegweiser* commented on the significance of music, stating that "what words are not able to utter, musical sound reechoes; it gives expression to the highest and the profoundest feelings of the human breast; it mirrors the tenderest emotions, the most secret moods of the heart—it expresses the soul of the soul."[13]

During the eighteenth century, the Puritans in New England and the Quakers in Pennsylvania checked the development of music, yet the German sectarians of Pennsylvania, though austere in their mode of life, fondly practiced the art of choral singing. The mixed chorus of the brothers and sisters of Ephrata and the music schools of the Moravians at Bethlehem invoked admiration and fostered the sacred flame. Philadelphia, with its large German population, early on began the cultivation of music and gave the first ambitious program of classical music on May 4, 1786. A noteworthy accomplishment was made in Boston with the founding of the Handel and Haydn Society in 1815. Real progress was made by this association when in 1854 a professional conductor was invited, the great German orchestral drillmaster Carl Zerrahn.

Johann Graupner had won the distinction of having established the Philharmonic Society in Boston in 1810–11, which became one of the finest orchestras of its time. For this reason Graupner is considered the father of orchestral music in America. New York began to show its mettle about the middle of the century with the foundation of the Philharmonic Society, and its rival, the famous Germania Orchestra, boldly began making tours, giving orchestral concerts in many eastern cities between 1848 and 1854.

Then came the period of the great German masters: Theodor Thomas, Anton Seidl, Leopold Damrosch, Wilhelm Gericke, Emil Paur, and many others, who developed a musical taste for the symphony and the grand opera. Current German conductors include Erich Kunzel of the Cincinnati Symphony Orchestra and Kurt Masur of the New York Philharmonic Orchestra.

In vocal music the efforts of the German-American singing societies must not be overlooked, as they have contributed greatly to the appreciation of German song and music in America. Moreover, they have been particularly successful in their maintenance of the German language. In 1849 the German-American singing societies formed the North American Federation of Singing Societies, a national federation which in 1999 celebrated its 150th anniversary in Cincinnati, where it was founded. Member societies also sponsor district song festivals, as do the individual member singing societies themselves. There were also conservatories and private music schools, very frequently founded or directed by German professors of music.

Among the many opera singers whose names stand out are Marcella Sembrich, Ernestine Schumann-Heink, Lotte Lehmann, Frieda Hempel, Maria Jeritza, and Elisabeth Schwarzkopf. Among the many conductors who have achieved national acclaim are Fritz Reiner, Fritz Kreisler, and Max Rudolf. One of the most famous composers is the German-American John Philip Sousa, whose numerous marches became very popular in America.

An interesting musician is Georg Drumm, who composed "Hail America" during the height of the anti-German hysteria of World War I in order to calm the frenzy. This ceremonial march was renamed "Hail to the Chief" in 1952, when it was first used for official purposes in the Eisenhower administration. Since that time, Drumm's march has become the leitmotif that "drums up" an impending entry on stage for all U.S. presidents.

Art and Architecture

German-American influences can be found in all branches of art, and it would be impossible here to do more than allude to a few outstanding artists. In painting, German influences have been quite strong. Among the early painters, the most distinguished was Emanuel Leutze from Württemberg, whose best-known work is *Washington Crossing the Delaware* (1851). It is interesting to note that this famous historic painting was completed in Düsseldorf on the Rhine and that the Continentals in the boat were painted from German models. Hence, the painting could be called *Washington Crossing the Rhine*.

Düsseldorf had a predominating influence on early painters. Another German-American, Albert Bierstadt, studied in that city and upon his return to America became fascinated by the Wild West. He produced numerous paintings of exceptional grace and beauty that created the image we have today of the West. These included works depicting the Rocky Mountains, Yosemite, and the Sierras. Other noteworthy German-American painters are Josef Albers, William Ritschel, Anton Otto Fischer, Franz Arthur Bischoff, Carl Rungius, Walt Kuhn, Max Ernst, Hans Hofmann, Ad Reinhardt, Franz Kline, Daniel Garber, Walter Emerson Baum, Max Kuehne, Julius Bloch, Carl Marr, Charles Ulrich, Louis Moeller, Frank Duveneck, Walter Y. Königstein, Friedel Dzubas, and Richard Lindner.

The works of Adolf Dehn of Minnesota portray not only his Minnesota German heritage, but also his sojourn in Vienna. In sculpture the works of William Rhinehart and Karl Bitter stand out. Especially significant is Albert Jaegers, a Cincinnati German who created the magnificent German-American National Monument in Germantown, Pennsylvania. In Minnesota the exquisite wood sculptures of the Swiss-German Ulrich Steiner adorns numerous locales.[14]

German-Americans have distinguished themselves in architecture also. Thomas U. Walter was appointed in 1851 by President Fillmore to superintend the extension of the Capitol in Washington. He designed the great iron dome and a number of public buildings, including the U.S. Treasury and the wings of the Patent Office. The Library of Congress was designed by architects Smithmeyer and Pelz in 1886. G. L. Heinz was the architect for the cathedral of St. John the Divine in New York. Since the 1930s, many German-Americans of the Bauhaus school of architecture became influential in the United States. Recently, Helmut Jahn of Chicago has become internationally well known for his architectural work.[15]

German-Americans contributed to the art of illustrating and engraving, and Alfred Stieglitz is known for his development of artistic expression in photography. Comic illustration and cartooning were brought to a high level by Thomas Nast, who was born in Landau. His brilliant cartoons in defense of the Civil War evoked praise from President Lincoln. His caricatures were not merely entertaining; they also had a serious message. In New York, he fought against the corruption of Tammany Hall with his vitriolic caricatures. Among his numerous cartoon creations were the donkey for the Democratic Party, the elephant for the Republican Party, the image of Uncle Sam, as well as the popular image of Santa Claus. Another cartoonist, almost as influential as Nast, was Joseph Keppler from Vienna, the founder of *Puck*. Equally effective was Eugene Zimmermann, the caricaturist of *Judge*. Of course, the comic series *Peanuts*, by Charles Schultz, also became a popular feature of the press.[16]

Politics

From Peter Minuit, Jacob Leisler, and Franz Daniel Pastorius in the seventeenth century to Henry Kissinger in the twentieth, German-Americans have taken an active role in American political life. However, the first politician who emerged as a real national spokesman of German-Americans was Carl Schurz, who began his long career in the 1850s (see chapter 7). Schurz's life is recorded in his fascinating three-volume memoirs, and his lifework is well presented in the six-volume edition of his speeches and memoirs, edited by Frederic Bancroft.[17]

In the twentieth century, two presidents were of German descent: Herbert Hoover and Dwight D. Eisenhower. There have been numerous congressional representatives from German-American stock, including Sen. Robert Wagner of New York, Sen. Everett Dirksen of Illinois, and Rep. Thomas Luken of Cincinnati, for example.

Historically, German-Americans have stressed the importance of the candidate and his or her principles, rather than the political party the candidate belongs to. They often claimed that Yankees supported the party, rather than examining the individual running for office. They expected good and clean government, which reflected both the religious and the political, especially the Forty-Eighter, heritage of German-Americans. German-Americans also had strong beliefs about the role of government, whose central task they felt was to guarantee and protect *persönliche Freiheit* (personal liberty). Government should, therefore, guarantee the individual's personal liberty to the fullest measure in accordance with the principles of basic law and order. This meant that any attempt to legislate the individual's personal liberty by laws, such as prohibition, would be regarded as an invasion of individual liberty. Such views continue to hold true today for German-Americans.[18]

Military Service

The record of German-American military service throughout the history of the United States has been discussed earlier and will not be repeated here. However, several comments are in order.

First, German-American regiments, battalions, and other units were first formed during the American Revolution and continued through the Civil War. They were first formed when the German-American element was relatively small, approximately 10 percent of the population. After the Civil War, as a result of the massive waves of immigration, German-Americans were in the process of becoming America's largest ethnic element and were numerically so large that they formed the largest single ethnic group in the U.S. armed forces.

A second aspect is that German-Americans have served in far greater numbers than would have been expected given their percentage (25 percent) of the population. In the nineteenth and twentieth centuries, a full one-third of American forces have been German-American.

In all wars from the American Revolution to the Gulf War, German-American officers have played an important role in terms of American military leadership—from von Steuben to Schwarzkopf.

Given this substantial role in American military history, it is difficult, if not impossible to imagine American involvement in the wars of the nineteenth and twentieth centuries without the services of German-American soldiers.[19]

Journalism

Well over five thousand German-American newspapers and journals have been published since the first one appeared in 1732, thereby making the German-language press the largest non-English press in American history. Chrisopher Saur founded one of the earliest, *Der Hoch-deutsche Pennsylvaniische Geschichtsschreiber*, in 1739. By 1762 there were five German newspapers in Pennsylvania, and even Benjamin Franklin had published one for a brief period of time. The number of journals and newspapers continued to grow, especially after the arrival of the Thirtyers and the Forty-Eighters in the nineteenth century.[20]

In cities and towns across the United States there were countless German-language newspapers. The largest ones were in New York, Chicago, Cincinnati, Milwaukee, St. Louis, and Philadelphia. Still published today is the *New Yorker Staats-Zeitung*, for a long time the most influential and most prestigious publication of its kind. Founded in 1834, it contains reports not only on German-speaking countries, but also on German-American communities across the country. Other contemporary German-American newspapers are *Nord-Ameriikanische WochenPostt* (Troy, Michigan), *Amerika-Woche* (Chicago), *Eintrachtt* (Chicago), and *Aufbau* (New York). Several of the major national German-American organizations publish journals and newspapers, such as the *German-American Journal*, published by the German-American National Congress; the *Ambassador*, published by the United German-American Committee-USA; and the *Steuben News*, published by the Steuben Society of America.

In 1890 there were 727 German-language publications. Today, there is still a substantial German-American press, but it no longer consists mainly of newspapers, but instead newsletters published by German-American societies. Whereas in the nineteenth century these societies supported the German-language press, they now support newsletters, a much more economical kind of publication. By the 1990s, based on the number of German-American societies, it is estimated that there are more than one thousand German-American newsletters, mainly in English, but sometimes in German or bilingual. Hence, the number of German-American publications has increased substantially. Some of these newsletters are even named for older German-language publications, such as *Der Neue Kurier*, named for *Der Cincinnati Kurier*, or *Der Neue Louisville Anzeiger*, named for *Der Louisville Anzeiger*. Then there are new publications, such as *Der Maibaum*, published in Hermann, Missouri.[21]

Two relatively new magazines dealing with German-American affairs but published in English are *German Life* and *in*. While *German Life* is published by an American company in Maryland, *in* is sponsored by the German government, printed in Germany, and distributed by an American firm in New Jersey.

German-Americans not only established a highly influential German-American press, they also have played an important role in the history of the American press in general. It was Johann Peter Zenger, an immigrant from the Palatinate, who in 1734 edited the *New York Weekly Journal* and established the principal of freedom of the press. Zenger had written a series of highly critical articles regarding the governor of New York, William Cosby, because of his dictatorial administration, whereupon he was arrested and held in jail for criminal libel. Zenger was defended by a famous lawyer, Alexander Hamilton, who argued that Zenger's statements were not unlawful because they were true and that the truth was not unlawful. Zenger was eventually acquitted, and he will always been remembered for this famous case that contributed to establishing freedom of the press in America.

Another significant name in the history of the American press is Joseph Pulitzer, who began his journalistic career in St. Louis with a German-American newspaper owned by Carl Schurz. Thereafter he published the *St. Louis Post-Dispatch* and later the *New York World*. He contributed to making the following features standard elements of daily newspapers: comics, women's sections, sports news, and illustrations. He also introduced promotional campaigns for the press, which included stunts and contests. Pulitzer also provided for the endowment of the

Columbia School of Journalism and for the establishment of the Pulitzer Prize, which has been awarded since 1917.

Oswald Garrison Villard was the well-known German-American publisher of the *New York Evening Post* and the *Nation*. As publisher of the *Post* from 1897 to 1918, Villard fought for many ideals, including opposition to the First World War, and he later published a volume dealing with his journalistic career, *Newspapers and Newspapermen* (1923).

Among the major newspapers published today, two were founded by German-Americans. The *New York Times* was founded in 1896 by Adolph S. Ochs, and *USA Today* was founded by Allen Neuharth in 1982. The Ridder family, who published the *New Yorker Staats-Zeitung*, later published English-language newspapers and is still involved with major papers, such as the *St. Paul Pioneer Press*. These indicate the continuing influence German-Americans exert in the realm of the American press.[22] For further introduction to the topic, see Henry Geitz, ed., *The German-American Press* (1992), as well as the bibliographies listed at this end of this volume.

Literature

Since the seventeenth century there have been over three thousand works written by German-American authors, and these works have been recorded in Robert E. Ward's *A Bio-Bibliography of German-American Creative Writers*.[23]

Among the significant colonial authors were Franz Daniel Pastorius and Johann Conrad Beissel. In the nineteenth century there were numerous writers, some of whose works became well known on both sides of the Atlantic. Karl Postl (pseudonym Charles Sealsfield) even became a best-selling author of the mid-nineteenth century in both America and Germany. Other well-known nineteenth-century authors were Caspar Butz, Martin Drescher, Karl Knortz, Konrad Krez, Konrad Nies, Heinrich A. Rattermann, Robert Reitzel, and Ernst Anton Zuendt. Leading authors in the early twentieth century were H. H. Fick, Georg Sylvester Viereck, and Otto Oscar Kollbrunner. In the 1930s many German authors came as émigrés to America, and some remained and became U.S. citizens. In this group was Nobel prizewinner Thomas Mann, who wrote some of his major works after he had become a U.S. citizen.

In the 1970s the Association of German-Language Authors in America published a poetry series as well as a literary journal. There is currently a series, *Deutschschreibende Autoren in Nordamerika*, which has published the work of German-language authors such as Irmgard Elsner Hunt, Gert Niers, Peter Pabisch, and others. There is also a literary organization, the Society for Contemporary Literature in German, which publishes a journal, *Trans-Lit*. Here one finds the works of contemporary German-American authors, including Peter Beicken, Lisa Kahn, and Margot Scharpenberg.

One of the most well-known German-American authors undoubtedly was L. Frank Baum, who wrote *The Wizard of Oz*. Another well-known author of children's literature was Theodore S. Geisel, who wrote more than fifty books, including the famous Dr. Seuss books, such as *The Cat in the Hat*. His works sold more than 100 million copies and have been translated into twenty languages, including Braille. There is a great number of German-American authors who have written and published their works in English, including Carol Ascher, Thomas Berger, Pearl Buck, Charles Bukowski, Theodore Dreiser, Stuart Friebert, John Gunther, Joseph Hergesheimer, John Jakes, Norbert Krapf, Ludwig Lewisohn, H. L. Mencken, Henry Miller, Joaquin Miller, Lisel Mueller, Charles Nordhoff, Conrad Richter, Theodore Roethke, John Godfrey Saxe, Herman George Scheffauer, Gertrude Stein, John Steinbeck, Bayard Taylor, Henry Timrod, Leon Uris, Kurt Vonnegut, and Paula Weber. Many of these are authors of major importance whose works illuminate various aspects of the German-American experience.

Many American authors, such as Cooper, Irving, Poe, Longfellow, Whittier, Thoreau, Melville, Whitman, and Twain, were influenced by German culture by means of their travels in German-speaking countries or their reading of German literature. The early history of this fascinating chapter of cross-cultural relations between Germany and America is traced in an encyclopedic work by Henry A. Pochmann, *German Culture in America: Philosophical and Literary Influences*.[24] A survey of German-American literature can be found in Don Heinrich Tolzmann, *German-American Literature* (1977).

German-Americans had a high interest in books and reading materials. *Der Goldne Wegweiser* advised that "everyone should have books. A house without books is rightly called a literary desert." It also advised that "if you have accumulated a number of books, it is most important that you use them well and preserve them well. By good use we mean not reading them through superficially, but rather studying them carefully. A book that is not worthy reading twice is not worth reading at all. Take good care of your books."[25]

Language and Linguistics

As a Germanic language, English contains numerous words of German origin. American English, or, as H. L. Mencken called it, American, has also incorporated the influences of many languages, especially those brought to America by various immigrant groups. Mencken wrote that the Germans have left an indelible mark on America, especially on English as it is spoken in the United States. Indeed, everyday vocabulary displays many German words and phrases.

American English not only has many words of German origin, but it also contains numerous loanwords that have been taken directly into the American vocabulary and reflect the linguistic impact of the German immigrations. German loanwords can be found in all areas and deal with all possible topics, but an area that appears to have the greatest concentration is that of dietary ingredients. This in itself is an indication of how German foodways have deeply influenced the American diet. Indeed, the influence has been so great that German words were incorporated directly into everyday language. These words are so ingrained in the vocabulary that they are used matter-of-factly as part of what constitutes basic elements of the American diet. Here is a partial list of such German loanwords: angst, auslese, bedeckt, beergarden, bierstube, bismarck, blitzkrieg, bock beer, bratwurst, concertmaster, cookbook, delicatessen, dummkopf, edelweiss, ersatz, flak, fahrvergnuegen, frankfurter, gemuetlichkeit, gesundheit, glockenspiel, gummi bear, hamburger, hasenpfeffer, hausfrau, hinterland, iceberg, kaffeeklatsch, kaputt, katzenjammer, kitsch, Kriss Kringle, kuchen, lager beer, leitmotif, liebfraumilch, lied, marzipan, meerschaum, misch-masch, mettwurst, muesli, noodle, ohm, ostpolitik, paraffin, pfannkuchen, plunder, poltergeist, pretzel, prosit, pumpernickel, rathskeller, riesling, rucksack, sauerbraten, sauerkraut, schnapps, schnitzel, Seltzer, smearcase, spaetzle, springerle, spritz, stein, stollen, streusel, strudel, thuringer, torte, verboten, waltz, wanderlust, weinstube, weissbeer, weltanschauung, weltschmerz, wienerwurst, wunderbar, wunderkind, wurst, yodel, zeitgeist, zigzag, and zwieback.

German loanwords also come into the American vocabulary via the media, where advertising slogans regularly make use of German words, such as *Fahrvergnügen*. Here the use of a German word connotes quality and is a marker indicating that the product is "Made in Germany." Another popular advertising gimmick is to create a compound noun by adding "fest" like a suffix to any kind of possible sale. Thus, a sale in November becomes a November-Fest.

One expression that is perhaps the most universally understood and used word of German-American origin is "O.K," or "okay." At the time of Henry Ford's Model T, the concept of mass production came into being, and the automobile was put together on an assembly line. The last man on the line was responsible for the final inspection and had to give his final approval. At first, he did so by signing his name, but so many cars were passing him that he began using a stamp with his initials on it. This individual with the Ford Motor Company was a German-American—Oskar Krause—and his initials were O.K.

German is and has been historically influential in molding and shaping the language spoken in America. This is a result not only of the substantial German immigrations, but also of the fact that German has been so widely spoken in the United States. Estimates of the percentage of the sixty million German-Americans who can speak and understand German today range from 10 to 30 percent. The percentage of those who can understand some German is most likely larger.

Where is German spoken? Obviously it is most widely spoken in the states and regions where the German-American element is predominant. The preservation of the German language has been especially strong among the Church Germans. German is also more strongly maintained in rural communities, which tended to remain stable and constant for generations and are usually close-knit. Finally, German tends to be spoken in two contexts: in the family and within the framework of ethnic institutions and organizations.

Who speaks German? The overwhelming majority of those who speak German is American-born, and most have never been to a German-speaking country. Their ancestors came to America anywhere from one to eight generations ago. Also, most have had no formal education in German but have mainly been taught by members of their families.

The history of German as an ethnic language reaches back to the beginnings of German immigration. It has most likely been spoken since 1608, when the first permanent German settlers arrived at Jamestown, and it is clearly, therefore, no more foreign to America than is English. The first recorded reference to a sermon given in German dates to 1657 in New Amsterdam, which was heavily settled by Germans. Also, German was one of the official languages of New Sweden. After 1683 German flourished with the beginnings of the German immigration. In the eighteenth century, the question arose about establishing German as an official language.

During the American Revolution, the Continental Congress had numerous proclamations and broadsheets printed in German, beginning in 1774 with the proceedings of the Continental Congress. The Articles of Confederation of the Continental Congress also appeared in German, and many more publications were issued in German. At the same time, the German language press had already been well established for several decades, and, in fact, the first announcement of the Declaration of Independence appeared on July 5, 1776, in Henry Miller's newspaper, the *Staatsbote*.

The question often arises as to whether there was a vote to make German an official language on a national basis, and the answer is that there almost was. In 1794 German-Americans from the state of Virginia petitioned the House of Representatives that U.S. laws be printed in German. The Speaker of the House, Frederick Muehlenberg of Pennsylvania, was also president of the German Society of Pennsylvania and desired very much to maintain his position in the House, which meant that he had to play politics.

At that time, there was a great deal of anti-immigrant sentiment due to the French Revolution and the fear of "foreigners," i.e., non-Anglos. Rather than supporting the German-American petition, Muehlenberg referred it to a committee, which meant death by pocket veto. It was then resubmitted but again was tabled by referral to a committee that was charged with investigating the matter. This petition was submitted at the same time that the question of the naturalization of immigrants was being discussed. Muehlenberg must have felt that to support such a petition would have weakened not only his position as the House Speaker, but also that of the naturalization legislation.

The myth that emerged from this was that German almost became a national language except for one vote, which was cast by Muehlenberg, but was not the case. Even if it had been brought to a vote, German would have been established not as the only U.S. language, but as a language equal with English in terms of printing laws and documents. The one-vote myth most likely derives from what happened in Pennsylvania. In 1828 a motion was defeated by one vote to make German equal with English. However, many states, such as Ohio (1817), recognized the importance of German and authorized the printing of state documents in German.

In 1843 a Pennsylvania-German representative in the House moved that the annual message be published in German, a motion that was defeated by three votes. An examination of who cast the votes is revealing. In the German Belt states, fifty-five were for and five against, and in the non-German Belt states, thirty-one for for and eighty-one against. Hence, the voting clearly was along ethnic lines.

In 1853 several issues of the *Congressional Globe* appeared in German. During the Civil War, there was another attempt to have documents published in German. This motion passed in the Senate but was defeated in the House when a nativist Anglo-oriented representative stated, "I submit the question whether we are to have a national language or not." In this resulting vote, the New England and Atlantic states voted against, and the Midwestern states voted for it. This was the last real attempt at the national level to petition for the publication of documents in German. However, numerous states did pass and retain regulations to print and publish documents in German. These remained in place until World War I, when they were revoked.

By the time of the Civil War, German-Americans moved to establish bilingual educational programs. In public schools, the heyday for German bilingual instruction was from 1840 to 1918, when German instruction was eliminated or banned across the country. In 1915 25 percent of high-school students were enrolled in German, but in 1922 only .6 percent were. By 1978 2.4 percent of high-school students were enrolled in German, or approximately 10 percent of the number that was enrolled before the First World War.

German instruction was reestablished after World War I, but only in secondary schools. However, as a reflection of the ethnic revival of the 1970s, a number of German bilingual schools were reestablished in Cincinnati, St. Louis, Milwaukee, Pittsburgh, and Chicago. Two all-German private schools were also established in Washington, D.C., and New York. By the 1980s there were close to one hundred Saturday schools in various cities that offered German instruction. German is also taught in private and parochial schools, especially by the Catholic and Lutheran churches, as well as by various sectarian groups.

German should be reintroduced at the elementary level, especially in those areas with a strong German heritage. As was the case in the nineteenth century, however, it is quite clear that German will not be reintroduced unless German-Americans apply the appropriate pressure to have it reinstated.

There are other institutions that support the German language today, including German-language publications (ca. 50), German radio programs (ca. 175), churches with German services (ca. 2,000), and numerous German-American societies. Recent studies indicate that German is more widely spoken than is realized. In spite of two world wars, it is rather surprising how much survived that first half of the twentieth century. This provides rich ground for the preservation and maintenance of the German language.

The historical importance of the German language to German-Americans is well expressed by *Der Goldne Wegweiser*, which stated that German

is one of the oldest, purest, and most cultivated of the living languages and surpasses most modern languages in richness and strength, in malleability and suppleness. It must therefore be especially important to our German compatriots in America that their descendants also learn not merely to understand their beautiful native language without difficulty, but to know it thoroughly and to speak it.

The guidebook noted that this certainly was "the most earnest wish of most of the citizens of this country who have immigrated from Germany."[26]

German-American Influences

In a recent work dealing with the significance and impact of the cultural capital brought to America by immigrants, Thomas Sowell observed that German emigrants did not simply leave their German-speaking homeland, but they took part of it with them, "preserving the culture not only for themselves, but also making it part of the larger culture" of America. He notes that "even the cultural mainstream of America began to take on features once peculiar to Germans." In his study of worldwide migrations, Sowell discusses German emigrations to America and to other areas around the world, noting, "In the long view of history, few peoples have made such cultural and economic contributions to so many lands in so many parts of the planet as the Germans." He especially cites the success and prominence of Germans in agriculture, business, industry, science, technology, and the professions. Their achievements in these areas were "fundamental to the rise of Germany as a world power and to the agricultural and industrial progress of other nations" that received German immigrations. German emigrants throughout the world have been "widely known for their industriousness, thrift, neatness, punctuality, and reliability in meeting their financial obligations, as well as retaining their own German language and customs."[27]

It is no easy task to summarize the manifold influences German-Americans have exerted on American society and culture, as they are so diverse and deeply interwoven into the very fabric of American life. This is due in part to the substantial percentage of the population that is German-American, but in many instances they have surpassed their expected contributions given their numbers. If you scratch the surface of something in America, the chances are high that a German origin is underneath. The German dimension is often overlooked or taken for granted as it is so deeply ingrained and accepted as a basic element of American life. What is American is often German-American in origin.

Notes

1. See Don Heinrich Tolzmann, ed., *German Pioneer Life* (Bowie, Md.: Heritage Books, Inc., 1992), pp. 54–73.

2. Albert B. Faust, *The German Element in the U.S.* (New York: Steuben Society of America, 1927), vol. 2, pp. 29–30.

3. For further references to business and industrial history, see Don Heinrich Tolzmann, ed., *German-Americana: A Bibliography* (Metuchen, N.J.: Scarecrow, 1977), pp. 296–304, and Don Heinrich Tolzmann, ed., *Catalog of the German-Americana Collection* (Munich: K. G. Saur, 1990), vol. 2, pp. 328–45.

4. Don Heinrich Tolzmann, ed., *New Ulm in Word and Picture: J. H. Strasser's History of a German-American Settlement* (Indianapolis: Max Kade German-American Center, Indiana University-Purdue University and Indiana German Heritage Society, 1997), p. 29.

5. Cited in Faust, *The German Element in the U.S.*, vol. 2, p. 251.

6. Colin B. Thompson and Charlotte Lang Brancaforte, eds., *The Golden Signpost: A Guide to Happiness and Prosperity* (Madison: Max Kade Institute for German-American Studies, University of Wisconsin-Madison, 1993), p. 70.

7. Susan Stern, *Those Strange German Ways* (Bonn: Atlantik-Bruecke, 1995), p. 104.

8. See LaVern J. Rippley, *Of German Ways* (Minneapolis: Dilon, 1970).

9. Faust, *The German Element in the U.S.*, vol. 2, p. 429.

10. For reference to the various religious denominations, see Tolzmann, *German-Americana*, pp. 187–239, and Tolzmann, *Catalog of the German-Americana Collection*, vol. 2, pp. 284–328.

11. Faust, *The German Element in the U.S.*, vol. 2, p. 223.

12. With regard to educational influences, see Tolzmann, *German-Americana*, pp. 240–50, and Tolzmann, *Catalog of the German-Americana Collection*, vol. 2, pp. 184–229. Also, see Henry Geitz et al., eds., *German Influences on Education in the United States to 1917* (Washington, D.C.: German Historical Institute, 1995).

13. Thompson and Brancaforte, *The Golden Signpost*, p. 246.

14. For further sources pertaining to the area of art, see Tolzmann, *German-Americana*, pp. 252–59, and Tolzmann, *Catalog of the German-Americana Collection*, vol. 2, pp. 229–42.

15. With regard to the Bauhaus, see Peter Hahn and Lloyd C. Engelbrecht, eds., *50 Jahre New Bauhaus: Bauhausnachfolge in Chicago* (Berlin: Bauhaus-Archiv, 1987).

16. Regarding Thomas Nast, see Morton Keller, *The Art and Politics of Thomas Nast* (New York: Oxford University Press, 1968).

17. See Carl Schurz, *Speeches, Correspondence and Political Papers of Carl Schurz*, selected and ed. Frederic Bancroft (New York: G. P. Putnam's Sons, 1913).

18. For a survey of political history, see Joseph S. Roucek, "The Germans," in Joseph S. Roucek and Bernhard Eisenberg, eds., *America's Ethnic Politics* (Westport, Conn.: Greenwood Press, 1982), pp. 161–69.

19. See Don Heinrich Tolzmann, ed., *The German-American Soldier in the Wars of the U.S.* (Bowie, Md.: Heritage Books, 1996).

20. For references dealing with the German-American press, see Tolzmann, *German-Americana*, pp. 159–86, and Tolzmann, *Catalog of the German-Americana Collection*, vol. 2, pp. 156–84.

21. For a recent directory of German-American organizations, see J. Richly, *Adressbuch deutsch-amerikanischer Vereine und Gesellschaften* (Chicago: J. Richly, 1989).

22. For an introductory history of the American press, see John W. Tebbel, *The Compact History of the American Newspaper* (New York: Hawthorn Books, 1963).

23. See Robert E. Ward, *A Bio-Bibliography of German-American Writers, 1670–1970* (White Plains, N.Y.: Kraus, 1985).

24. See Henry A. Pochmann, *German Culture in America: Philosophical and Literary Influences, 1600–1900* (Madison: University of Wisconsin Press, 1957).

25. Thompson and Brancaforte, *The Golden Signpost*, p. 99.

26. Ibid., p. 337.

27. Thomas Sowell, *Migrations and Cultures: A World View* (New York: Basic Books, 1996), pp. 35, 74, 78, 103, 105.

Sources

Works dealing with particular topics and aspects of German-American history can be found in the notes. To locate further sources, references to the major bibliographical guides are provided here.

General Bibliographies

Sources in German-American history are recorded in several bibliographies. Works published through 1940 can be found listed in Henry A. Pochmann, *Bibliography of German Culture in America to 1940* (Madison: University of Wisconsin Press, 1953). The post-1940 period is covered by two bibliographies. Comprehensive coverage is provided by Arthur R. Schultz, *German-American Relations and German Culture in America: A Subject Bibliography 1941–1980* (White Plains, N.Y.: Kraus International, 1985). A selective bibliography for works published after 1940 is found in Don Heinrich Tolzmann, *German-Americana: A Bibliography* (1975; reprint, Bowie, Md.: Heritage Books, 1995). Works published after the dates covered by the last two bibliographies can be found listed in the annual bibliography published by the Society for German-American Studies, Dolores and Giles Hoyt, eds., "Annual Bibliography of German-Americana: Articles, Books, Selected Media, and Dissertations," *Yearbook of German-American Studies* (Lawrence, Kan.: Society for German-American Studies, 1989).

409

There are also several other useful bibliographies that provide selective coverage of works dealing with German-American history. The colonial period was thoroughly covered by Emil Meynen, *Bibliographie des Deutschtums der kolonialzeitlichen Einwanderung in Nordamerka: Ins besondere der Pennsylvanien-Deutschen und ihrer Nachkommen, 1683–1933* (Leipzig: Harrassowitz, 1937), although it is outdated. Two especially useful selective bibliographies are: Michael Keresztesi and Gary R. Cocozzoli, *German-American History and Life: A Guide to Information Sources* (Detroit: Gale Research, 1980); and Margrit B. Krewson, *Immigrants from the German-Speaking Countries of Europe: A Selective Bibliography* (Washington, D.C.: Library of Congress, 1991).

The German-American press is recorded in a state-by-state listing in Karl J. R. Arndt and May E. Olson, *German-American Newspapers and Periodicals, 1732–1968* (Pullach: Verlag Dokumentation, 1973), and early German-American imprints are listed in Karl J. R. Arndt and Reimer C. Eck, *The First Century of German Language Printing in the United States of America: A Bibliography Based on the Studies of Oswald Seidensticker and Wilbur H. Oda* (Göttingen: Niedersächsische Staats- und Universitätsbibliothek, 1989).

A useful guide to works dealing with the ancestral homelands of German-Americans can be found in Margrit B. Krewson, *The German-Speaking Countries of Europe: A Selective Bibliography* (Washington, D.C.: Library of Congress, 1989), which provides references for the German-speaking countries in the following categories: bibliographies and reference works, description and travel, economy, education, history, intellectual and cultural life, literature, military policy, politics and government, religion, society.

Primary Sources

There are several published catalogs to some of the major German-Americana collections, which provide further access to source materials dealing with German-American history. Access to the holdings of the Max Kade German-American Document and Research Center at the University of Kansas-Lawrence is provided by Erich P. Albrecht and J.

Anthony Burzle, *Max Kade German-American Document & Research Center Catalogue, October 1976* (Lawrence: University of Kansas, 1976); and J. Anthony Burzle and Helmut E. Huelsbergen, *Max Kade German-American Document & Research Center Catalogue-Addenda* (Lawrence: University of Kansas, 1982).

The University of Cincinnati's holdings are listed in Don Heinrich Tolzmann, *Catalog of the German-Americana Collection, University of Cincinnati* (Munich: K. G. Saur, 1990), which not only records library holdings, but also indexes the major German-American historical and literary journals. The materials at the University of Illinois are found in Donna-Christine Sell and Dennis Walle, *Guide to the Heinrich A. Rattermann Collection of German-American Manuscripts* (Urbana: University of Illinois Library and the Graduate School of Library Science, 1979).

A selection of Library of Congress holdings are found in Margrit B. Krewson, *German-American Relations: A Selective Bibliography* (Washington, D.C.: Library of Congress, 1995), and those of the Center for Research Libraries can be found in Adriana Pilecky-Dekajlo, *German-American Newspapers and Periodicals Held by the Center for Research Libraries* (Chicago: Center for Research Libraries, 1995). Holdings of the New York Public Library are listed in Don Heinrich Tolzmann, ed., *Americana Germanica: Paul Ben Baginsky's Bibliography of German Works Relating to America, 1493–1800* (Bowie, Md.: Heritage Books, 1995). Materials dealing with the Germans from Russia are recorded in Michael Miller, *Researching the Germans from Russia: Annotated Bibliography of the Germans from Russia Heritage Collection at the North Dakota Institute for Regional Studies, North Dakota State University Library: With a Listing of the Library Materials at the Germans from Russia Heritage Society* (Fargo: North Dakota State University, Institute for Regional Studies, 1987).

Although there are other collections with a national focus, as well as many with a regional or special focus in German-American history, the aforementioned are the major ones with a published catalog of their holdings. The location of these other collections, as well as libraries with German-Americana in their collections, can be found in Anne Hope and Joerg Nagler, *Guide to German Historical Sources in North American Libraries and Archives* (Washington, D.C.: German Historical Institute, 1991).

Those unable to access these collections should consult a microfilm collection of primary sources of German-Americana: *The Immigrant in America Microfilm Collection: Unit 5, The Germans* (Woodbridge, Conn.: Research Publications, 1984), Reels 148–80. This contains many of the basic nineteenth- and early twentieth-century German-language histories.

Secondary Sources

There are a number of general histories available, and these can be found listed in the bibliographies cited above. However, several more should be mentioned here. An older work, still considered a basic source, is Albert B. Faust, *The German Element in the U.S.* (New York: Steuben Society of America, 1927). Another older work, recently reprinted, is Don Heinrich Tolzmann, ed., *German Achievements in America: Rudolf Cronau's Survey History* (Bowie, Md.: Heritage Books, 1995). A recent survey is LaVern J. Rippley, *The German-Americans* (Boston: Twayne, 1976). A more recent but brief introduction can be found in Willi Paul Adams, *The German-Americans: An Ethnic Experience*, trans. and adapted by LaVern J. Rippley and Eberhard Reichmann (Indianapolis: Max Kade German-American Center, Indiana University-Purdue University, 1993).

A concise essay on German-American history by Kathleen Neils Conzen is found in the *Harvard Encyclopedia of American Ethnic Groups* (Cambridge: Harvard University Press, 1980). A popular history is Richard O'Connor, *The German-Americans* (Boston: Little, Brown, 1968). Another recent work of general interest is Dorothy and Thomas Hoobler, *The German-American Family Album* (New York: Oxford University Press, 1996). Other useful general works are: Frederick C. Luebke, *Germans in the New World: Essays in the History of Immigration* (Urbana: University of Illinois Press, 1990); Günter Moltmann, ed., *Germans to America: 300 Years of Immigration, 1683–1983* (Stuttgart: Institute for Foreign Cultural Relations, 1983); Christine M. Totten, *Roots in the Rhineland: America's German Heritage in Three Hundred Years of Immigration, 1683–1983* (New York: German Information Center, 1988);

Frank Trommler and Joseph McVeigh, eds., *America and the Germans: An Assessment of a Three Hundred Year History* (Philadelphia: University of Pennsylvania Press, 1985).

Two useful biographical works are Gerard Wilk, *Americans from Germany*, ed. Don Heinrich Tolzmann (Indianapolis: Max Kade German-American Center, Indiana University-Purdue University, 1995), and Charles R. Haller, *Distinguished German-Americans* (Bowie, Md.: Heritage Books, 1995). Other general works, as well as works dealing with more specific topics, can be found in the aforementioned bibliographies.

Finally, reference should be made to the quarterly *Newsletter* and the *Yearbook of German-American Studies*, published by the Society for German-American Studies for the latest news, information, and references dealing with the field of German-American Studies. The former contains news and information about the various organizations, institutes, and research centers affiliated with the society.

Fields of Distinction

In a recent biographical study by Charles R. Haller entitled *Distinguished German-Americans* (1995), he identified 2,300 German-Americans who distinguished themselves for their contributions to American society. The study lists the following areas in which German-Americans are noted for having made their major contributions:

- ✦ Art and Artists
- ✦ Baseball, Brewers and Other Sporting Personalities
- ✦ Pioneering Clergymen and -women
- ✦ Educators and Intellectuals
- ✦ Engineers and More Engineers
- ✦ The Entertainment World
- ✦ The World of High Finance and Big Business
- ✦ German-American Officials in Government
- ✦ Medical Sciences in America
- ✦ The World of Pop to Classical Music
- ✦ The Printing and Publishing World
- ✦ The Natural Sciences
- ✦ Men and Women at War

Prominent
German-Americans

Further information on many of these can be found in *The Dictionary of American Biography*, a standard biographical reference source, as well as the bibliographies listed at the end of this volume.

Josef Albers, 1888–1976, painter
John Peter Altgeld, 1847–1902, governor of Illinois and prison reformer
Mathilde Anneke, 1817–1884, Forty-Eighter and author
Karl J. R. Arndt, 1903–1991, scholar, author, educator
John Jacob Astor, 1763–1848, financier and fur trader
Leon "Bix" Beiderbecke, 1903–1931, jazz musician
Judah P. Benjamin, 1811–1884, secretary of state for the Confederacy during the Civil War
Emil Berliner, 1851–1892, inventor of the phonograph using disc records
Maximilian Berlitz, 1852–1921, founder of language schools
Albert Bierstadt, 1830–1902, artist and painter
Walter P. Chrysler, 1875–1940, automobile manufacturer
George Armstrong Custer, 1839–1876, Civil War and frontier general
Adolf Dehn, 1895–1968, artist and painter
Johann de Kalb, 1721–1780, Revolutionary War general
Marlene Dietrich, 1901–1992, actress
Everett M. Dirksen, 1896–1969, U.S. senator from Illinois
Theodore Dreiser, 1871–1945, novelist

Albert Einstein, 1879–1955, physicist

Dwight D. Eisenhower, 1890–1969, 34th U.S. president

Albert B. Faust, 1870–1951, historian

Lyonel Feininger, 1871–1956, artist

Lion Feuchtwanger, 1884–1958, author

Heinrich H. Fick, 1849–1935, educator and author

Carl Follen, 1795–1840, first professor of German in the United States (Harvard), pioneer of German gymnastics, and abolitionist

Henry C. Frick, 1849–1919, industrialist

Henry L. Gehrig, 1903–1941, baseball player

Oscar Maria Graf, 1894–1967, author

Walter Gropius, 1883–1969, architect and founder of the Bauhaus

George Grosz, 1893–1959, painter of socially critical themes

Franz Josef Grund, 1798–1863, author, journalist, and politician

Oscar Hammerstein, 1847–1919, producer of grand opera, vaudeville and musical comedies

Oscar Hammerstein II, 1895–1960, lyricist

Friedrich Hecker, 1844–1881, Forty-Eighter, community leader, Civil War officer

Johann G. E. Heckewelder, 1743–1823, Moravian missionary and frontier pioneer

Henry J. Heinz, 1844–1919, food packer

Karl P. Heinzen, 1809–1880, Forty-Eighter, editor, publisher, and abolitionist

Johann Martin Henni, 1805–1881, founded first German Catholic newspaper in the United States and became bishop/archbishop of Milwaukee

Nicholas Herkimer, 1728–1777, Revolutionary War general

Milton S. Hershey, 1857–1945, founder of Hershey chocolate

Michael Hillegas, 1729–1804, first U.S. treasurer

Herbert C. Hoover, 1874–1964, 31st U.S. president

Theodore Huebener, 1895–, scholar, author, educator

Abraham Jacobi, 1830–1919, founder of American pediatrics

Otto Kahn, 1867–1934, banker

Micahel Kalteisen, 1729–1807, war hero and founder of the Charleston German Society

Johann Kelpius, 1673–1708, mystic and leader of sectarians

Henry Kissinger, 1923–, statesman

Edward Kleinschmidt, 1875–1977, inventor

Otto Klemperer, 1885–1973, conductor

Gustav Koerner, 1809–1896, lieutenant governor of Illinois

Konrad Krez, 1828–1897, Forty-Eighter, Civil War officer, and poet; author of well-known poem *Da waren Deutsche auch dabei*, which became known as the German-American national anthem

Fritz Lang, 1890–1976, film director

Lotte Lehmann, 1885–1976, star of the opera and concert stage

Jacob Leisler, 1640–1691, political leader of New York

Emanuel Leutze, 1816–1868, influential painter of American historic themes

Francis Lieber, 1800–1872, educator, editor, author

Ernst Lubitsch, 1892–1947, filmmaker

Christopher Ludwig, 1720–1801, Superintendant of Baking during the Revolution

Maria Ludwig, 1754–1832, Revolutionary War heroine known as Molly Pitcher

Thomas Mann, 1875–1955, literary author

H. L. Mencken, 1880–1956, editor, author, critic

Christian Metz, 1794–1867, founder of the Amana Colonies

Hans Otfried von Meusebach, 1812–1894, founder of Fredericksburg, Texas

Peter Minnewit (Minuit), 1580–1638, first director-general of the Dutch colony of New Amsterdam, as well as founder of New Sweden

Henry Muehlenberg, 1711–1787, father of the Lutheran Church in America

Friedrich Muench, 1799–1881, pastor and senator from Missouri

Hugo Muensterberg, 1863–1916, scholar and author

Thomas Nast, 1840–1902, artist and caricaturist

Wilhelm Nast, 1807–1899, founder of the German-American Methodist Church

Reinhold Niebuhr, 1892–1970, theologian

Gert Niers, 1943, German-American author and editor of German-American newspapers

Konrad Nies, 1861–1921, author known as the German-American Literary Knight

Chester W. Nimitz, 1885–1966, World War II naval commander

Jacob Nix, 1822–1897, Forty-Eighter and Commandant of the defense of New Ulm during the Sioux Uprising

Anna Ottendörfer, 1815–1884, publisher of the *New Yorker Staats-Zeitung*

Erwin Panofsky, 1892–1968, art historian and writer

Franz Daniel Pastorius, 1651–1719, founder of the first permanent German settlement in America

John Pershing, 1860–1948, World War I general

Wilhelm Pfaender, 1823–1905, cofounder of the first Turner Society in the United States, and chief founder of New Ulm, Minnesota

John A. Quitmann, 1798–1858, politician, soldier, and lawyer

Johann Georg Rapp, 1757–1847, founder of the Harmonite religious sect

Heinrich A. Rattermann, 1823–1923, historian

Walter Rauschenbusch, 1861–1918, theologian

Erich Maria Remarque, 1898–1970, author

Walter Reuther, 1907–1970, labor union leader

Edward V. Rickenbacker, 1890–1975, World War I aviator

David Rittenhouse, 1732–1796, inventor of astronomical instruments

John D. Rockefeller, 1839–1937, industrialist

Johann A. Roebling, 1806–1869, engineer and bridge builder

Julius Rosenwald, 1862–1932, merchant and philanthropist

George Herman (Babe) Ruth, 1895–1948, baseball player

Christopher Saur, 1693–1758, colonial printer and publisher

Fritzi Scheff, 1882–1954, grand opera soprano, popular singer

Jacob Schiff, 1847–1920, banker and philanthropist

Michael Schlatter, 1716–1790, German Reformed Church leader

Arnold Schoenberg, 1874–1951, originator of the "twelve-tone" musical method

Charles Schott, 1826–1901, civil engineer

Ferdinand Schuhmacher, 1822–1908, originated process for manufacture of oatmeal

Elisabeth Schumann, 1885–1952, grand opera soprano

Carl Schurz, 1829–1906, Forty-Eighter, Civil War general, statesman, U.S. senator from Missouri, and Secretary of the Interior

Charles Sealsfield, 1793–1864, pen name of well-known novelist Karl
  Postl
Oswald Seidensticker, 1825–1894, scholar and historian
Joseph Seligmann, 1819–1880, financier
Franz Sigel, 1824–1902, Civil War general
August C. Spangenberg, 1704–1792, bishop of the Moravian Church
Claus Spreckels, 1828–1908, industrialist
John Steinbeck, 1902–1970, novelist
Charles P. Steinmetz, 1865–1923, electrical engineer, inventor
Henry Steinway, 1797–1871, piano and organ builder
Alfred Stieglitz, 1864–1946, master of photography
Levi Strauss, 1829–1902, inventor of world-famous blue jeans
Clement Studebaker, 1845–1912, car manufacturer
John A. Sutter, 1803–1880, owner of land where the California gold rush
  began
Theodore Thomas, 1835–1905, musician and conductor
Paul Tillich, 1886–1965, theologian
Ludwig Mies van der Rohe, 1886–1969, architect and director of the
  Bauhaus
George S. Viereck, 1884–1962, author, editor, publicist
Wernher von Braun, 1912–1977, space scientist
August von Willich, 1810–1878, Forty-Eighter, journalist, Civil War
  officer
Baron Friedrich Wilhelm von Steuben, 1730–1794, Revolutionary War
  general
Robert F. Wagner, 1877–1953, pioneer of labor legislation
Lillian D. Wald, 1867–1940, social worker, organized Henry Street Set-
  tlement
Bruno Walter, 1876–1962, conductor
Carl F. W. Walther, 1811–1887, founder of the Lutheran Church-Missouri
  Synod
Robert E., Ward, 1937, scholar, education, and founder of the Society for
  German-American Studies
Kurt Weill, 1900–1950, composer
Wilhelm Weitling, 1808–1871, founder of the New York *Arbeiterbund*
  labor organization

Franz Werfel, 1890–1945, author

George Westinghouse, 1846–1914, manufacturer, inventor of the air brake

Friedrich Weyerhaeuser, 1834–1911, businessman

Wendell Willkie, 1892–1944, politician

Rabbi Isaac M. Wise, 1819–1900, Jewish religious leader

Kurt Wolff, 1887–1964, publisher

David Zeisberger, 1721–1808, Moravian missionary and frontier pionier

Johann Peter Zenger, 1697–1746, printer who established the principle of freedom of the press

Nikolaus von Zinzendorf, 1700–1760, bishop and missionary

A Chronology of German-American History

1608	Around October 1, the first permanent German settlers arrive at Jamestown, Virginia, on the *Mary and Margaret*.
1626	Peter Minuit becomes director of the Dutch colony New Amsterdam (New York) and purchases Manhattan Island.
1633	First publication encouraging immigration to America appears in Germany.
1638	Minuit establishes New Sweden, which like the Dutch colony is settled by many Germans.
1676	Nikolaus de Myer becomes mayor of New York.
1683	On October 6, a group of German Mennonites under the direction of Franz Daniel Pastorius arrive in Philadelphia, where they establish the first permanent German settlement in America—Germantown.
1688	Germantowners led by Pastorius issue the first protest in America against slavery.
1689	Germantown is incorporated with Pastorius as the first burgomaster.
1690	The first paper mill in America is established at Germantown by William Rittinghausen (later Rittenhouse).
1691	The first elected governor of New York, Jacob Leisler, is falsely accused of treason and executed by the British.
1694	Johann Kelpius leads a group of mystics to establish a brotherhood near Philadelphia.

1701	The first fair is held at Germantown.
1702	The first German-American school is established at Germantown.
1708	Josua Kochterthal leads the first group of Palatines, which becomes the first major wave of German immigration.
1710	Germans and Swiss-Germans settle in North Carolina.
1714	German miners under Christopher von Graffenried come to Virginia.
1719	The first German Baptist Dunkards arrive at Germantown.
1720	Augsburg and Marienthal are established in Louisiana.
1727	Germans number approximately 20,000 in Pennsylvania.
1730	Benjamin Franklin prints the first collection of Pennsylvania-German songs for Conrad Beissel, a Palatine Seventh-Day Dunkard.
1732	The first German-language newspaper in America, the *Philadelphische Zeitung*. Beissel founds the Ephrata Cloister near Lancaster.
1733	The Schwenkfelders from Silesia settle in Pennsylvania.
1734	The Salzburger Protestants arrive in Georgia.
1735	Under the leadership of August G. Spangenberg, the Moravians found their first settlement. John Peter Zenger, publisher of the *New York Weekly Journal*, wins the first battle for the freedom of the press.
1738	Printer Christopher Saur opens his shop in Germantown.
1739	Caspar Wistar builds a glassmaking plant at Salem, New Jersey. Saur publishes the *Germantauner Zeitung*. Beissel issues the first hymnal in America.
1741	President Eisenhower's ancestor, Hans Nicholas Eisenhauer, arrives from the Palatinate.
1742	Bethlehem, Pennsylvania, is established as a Moravian town by Count von Zinzendorf.
1743	Saur prints the first Bible in America in a European language (German).
1744	The Collegium Musicum orchestra of the Moravians is founded in Bethlehem.
1746	The Moravians establish their first school for girls.

1747	The first German Reformed Church is established by the Rev. Michael Schlatter.
1748	The Rev. Henry Melchior Muehlenberg takes the lead in promoting the formation of a Lutheran Synod. The largest German book of the colonial period is published, a German edition of *The Martyr's Mirror* (1,514 pages).
1750	The first pedagogical work in America is published by Christopher Dock, his *Schulordnung*.
1759	The first music store in America is opened in Philadelphia by Michael Hillegas.
1762	Henry Miller begins publishing the newspaper the *Staatsbote*.
1764	The German Society of Pennsylvania, the oldest German-American society in the United States, is formed to assist German immigrants and German-Americans.
1767	David Rittenhouse constructs the first planetarium in America.
1771	Saur establishes the first foundry for making type.
1776	The first announcement of the Declaration of Independence appears in the *Staatsbote*. German-American regiments and military units are raised. The first Christmas trees in America are erected by Hessian troops.
1778	Baron von Steuben trains the Continental Army. The Independent Troop of the Horse is established as a German-American bodyguard unit for Washington.
1779	Von Steuben completes his *Blue Book* of regulations for the army.
1783	One of the first people to become an American tycoon arrives in America—John Jacob Astor from Baden. He establishes the American Fur Company in 1808, and by the 1830s he is the richest man in the United States. The first German brass band is founded in America. Some 5,000 Hessians remain in America after the Revolution. The German Society of Maryland is formed.
1784	The German Society of New York is established.
1785	The Treaty of Amity and Commerce between the United States and Prussia is signed.

1789	Frederick A. Muehlenberg becomes the first Speaker of the House of Representatives and signs the Bill of Rights.
1792	Rittenhouse is appointed director of the U.S. Mint.
1794	Virginia Germans petition Congress to print and publish documents in German.
1798	Johann Graupner arrives in Boston and becomes the father of orchestral music in America.
1800	German-Americans vote overwhelmingly for Thomas Jefferson and help elect him to the presidency.
1804	Georg Rapp establishes the settlement of Harmony, Pennsylvania.
1812	German-American units fight in the War of 1812.
1815	The Handel and Haydn Society is founded by Boston's Germans.
1817	The Wartburg Fest is held in Germany at Wartburg to protest Prince Metternich and the reactionary princes in the German states, which leads to continued suppression and immigration. German separatists establish Zoar in Ohio.
1819	A steamer crosses the ocean in twenty-six days, opening a new era in transportation.
1820	Joseph Heister serves as governor of Georgia.
1823	First all-German singing society is formed in Cincinnati.
1825	Charles Follen becomes the first professor of German in America at Harvard. German gymnastics are introduced by Karl Beck.
1826	Francis Lieber directs the Turner Guymnasium in Boston and begins editing the *Encyclopedia Americana*, based on the Brockhaus *Conversations-Lexikon*.
1829	Gottfried Duden publishes his highly influential book about the United States, which encourages many to immigrate.
1832	The Hambacher Fest, like the 1817 Wartburg Fest, is held to protest sociopolitical conditions and the lack of unity in the German states; leads to immigration of the Thirtyers, including J. G. Wesselhoeft, Gustav Koerner, and Friedrich Muench.
1830s	German-Americans introduce the custom of gaily decorated Christmas trees.

1834   There are more than five hundred German-language schools in America, the largest non-English-language system in the United States.

1835   The Giessen Society is formed, which aims to establish a New Germany in America. The first German-American singing society is established in Philadelphia. Wilhelm Wesselhoeft introduces homeopathy to the United States.

1836   Hermann, Missouri, is founded and becomes noted for its fine wines.

1837   The Pittsburgh Convention takes place, the first national conference of German-Americans. The Pennsylvania legislature begins publishing its laws and the governor's message in German.

1838   First major immigration of German Lutherans to Missouri.

1839   Theodore Bernhard organizes and introduces the first system of free textbooks in America at Watertown, Wisconsin.

1840   The first German bilingual programs in public schools are established in Cincinnati, Ohio. German Lutherans found Concordia College in Fort Wayne, Indiana.

1841   Under the pen name of Charles Sealsfield, Karl Anton Postl publishes his famous book, *Das Kajütenbuch*.

1844   The first German settlers are brought to Texas under the direction of Prince Carl von Solms-Braunfels, with the support of the Mainzer Adelsverein.

1846   Maximilian Schaefer establishes the first great lager beer brewery in America.

1846/47   German-American units fight in the Mexican War.

1847   C. F. W. Walther organizes the Lutheran Church-Missouri Synod.

1848   After the revolution of 1848, thousands emigrate to America. The Forty-Eighter Friedrich Hecker is greeted by twenty thousand German-Americans in New York. Founding of the first Turner Society in America at Cincinnati, Ohio.

1849   The first national German-American association is formed in Cincinnati, Der Nord-Amerikanische Sängerbund. In New York, Eberhard Faber establishes the pencil business that still carries his name.

1850   Wilhelm Weitling organizes the labor movement in New York. Strauss produces the first jeans.

1851   Konrad Krez, a Forty-Eighter, arrives in America; becomes famous as the author of the poem *Da waren Deutsche auch dabei*. The famous painting *Washington Crossing the Delaware* is painted by Emanuel Leutze.

1852   Carl Schurz arrives in America. The Studebaker company begins production of wagons.

1853   Gustav Koener, a Thirtyer, is elected lieutenant governor of Illinois. Heinrich Steinweg arrives in America and founds Steinway & Sons in New York.

1855   Castle Gardens opens as a processing center for immigrants in New York.

1856   Mrs. Carl Schurz establishes the first kindergarten in the United States in Watertown, Wisconsin.

1859   Abraham Lincoln secretly acquires the *Illinois Staatsanzeiger*, which endorses him in the 1860 election.

1860   German-Americans strongly support Abraham Lincoln for the presidency. Schurz and other German-Americans, especially Gustav Koerner, campaign for Lincoln; Schurz goes on a 21,000-mile speaking tour through the entire Midwest.

1861   Carl Schurz as U.S. ambassador to Spain seeks support for the Union. German-Americans fight on both sides in the Civil War. One-fourth of the Union army consists of German-Americans.

1862   The Turner town of New Ulm is attacked on the frontier, and the defense is organized by Jacob Nix.

1870s   Milwaukee becomes a German-American brewing center.

1871   The unification of Germany as a federation of twenty-five member states. The king of Prussia, Wilhelm I, becomes the kaiser of Germany, with Bismarck as chancellor. Thomas Nast, the first great American caricaturist, is instrumental in the destruction of the Boss Tweed political machine in New York.

1873   The New York Oratorio Society is founded by Leopold Damrosch.

1874   Alfalfa is introduced by Wendelin Grimm.

1876   The suspension bridge at Cincinnati is completed by Johann A. Roebling.

1877   Schurz becomes the Secretary of the Interior in the Hayes administration, the first German-born member of the cabinet, and advances civil service reform and the revision of the prevailing Indian policy.

1878   The National German-American Teachers Seminary is founded in Milwaukee. Damrosch founds the New York Symphony Society. Bismarck's antisocialist legislation causes immigration of socialists to America.

1883   The celebration of the German-American Bicentennial is organized in Philadelphia by Oswald Seidensticker, by H. A. Rattermann in Cincinnati, and these become the basis for the annual German Day celebrations that are established across the country by the 1890s. The Brooklyn Bridge is completed by Washington Roebling. Germans from Russia come to America.

1886   Ottmar Mergenthaler invents the lintotype machine, which revolutionizes the printing industry. The Haymarket Riot leads to suppression of German-American socialists.

1887   Emil Berliner invents the first sound recording on disc.

1892   Ellis Island is opened and remains an immigration center until it closed in 1954 after it has processed 20 million immigrants.

1892–93 German-Americans are elected governors of Illinois and Kentucky.

1898   Admiral Winfield Schley destroys the Spanish fleet at Santiago, Cuba, during the Spanish-American War.

1901   The National German-American Alliance is formed as the umbrella organization for German-American societies and is led by Dr. Charles Hexamer, the son of a Forty-Eighter.

1903   The first production of Wagner's *Parsifal* outside of Bayreuth is held in New York.

1906   The death of Carl Schurz, statesman, author, and Forty-Eighter.

1907	Gustav Mahler conducts the Metropolitan Opera on the invitation of Heinrich Conried, manager of the Met.
1909	St. Louis Germans introduce the "hamburger" to America.
1914	Mass meetings of the German-American Alliance propose that the United States not become involved in the war in Europe.
1916	The 75th anniversary of the establishment of the first German bilingual public-school program in America.
1917	The United States declares war against Germany, which results in a tragic anti-German hysteria across the country.
1918	The first well-known case of a German-American lynching (Robert Prager) takes place on April 5, 1918, in Collinsville. One-third of U.S. troops are German-American and are commanded by General Pershing. The German-American Alliance is forced to disband as a result of the anti-German hysteria. The Armistice is signed. Prohibition is enacted as part of the hysteria, as most brewers are German-American and support the German-American press and societies.
1919	The Treaty of Versailles is signed but is rejected overwhelmingly in the German-American press. The Steuben Society is formed to represent German-American interests.
1923	Charles P. Steinmetz becomes one of the greatest electrical wizards in the employ of General Electric Corporation. The death of Heinrich A. Rattermann (1832–1923) of Cincinnati, known as the "Father of German-American History" because of his numerous historical publications.
1928	Herbert Hoover becomes the first president of German descent.
1929	Some of the great baseball stars are German-Americans, including Babe Ruth, Lou Gehrig, Honus Wagner, and Frank Fritsch.
1930	There were 300,000 Russian-born German-Americans, an indication of the substantial immigration from Russia; band leader Lawrence Welk becomes the most prominent member of this group.
1933	The beginnings of a new immigration as result of the Third Reich. The Steuben Society together with German-American societies and the German-American press oppose Nazism.

1934	The Carl Schurz Association publishes *The American-German Review* and assists recently arrived immigrants.
1935	Sen. Robert Wagner introduces the Labor Relations Act, which is signed into law by Roosevelt.
1936	The Bauhaus is reestablished in Chicago as the New Bauhaus.
1941	Hitler declares war against the United States, which again results in anti-German sentiment resulting in the internment of more than ten thousand German-Americans. One-third of U.S. troops are German-American, and commanders of German descent include Eisenhower, Spaatz, Nimitz, and Krueger.
1945	The end of the war brings numerous rocket scientists to the United States. Also, large numbers of Germans are driven from their homes in eastern and southeastern Europe and come to America. German-Americans strongly support the CARE program to bring assistance to Germany.
1948–49	The Western, largely American, airlift breaks the Soviet blockade of West Berlin.
1950	Wernher von Braun becomes head of the U.S. Army Ordinance Guided Missile Center and paves the way for the U.S. space program.
1952	Eisenhower is elected president.
1953	The Nobel Prizes for medicine and physiology go to Hans A. Krebs and Fritz Lippmann. On June 17, Soviet troops suppress a popular uprising in East Berlin and other cities in East Germany.
1955	The Federal Republic of Germany joins NATO.
1957	The founding of the European Economic Community in the Treaty of Rome.
1958	The German-American National Congress is formed.
1960	By this date German-Americans have contributed a total of $350 million in CARE packages to Germany.
1961	The infamous Berlin Wall is built.
1963	President John F. Kennedy visits the Berlin Wall and declares solidarity with the German people.
1968	Formation of the Society for German-American Studies.

1969   America lands the first man on the moon through the work of German-American space scientists under the leadership of Wernher von Braun.

1973   Henry Kissinger becomes secretary of state and wins the Nobel Peace Prize. The two German states join the United Nations.

1974   Formation of the Association for German-language Authors in America, which published a poetry series and a literary journal and contributed to an upswing in German-American literature.

1976   The celebration of the American Bicentennial heralds the beginning of the ethnic revival. German-American represen-tatives attend the White House Conference on Ethnicity.

1977   The United German-American Committee of the USA is formed.

1980   The U.S. Census reports that German-Americans are the nation's largest ethnic element.

1982   Helmut Kohl is elected chancellor of the Federal Republic of Germany.

1983   The German-American Tricentennial is celebrated across the country.

1987   German-American Day is reestablished by congressional and presidential resolutions and proclamations on October 6. President Reagan visits Berlin and challenges: "Mr. Gor-bachev, tear down this wall."

1988   The German-American Joint Action Committee (GAJAC) is formed to coordinate cooperation between the major Ger-man-American national organizations, as well as to coordi-nate national planning for the annual German-American Day.

1990   The U.S. Census again reports that German-Americans con-stitute the largest single ethnic element in America. Germany is reunited on October 3, which is celebrated in conjunction with German-American Day.

1992   The 35th annual Steuben parade takes place in New York City, the largest and oldest German-American parade in the United States.

1995 The first national celebration of German-American Heritage Month from mid-September through mid-October is organized by the German-American Joint Action Committee.

1997 The tenth anniversary of the establishment of German-American Day.

1998 The 150th anniversary of the 1848 revolution and the founding of the first Turner Society in America at Cincinnati, Ohio.

1999 The 150th anniversary of the founding of the North American Sängerbund, a national association of German-American singing societies, at Cincinnati, Ohio.

2006 The 100th anniversary of the death of the major German-American politician of the nineteenth century, Carl Schurz.

2007 The 20th anniversary of the establishment of German-American Day.

2008 The 400th anniversary of the arrival of the first permanent German settlers at Jamestown, Virginia.

German Place Names in the United States

Alabama: Altoona, Bremen, De Kalb, Geiger, Geneva, Kellerman, Linden, Newbern, Salem, Vredenburgh

Alaska: Newbern

Arizona: Ehrenberg, Hayden, Humboldt, Kohl's Ranch

Arkansas: Altheimer, Bergman, Bingen, Bismarck, Busch, Elmendorf, Engelberg, Hamburg, Hanover, Salem, Stuttgart, Ulm, Waldenburg

California: Anaheim, Bockweiler, Carlsbad, Donner Pass, Gerber, Hamburg, Humboldt, Kern, Linden, Lucerne, Spreckels, Sutter, Wagner, Weimar

Colorado: Custer, Lucerne, Strasburg, Walsenburg, Wattenberg

Connecticut: Berlin, East Berlin, Hamburg, Hanover, Salem

Delaware: Frankford, Nassau, Winterthur

Florida: Altoona, Astor, Geneva, Gotha, Salem

Georgia: Augusta, Berlin, Bremen, Brunswick, Geneva, Rhine, Vienna

Idaho: Bern, Geneva

Illinois: Albers, Altona, Astoria, Augsburg, Berlin, Bismarck, Colmar, Custer Park, De Kalb, Edelstein, Emden, Frankfort, Frankfort Heights, Frankfort Park, Gallatin, Geneva, Germantown, German Valley, Hamburg (two locations), Hanover, Hanover Park, Hecker, Humboldt, Lindenwood, Millstadt, Munster, New Baden, New Berlin, New Minden, New Salem, Opheim, Palatine, Posen, Salem, Schaumburg, Sigel, Strasburg, Sutter, Teutopolis, West Baden, West Frankfort, West Salem, West Vienna, Vienna

Indiana: Altona, Berne, Bremen, Brunswick, Darmstadt, De Kalb, Elberfeld, Frankfort, Fulda, Geneva, Hanover, Haubstadt, Helmer, Leipsic, Linden, Lucerne, Monrovia, New Salem, North Salem, Oldenburg, Pershing, Raub, Salem, Schneider, Stroh, Switzerland, West Baden Springs, Westphalia

Iowa: Allendorf, Altoona, Bettendorf, Bode, Celwein, Geneva, Graf, Guttenberg, Hamburg, Holstein, Humboldt, Linden, Luther, Luxemburg, Minden, New Vienna, Reinbeck, Salem, Schleswig, Westphalia

Kansas: Alma, Altoona, Bavaria, Bern, Bremen, Dresden, Elbing, Frankfort, Goessel, Hanover, Hollenberg, Humboldt, Liebenthal, Marienthal, Oberlin, Olpe, Olsburg, Pfeifer, Richter, Stark, Strauss, Stuttgart, Welda, Westphalia, Zurich

Kentucky: Bernstadt, Brandenburg, Bremen, Büchel, Custer, Frankfort, Gallatin, Germantown, Heidelberg, Luther, Muhlenberg, Salem, Steubenville, Switzer

Louisiana: Des Allemandes, Bastrop, Geismar, Hamburg, Jena, Minden, Oberlin, Vienna, Waldheim, Zimmermann

Maine: Alfred, Brunswick, Dresden, Frankfort, Fryeburg, Hanover, Lubec, North Lubec, Vienna, West Lubec

Maryland: Berlin, Brunswick, Germantown, Hanover, Silesia, Vienna, Waldorf

Massachusetts: Astor, Berlin, Hanover, Hanover Center, Lunenburg, North Hanover, Salem, Saxonville, South Berlin, South Hanover, West Berlin, West Hanover

Michigan: Arnheim, Bach, Bauer, Bergland, Brunswick, Custer, Eckermann, Frankenmuth, Frankfort, Hamburg, Hanover, Herman, Hermannsville, Hessel, Humboldt, Linden, Luther, Minden City, Steuben, Vienna, Vriesland, Waldenburg, Westphalia

Minnesota: Augsburg, Berlin, Bismarck, Bock, Cologne, Danube, Dassel, Eitzen, Essig, Flensburg, Franconia, Frankfort, Friburg, Friedland, Fulda, Geneva, Germania, Germantown, Gotha, Hagen, Hamburg, Hanover, Heidelberg, Herman, Hoffmann, Humboldt, Karlstadt, Krain, Lastrup, Moltke, Nassau, Nessel, New Germany, New Munich, New Ulm, North Germany, Posen, Potsdam, Prosit, Rheiderland, Schroeder, Stark, Waldorf, Weimar, Willmar, Wirt, Zimmermann

Mississippi: Ackerman, De Kalb, Germania, Gluckstadt, Hamburg, Heidelberg, Hermanville, Oldenburg

Missouri: Altenburg, Altona, Baden, Berger, Bismarck, Brunswick, Deicke, Detmold, Diehlstadt, Dresden, Duenweg, Emden, Frankford, Freistatt, Friedensburg, Friedheim, Gallatin, Hamburg, Heidelberg, Hermann, Holstein, Kiel, Koenig, Kohler City, Krakau, Lippstadt, Lucerne, Mehlville, Millheim, Mindenmines, New Hamburg, New Offenburg, Oldenburg, Pershing, Pyrmont, Rhineland, Schubert, Stolpe, Strasburg, Swiss, Vienna, Weber Hill, Weingarten, Westphalia, Wittenberg, Zell

Montana: Custer, Fromberg, Gallatin, Hanover, Klein, Opheim, Silesia, Ulm, Wagner, Zurich

Nebraska: Brunswick, Custer, Geneva, Gering, Herman, Holstein, Humboldt, Minden, Salem

Nevada: Gerlach, Humboldt, Minden, Schurz

New Hampshire: Berlin, Franconia, Hanover, North Salem, Salem

New Jersey: Berlin, Cologne, East Brunswick, East Hanover, Hamburg, Linden, Lindenwald, New Brunswick, North Brunswick, Roeblin, South Brunswick, Vienna, West Berlin

New Mexico: Carlsbad, Hanover, Salem

New York: Frewsburg, German Flatts, Germantown, Hamburg, Herkimer, Lake Luzerne, Moravia, New Berlin, Newburgh, New Paltz, Rhinebeck

North Carolina: Brunswick, Charlotte, Germantown, Linden, Little Switzerland, Mecklenburg, New Bern, New Hanover, Swiss, Wallburg, West New Bern

North Dakota: Berlin, Bismarck, Bremen, Dahlen, Dresden, Fryburg, Hamberg, Hannover, Heil, Karlsruhe, Munich, New Leipzig, Osnabruck, Strasburg

Ohio: Arnheim, Bachman, Batavia, Bergholz, Berlin, Berlin Center, Berlin Heights, Berlinville, Berne, Bonn, Bremen, Brunswick, Deucher, Dresden, Erhart, Frankfort, Fulda, Funk, Geneva, Geneva on the Lake, Germano, Germantown (two locations), Glandorf, Gnadenhutten, Gutman, Hageman, Hamburg (two locations), Hammansburg, Hanover, Hanoverton, Hartville, Helmick, Humboldt, Kunkle, Landeck, Leipsic, Lindentree, Lindenwald, Lorain, Lower Salem, Maria Stein, Millersburg, Minster, New Bavaria, New Bremen, New Germany, New Hagerstown, New Riegel, New Strasburg, New Vienna, North

Berne, Oberlin, Phillipsburg, Potsdam, Reinersville, Rickenbacker, Rossburg, Salem, Sandusky, Schoennbrunn, Schumm, Speidel, Steuben, Steubenville, Strasburg, Vienna, Wahlsburg, West Leipsic, West Salem, Winesburg, Yost, Zahns, Zanesfield, Zanesville, Zoar

Oklahoma: Berlin, Custer, Hoffmann, Krebs, Luther, Springer, Unger, Verden

Oregon: Astoria, Birkenfeld, Coburg, Donn und Blitzen River, Heppner, Newberg, Salem

Pennsylvania: Ackermanville, Altoona, Armbrust, Baden, Baum, Berlin, Berlinvile, Berne, Bohemia, Brandt, Brandywine, Breslau, Colmar, Custger City, East Berlin, East Germantown, East Hanover, Ehrenfeld, Francford Springs, Franconia, Frankford, Friedens, Friedensburg, Fritztown, Geneva, Germania, Germania Station, Germansville, Germantown, Hamburg, Hanover, Hanoverdale, Hanover Junction, Heidelberg, Helfenstein, Herman, Humboldt, Kellertown, King of Prussia, Knapp, Koppel, Landenberg, Leisenring, Linden, Lititz, Manheim, Millheim, Mittenberg, New Berlin, New Berlinville, New Geneva, New Germantown, New Hamburg, New Hanover, Nuremberg, Osterburg, Saxonburg, Schoenback, Sigel, Strasburg, Upper Berne, Upper Strasburg, Waltersburg, Wurtemburg

South Carolina: Augusta, Bamberg (two locations), Ehrhardt, Salem, Walhalla

South Dakota: Brandt, Custer, Frankfort, Humboldt, Kranzburg, Salem, Vienna, Wagner, Witten, Zell

Tennessee: Brunswick, De Kalb, Dresden, Gallatin, Germantown, Hohenwald, Humboldt, Linden, Mosheim, Newbern, Wartburg

Texas: Alice, Bastrop, Bergheim, Castell, De Kalb, Elmendorf, Fischer, Fredericksburg, Geneva, Heidenheimer, Hochheim, Kaufmann, Keller, Kleberg, Klein, Knickerbocker, Linden, Lohn, Lueders, Minden, Muenster, New Baden, New Braunfels, New Ulm, Nimitz, Nordheim, Olden, Schertz, Schleicher, Schroeder, Schulenburg, Uhland, Waelder, Walburg, Weimar, Wetheimer

Utah: Altonah, Salem

Vermont: Berlin, Lunenburg

Virginia: Augusta, Brunswick, Caroline, Charlotte (two locations), Cologne, Franconia, Germania, Hanover, Hanover Junction,

Hanovertown, Keller, Linden, Lunenburg, Mecklenburg, Salem (two locations), Strasburg, Vienna

Washington: Bingen, Custer, Elbe, Geneva, Keller, Lind

West Virginia: Augusta, Berlin, Frankford, Hanover, Herold, Linden, Manheim, Minden, Nimitz, Salem, Swiss, Vienna, Wetzel

Wisconsin: Altoona, Amberg, Berlin, Custer, Freistadt, Friesland, Germania, Germantown, Hamburg, Hanover, Kiel, Knapp, Kohlsville, Kolberg, Leipsig, Linden, New Berlin, New Franken, New Glarus, New Holstein, New Munster, Rhinelander, Saxon, Saxon Harbor, Steuben, Teutonia, West Salem, Weyerhaeuser, Wittenberg

Wyoming: Ulm

Sister-City Relationships

Ansbach and Bay City, Mich.
Arolsen and Hermann, Mo.
Augsburg and Dayton, Ohio
Bad Zwischenahn and Centerville, Ohio
Baumholder and Irving, Tex.
Berlin and Los Angeles, Calif.
Berlin-Spandau and Boca Raton, Fla.
Bexbach and Goshen, Ind.
Billerbeck and Englewood, Ohio
Bingen and Bingen, Wash.
Braunfels and New Braunfels, Tex.
Coburg and Garden City, N.Y.
Crailsheim and Worthington, Minn.
Dorfen and Constantine, Mich.
Dortmund and Buffalo, N.Y.
Düsseldorf and Minneapolis, Minn.
Eberbach and Ephrata, Pa.
Esslingen and Sheboygan, Wisc.
Freiburg and Fryburg, Pa., Whittier, Calif.
Friedrichshafen and Peoria, Ill.
Friolzheim and Williamsville, N.Y.
Füssen and Helen, Ga.
Garmisch-Partenkirchen and Aspen, Colo.
Gescher and Arvado, Calif.
Giessen and Springfield, Ill.
Glückstadt and Fredericksburg, Tex.
Gottelfingen and Botkins, Ohio
Gunzenhausen and Frankenmuth, Mich.
Hamburg and Chicago, Ill.
Hamm and Chattanooga, Tenn., and Santa Monica, Calif.
Heidenheim and Cleveland, Ohio
Hof and Ogden, Utah
Kaiseralautern and Davenport, Iowa
Leinfelden-Echterdingen and York, Pa.
Leonberg and Seward, Nebr.
Lichtenfels and Vandalia, Ohio

Linz am Rhein and Marietta, Ga.
Lübeck and Spokane, Wash.
Lüdinghausen and Deerfield, Ill.
Ludwigshafen and Pasadena, Calif.
Lüneburg and Thomasville, Ga.
Mainz and Louisville, Ky.
Malsch and Dinuba, Calif.
Mannheim and Manheim, Pa.
Marl and Midland, Mich.
Melsungen and Elmira, N.Y.
Memmingen and Glendale, Ariz.
Messstetten and Toccoa, Ga.
Mörzheim and Frederick, Md.
Munich and Cincinnati, Ohio
Neu-Bernburg and Alexandria,
    Minn.
Neustadt and Hays, Kans.
Offenburg and Easton, Pa.
Offerdingen and Dester, Mich.
Passau and Hackensack, N.J.
Pinneberg and Rockville, Md.
Porta Westfalica and Waterloo, Ill.
Ratlingen and Vermillion, S. Dak.
Regen and Brownsville, Tenn.

Regensburg and Tempe, Ariz.
Rodental and Eaton, Ohio
Saarbrücken and Pittsburgh, Pa.
Schifferstadt and Frederick, Md.
Seevetal and Decatur, Ill.
Soest and Mishawaka, Ind.
Soltau and Coldwater, Mich.
Stade and Swarthmore, Pa.
Stuttgart and St. Louis, Mo.
Sulzfeld and El Cajon, Calif.
Tegernsee and Ketchum, Idaho
Ulm and New Ulm, Minn.
Walldorf and Astoria, Ore.
Wesel and Hagerstown, Md.
Wiesloch and Sturgis, Mich.
Wiernsheim and New Harmony,
    Ind.
Wilhelmshaven and Norfolk, Va.
Winterlingen and Shiner, Tex.
Wolfach and Richfield, Ohio
Wolfenbüttel and Kenosha, Wis.
Worms and Mobile, Ariz.
Würzburg and Rochester, N.Y.

Census Data, 1790–1990

The 1790 U.S. Census

I n the table[1] here given, the census figures (of 1790), for the county are given first, then the estimate of the German population the total population of each state is added in a column to the right.

	German	Total Population in 1790
New England:		
Maine, Lincoln County (29,962)	1,500	96,540
Massachusetts, Suffolk County (44,875)	1,000	
Franklin County (present name)	500	
Total	3,000	378,787
New York: Counties—		
Dutchess (45,266), ⅓	9,000	
Montgomery (28,848)	20,000	
Schoharie (9808 in 1800)	3,000	
All other counties	5,000	
Total	37,000	340,120

1. Cf. Census *Report*, volume i. Population, part i, table iv—Population of States and Territories by counties, at each census, 1790–1900, pp. 9 ff. (1901).

443

New Jersey:

Hunterdon (20,153), Morris (16,216),		
Somerset (12,296); one-third of total	16,000	
All other counties	4,000	
Total	20,000	184,139

Pennsylvania:

Allegheny (10,309) ⅓	3,700	
Berks (30,179) ½	15,000	
Cumberland (18,243) ⅖	7,000	
Dauphin (18,177) ⅖	7,000	
Franklin (15,655) ⅓	5,300	
Lancaster (36,147) 70%	25,000	
Montgomery (22,929) 50% plus	12,000	
Southampton (24,2,50) ⅓	8,000	
Philadelphia (54,3391) ⅓ plus	20,000	
Washington (23,866)	7,000	
York (37,747)	25,000	
Other counties. (Bucks Center, Chester,		
Delaware, Fayette, Huntington,		
Luzern, Monroe, Northumberland)		
(152,285) ⅙	25,000	
Total	160,000	434,373

Maryland:

Baltimore (38,937) ⅓	13,000	
Allegany (4,809) ⅓	1,600	
Frederick (30,791) ⅔	20,000	
Washington (15,822)	6,400	
All other counties	2,000	
Total	43,000	319,728

Delaware:

Newcastle (19,688)	3,000	59,096

Virginia:

Augusta (10,886) ⅓	3,600	
Botetourt (10,524) ⅕	2,000	
Culpeper (22,105) ¼	5,000	
Fairfax (Alexandria) (12,320) ¹⁄₁₀	1,200	
Fauquier (17,892) ⅓	5,500	
Orange (9,921) ⅓	3,200	
Rockingham (7,449)	3,500	
Shenandoah (10,510)	6,000	
Spottsylvania (11,252) ⅓	3,000	
Other counties (Henrico, Mecklenburg, etc.)		
(37,500)	2,000	
Total	375,000	691,737

West Virginia:

Berkeley (19,713) ⅓	6,000	
Greenbrier (6,015)	2,000	
Hampshire (7,346)	2,000	
Hardy (7,336)	2,000	
Harrison, Ohio, Pendleton, etc.		
(together 10,000)	3,000	
Total	15,000	55,873

Georgia:

Efflugham (2,424)	1,800	
Chathain (10,769) ⅓	3,500	
Richmond (11,317) ⅓	3,700	
Total	9,000	82,548

North Carolina:

Craven (10,469)	3,000	
Guilford (7,191)	1,500	
Iredell (5,435)	1,800	
Lincoln (9,224)	2,200	
Mecklenburz (11,395)	2,500	
Stokes (8,528)	5,000	
Rowan (15,828)	3,000	
Montgomery, Randolph (12,000) ¹⁄₁₂	1,000	
Total	20,000	393,751

South Carolina:

Abbeville (9,197) $\frac{1}{4}$	2,500	
Beaufort (18,753) $\frac{1}{4}$	4,600	
Charleston (46,647) $\frac{1}{10}$	4,500	
Edgefield (13,289) $\frac{1}{4}$	3,000	
Newberry (9,342) $\frac{1}{4}$	2,400	
Orangeburg (18,513) 60%	11,000	
Richland (3,930) $\frac{1}{3}$	1,000	
Other counties	1,000	
Total	30,000	249,073

The summary of results is as follows:

New England	3,000
New York	37,000
New Jersey	20,000
Pennsylvania	160,000
Maryland	43,000
Delaware	3,000
Virginia and West Virginia	50,000
North Carolina	20,000
South Carolina	30,000
Georgia	9,000
Total	375,000

German Immigration by Decade

Decade Jahrzehnt	Total Immigration	German Immigration	German as Percentage of Total Immigration
1820–29	128,502	5,753	4.5
1830–39	538,381	124,726	23.2
1840–49	1,427,337	385,434	27.0
1850–59	2,814,554	976,072	34.7
1860–69	2,081,261	723,734	34.8
1870–79	2,742,137	751,769	27.4
1880–89	5,248,568	1,445,181	27.5
1890–99	3,694,294	579,072	15.7
1900–09	8,202,388	328,722	4.0
1910–19	6,347,380	174,227	2.7
1920–29	4,295,510	386,634	9.0
1930–39	699,375	119,107	17.0
1940–49	856,608	117,506	14.0
1950–59	2,499,268	576,905	23.1
1960–69	3,213,749	209,616	6.5
1970	373,326	10,632	2.8
Total	45,162,638	6,917,090	15.3

U.S. Bureau of the Census

Geographical Distribution of German-born Americans

Region	Percentage of German-born			
	1850	1880	1920	1960
New England States	1.2	1.8	3.0	3.9
Middle Atlantic States	36.0	30.0	30.1	38.5
East North-Central States	39.1	39.8	35.1	25.3
West North-Central States	9.0	16.6	17.4	7.1
South Atlantic States	6.6	3.6	2.4	5.8
East South-Central States	3.0	2.0	1.0	0.9
West South-Central States	4.6	2.9	2.8	2.2
Mountain States	—	0.8	2.0	2.9
Pacific States	0.6	2.5	6.1	13.2

Numbers of German-Born in Selected Cities, 1850—1950

City/State	1850	1860	1870	1880	1890	1900	1910	1920	1930	1940	1950
New York	56,141	119,984	151,203	163,482	210,723	324,224	278,137	194,155	237,588	224,749	185,467
Chicago	5,035	22,230	52,316	75,205	161,039	203,733	182,289	112,288	111,366	83,424	56,635
Philadelphia	23,020	43,643	50,746	55,769	74,974	73,047	61,480	39,766	37,923	27,286	19,736
Milwaukee	7,271	15,981	22,509	31,483	54,776	68,969	64,816	39,771	40,787	28,085	18,259
Los Angeles	—	—	—	—	2,707	4,032	9,684	10,563	18,094	17,528	17,302
Detroit	2,838	7,220	12,647	17,292	35,481	42,730	44,675	30,238	32,716	23,785	17,046
San Francisco	—	6,346	13,602	19,928	26,422	35,303	24,137	18,514	18,608	14,977	12,394
Cleveland	—	9,078	15,855	23,170	39,893	44,225	41,408	26,476	22,532	15,427	9,629
Saint Louis	22,571	50,510	50,040	54,901	66,000	59,973	47,766	30,089	22,315	14,120	8,112
Buffalo, N.Y.	—	18,233	22,249	25,543	42,660	49,812	43,815	20,898	18,816	12,483	7,775
Baltimore	19,274	32,613	35,276	34,051	40,709	33,941	26,024	17,461	13,568	9,744	6,943
Cincinnati	33,374	43,931	49,446	46,157	49,415	38,308	28,426	17,833	13,944	8,856	6,013
Pittsburgh	—	6,049	8,703	15,957	25,363	36,838	29,438	16,028	14,409	9,805	5,898
Rochester, N.Y.	—	6,451	7,730	11,004	17,330	15,685	14,624	10,735	10,287	7,302	5,012
Newark, N.J.	3,822	10,595	15,873	17,628	26,520	25,251	22,177	14,041	12,508	7,813	4,977
Jersey City, N.J.	—	1,605	7,151	10,151	16,086	17,838	16,131	11,113	9,631	3,681	
Boston	1,777	3,202	5,606	7,396	10,362	10,739	8,701	5,915	5,381	3,851	3,289
Columbus, Ohio	—	—	3,982	4,416	6,882	6,296	5,722	4,098	3,582	2,422	—
Louisville, Ky.	7,357	13,374	14,380	13,463	14,094	12,383	8,471	4,748	3,219	1,953	—
Albany, N.Y.	2,875	3,877	5,168	6,648	7,605	5,963	4,620	3,068	2,513	1,687	—
New Orleans	11,425	19,752	15,224	13,944	11,338	8,743	6,122	3,418	2,159	1,403	—

U.S. Bureau of the Census

German Born and Their Children in Selected Counties and Townships, 1860

State County Township	German Born	Native Born Children			
		Both Parents German		One Parent German	
		Number	Ratio of Increase	Number	Ratio of Increase
			%		%
Missouri					
Perry	1329	1120	94.27	1250	94.06
Brazeau	597	484	81.07	494	82.75
Cinque Homme	391	369	94.37	431	110.23
Cole	1508	1386	91.91	1264	83.82
Jefferson City	527	337	63.95	392	74.38
Marion	23	21	91.30	21	63.94
Jefferson	1431	899	62.82	1084	75.75
Rock	739	477	64.55	538	72.80
Michigan					
Bay	552	263	47.64	307	55.62
Bangor	196	87	44.39	101	51.53
Bay City	279	122	43.73	142	50.90
Saginaw	2557	1660	64.92	1697	66.37
Frankenmuth	465	504	108.39	504	108.39
Kochville	264	207	78.41	207	78.41
East Saginaw	664	288	43.37	302	45.48
Clinton	398	403	101.28	423	106.28
Westphalia					
Minnesota					
Carver	1790	885	49.44	930	51.96
Chaska	251	162	64.54	179	71.31
Brown	832	363	43.63	388	46.63
New Ulm	396	187	47.22	202	51.01
Stearns	1650	1021	61.88	1069	64.79
Wisconsin					
Portage	321	160	49.84	172	53.58
Stevens Point	105	52	49.52	60	57.14
Shawano	158	50	31.65	60	37.97
Marathon					
Berlin	505	78	15.45	82	16.24
Stettin	169	54	31.95	58	34.32

Nebraska 1870

Hall	334	128	38.32	135	40.42
Cedar	339	180	53.10	234	69.03
St. Helena	260	147	56.54	176	67.69
Cuming	931	608	65.31	666	71.54

German Born in Eleven Cities and Surrounding Counties 1870 and 1900[*]

City	County	1870				1900			
		City		County (without City)		City		County (without City)	
		Total Pop. (Germans)	%	Total Pop. (Germans)	%	Total Pop. (Germans)	%	Total Pop. (Germans)	%
Cincinnati	Hamilton	216,239 (49,446)	22.87	44,131 (5,827)	13.20	325,902 (38,219)	11.73	83,577 (7,584)	9.07
Cleveland	Cuyahoga	92,829 (15,855)	17.08	39.181 (4,079)	10.41	381,768 (40,648)	10.65	57,352 (5,139)	8.96
Columbus	Franklin	31,274 (3,982)	12.73	31,745 (1,723)	5.43	125,560 (6,296)	5.01	38,900 (1,394)	3.58
Dayton	Montgomery	30,473 (4,962)	16.29	33,533 (2,424)	7.23	25,333 (6,820)	7.99	44,913 (2,604)	5.81
Toledo	Lukas	31,594 (5,341)	16.91	15,138 (1,463)	9.66	131,822 (12,373)	9.39	21,737 (1,663)	7.65
Indianapolis	Marion	48,244 (5,286)	10.96	23,695 (1,250)	5.32	169,164 (8,632)	5.10	28,063 (1,007)	3.59
Chicago	Cook	298,977 (52,316)	17.50	50,989 (13,132)	25.75	1,698,575 (170,738)	10.05	140,160 (18,915)	13.50
Detroit	Wayne	79,577 (12,647)	15.89	39,461 (4,413)	11.18	285,704 (32,027)	11.21	63,089 (8,257)	13.09
Milwaukee	Milwaukee	71,440 (22,599)	31.63	18,490 (6,420)	34.70	285,315 (53,854)	18,88	44,702 (10,098)	22.59
Kansas City, Mo.	Jackson	32,216 (1,884)	5.85	22,825 (426)	1.87	163,752 (4,816)	2.94	31,441 (560)	1.78
St. Louis	St. Louis	310,864 (59,040)	18.99	40,325 (6,896)	17.10	575,238 (58,781)	10.22	50,040 (4,856)	9.70

[*]Data for cities from *Ninth Census*, 1, pp. 388–390; *Twelfth Census*, 1, pp. 796–803. Data for counties without cities computed.

Leading Nationality Groups in the United States 1850—1900 Percentage of Total Foreign Born

Year	Germany		Ireland		Great Britain	
	Number	% of foreign born	Number	% of foreign born	Number	% of foreign born
1850	583,774	26.0	961,719	42.8	278,675	12.4
1860	1,276,075	30.8	1,611,304	38.9	433,494	10.5
1870	1,690,533	30.4	1,855,827	33.3	555,046	10.0
1880	1,966,742	29.4	1,854,571	27.8	664,160	9.9
1890	2,784,894	30.1	1,871,509	20.2	909,092	9.8
1900	2,666,990	25.8	1,618,567	15.6	842,078	8.1

From *Twelfth Census of the United States, 1900*, 1, p. clxxi.

German Born and Children of German Parentage in 1900

State	German Born	Both Parents Born in Germany	One Parent Native One Parent Born in Germany
Ohio	204,160	331,518	702,578
Indiana	73,546	131,121	283,576
Illinois	332,169	438,964	944,329
Michigan	125,074	167,384	357,629
Wisconsin	242,777	333,759	709,969
Minnesota	117,007	172,051	355,268
Iowa	123,162	177,952	381,716
Missouri	109,282	185,931	399,822
North Dakota	11,546	14,406	32,393
South Dakota	17,873	25,867	55,860
Nebraska	65,506	88,333	191,928
Kansas	39,501	56,172	131,563
North Central Division	1,461,603	2,123,458	4,546,631

From *Twelfth Census*, pp. clxiii, cxcv, 814.

The 1900 U.S. Census

The following table, taken from the Census Report of 1900,[1] will show exactly where the Germans are located and compare them with the two next largest elements, the Irish and the English: —

German Population Distributed Over the United States

	Germans	Irish	English
The United States:	2,666,990	1,618,567	842,079
North Atlantic Division—	883,908	1,113,876	435,031
Maine	1,356	10,159	4,793
New Hampshire	2,006	13,547	5,100
Vermont	882	7,453	2,447
Massachusetts	31,395	249,916	82,346
Rhode Island	4,300	35,501	22,832
Connecticut	31,892	70,994	21.569
New York	480,026	425,553	135,685
New Jersey	119,598	94,844	45,428
Pennsylvania	212,453	205,909	114,831
South Atlantic Division—	72,705	36,606	20,274
Delaware	2,332	5,044	1,506
Maryland	44,990	13,874	5,299
District of Columbia	5,857	6,220	2,299
Virginia	4,504	3,534	3,425
West Virginia	6,537	3,342	2,622
North Carolina	1,191	3 371	904
South Carolina	2,075	1,131	474
Georgia	3,407	2,293	1,514
Florida	1,812	797	2,231

1. *Twelfth Census Of the United States*, 1900, vol. i (Population), part i, pp. clxxiii–clxxiv, table lxxxii.

North Central Division—	1,461,603	349,805	260,369
Ohio	204,160	55,018	44,745
Indiana	73,546	16,306	10,874
Illinois	332,169	114,563	64,390
Michigan	125,074	29,182	43,839
Wisconsin	242,777	23,544	17,995
Minnesota	117,007	22,428	12,022
Iowa	123,162	28,321	21,027
Missouri	109,282	31,832	15,666
North Dakota	11,546	2,670	2,909
South Dakota	17,873	3,298	3,862
Nebraska	65,506	11,127	9,757
Kansas	39,501	11,516	13,283
South Central Division—	109,743	31,640	22,183
Kentucky	27,555	9,874	3,256
Tennessee	4,569	3,372	2,207
Alabama	3,634	1,792	2,347
Mississippi	1,926	1,264	798
Louisiana	11,839	6,436	2,068
Texas	48,295	6,173	8,213
Indian Territory	842	397	779
Oklahoma	5,112	987	1,121
Arkansas	5,971	1,345	1,394
Western Division—	135,459	83,532	102,656
Montana	7,162	9,436	8,077
Wyoming	2,146	1,591	2,596
Colorado	14,606	10,132	13,575
New Mexico	1,360	692	968
Arizona	1,245	1,159	1,561
Utah	2,360	1,516	18,879
Nevada	1,179	1,425	1,167
Idaho	2,974	1,633	3,943
Washington	16,686	7,262	10,481
Oregon	13,292	4,210	5,663
California	72,449	44,476	35,746

The 1990 U.S. Census
German-American Census Statistics

States	Total Population	German Pop.	% by State	% of Total
United States	248,709,873	57,947,374	23.30%	23.30%
California	29,760,021	4,935,147	16.58%	1.98%
Pennsylvania	11,981,643	4,314,762	36.31%	1.73%
Ohio	10,847,115	4,067,840	37.50%	1.64%
Illinois	11,430,602	3,326,248	29.10%	1.34%
Texas	16,986,510	2,949,686	17.36%	1.19%
New York	17,990,455	2,898,888	16.11%	1.17%
Michigan	9,295,297	2,666,179	28.68%	1.07%
Wisconsin	4,891,769	2,630,680	53.78%	1.06%
Florida	12,937,926	2,410,257	18.63%	.97%
Indiana	5,544,159	2,084,667	37.60%	.84%
Minnesota	4,375,099	2,020,975	46.19%	.81%
Missouri	5,117,073	1,843,299	36.02%	.74%
New Jersey	7,730,188	1,407,956	18.21%	.57%
Iowa	2,776,755	1,394,542	50.22%	.56%
Washington	4,866,692	1,389,914	28.56%	.56%
Maryland	4,781,468	1,218,257	25.48%	.49%
Virginia	6,187,358	1,186,056	19.17%	.48%
North Carolina	6,628,637	1,110,581	16.75%	.45%
Colorado	3,294,394	1,063,694	32.29%	.43%
Kansas	2,477,574	968,078	39.07%	.39%
Oregon	2,842,321	878,555	30.91%	.35%
Arizona	3,665,228	878,088	23.96%	.35%
Georgia	6,478,216	810,165	12.51%	.33%
Kentucky	3,685296	798,001	21.65%	.32%
Nebraska	1,578,385	794,911	50.36%	.32%
Tennessee	4,877,185	724,059	14.85%	.29%
Oklahoma	3,145,585	714,184	22.70%	.29%
Louisiana	4,219,973	507,453	12.03%	.20%
South Carolina	3,486,703	500,089	14.34%	.20%
Massachusetts	6,016,425	497,462	8.27%	.20%
West Virginia	1,793,477	468,927	26.15%	.19%
Connecticut	3,287,116	450,247	13.70%	.18%
Alabama	4,040,587	430,442	10.65%	.17%
Arkansas	2,350,725	400,234	17.03%	.16%
South Dakota	696,004	355,102	51.02%	.14%
North Dakota	638,800	324,923	50.67%	.13%

Utah	1,722,850	299,414	17.38%	.12%
Montana	799,065	285,385	35.71%	.11%
Nevada	1,201,833	279,693	23.27%	.11%
Idaho	1,006,749	278,615	27.67%	.11%
New Mexico	1,515,069	234,000	15.44%	.09%
Mississippi	2,573,216	224,674	8.73%	.09%
Wyoming	453,588	158,469	34.94%	.06%
Delaware	666,168	138,128	20.73%	.06%
Alaska	550,043	127,103	23.11%	.05%
New Hampshire	1,109,252	118,003	10.64%	.05%
Maine	1,227,928	108,859	8.87%	.04%
Hawaii	1,108,229	102,714	9.27%	.04%
Rhode Island	1,003,464	73,425	7.32%	.03%
Vermont	562,758	59,090	10.50%	.02%
District of Columbia	606,900	39,218	6.46%	.02%
Total Statistics	248,709,873	57,947,374	23.30%	23.30%

Index

*Don Heinrich Tolzmann
with former president
Ronald Reagan.*
Photo courtesy of the author.

About the Author

Dr. Don Heinrich Tolzmann is recognized as the "father of German-American Day," the now official and annual celebration that honors the contributions of German-Americans to American life and culture. In 1989, in Cincinnati, Ohio, he organized the first German-American Heritage Month centered on German-American Day. As curator of the German-Americana Collection and director of German-American Studies at the University of Cincinnati, he has led the movement to create a national and international awareness of the important, but for so long neglected, role played by German-Americans in the development of the American way of life. He is the author and editor of numerous books dealing with German-American history, literature, and culture.

He edits a monographic series (*New German-American Studies*), has served as Ohio editor of the *New Yorker Staats-Zeitung*, editor of the *Zeitschift für deutschamerikanische Literatur*, and is on the editorial board of the *Yearbook for German-American Studies*. As an active, dedicated, and informed member of most regional and national German-American organizations, he has frequently been called upon to represent German-American interests to the administrations in Washington, D.C.

He is the recipient of the Friendship Award of the Federal Republic of Germany as well as that country's Federal Cross of Merit (*Bundesverdienstkreuz*), the Ohioana Book Award, the Ficken Award from Baldwin-Wallace University, and the German-American of the Year Award from the Federation of German-American Societies. In addition, he has served for many years as president of the Society for German-American Societies. By promoting the development of teaching units for use in schools and strengthening academic and personal ties between Germany and the United States, Dr. Tolzmann has performed exemplary service in raising community, state, and regional awareness of the many contributions to American society made by German-Americans.